Sports in America

Tales of the South Pacific
The Fires of Spring
Return to Paradise
The Voice of Asia
The Bridges at Toko-Ri
Sayonara
The Floating World
The Bridge at Andau
Hawaii
Report of the County Chairman
Caravans
The Source
Iberia
Presidential Lottery
The Quality of Life
Kent State: What Happened and Why
The Drifters
A Michener Miscellany: 1950–1970
Centennial
Sports in America

with A. Grove Day
Rascals in Paradise

James A. Michener

Sports in America

Random House  *New York*

Library of Congress Cataloging in Publication Data

Michener, James Albert, 1907–
   Sports in America.

   1. Sports—United States. 2. Physical education and training—United States. I. Title.
GV583.M5   796'.0973   75–40549
ISBN 0–394–40646–X

Manufactured in the United States of America
  98765432
First Edition

Grateful acknowledgment is made to the following for permission to reprint the specified selections:

Addison-Wesley Publishing Company, Inc.: Adaptations of Tables 4–3, 6–1, 6–6, and 7–1 from pages 80, 81, 119, 133, 150 and 151 of *A Geography of American Sport* by John F. Rooney, Jr. Copyright © 1974 by Addison-Wesley Publishing Company, Inc.

American Alliance for Health, Physical Education & Recreation (1201 16th St., N.W., Washington, D.C.): Chart entitled "Percentile Norms for a Thirteen-Year-Old American Boy" from *AAHPER Youth Fitness Test Manual,* 1976 Revised Edition.

American Council on Education and Mr. George H. Hanford: Excerpts from "An Inquiry into the Need for and Feasibility of a National Study of Intercollegiate Athletics" by George H. Hanford from *A Report for the American Council on Education.*

THIS BOOK IS DEDICATED TO THREE MEN WHO HELPED ME
UNDERSTAND AMERICAN SPORTS

ED PISZEK, owner of the Philadelphia Firebirds hockey team

JOE ROBBIE, managing director of the Miami Dolphins football team

ROBIN ROBERTS, of baseball's Hall of Fame

Contents

Author's Note

The writing of this book was aided considerably by the research help provided by Joseph Avenick. A former sportswriter for various newspapers, he has an affection for games, a familiarity with the players, a knowledge of their records, and an acquaintance with the literature about them. He also has strong verbal preferences and insists that students never *graduated;* they *were graduated by* their schools. Working with him was both instructive and enjoyable.

Sports in America

I

Basic Principles

This book was written by a man who loves sports.

It would not be extravagant to say that twice in my lifetime sports have made the difference between life and death, and I must therefore treat them with respect. The first incident occurred when I was a boy, and it was spiritual in significance. The second took place when I was fifty-eight, and was completely physical.

Like many future athletes, I came from poor surroundings. Many of the boys with whom I played got into serious trouble and found themselves sentenced to Glen Mills, the local reformatory. I can still remember with awe the account of one street-mate who returned from Glen Mills: 'As soon as the door slams behind you, a guard knocks you down, other guards grab you, and they beat you with a leather strap.'

'Why?' I asked.

'To let you know who's boss.'

I developed a healthy fear of Glen Mills and determined not to find its door slamming behind me, but at the same time I was drifting into dangerous companionships. I knew that I was falling, almost against my will, onto perilous terrain.

I was saved by athletics, and by the generosity of a remarkable man. George Murray was an almost illiterate roofer who never earned more than a few dollars a day. An extremely shy man, he never married, but took upon himself the fathering of disadvantaged boys. He formed what was known as the Doylestown Boys' Brigade, which had bits of military fol-de-rol and a tenuous allegiance to the Presbyterian Church. Most important for us, he gained access to a defunct meeting hall which had been erected for some aborted purpose. The second floor of this rather small building he converted into a basketball court, and there I spent my youth.

The court had every conceivable deficiency. The baskets were hung flat against the end walls, which meant that those of us accustomed to using them mastered the art of dashing headlong at the wall, planting our right foot high against the planking, and vaulting upward toward the basket, ending high above the rim so that we could then dunk the ball downward. This was a shot fairly hard to stop by a bewildered defender who had never before seen such a court.

The ceiling was unusually low, with a wide, heavy rafter right above the basket, and we became expert in speeding down the floor, and with maximum force slamming the ball vertically upward, so that it caromed back down through the basket. This, too, was a shot difficult to stop if you were not accustomed to it.

On this bizarre floor the Doylestown Boys' Brigade fielded teams with far more than normal skills. We once went for a period of three years without losing a home game, even though we played teams that had better reputations and much taller players. At the time I thought we were pretty good, but now, looking back on those years, I realize that even superlative opponents would have required about three-quarters of a game to familiarize themselves with our peculiar floor and its strange rules. Our victories were tarnished.

'Wait till we get you on a real court!' our defeated opponents sometimes threatened as they left our little bandbox, but I noticed that when they did get us on their own court we were apt to be so much better trained and so determined that we defeated them there too.

As a result of this roofer's concern for boys, a constant supply of young fellows like me was provided the local high school, which also produced championship teams, even though it consistently competed against schools that were markedly bigger. But now my life fell under the control of a much different man, who, in a very real sense, determined my future.

J. Allen Gardy was a tall, moderately gifted athlete who had played basketball for nearby Lehigh University. He was a printer by profession, a publisher of a hunting magazine by avocation, and an amateur coach of high school basketball out of the goodness of his heart. At the precise time in my life when I required strong guidance, he threw me a basketball and said, 'Let's see if you can make a lay-up.'

He was a simplistic man to whom everything was either good or bad, and he knew the difference. Fried foods were bad, and alcohol, and cigarettes, and fooling around with girls, and talking back to teachers, and staying up late before an important game, and anything that was ungentlemanly or unsportsmanlike. He subscribed to the highest possible standards, and observed them himself. You could go to him with any problem and get an immediate, clear-cut decision.

J. Allen Gardy knew, and his knowledge covered the universe. Like most coaches, he considered Democrats bad, and labor union people, and troublemakers, and college professors, and radicals, and anyone not wholeheartedly in support of the good society as he experienced it.

But most of all, he knew how to encourage young boys to develop themselves to their fullest, to compete ruggedly, to observe the basic rules of sportsmanship. He held us to rigorous performance, made us run more practice laps than any other coach in the region, and drilled us incessantly on fundamentals.

As a consequence of Coach Gardy's attention, we went several years without losing a home game and won the vast majority of our away games, even though we consistently played teams from larger towns and cities. Our high school court was a spacious one, and we simply ran the other teams ragged, but when we were thrown into little jewel boxes, as at Lansdale and Perkasie, our previous training on Uncle George's tiny court stood us in good stead. All of us could climb the back wall and dunk the basketball. All of us could ricochet shots off low ceilings, and we customarily won just as easily on small courts as on large.

Looking back on those hectic and triumphant years, I am not sure that we gave our competitors a fair shake. We were unfair for a reason not of our making. A few years before I entered high school a Doylestown boy had been killed playing football—killed right on the playing field. The ensuing revulsion was so great that football was banned during my years at school.

As a consequence, we spent our fall term getting ready for basketball, and by the time the season opened we were so advanced in our training that we were almost professionals. Year after year we were something like 12–0 or 14–1 in game standings before the opposition was really ready to play. In the later stages of the season, when the opposing teams were beginning to settle down, they sometimes drubbed us, but by then we were so far ahead in the standings, we could not be overtaken.

We played each Tuesday and Friday, a brutal schedule, and often totaled as many as twenty-seven or thirty games a season. It was our whole life, and our constant guide was Coach Gardy, that quiet, resolute man who could answer any question. At a time when my personal life was chaotic and required a firm hand, he was there, a surrogate father, a stern counselor, a man who never doubted that good things lay ahead for me.

If there was ever an American boy who was saved by sports, it was I. Gardy was helpful in getting me an athletic scholarship to Swarthmore, so that even my future education depended upon sports. He encouraged me to play baseball—good field, fair hit—and gave me a tennis racket, which I could otherwise never have afforded, thus introducing me to the game which has been my constant companion and chief delight.

But there was something more. In Uncle George's small gym and Coach Gardy's larger court we won championships and I came to regard myself as a champion. I carried myself a little taller, worked a little harder in school, built a confidence that was crucial. I drew away from the boys who were headed for reform school and patterned myself after those who were headed for college.

I was a heavy scorer in days when a game that ended 23–17 in our favor was reported as 'another runaway,' and I garnered more praise than I deserved, but I can never forget those wintry Saturday mornings, after some sterling victory, when I would saunter into the middle of town, and everyone would know how many goals I had scored the night before. I remember particularly the Saturday in 1924 when we came home with the championship. In the last moments of the game on Friday night I had thrown the ball a disgraceful distance with no hope of scoring, and somehow the ball had dropped into the net and we had won, 16–14. That Saturday I had to explain to the men of our town how I had made that last, unbelievable shot, and the men said, 'The whole town is proud of you.'

Young people need that experience of acceptance; it can come in a variety of ways, of which athletics is only one. For example, they need to know that their parents approve of them; they need occasional praise from an older person. But in the United States it is sports that have been elected primarily to fill this need.

It was remarkable, I now realize, that during those years of athletic achievement in high school I was also earning straight A's in my classwork but I cannot recall a single instance in which any member of my community gave me any accolades for such accomplishment. In Doylestown, in those days, all that mattered was sports, and even today across America things are not much different.

Assessing those distant days as honestly as I can, I must confess that our team was never really first rate. No boy I ever played with or against could even make a first-class team today, and if our team were to play a modern high school, the score would be something like 97–22, with us losing.

And yet, in our little world we were champions, and from that simple fact radiated an inner confidence that has never left me. I could never become a bum, because I was a champion. Realizing this, I was able to lift myself onto a level of existence I could not have otherwise attained.

The second time sports saved me came in the autumn of 1965, when I was knocked down by a massive coronary infarction. Five hours elapsed before I reached a hospital, and several times in that period I was sure I was going to die.

I had the good fortune to have as a family friend Dr. Paul Dudley White, the cardiologist who treated President Eisenhower. My wife and I had met him while serving on a cultural committee visiting Soviet Russia, and in the idle periods of the conference he had given me a concentrated course on heart attacks.

'Some years ago I was summoned by the Pentagon,' he said. 'They had an aggravating problem. They were sending to duty in Alaska some of their finest young colonels, men in their late forties and apparently in perfect health. Well, these eager colonels were going out onto the ski slopes and dropping dead at an alarming rate.

'A group of heart specialists like me went to work, and we put all the cases we could find into a computer, but it told us nothing. There was no single cause why healthy young colonels should be dropping dead on ski slopes. But we were able to construct a profile of factors which, while not causative individually, were predictive if they clustered.'

'What were they?' I asked.

'Cholesterol in the blood. Gross overweight. Smoking. History of diabetes. Previous attack of gout. And three special factors which were of acute significance. One, high blood pressure. Two, a father or an older brother who had died of a heart attack. Three, body type.'

'What's body type?'

'Ectomorph. Endomorph. Mesomorph. An ectomorph is tall and skinny, like Abe Lincoln, or Kenneth Galbraith on our committee. They very rarely have heart attacks. The endomorph is pear-shaped, or round and chubby, like Pierre Salinger. You know, there's not a pound of improper weight on that man. That's the way he's supposed to be. They don't have many attacks either. It's the mesomorph that gets them.'

'What's a mesomorph look like?' I asked.

He leaned back and studied me carefully. 'You,' he said. 'Big chest. Heavy bones. Shoulders curving in. The mesomorph is probably a throwback to the apes. You're the good athletes, the hypertensives, the ones who work eighty hours a week. And play hard.'

I remember distinctly—we were in Leningrad at the time—that he poked me in my protruding apelike chest. 'You're almost a caricature of the mesomorph. You're a prime target for a heart attack.'

'I had a high school coach who steered me away from smoking, drinking and fried foods. I have very low blood pressure.'

'Gout?'

'Yes.'

'I thought so. That's the disease of the intellectual perfectionist. Your father or brother die young?'

'I don't know about my parents.'

'You're not conspicuously overweight, but gout indicates you're a man with a good deal of inner tension. How about your cholesterol?'

'I don't know that word.'

'You'll be learning it. But I'll bet you drink a great deal of milk.'

'Yes. Always have.'

'Cut it out. Lose weight. And learn to relax, or you may find yourself within the profile.'

'Is the profile as predictive as that?'

'I'll tell you what, Michener. If any man told me that he smoked two packs a day, that he had diabetes, that his cholesterol was high, and that his father and brother had dropped dead of heart attacks, I'd advise him to go into a hospital right away. He'd be terribly sick.'

'Should I quit playing tennis? I play a very tough game.'

'Absolutely not!' he had concluded. 'Exercise as much as you can. It may save your life.'

When Dr. White reached the hospital, my wife asked him if my playing tennis had caused the attack. 'Heavens no!' he said. 'The only reason Jim is alive right now is that robust exercise forced his heart to set up alternative feed lines. Normally, with that much damage he'd be dead, but his heart had already constructed those bypasses, and they're keeping him alive now.'

It was fortunate for me that I had my attack in 1965 and not twenty years earlier, for in those uninformed days I would have been converted into a cardiac basket case, coddling myself and living in a kind of suspended animation. Dr. White realized that historically one of the greatest dangers of a heart attack, if the patient survived, was what doctors did to him in the postattack period.

'My advice is radical,' he told me. 'If, during the first six weeks after a severe attack, you try to do even little things, you're foolish, for the heart fibers require time to knit together. But after the mending has occurred, if you don't try to do everything you did before, in moderation, you're even more foolish.'

Dr. White had developed this theory himself, and had proved it by the manner in which his patients resumed a full life after even the most devastating attacks. We forget that Dwight Eisenhower had his attack during his first term, and that after his attack he conducted the 1956 campaign and served four additional years in the world's most demanding office. Lyndon Johnson recovered from his attack, served in the Senate and then the Presidency.

White told me that he had been much influenced by an Israeli cardiologist who, working by himself, had developed a comparable theory. 'This man will not treat a cardiac patient unless the patient agrees, upon recovery, to perform some athletic feat much more strenuous than anything attempted previously. Like climbing Mount Tabor or rowing five miles or hiking twenty. He tells his patients, "If you drop dead climbing, all it means is that you'd surely have dropped dead sitting at your desk." '

Under Dr. White's regime I was soon playing tennis again, very vigorously, but not singles. I traveled six times around the world. I researched and wrote six difficult books. I ran for office and served in various demanding jobs. And I took a nap almost every afternoon, as he prescribed, and laid off eggs, cheese and milk, which I crave.

I am convinced that hearty athletic competition saved my life in 1965. I am convinced that vigorous athletic participation has kept me healthy and viable in the succeeding years. I suspect that under the old-style restrictive regimen of no exercise, I would now be either dead or a vegetable-like cardiac cripple. The wild games I have played these last ten years, plus the endless walks up and down hills, have kept me in good spirit and eager to tackle new work.

My debt to sports is therefore considerable, and the reader will understand why I might want to write about them, but the justification for this book goes far beyond anything personal. Sports have become a major force in American life. We devote more money and time to them than we realize. They consume a major portion of our television programming, and our newspapers allocate tremendous space to their coverage. They dominate the dreams of ghetto children, who see them as their traditional way of escape; they have become a fetish to our black community, distracting it from more serious solutions to problems. Their effect upon our schools and colleges is oftentimes deplorable, and they have been accused of generating at least some of the violence that assaults us.

Yet the critical analysis of school sports has been grossly neglected. Universities whose major moral positions have been dictated by sports have not encouraged their faculties to analyze the problems they create; it is easier to find a good study on the effect of the Flemish language on the children of Antwerp than to discover from articles in learned journals what really goes on in the sports department of the university in which the scholars reside.

In discussing sports in American life, I shall try to apply specific definitions to seven recurring words, but they are of such common usage and appear in so many alternate meanings that I cannot guarantee consistency.

Health. The general condition of the body with reference to soundness and vigor; freedom from disease or ailment. Many definitions of this word include *mental health,* but when I intend to indicate it, I shall say so.

Physical fitness. The general state of one's health; especially the ability to utilize one's equipment, such as muscles, strength, dexterity, endurance, etc., at a satisfying level of proficiency.

Sports. Of the three dozen definitions to be found in even a medium-sized dictionary, I restrict my usage to two: 1) an athletic activity requiring physical prowess or skill and usually of a competitive nature (baseball, football, tennis, Olympic field sports, fencing, boxing, etc.); 2) any form of activity carried on out of doors, often not of a competitive nature (hunting, fishing, horseback riding, sailing, birdwatching, etc.) Bridge, chess, backgammon, pinochle and the like are not sports.

Game. Again one has a host of definitions to choose from. I restrict my usage to: a competitive activity involving skill, chance or athletic prowess on the part of two or more persons who play according to a set of rules, for their own enjoyment or for the entertainment of spectators. (Football, ice hockey, bridge, chess and their sort are games. Hunting, fishing, birdwatching and jogging are not.)

Physical education. Systematic instruction in exercise, physical fitness, health practices and hygiene conducted as part of a school or college program.

Athletics. A most imprecise word. I shall use it in the sense of 'the organized program of games in a school, college or university.' The athletic department supervises organized games, as contrasted to the physical education department, which supervises physical fitness, hygiene, etc.

Lifetime sports. This recently coined phrase is a useful shorthand. It designates sports which can be engaged in at all ages (tennis, golf, bowling, birdwatching) as distinguished from those which cannot (football, pole vaulting, boxing.)

Every statement I make henceforth will be subject to three criteria, and I hope the reader will keep these in mind, because they will explain some of the arguments I advance.

I. *Sports should be fun for the participant.* They should provide release from tensions, a joyful exuberance as the game progresses, and a discharge of those aggressions which, if kept bottled up, damage the human being. If sports become a drudgery, or a perverted competition, or a mere commercial enterprise, something is wrong. I believe that sports should be fun whether one is actively participating, like the ancient Greeks, or watching, like the ancient Romans. In either case they ought to provide a spiritual catharsis, which cannot occur if participants are overly dedicated to winning, or if spectators allow their partisanship to get out of hand. This criterion of fun will become especially important when we inspect Little Leagues in baseball and Pop Warner teams in football, but it will also apply at every other level of sports in America. If the game isn't fun, it has lost at least half its justification, and there are many signs that in America some sports are no longer fun, to either the participant or the spectator.

II. *Sports should enhance the health of both the individual participant and the general society.* I place this criterion at the apex of my value system. For me it takes precedence over everything else, and most of my conclusions will be incomprehensible if this goal is forgotten. I believe without question that the general health of the nation ought to be a concern of those who govern the nation, and the way in which we have allowed national health standards to decline in recent decades is a scandal for which schools, colleges and universities will one day be called to account. Specifically, a sport, to be effective, should place a demand upon big muscles, lung capacity, sweat glands, and particularly the heart. If it does not, much of the potential value of that sport is lost. Of course, prudent limits should be observed. Not many should engage in a marathon run of 26 miles 385 yards, because that requires too much exertion. But I cannot consider croquet a serious sport, because it requires none. A rigorous application of this criterion to all the sports we engage in will produce surprising results, and in a later chapter tables will be given showing that some of our most popular sports contribute little, whereas others of small reputation contribute much. For myself, I no longer have much interest in any sport that does not generate a vigorous sweat.

III. *Sports have an obligation to provide public entertainment.* I am by nature a participant rather than a spectator, and my whole sympathy lies with the sandlot where boys are playing rather than the stadium where professionals are offering an exhibition. One might therefore expect me to be prejudiced against spectator sports, and I might have been had I not spent much of my adult life abroad, studying various cultures and countries. The more I learned, the more apparent it became that all societies in all periods of history have needed some kind of public entertainment, and it has usually been provided by sports.

Ancient Greece had its Olympiad and Rome its Colosseum. In the most distant corners of Asia Minor, I saw amphitheaters constructed by these civilizations because the rulers knew that the general citizenry required some kind of public entertainment. In Mérida, in western Spain, I visited the enormous flat plain that had once been walled to a height of four feet and waterproofed so that when a river was led into the area a small lake resulted on which actual ships could engage in simulated naval battles. In Crete young men and women skillfully leaped on and off the backs of charging bulls, and I have always been impressed by the frequency with which games are mentioned in the Bible. Some of the most effective analogies of St. Paul were borrowed from the arena. Shakespeare, too, found examples in sports, and I have found only one society in which sports were not a functional part. The Hebrews of Biblical time held a low opinion of games and said so, but when they entered Greek and Roman society they became advocates, like their neighbors. The most dramatic example of a spectator sport I have ever witnessed occurred in the most primitive society I have known, one of the savage islands in the New Hebrides group. There the entire community gathered at the bottom of a cliff to watch admiringly as young men of the village climbed to the top of the cliff, and then to the top of a tall tree at the edge of the cliff. Posing there, the athlete would utter a defiant scream, then throw himself headfirst toward the rocks below, trusting that the vine rope attached to his heels would bring him up short just before he crashed onto the rocks. In all ages societies have looked to sports for entertainment, so that when the State of Alabama demands that its university provide first-class, big-time football, it is acting within a historical tradition, and when the State of Louisiana spends $163,000,000 to build a Superdome, it is aping only what Greece and Rome did ages ago. I am completely in favor of public sporting spectacles, for they fill a timeless need, but I am confused as to who should provide them and under what type of public sponsorship.

While doing research for this book I sometimes outlined these three criteria to public groups. Frequently I was asked, 'Why don't you have one about sports building character?' Originally I had that as my fourth criterion, but the more I considered it, and the more I weighed the evidence that has been forthcoming in recent years, the more doubtful I became as to its validity, and here we come to the nitty-gritty of this book.

In favor of including character-building as one of the great contributions of sports is this kind of evidence: The Duke of Wellington has been quoted as having said, 'The battle of Waterloo was won on the playing fields of Eton.' General MacArthur was lavish in his praise of West Point and its playing fields. The men who played for Vince Lombardi testified to the fact that he made them better men than they were when they joined his team. A thousand masters of ceremonies have introduced their local coaches as molders of character first and athletes second. Aging alumni, returning to their colleges, pay tribute first to long-dead coaches and much later to certain memorable professors. Hundreds of professional athletes have testified to the impact their high school coaches had on them. And I myself, a few pages back, stated that my character was formed in part by athletics.

On the other hand, emerging evidence begins to erode the legend that participation in sports automatically builds character. The present Duke of Wellington has disclosed that within his family it has long been known that the famous duke never made his statement about the playing fields of Eton. That attractive quotation did not surface until forty-one years after the Battle of Waterloo, and then in the book of a Frenchman known for his ability to turn a neat phrase.

I often thought about this during my navy service in World War II. I noticed that whenever an admiral had played on the football team at Annapolis, a great deal was made of the fact, and there were numerous stories to the effect that he had acquired his capacity for leadership and military strategy from playing football. The same was true, to an even greater degree, of generals who had played at West Point, and this impressed the public, as it did me.

But then I began to look at the record, and many of the finest admirals and generals had never stepped on a football field, or a baseball field either. Some of the greatest had been primarily scholars, who had paid commendable attention to their bodies and who now even during the heat of war took care to get their daily exercise. Leadership and military brilliance, I discovered, had very little to do with football training. Some of the great leaders had played on teams; more had not. Capacity for leadership came principally from the fact that they were well-disciplined, intelligent men to begin with, and those who had happened to play football played it well, as now they fought well.

I had also begun to suspect the legend that playing on a university football team, or basketball or baseball, created civic leaders. In company after company that I knew, the guiding man had played no organized games in college, although he was apt to play golf in his later years. I found little correlation between being a quarterback in college and a quarterback in life. Some college athletes graduated into good jobs and became absolutely topnotch human beings; but a larger number of topnotch leaders had never participated in organized college sports. And as every college graduate knows, a distressing number of college athletes failed to find themselves in adult life. For them the adulation of college athletics was a positive deterrent; it was an albatross which they could never shake off. For them football was not character-building; it was character-destroying.

For some twenty years I kept these tentative suspicions to myself, insecure in my evidence and suspicious that I might be reasoning from inadequate data. Certainly, the whole popular legend was that athletics did build character, and it had done so for me. So I kept silent.

And then, a few years ago, a slow but constant trickle of books and stories began to surface, calling into question the assumptions we had accepted automatically before. The intellectuals' agitation of the 1960s, with their attack on all fronts against the establishment, made it inevitable that sports should be subjected to a more severe scrutiny, and the result was spectacular.

I do not believe that anyone has the right to be doctrinaire on this question of character-building unless he has read at least some of the following books, most of which have appeared in paperback. He can reject them as sensational. He can deny their argument as prejudiced. He can inveigh against them as anti-American. And he can dismiss the individual authors as sensation mongers. But he cannot ignore the basic questions they raise.

Paul Hoch. *Rip Off the Big Game: The Exploitation of Sports by the Power Elite.* A Canadian Marxist launches a frontal attack on almost every hallowed preconception of American sports. I know of no book which so totally rejects all the beliefs I sustained from my early experience. Always infuriating, sometimes unfair, grotesquely anti-capitalist, it is nevertheless a good book to read if you want the cobwebs blasted from your eyes.

Harry Edwards. *The Revolt of the Black Athlete.* One of the first hard-nosed analyses of what the black athlete gains and loses when he becomes a part of big-time sports. Edwards, himself a black athlete, was bitterly criticized for having led the strike of black athletes at the Mexico City Olympics, but here he raises fundamental questions which destroy many illusions previously held by well-intentioned whites.

Martin Ralbovsky. *Destiny's Darlings. A World Championship Little League Team Twenty Years Later.* A carefully researched, compassionate portrait of the Schenectady Little League team which won the world championship at Williamsport in 1954. Vivid portraits of the players and coaches, then and now. In no sense scandalmongering, this book nevertheless raises important questions and indicates solutions.

Dave Meggyesy. *Out of Their League.* A cynical attack on college football (Syracuse) and professional (St. Louis). Shows a superjock as he slowly wakens to the realities of big-time sports. An eye-opener whose theses have been disputed by critics who castigate Meggyesy as a no-talent ingrate.

Robert Vare. *Buckeye, a Study of Coach Woody Hayes and the Ohio State Football Machine.* A good book to read regarding character-building and the problems attached to the vigorous recruiting of high school athletes.

Gary Shaw. *Meat on the Hoof.* A shocking personal account of how high school stars are recruited into the University of Texas and then abused when they don't make the first team and shamed into voluntarily surrendering their scholarships. Some critics have accused Shaw of being a crybaby who couldn't make it, but the basic accusations have not yet been refuted. If you can read only one book of adverse criticism, read this one for an inside look at what 'big-time football' means.

David Wolf. *Foul! The Connie Hawkins Story.* A sad, angry guided tour through the irresponsibility of big-time basketball. The conductor, Connie Hawkins, is a talented black college star who becomes a case history in exploitation, gambling, disenchantment and legal gymnastics. Anyone misty-eyed about the influence of a benign coach must read Chapter 15. Of course, if you do, you'll read the rest of the book.

Peter Gent. *North Dallas Forty.* A shocking fictional account of what life is supposed to be like when playing for the Dallas Cowboys. Gent, a football star at Michigan State and with the Cowboys, writes with an insider's know-how, but his unrelieved emphasis on brutality, venality, drugs and sex sometimes seems unreal. My comment on finishing the book: 'If they had that much sex that constantly, how did they have the energy to suit up for the Sunday game?' A book for those who retain a schoolboy's dedication to sports.

Dan Jenkins, *Semi-Tough.* A rollicking, hilariously written novel about big-time football, less brutal in its approach than *North Dallas Forty,* but based on the same assumptions. Difficult reading for those who still believe that sports build character.

I assure the reader that later on I shall be citing an equal number of books highly favorable to sports, but I believe that familiarity with some of the above books, or at least the tenor of their criticisms, is essential.

If the militaristic type of leadership evidenced in the Little League book, in the biography of Woody Hayes and the study of football at the University of Texas is what sports idealize and sponsor, then our democracy is doomed. If the professional football players presented in the two novels epitomize the kinds of all-Americans graduated by Oklahoma, Notre Dame and Michigan, our civilization has progressed to a point that leaves us some thousand leagues behind the Roman Empire.

As I was typing these doubts, and wondering if I was being fair, *The New York Times* carried this brief notice about New York City basketball, with no headline, as if the story were too ordinary to deserve comment:

> New York, February 7, 1975. Another Public Schools Athletic League basketball team has forfeited its spot in the playoffs. Brandeis High School, which gained a playoff spot when Franklin gave up all its victories, admitted yesterday that one of its players was in his fifth year in high school and was thus ineligible. Franklin's forfeits had been for the same reason. This week, in addition to Franklin and Brandeis, Bayside forfeited two games and George Washington forfeited all its games.

Thus in one week, four major high schools in one city admitted that they had been playing ineligible players, and the nature of that offense is such that at least some officials in each school must have known about it. But the lure of fielding a winning team is so great, and the rewards to any coaching staff so attractive, that outright cheating is condoned. A coach whose team goes 23–2 but who gets reprimanded for playing an ineligible player, or two or three, suffers a momentary rebuke, but he also gains long-lasting accolades for having produced a winner. And if such coaches are building character, I must not understand the meaning of that word.

I am very doubtful that big-time sports, whether high school, college, university or professional, do much to alter or enhance the character of the young men who participate. Those who enter the system with strong characters formed at home and who fall under the guidance of a good coach emerge strengthened in their convictions. Later on I shall refer to several who have had this experience.

But if the boy already has a weak character, and if he falls into the hands of an irresponsible coach, the effect of sports can be disastrous, and he may well wind up a weaker person than when he began. I know of many such and will be referring to a few.

Three conclusions have been offered to this problem. Heywood Hale Broun, who has written much in this field, has said, 'Sports do not build character. They reveal it.' Darrell Royal, of Texas, phrased it this way: 'Football doesn't build character. It eliminates the weak ones.' And a comedian has said, 'Sport develops not character, but characters.' A sentimentalist, remembering only the best, can be forgiven if he argues that sports do build character. The most I will concede is that a balance is reached, the Fellowship of Christian Athletes offsetting the savagery, the drugs, the broken contracts, the chicanery and the awful abuses in recruiting high school athletes. The literature on this subject is ably summarized in Charles R. Kniker's 'The Values of Athletics in Schools: A Continuing Debate,' in *Phi Delta Kappan,* October 1974.

The days of bland acceptance of sports are past. The entire program in this country will have to be subjected to most careful scrutiny and the most biting criticism. Those who defend sports and their enormous budgets will have to justify them as never before and many hallowed preconceptions will be challenged. From the nine critical books cited, and from other sources, including especially the daily press and to less extent television and radio, the following major accusations against sports as now conducted are being made:

• Children are being introduced into highly organized sports too young.

• Adults conducting children's programs place too much stress on winning.

• Girls and women are unjustly deprived of an adequate share of the sports budget.

• The popular contention that sports are an escape hatch for ghetto youth is overstated.

• Small colleges ought to quit trying to field two-platoon football teams.

• Most medium-sized universities are spending too much money trying to maintain big-time football programs and many should deescalate to something more manageable.

• Large universities with successful big-time programs should finance them more realistically.

• The recruiting of high school athletes is a national scandal.

• Television threatens to engulf many of the inherent values of sports.

• The media, up until recent years, have been delinquent in reporting the facts about sports.

• It is improper for political units like cities, counties and states to use public money to pay for large stadiums which are then turned over to professional teams for a fraction of a realistic rental.

• The federal government may have to intervene to provide guidance for national sporting programs, including supervision of professional contracts with players, the awarding of franchises to cities, and sponsorship of our Olympic teams.

• Throughout our sports programs there is an undue emphasis on violence.

• Even if, as some charge, the excesses of sports merely reflect the excesses of our society, that is no justification. Sports, as an idealistic exercise, should transcend any meannesses in our society and offer a more responsible ideal.

These are the conditions with which our society must grapple in the next decades, and naturally they form the basis for this book. I should like to add two other criticisms that may be the most important.

• Our present program for sports has deplorably evaded its responsibility for improving the health of individuals and of the general society.

• Especially grievous has been the lack of any program to encourage young people to continue sports activity into adult life. Such a vigorous program could prolong many lives and make each day lived more meaningful and enjoyable. We place an undue emphasis on gifted athletes aged fifteen to twenty-two, a preposterous emphasis on a few professionals aged twenty-three to thirty-five, and never enough on the mass of our population aged twenty-three to seventy-five.

II

Ways of Participating

Much of the attractiveness of sports derives from the variety of experiences they offer, and this explains in part their grip upon the American audience. I propose to cite eight case histories illustrating different ways adults respond to the stimulus of sports. The names used are fictitious but the cases are real.

The Spectator

Herman Fly was born in northwest Philadelphia in 1904. His father was a baker who had learned his trade in Germany, a no-nonsense man who frowned upon his son's desire to play in the street with other boys. He wanted Herman to learn baking, but the boy had no desire to rise at two each morning to bake the day's cinnamon buns.

Instead he joined the games the neighborhood boys were playing, and in this way learned that he was German. It came about when they chose up sides, for in the custom that then prevailed in the major-league training camps, every baseball player was either on the Irish side or the German. Slavic, Polish and black players had not then been welcomed into organized baseball.

Herman was proud to be one of the Germans, and it seemed natural to him that he should be eternally opposed to the Irish, but in the late summer of 1913 such rivalry was forgotten. The Athletics won the American League championship and headed for the World Series with the National League champion, New York. Herman was caught up in the frenzy and surprised his father one night by announcing, 'I'm an Athletics.'

When the Series started, Herman and the other boys gathered each afternoon to stand in front of Dobblemayer's tobacco shop, where a large board, painted white, had been converted into a scoreboard showing the progress of the game being played that day.

Mr. Dobblemayer received each half-inning score by telephoning the *Philadelphia Bulletin,* then posting it in black crayon. The crowd outside could see him talking into the phone and watched as he nodded gravely. Like a judge, he would then walk solemnly to the scoreboard, but if he lingered at the phone when the A's were at bat an exciting rumor would circulate among the knowing: 'Something big is happening, you watch.' And occasionally when the man at the *Bulletin* reported an A's rally, Mr. Dobblemayer would allow a half-smile to cross his lips as he marched to the scoreboard to draw a 1 or a 2.

Shibe Park, the new home of the Athletics, was only ten blocks away, yet this slow system of reporting scores continued until 1927, when radio took over, and Herman Fly always visualized the World Series as taking place on the board hung outside Mr. Dobblemayer's tobacco shop.

His first Series was, in some respects, his finest, for the A's soundly defeated John McGraw's Giants. It was this McGraw who had said contemptuously of the Philadelphia team when it entered the league, 'Well, I guess we have another white elephant on our hands,' and Connie Mack, owner of the A's, had adopted that as his team insignia. It was during this Series, when Herman first learned to hate McGraw, that his abiding antipathy for any New York team developed.

His antagonism had much to feed on that year. Chief Bender, the big Indian pitcher, defeated New York twice, and in the final game Eddie Plank allowed McGraw's men only two hits, administering a shellacking to the great Christy Mathewson. But it was the Hundred Thousand Dollar Infield of the A's that won young Herman's heart, for McInnis, Collins, Barry and Baker rattled hits off the wall, winning one game by the lopsided score of 8–2.

So the A's won the Series, four games to one, and Herman Fly was hooked on baseball. It became the most compelling experience of his life. Each evening during the season he would wait eagerly for the sports extra of the *Bulletin* to share the delicious thrill of discovering how his team had done that day. Home Run Baker became his hero—eight home runs one year, twelve another—but he also liked Eddie Collins, the smooth second baseman. 'We may win the championship forever,' Herman told the German and Irish boys with whom he played.

But in the fall of 1914 he had his first experience with that sense of loss which true sportsmen sooner or later know if they identify too closely with a team they love. The A's had coasted to the pennant and were predicted to win easily over the Boston Braves, a parvenu team which had been extremely lucky to win the National League race. In October, Herman and his gang gathered outside the tobacco store to share in the massacre, but the first day was a disaster. Boston won 7–1. They won the next game, too. And the next. And on the last day Herman's team of mighty sluggers picked up seven hits, yet lost, 3–1.

That was the end of the Athletics, and of Herman Fly's dream of endless victories. Connie Mack sold off the Hundred Thousand Dollar Infield: Eddie Collins to the White Sox, Jack Barry to the Red Sox, Home Run Baker to the Yankees, and finally, Stuffy McInnis to the Red Sox. The sterling pitchers went, too: Chief Bender to an outlaw league; Eddie Plank to the St. Louis Federals; Joe Bush to the Red Sox; Bob Shawkey to the Yankees; and the great Herb Pennock to the Red Sox.

Then came the years of disaster. In 1915 Herman Fly saw his beloved team drop to last place, 58½ games behind the leaders, the most disastrous one-season drop from first to last in baseball history. For seven years the A's languished in the cellar, and it was during this arid spell that Herman learned what it meant to be a Philadelphia fan: he cursed the inept players but never once did he desert the team.

'They'll come back,' he predicted. 'Next year they'll have the pitching.' It became a mania with him, and when he landed a job with the Baldwin Locomotive Works on Broad Street he spent every Saturday and holiday at Shibe Park, if the A's were playing at home. And often he would take a day's sick leave to watch his champions, for they were always that to him.

'I saw this team when it swept everything before it,' he told his fellow workmen. 'I saw the Hundred Thousand Dollar Infield. McInnis, Collins, Barry, Baker.' He had never actually seen that infield, but like a true fan, he thought he had.

And then about 1924 Herman's loyalty began to be repaid. The A's quietly picked up some players who were destined for greatness: Max Bishop at second base, Bing Miller, who had come in 1922, in right field, and particularly a slugging Pole named Aloysius Szymanski, to be known as Al Simmons, who would bat .392 one year, .334 lifetime. The pitchers were improving too: Walberg and Rommel were there already; Earnshaw and Grove were about to appear.

'I can smell a championship,' Herman said at the beginning of 1924, and although the A's would finish only fifth that year, they did play one double-header with Boston which Herman always said was 'the greatest one day of baseball a man's ever seen.'

The games took place on Wednesday afternoon, May 28, 1924. Howard

Ehmke had been announced as the pitcher for Boston, and this of itself would have filled the park, for last year he had thrown a no-hitter against the A's. 'It was really a one-hitter,' Herman explained to the two men from the locomotive factory as they rode the streetcar to the games. 'Bugger Welch had a single, but the Boston left fielder got his glove on the ball, and late in the game, when it looked like Ehmke might carve a no-hitter, the scorers changed the single into an error.'

Now Ehmke, the constant nemesis of Philadelphia, was to pitch again, and he picked up where he had left off the year before. With two out in the ninth inning, he had another no-hitter going, 1–0, in precisely the same circumstances as before. Early in the game Bugger Welch had scratched a single, but Bobby Veach, the left fielder, had played the ball badly, and a rumor passed through the bleachers that if Ehmke got the last man out, the single would be changed to an error, and he would have a second no-hitter against the A's.

But with two out, Ehmke walked Harry Riconda, the A's third baseman, and that brought to the plate Bugger Welch, still bitter about having been robbed of a hit last year and about to be robbed of another hit. As to what happened next, Herman told the story through the years: 'It's two out, a no-hitter working, a man on first because of a walk. Bugger Welch up, swingin' his mighty bat. Count goes to three and one and Ehmke supposes Welch will take the next one, hopin' it'll be a ball. Right down the middle. One swing and out of the park. It landed two seats away from me in left field, and I mighta caught it but a big geezer moved in front of me. But you know what I remember best about that hit? Howard Ehmke stood on the pitcher's mound and watched the ball come into the stands. Then he skimmed his glove like a little boy skippin' stones, and it went right into the boxes and he didn't give a damn. He just walked into the dugout and kicked the waterbucket.'

The second game was almost as interesting. On the first pitch in the first inning, Ira Flagstead blasted a home run into almost the same spot that Welch's had landed. 'I coulda caught that one, too,' Herman told his friends, 'but this big geezer steps in front of me. There was no more scorin' that day. First game 2–1, second game 1–0, both games settled by home runs on back-to-back pitches. Best day of baseball a man could see.'

In later years, however, an added piquancy accrued to this strange doubleheader, and Herman Fly was one of the first to remark upon it. 'Who were the Boston pitchers that day? Howard Ehmke and John Picus Quinn. And it was only when these two cunning old-timers were picked up by the A's that our great championship really melded.'

Ehmke came in 1926, Quinn in 1925, and from then on, one of baseball's finest teams began to coalesce. Second place in 1927, second place in 1928 by 2½ games, first place in 1929 by the huge margin of 18 games, and first again in 1930 and 1931.

For the rest of his life Herman Fly would be able to recite the roster of that poetic, powerful and pleasant team: 'I can see them now, gettin' ready to play the Yankees. Foxx, Bishop, Boley, Dykes in the infield. Simmons, Haas, Miller in the garden. Mickey Cochrane behind the plate, and there never was a better. And a pitchin' staff to make a manager dream. Grove, Earnshaw, Walberg, Rommel, Ehmke, Quinn.'

In these years Herman Fly earned only a modest salary at the locomotive works. He was married, had two children and attended church regularly, but the spiritual focus of his life was the baseball team, and whenever it appeared certain that the A's would win the pennant he dipped into his savings and bought himself a set of tickets for the World Series. He was in the bleachers, therefore, on that memorable afternoon, October 12, 1929, when the strangest game in World Series history was played, and he was not loath to recount it to his friends.

'The A's had won the first two in Chicago, but in the third game at Shibe Park, Guy Bush throws himself a masterpiece and wins, 3–1. The fourth game, with me sittin' almost where I was durin' that famous doubleheader, is a disaster. The Cubs blast Quinn, Walberg and Rommel for ten hits includin' a home run and who knows how many doubles and they lead by 8–0 with three innin's still to go, and Charlie Root pitchin' himself another masterpiece.

'But in the bottom of the seventh, with no hope, Al Simmons swings from his toes and lands the ball on the roof in left field. Foxx singles, Miller singles, Dykes singles and a guy near me yells, "We got a rally goin'," and I yelled back, "Don't be stupid." But now Boley singles and the runs start comin' in. Then George Burns, the old Cleveland castoff, he bats for Rommel and he flies out. Remember this, because it's important.

'Then Mule Haas hits a home run inside the park, and suddenly the score is 8–7 and I'm yellin' to the guy, "We sure do have a rally goin'," and he yells back, "You watch! We're gonna win it," and this time I don't contradict him, because even if I did, he couldn't hear me.

'Then Cochrane draws a pass, but Al Simmons gets his second hit, a single to left. Jimmy Foxx gets his second hit, a single to center, and bazooo! The score's tied! Miller gets hit by a pitched ball, and Jimmy Dykes gets *his* second hit, a screaming double to left, which scores two more runs and makes the game 10–8 our favor.

'Then George Burns strikes out, and becomes the only man in history to make two outs in one innin' in a World Series, or so I'm told. And Boley strikes out too, and the famous innin' is over. Ten runs at one smack by a team climbin' out of the pits of hell.'

In 1931 Herman Fly became the quintessential Philadelphia rooter: he learned the meaning of tragedy. His A's had a chance for a third straight pennant, and Herman followed his club attentively as they forged ahead of Washington and New York, but what the men in the foundry really talked about was the amazing skein of victories being strung together by Lefty Grove, believed by all A's rooters to be the greatest left-hander in baseball history.

Thirteen wins in a row. Then an easy 8–1 victory over Detroit for number fourteen. Then a pitching duel with Wes Ferrell of Cleveland, which Grove won 4–3 for number fifteen. Then a marvelous pitching performance in Chicago and a 4–2 win which tied him with Smoky Joe Wood and the great Walter Johnson as the American League pitcher with the most victories in a row, sixteen.

'Never saw him greater,' Herman said of Grove in those wildly exciting days. 'And look at the easies he has comin' up. St. Louis Browns, and they ain't goin' anywhere. It's a cinch he'll beat 'em Sunday and set a new league record. Then home for a long stand, and he'll easy win two more and tie the world record. Nineteen in a row, then one more and he stands alone.'

Herman Fly would never forget the first game of the doubleheader played in St. Louis on Sunday, August 23, 1931. Grove went up against a so-so pitcher named Dick Coffman, and Herman told the men who had gathered to drink beer, 'Lefty is a shoo-in.'

But Coffman pitched a superlative game, allowing the A's only three scrawny hits. Grove was equal to the occasion, pitching his own masterpiece. The score should have gone into the tenth inning 0–0, with Grove a good bet to win in overtime, except that disaster loomed.

Al Simmons, one of the greatest, had injured his foot and had gone home to Milwaukee to tend it. In his place in left field the rookie Jimmy Moore had started, and in the third inning, with two outs and Fred Schulte on first, Oscar Melillo, the Browns' second baseman, hit a routine liner into left which Simmons would have gobbled up for the third out. Jimmy Moore, however, attempted a fancy catch, the ball went over his head, and by the time center fielder Doc Cramer got to it, Schulte had scored the game's only run. Grove's once-in-a-lifetime chance to set a new world's record was lost, and all because a rookie replacement had tried to act like an old-timer.

'What eats my guts out,' Herman Fly muttered for weeks after that disaster, 'is that Grove went on to win his next three games, includin' that fantastic game in Boston, 2–0, when he gave the Red Sox only three hits and didn't let a man get to second. God Almighty, if he'da won in St. Louis that Sunday, he'da had twenty in a row, and his record woulda stood forever.'

Often when he thought of the disaster that had overtaken his hero, he would drop his head and mutter, 'I could strangle Jimmy Moore,' and tears would come into his eyes. Forever after, when he thought of Grove, the marvelous stringbean, he visualized that sad moment when Jimmy Moore miscalculated an easy out. 'Except for that,' Herman often said, 'old Lefty woulda swept all before him. One pukey error.' He continued to visualize himself strangling Jimmy Moore. But then his attention was distracted by the way the St. Louis Cardinals tore the A's apart in the World Series. It was disgraceful, with Pepper Martin stealing the glove off Cochrane's hand.

'It's been a bad year,' Herman moaned as the fate-ridden season ended, and he sensed that it might be the harbinger of worse to come.

In 1935 everything turned sour. Once more Connie Mack sold off his stars, all of them, and it grieved Herman to see Boston come into town with Grove and Foxx, or Detroit with Mickey Cochrane, still the best catcher in baseball. Eighth place one year by 34 games, once by 49, and later by 55, by 60. The team was so inept that fans conducted contests to see who could invent the silliest sayings about it: 'One day Elmer Valo actually got to third base, and he asked the umpire, "Where do I go from here?" '

But now the quality of the true Philadelphia rooter manifested itself. Herman Fly and men like him kept coming out to the games, kept hoping that some miracle would again lift their team from last to first. They bled, they cursed, they left the park humiliated, but they kept supporting the team. In later years Herman would grow furious when he read that Baltimore or Boston would support only a winner. 'Hell,' he growled, 'if we waited in Philadelphia for a winner, we wouldn't support nobody.'

In 1954 the miserable news broke that the Athletics were finally leaving the city. Connie Mack was long since broke. The team showed no possibility of recuperation, and other cities were eager to try their hand at rejuvenation in a new setting. Herman Fly felt as if a major part of his life were ending, as indeed it was.

But then an extraordinary reaction took place: although the A's now played in Kansas City, they remained his team, and when they moved to Oakland and their fortunes began to revive, Herman felt a surge of pride. 'My old team's comin' back,' he told his friends. When the A's won three pennants in a row, and did so well in the World Series, he basked in their glory as if they were still playing in Shibe Park. 'I told you they'd be winners again.' Even though he had not seen them play a single game since 1954, for they did not play National League teams like the Phillies, they were still his team.

But as a dedicated spectator, who derived positive good from sitting in a crowd and cheering for his team, he required a club to support, and when the A's left Philadelphia some of his friends suggested that he transfer his loyalty to the Phillies, but he spurned them. 'Worst team in baseball history.

In their entire career they won just one World Series game, back in 1915. To hell with such a team.'

Later he transferred his affections to the 76ers basketball team, but this, too, was an agonizing experience, for every year the team would show real promise, only to collapse in the play-offs against the Boston Celtics. After one real debacle he growled, 'I would like to punch Wilt Chamberlain right in the nose,' and a friend asked, 'What you goin' to use, a stepladder?'

When he was seventy years old, in 1974, his grandson insisted that he see a hockey game, and after ten minutes in the bright new arena at the other end of Broad Street, he understood what the game was all about, and he became a fierce partisan, screaming in support of the rowdy team known as the Broad Street Bullies. He pointed out, correctly, that when the Boston Bruins played rough it was called 'vigorous checking,' but when the Flyers used the same tactics it was 'unnecessary brutality.'

Tickets to the hockey games were difficult to get, but during the regular season he managed a few. When the play-offs came, it was hopeless, and he watched those brilliant games on television with mounting fury. First Atlanta, and the Philadelphia team won. Then a bruising series with New York, and again his team won. Then the culmination with Boston, the best team in the world, and in a final game of uninterrupted brilliance, Philadelphia won, 1–0.

When the last moment of that game ended, Herman Fly gave a shriek, turned off his television, and stormed out into the streets. Hundreds did the same, then thousands and finally more than a million and a half. They roared up and down Broad Street, smashing windows, kissing girls, overturning automobiles. They sang and drank beer and hugged one another and became a town gone wild, absolutely wild, and long after dawn Herman returned home, exhausted and very happy.

'You look like a ten-day drunk,' his wife said.

'It's worth it, to have a championship again,' he replied.

He couldn't get to sleep. He sat on a chair in his room, his head bowed as if he were praying. From time to time he would shake his head and mutter, 'I've seen 'em all. McInnis, Collins, Barry, Baker. Foxx, Bishop, Boley, Dykes. Wilt Chamberlain, Hal Greer, Billy Cunningham. And now Bobby Clarke and Bernie Parent.'

Deeply satisfied, he nodded his bald head, a man of seventy no longer working. 'But the day I remember best isn't that ten-run inning in the World Series. It's that doubleheader. My, my. A no-hit game ruined in the ninth inning with two outs. And the next game 1–0 on Ira Flagstead's home run. That was a day to remember.'

But then the sadness of the passing years caught up with him and he gritted his store teeth: 'By God, I'd like to strangle Jimmy Moore.'

*   *   *

Herman Fly never once knew the joy of active participation, but that he derived spiritual pleasure from being a mere spectator, there can be no doubt. In an age when big-league franchises were being callously shifted in order to pick up a few more dollars, he was unique in continuing to pay his devotion to a team which had abandoned him; many fans refused to do this and turned away from sports in bitterness.

Fly's health was affected neither favorably nor unfavorably by his attendance at games. Possibly he derived some good from sitting in sunlight and fresh air, but not much. At the later basketball and hockey games he inhaled a lot of other people's smoke, but the damage was minimal. His furious partisanship could have endangered his heart, but his hard work at the locomotive plant had established alternate feed lines. In fact, the excitement stimulated his circulation.

For the small amount of money he spent each year on his admissions, Fly received a maximum return. For him, sports were a bargain.

The Bettor

While working on this book I enjoyed opportunities that would rarely be accorded the average fan, and I was always mindful of that fact. I was allowed to work out with a professional football team. I was invited into the inner sanctum of another NFL team and watched many inside operations. I met with our leading coaches, attended seminars of college presidents concerned with sports, followed baseball teams closely, and watched private practices in college basketball.

I was able to travel, too, and experience big-game fishing in Hawaii, the Super Bowl in New Orleans, a rodeo in a little town in Montana, auto races everywhere, trotting races at a beautiful rural track in upper New York, and soccer's World Cup in Munich.

If I like sports, it is partly because I have been privileged to see them at their best, but no experience was more meaningful than an invitation I received from a man who made his living gambling on horses. 'If you want to see what it's like, live with me for a while.'

I shall call him simply the Pole, because that's what he called himself. He lived in a neat garden apartment at the edge of Camden, New Jersey, where he was within driving distance of six major race tracks: Garden State, Monmouth and Atlantic City in New Jersey; Liberty Bell and Keystone across the river in Pennsylvania; and beautiful Delaware Park across the bridge in Delaware. The meetings at these tracks were so coordinated that he could attend one almost every day in the year, and he did so.

He asked me, 'Try to get to my place before eight in the morning, because I want you to see just what we do.' I asked who the *we* were, and he said, 'You'll see.'

I left home about six and drove down the turnpike to the Camden exit, then out to the edge of the city, where the Pole was waiting for me. He led me to his quarters, a fine, clean apartment decorated with watercolors his wife had done before she died. He was a good cook, and as soon as we got to his apartment he started breakfast, a rather large one for the two of us, I thought.

At quarter to nine, as they did every day of the year, the Italian and the German arrived, the first a short, intense man in his early fifties, the second a very tall, thin man in his late forties. The Pole, a hefty man who had held many jobs from which he was now retired, was just past sixty.

His visitors had brought with them three copies of that day's *Daily Racing Form,* and before breakfast was served, each man opened his *Form* and studied it in silence. They were comparing the offerings at the various tracks running that day, and with a skill that I would never understand or master, they decided which track offered them the best opportunities for betting. They then discussed their conclusions, each man stating his opinion, and in the end it was decided that on this day they would head for Liberty Bell.

These men earned their livings betting on horses. Each had a small assured income from either retirement benefits or a night custodian's job, but primarily they spent only such money as they earned at the track. For them betting was deadly serious, and although they were pleased to talk with me about other aspects of their lives, they wanted no levity about horses and refused to tell me how much actual money they bet or on what horse. They did not even tell one another. They would share the most intimate thoughts about a race, the jockey, the past performances, the way the horse did on grass or on a wet track. But when the final moment came, they moved apart and each man bet his own conclusions.

They bet in three radically different ways. The Pole, a conservative, looked for the races that promised higher than usual returns on place and show bets, and he was supposed to be uncanny in his ability to spot a race in which the odds were more favorable than the facts would warrant. He rarely bet to win, although sometimes he would go across the board on a horse that seemed sure to place and with a good chance to win. There were refinements to his system that I did not penetrate; although he explained them to me several times, they required so much concentration and study of the *Racing Form* that I was soon lost in paper work.

The Italian played only the gimmick bets: the Daily Double (the winners in the first two races), the Exacta (first two finishers in one race) and the

Trifecta (first three finishers in one race). 'What's the good of betting $2 and getting back $3.20, like him?' he asked contemptuously, indicating the Pole. Betting every gimmick race on the card, the Italian's winnings were sensational . . . once or twice a month. I was with him when he won something like $372 for a $10 bet in the Daily Double, and $194 for a $2 bet. He was also very strong in picking the Trifecta on the ninth race, and when he did this, ending the day with a big hit, he invariably invited his two companions to a good dinner at one of the fine restaurants in the area.

The German looked for special situations. He would bet either the gimmicks, or to win, or across the board, or even sometimes to show. All he required was some bit of knowledge the general public did not have. When he acquired this edge, he was willing to gamble heavily on it. But when he felt himself just one of the general mass, he would ignore that race, and on some days he might bet only once or twice out of nine races. I gained the impression that perhaps he did better, in the long run, than either of the other two.

It was the German who set the philosophical stage for my betting experience, but before we get to that, let's finish with the breakfast. Every morning when the meal was about ready the Pole would ask the Italian how he liked his eggs, and every morning the Italian would reply, 'On a plate.' Then, chuckles behind them, the Pole would disappear into the kitchen and shortly thereafter summon the others to the table. There he would serve them eggs, sausage, fried potatoes, Danish and coffee. The German always had milk. They would eat heartily, for that was the last meal they would have till about eight at night.

During breakfast they would discuss the nine races at Liberty Bell, or wherever they were headed, and I could see each man confirming himself in his predilected way of betting. The Pole would be looking for horses with slight edges that he might capitalize upon across the board. The Italian was forming up his ideas about the Daily Double, his first big responsibility of the day. And the German would be studying speed ratings, jockey switches, trainers' habits, weather and the multitude of other factors reported in the *Racing Form*. At this stage they would be exchanging information rather freely, and I was invited to listen and make use of it as I deemed best. (During our entire relationship, which was a most congenial one, they never advised me specifically concerning a single horse. If, as a consequence of their stated opinions, I came to like one enough to bet on it, that was my decision, not theirs.)

After breakfast there was a more leisurely study of the *Form*, but with each man zeroing in on some peculiarity he had noticed, and now there was no exchange of information. The room was hauntingly quiet, and it was definitely each man for himself.

At about eleven-thirty they would clean up the apartment, washing the breakfast dishes before they left, and would head for the car so as to be inside the race track well before one-thirty, post time for the first race, which would also be the first leg of the Daily Double.

At the track each man would pay $2 or $2.25 entrance money and 35¢ for the program, which gave last-minute changes and the track handicapper's selections. These two fees, added to the $1 apiece already paid for the *Racing Form,* meant that each man started the day a total of $3.35 or $3.60 in the hole, plus the 50¢ or $1 parking fee paid by whoever drove.

I asked why they were willing to pay this initiation fee, as it were, and the Italian introduced me into some of the niceties of betting for a living. 'I'd prefer to stay home and bet with my bookie, but if I do, four bad things can happen. No matter how high the odds are at the track, and we'll see some sixty-to-one shots, the bookie has a rule that he will never pay higher than thirty-to-one on win bets and fifty-five-to-one on gimmicks. Also he won't accept place and show bets unless an equal amount is bet to win. So you miss your chance at a real killing. And if you win too often, he won't let you bet with him any longer. And if too many people win one day, you may never see him again. To get the best betting odds, you simply gotta go to the track.'

'Also,' said the German, 'you gotta be at the track to pick up your last-minute bits of information.' I was to learn that the German never placed any bet until the last thirty seconds before a race began. He was especially sensitive to the ebb and flow of heavy money, which altered the visible odds on the horses, and if a great chunk of what he called 'smart money' were suddenly dumped on a horse to lower the odds appreciably at the last minute, he might rush in and climb aboard, aware that some kind of special knowledge was operating that day.

Each day as we entered the race track he would look up at the portals and tell me, 'Remember, Michener, more than a million dollars will be bet here today. By slobs who don't know anything about racin'. There's no reason why us fellows who do know somethin' shouldn't pick off our share of that loot.'

The Pole, when I'd asked apprehensively if any of the races were fixed, told me not to worry about my money. 'Whether they're fixed or not doesn't matter, Jim. At most, they manipulate one race a day, and even then, whether the fix is a tampered horse that's supposed to lose because, say, they put bad shoes on him, or whether it's a hyped horse that's supposed to win, everything doesn't always go according to plan, because the horse that's supposed to win doesn't know it. Nobody's figured out how to tell him yet.'

I was astonished by the fact that my three gamblers almost never watched a race. They gathered in a corner under the grandstand, joined by seven or eight other gamblers who attended the tracks regularly, and there they would stand all afternoon, lying to one another, studying the past performances for the upcoming race, moving cautiously to the betting windows with an eye on the tote board in the last two or three minutes, and placing their bets in the severest secrecy.

They cashed their winning tickets in the same secrecy, and during the entire time I was with them I never heard one of my three or any of the other seven or eight report honestly on whether he had won or lost a specific race or on how he was doing generally. The standard reply, used by all of them, was, 'I'm makin' expenses.'

While these classic and silent men pursued their trade, I was being introduced to two of the most fascinating people at the track. The Super Stooper was a tall, thin man who wore a sharp spike attached to the toe of his right shoe. He spent his afternoon prowling the grandstand, keeping his eyes on the floor, turning over castaway tickets with the spike, looking for winning tickets whose one-time owners had mistakenly thrown them away.

The introduction was sedate and formal: 'Super, this is James Michener, the writer. He'd like to work with you for a while. Mr. Michener, this is the Super Stooper.' He nodded gravely and indicated that I would be welcome to join him, if I didn't slow him down too much with my questions.

'Do you ever find tickets worth real money?'

'Would I wear a nail in my toe if I didn't?'

When the Super Stooper did not intend answering a question, he would interrupt his constant staring at the floor and look at me as if I were an imbecile. Without further comment he would resume his inspection of the fallen tickets.

'What kind of situation is best for you?'

'The race ends, a losing jockey claims foul against the winner. Confusion. A lot of people have already thrown away their tickets. If it's the last race, some of them are already on the bus. On a good day, maybe three objections.'

'On an average day, why might I throw away one of my tickets?'

He looked at me as if to calculate the level of my stupidity, then said, 'You get three different tickets, to win, to place, to show. Your horse wins, so you throw the other two away.'

'Are people that dumb?'

'You could be. Easy.'

'You ever bet on a race yourself?'

He gave me the stare and resumed his endless search for the big winning ticket that some stupid customer had thrown away. The Italian told me that each week the Super Stooper would find himself quite a few $3.60 and $4.20 winners.

But the bettor who won my heart was Frank the Tank. (At the tracks they really did use such names. One bettor I got to know very well who went by the monicker Nobbles was squiring a married lady to whom he referred invariably as Yamma, so if the name were overheard in the wrong places, the sex wouldn't be apparent.)

Frank the Tank was a muscular, barrel-like specimen who appeared every afternoon only at the end of the eighth race, for it is the custom at eastern race tracks to throw open the gates at the conclusion of that race, giving anyone who wished to enter free access to the betting windows for the ninth and final race. That late in the day a bettor could park free in the track lot and have little trouble finding a discarded program and *Racing Form.* Frank the Tank bet only the ninth race, for which, through the years, he had acquired a special proficiency.

From the moment he walked in, he would position himself on the outside apron overlooking the finish line. This allowed him both a clear view of the place and show pools on the tote board and quick access to the betting windows. He was unbelievably sensitive to any changes in odds which might give him an edge, and he watched right down to the last second before placing his own bet, which I judged to be considerable, say $50 or $75.

Once he explained his system. 'In the ninth race everything is different. The big winners have gone home. The big losers are still here, tryin' to make a recovery. They throw a lot of money into the pool on horses that ain't got a chance of winnin'. To get even, the big loser has to bet on long shots, which means the bad horses are drawing lots of money. If a good horse wins, he will pay better odds than normal for place or show. Also, the really stupid bettors are puttin' all their money on the Trifecta moon shot, so they ain't clutterin' up the place and show lines, 'cause this late they can't get even with place and show. Also, in the ninth race lotsa times they run broken-down horses at strange distances, so it's a real grab bag and form don't mean that much. The money can be seen right there on the board if you got a keen eye.'

Frank the Tank spent his entire life waiting outside Philadelphia-area race tracks for his free ninth race. On those days when he judged the ninth to be totally banal, with no edge to the knowing bettor, he was quite content to stand pat and watch other people bet. But whenever he had a slight edge in knowledge, and when it was confirmed by the *Daily Racing Form,* he would plunge.

I liked Frank and was with him one day when he hit a big winner in the ninth at Delaware Park. From somewhere he had picked up a tip that one of the trainers was trying to slip a very speedy horse into a cheap race, but had not given winning instructions to the jockey. This meant that another horse, on whom the odds were rather long, had a good chance maybe to win, but at least to either place or show. So Frank bet his bundle on this second horse, and whether the trainer was trying to win with the favorite or not, the jockey was, and the first horse came home a winner . . . at very short odds, something like $3.80. But Frank's horse came in at $10.60 to place and $6.60 to show.

I had two superb moments at the race tracks. On the last morning the four of us were together, I had my own *Racing Form,* and by diligently applying the lessons I'd learned, I actually picked a filly in the first race who was destined to win. I was tipped off by various facts: she was dropping from a $10,000 race to $5,000, which was helpful. She ran much better in wet weather than dry, and today was going to be dry but at the end of a wet spell. And she had finished her last three races in fourth position but against better opposition. She was a maiden, meaning that she—or it could be a he —had not yet won a race, but her times were consistent and she was being ridden on this day by a jockey who was among the leaders at the meet but hadn't been winning lately. I judged that horse and jockey alike were about due, and as we ate I outlined my thinking to my three mentors.

'He's catchin' on,' the German said approvingly, but none of the three liked my selection, mainly because the first race was for maiden fillies, and in such a race anything is likely to happen, since none of the competitors has ever won and since fillies are more unpredictable than colts. But when we reached the track and I bet my $5 across the board on number nine and she won by three lengths at $10.40 for $2, a good win price, I was touted through the professional fraternity as a comer. The Italian, who never missed a trick, had, against his own better judgment, decided to crank my selection into his Daily Double bets—a fact which he told me much later —and made himself $166.

The second good moment came at Atlantic City some three months after I had spent my apprenticeship with the bettors. I was that day a guest of the management and the eighth race had been named in my honor, which meant that I was to hand out the trophy in the winner's circle. After I did so, and after the flash bulbs had subsided and I was walking back to the plush clubhouse from where I was watching the races, I heard a loud 'Pssst!' and I looked into the grandstand area and there were my mentors, the Pole, the Italian, the German.

'Hey, Jim!' the latter yelled as I went to the fence separating the wealthy customers from the rabble. 'Look who we got with us!'

It was the Super Stooper, his eyes bleary from the unaccustomed sunlight. 'You have any luck?' I asked him.

'He's makin' expenses,' the Italian interjected.

And then, shuffling in past the open entrances loomed Frank the Tank on his way to master the ninth race. He was wearing sneakers that day, lest he have to hurry to the windows in the last few seconds. He did not see me, for his eyes were glued to the tote board; he had probably picked up inside information which would give him an edge.

I am always surprised when I hear that horse racing is the principal public sporting event in America. In a typical year it collects over seventy million paid admissions. Next is the forty-five million at auto racing, thirty million at college football. Having attended a good many races in the course of my study, and at a rather intense level, I can understand the popularity. The nine races go off on time. Each produces a known winner and a certain bunch of losers. The race tracks tend to be handsome, well-run places, with posh restaurants for those who can afford them and rather good beef sandwiches for the hoi polloi. And for people like me, who love the printed word and the calculation of possibilities, there is the *Daily Racing Form* with its multitude of ascertainable facts and its delicious implication that picking the winner is a science. Also, there are the handsome horses, the keen-witted little jockeys, the canny old trainers, and in harness racing the amazingly complex drivers, who can continue racing well past the age of sixty. Racing is indeed 'The Sport of Kings,' but I suspect that a good four-fifths of its appeal is the organized gambling that accompanies it, which may be sadly true of other sports also, like football, where the gambling is just as well organized but wholly illegal.

Few spectators of any sport derive the joy that my three gamblers do from racing: the camaraderie of getting to the track, the close association with other gamblers, the intense excitement repeated nine times, and the general graciousness that governs the track. I learned about this when I occupied a folding chair which I thought had been provided by the management. The Italian, horrified by this breach, whispered, 'That belongs to somebody! Get off, quick, before they come back.'

My three gamblers derived few if any health benefits from their hobby. They rarely saw the outdoors, or the sun, or the race-track gardens. They got little fresh air. They rarely moved about, and the idea of exercise would have stunned them. They were unusually tense, but the episodic emotional release at either victory or defeat undoubtedly helped them discharge both their aggressions and their tensions.

The Vigorous Participant

Artemius Crandall grew up in the black section of a small Texas town. He had no father, but lived with his mother and her four other children in a mean house on a mean street. From his earliest days he could run and wrestle, and his obvious skill at games attracted much favorable attention from the black men who watched the boys at play.

One of them advised a white carpenter for whom he worked that 'there's this here Crandall kid at the edge of town who's faster than a deer.' The white man, an enthusiastic supporter of the high school football team, took it upon himself to scout the Crandall boy, and what he saw he liked.

He went to the high school coach and said, 'Vernor, I've spotted you an all-time winner, but we got to keep him under cover before one of the other schools hears about him.'

So the carpenter and the coach went to see Mrs. Crandall and gave her some money to help with the other children, and they told her that they felt sure her son Artemius could be a real star on the local team, if he kept his nose clean.

'He's a good boy,' she assured the two men, and she was right.

Artemius was then thirteen years old, a slim-hipped, broad-shouldered boy five-feet-ten and with every indication he would grow another six inches. He had a short neck, the kind that doesn't injure easily, and extremely quick reactions, including a remarkable peripheral vision, so that he could both see an oncoming object and adjust to it quickly.

And he behaved himself. He had broken into no stores, stolen nothing, molested no girls. Had he been a white boy in a town like Waco or Lubbock he could have been an honor student. In his little town his teachers taught him practically nothing, and even without the intervention of the carpenter and the coach, he knew that unless he excelled in football he was doomed to the nothingness he saw among the black men of his community.

The white men now faced a difficult decision. They had been insisting for some years that their town have a big-time football team, one they could be proud of, and they saw in Artemius Crandall and some other boys of promise a chance to achieve greatness. But to field a winner required some nice tactical decisions, and they discussed what age to make Artemius, who was thirteen. If they made him twelve, he could play when he was more mature, but if he was fourteen, he could start a year earlier. They decided on twelve, so that he would be coming along with two other very good prospects, and his birth papers, fragmentary at best, were reissued to make him seem a year younger than he really was.

They also looked after his grades, convincing his teachers to give him all A's and B's, even though his schooling up to then had left him largely illiterate. He wanted to play basketball and baseball too, but they convinced him that he might damage his football chances if he did that, so they kept him working winter, spring and summer on football until he became a phenomenon.

Unfortunately, he became so good at breaking tackles and cutting either left or right that it was impossible to keep his existence secret. Scouts from a neighboring city of some size heard from a traveling salesman, whom they paid to bring them such news, that 'a kid named Artemius Crandall is tearin' things up out on the prairie,' and they slipped a couple of experts into the crowd one afternoon when Artemius was playing, and these men saw immediately that this kid was an all-time winner.

What to do? To waste such talent in a hick town was disgraceful when the boy might have a chance to play for the state championship. So it was decided to look into the matter. The men from the city decided that it would be too costly to relocate the whole Crandall family. However, Mrs. Crandall had a bachelor brother, and the men persuaded him to move into the city and to bring his nephew Artemius along.

When the rural high school coach heard about the proposed hijacking, he raised the devil, but the coach from the city appeared in a black Chrysler and talked sensibly with the boy's mother. 'What do you desire for your son?' he asked with extreme politeness. 'If he comes with us . . . front page coverage . . . state-wide television . . . a sure scholarship to the University of Texas . . . maybe a doctor or a lawyer.'

He painted such a glowing vision of the boy's future that Mrs. Crandall could not resist. Her son would move to the city with his uncle.

'I'll go to court if they try to steal him that way,' the rural coach shouted, but he knew he was licked. The city coach had affidavits proving that Mrs. Crandall was too poor to support all her children, whereas provision would be made so that the boy's uncle could do so. The latter was true, since businessmen who were determined to bring the state championship to the city had found jobs for both uncle and nephew, so that each was making four times as much money as Mrs. Crandall had ever made in her life.

As a high school player, Artemius Crandall was a sensation, a running back of speed and skill. Of course, because of his spurious birth date he was playing against boys a year younger than himself, except that some of their certificates had been shifted too. His team went 11–1, 11–0, and 11–1 while he played on it, and two years out of three it won the Texas championship. The only thing that might have marred his record was the fact that late in his senior year the disgruntled carpenter from his hometown told the coach of another team that was battling Crandall's for the championship that the star halfback's true age was nineteen, and that his birth certificate had been jimmied. This created a temporary scandal, but since Crandall's hometown was proud of the boy's accomplishments, the officials repulsed the rumor, and his career was saved.

He had no trouble academically. Although he could barely read or write, teachers in his new school gave him the same high marks he had been receiving in the country town, and he was able to graduate with a B-plus average. In deportment he remained an almost ideal young man, and his coach said of him, 'Probably the finest young football player in the State of Texas, all things considered. I'd be proud to have him as my son.'

Crandall's real trouble started in the latter weeks of his junior year, when he already held most of the state records for rushing. Informal scouts, representing numerous universities, began running into Crandall accidentally. He would be entering a supermarket to buy a quart of orange juice and a stranger would ask, 'Aren't you Artemius Crandall, the famous halfback?' Such a question was flattering, and Crandall would nod, whereupon the man would say, 'I'm Ed Garver. Went to Baylor myself, and if you ever want to go to a real great school, get in touch with me.'

In this way he met alumni from Texas, TCU, Rice, Arkansas and Oklahoma. No one made any specific promises, because that was illegal, but hints were dropped and two different men stopped by to see Artemius' uncle, to see if he would like to move to this university town or that to a much better job. His uncle said he liked it where he was.

Things might have gone badly for Artemius had not his uncle proved to be a man of character. From the first he had known what these white men were up to, for he had early on spotted the unusual ability of his nephew. He knew that Artemius was a marketable item and had agreed to move to the city only because such a setting would enable his nephew to command a higher price.

As soon as the scouts began to converge, he laid the facts on the table for Artemius to study. 'What we're after,' he said forcefully, 'is for you to get yourself a big-time contract like O.J. Simpson or John Brockington. They did it, Artemius, so can you. What university you go to don't matter, Artemius. So long as you get a coach like Bear Bryant or Woody Hayes who can land you that contract. So you listen, boy, listen to all of them, but in the back of your mind you keep askin' just one question, "Can this dude get me a big-time contract?" What he can do for you in the next four years ain't much. But what he can do for you at the end of four years, that's everything.'

Most of the scouts who visited the uncle considered him a lout, a big, hulking black man who stayed in the shadows. They suspected he had been moved into the city with his nephew so that the boy could play football there, and they laid plans to bring both of them to their campuses. That the uncle would come along they did not doubt and were prepared to pay him handsomely for doing so.

One coach was different. Honest John Taggart, from the University of Jefferson* flew into the city in a Lear jet owned by Western United, a food

*A fictitious place, as explained in Chapter VII.

processing chain. At the airport two large black Cadillacs, also owned by Western United, were waiting, and when they pulled up before the modest house in which Artemius and his uncle lived, children in the street started yelling, 'They comin' to see the football hero!' And Honest John stopped, bent over, talked with the children, and said 'You're right. We're coming to see the finest football player in the nation.' He knew the children would repeat this through the neighborhood.

Once inside the house, Coach Taggart saw that this whole arrangement was dominated by the stubborn integrity of the uncle, so before he even spoke of football, or what his university could do for Artemius, he said to the uncle, 'Mr. Carter, they told me back in Jefferson you were the man who had held this fine boy together. Mr. Carter, I know of no finer service a man can perform than to look after the children of his widowed sister.'

'She ain't widowed,' Carter said. 'Her husband left her.'

'With five children,' Coach Taggart said sadly. It was his business to know everything possible about a prospect, because if he could land only two or three boys like Artemius Crandall, his reputation, his income and indeed his job would be secure for another two or three years, and since he earned more than $125,000 a year, it was vital that he land Artemius.

Even so, his sadness at the plight of Mrs. Crandall was not feigned. In America, the black high school athletes on whom the success of a university football team depended were apt to be from broken homes, from disadvantaged backgrounds, and even though Taggart saw so much of this, it always grieved him. There ought to be a better system, but until it was devised, he would continue to use this one to his advantage.

'Does your nephew have good grades?' he asked.

'He does, but they give him the grades.'

'Mr. Carter, suppose your nephew decides to join us, do you know what he gets first of all?'

'I'd like to know.'

'A tutor. A full-time, well-paid tutor whose sole job it will be to teach your nephew how to cope with his university studies. Because, Mr. Carter, when your boy leaves us, we want him to have an honest education . . . lawyer . . . business executive . . . whatever he wants to be, he can be.'

'What he wants, Mr. Taggart, is a damned good contract with a top professional team.'

Coach Taggart coughed. 'Have you followed the results of the last three drafts? Our men stand way at the top, year after year. And do you know why, Mr. Carter? Because at Jefferson we teach them football. We teach them to hit.'

Abruptly he turned to Artemius and said, peremptorily, 'Stand up, young man.' From his chair he said, 'You look even stronger than they told me.'

Then he rose, walked over to the boy, and stared him right in the eye. 'If you have character as well as strength, you might be able to play for Jefferson. But let me warn you about this. When you get to Jefferson, you find yourself among a hundred and ten young men just as tough as you are, and, son, to make our team you have to put out. I'd like you to see your future teammates.'

He promised that during the season the Western United jet would come back to pick Artemius and his uncle up for a visit to Jefferson. Then, abruptly, he resumed his discussion with the uncle.

'Mr. Carter, I'm aware that certain other coaches, whom I will not mention, have offered you jobs in their towns. Now, obviously, my good friends here from Western United can equal their offers any day in the week, but I see you as a man who's made his own way. You have a nice house here, clean, well organized. You don't need help from us, and I'm not going to insult you by proposing that you change your residence just to please us. Now, you can have a job with the Western United plant out in the industrial park, but only if you want it. What I propose is something quite different. I would like these two good gentlemen to find your sister a job at their plant near Lubbock. She'd have to move—take the children with her—but we'd help with the expenses. The thing of it is, you'd not only be assuring Artemius of the best education he can possibly get, but you'd be taking care of his four brothers and sisters, and, Mr. Carter, frankly I think you're the kind of man to whom that would be important.'

It was. The University of Jefferson, in order to entice a great high school halfback to enroll, found the uncle a well-paying job, moved the mother and her four children to a rent-paid house near Lubbock, found her a job, gave her son a full scholarship, six suits of clothes, a Pontiac hardtop, eight hundred dollars a year spending money, ten tickets to each football game, which he could sell for one hundred and twenty dollars a week, plus a full-time tutor to teach him to read and write. In total, such a scholarship would provide $6,800 a year, for four years.

Crandall was worth it, a sensational back and one of the easiest men to coach Honest John Taggart had ever unearthed. He had an instinctive feel for open space, which all the great halfbacks had, but he was unusual in that he could sense where the line would open up while it was still a solid mass, and he would plunge for that spot, satisfied that something would give. When it did, he was off for eighteen or twenty yards, and if things broke wide open, he'd score.

He was also a likable person, modest, not talkative, but never surly. He loved the game of football so much that he would gladly have played for nothing, and he sometimes said so. He was gratified, in the late spring of his junior year, to find that the university publicity department had selected him as the man to push for all-American honors in his senior year.

This meant a host of color photographs, many interviews, the construction of human-interest stories, and even the making of a color film which would be distributed to television stations. One of the coaches calculated that Jefferson had spent at least $11,000 on the brochure extolling Artemius Crandall, but he judged the money well spent if Crandall landed an all-American designation. It would help in recruiting next year.

The only negative aspect of Crandall's stay at Jefferson was reported by his tutor: 'Coach Taggart, he doesn't even know the multiplication table. I know you count on me to get him through his classes, but algebra and calculus! They're simply impossible. He can't even subtract, let alone fractions.'

So a plan was devised whereby Artemius took a smattering of unrelated courses in the easiest possible subjects, plus four apparently difficult courses in which the professors were what was known as 'slaves to the athletic department' in that they gave any boy on scholarship a passing grade, and to those who needed it an A or a B to offset low grades in some other class.

At the beginning of Crandall's senior year, in a major American university, he had an education at about the fifth-grade level of a good public school. Even counting the gratuitous marks given him by 'the slaves,' he had credits which would place him at the second semester of his freshman year, because his scattered courses added up to no reasonable program, and he had no major. There was not the slightest chance that he would graduate with his class or ever.

But he was an adornment to the university, a young man positively loved by the alumni, by the sportswriters and by the television audience. For he was essentially a bright young man, with solid instincts inculcated by his mother and her sharp-minded brother. He could have been educated, for he obviously could learn, but from the seventh grade on, there had been no necessity for him to study, because, as in so many American schools, any boy who could play football or basketball was so precious a commodity that it was best if he not be bothered with books.

Nor did he need them. At the end of his senior football season he stood high in the competition for the Heisman Trophy, and went number eleven in the January draft for the National Football League.

He was picked up by Kansas City, a team which sorely needed a running back, and both he and his future coaches felt certain that he would make it big in the pros.

When he reported to training camp the following summer, his quiet competence impressed everyone, and several sportswriters from western papers ticketed him as 'another Leroy Kelly.' It was clear that he would make the cut, and by the end of the camp he was ready to take his place in the Chiefs' backfield for the exhibition games.

As the season started, he saw something of which he had not been aware before. Crandall looked over the roster of the Chiefs: forty-seven players on the active list, and only three of them over the age of thirty; one was a center, one a place kicker, one a reserve quarterback. And then it dawned on him that running backs, with their fragile knees, do not last into their thirties. He would have five or six good years, and then he would be finished.

'What'm I gonna do then?' he asked himself. 'Hell, I don't know nothin'.' He wondered if he could get a coaching job, even in Texas.

But the big games were about to begin. Kansas City was on the way back to its days of greatness. There was a thrill to any football season, exceeding all other things he knew, and this year was bound to be one of the best.

That Artemius Crandall found joy in football there can be no doubt. It was exhilarating to crash into linebackers or to zigzag downfield for a long pass. He felt himself to be a lithe young animal, tougher and swifter than most, and he was competing against the best in his profession.

His basic health was not threatened by the violence of the game; indeed, it was enhanced. He took care of himself, taping his ankles before even the most casual practice. He watched his diet, got more than the average sleep, and while reckless on the field, challenging even the most mammoth tackles and linebackers, he was never so in his private life. He was aware that a knee could pop at any time, but when it did he would have it operated on immediately, for he had observed that men who postponed the knife damaged both their knees and their careers. In the off season he kept in condition by playing paddleball, a vigorous game he intended cultivating after his retirement.

In high school and college he provided solid entertainment for spectators and was paid accordingly. By prevailing American standards he was a more significant product of Jefferson University than any of its future doctors, lawyers or professors, and if perchance he prospered in the professionals, he stood a good chance of becoming a true folk hero.

On the debit side there was the likelihood that he would find himself at age thirty-three with no education, no job and no prospect of any. Then he would have to acknowledge that the system had treated him poorly. It had used him as a paid gladiator. The bright intelligence he had displayed as a boy had been intentionally dissipated.

The Moderate Participant

One dark and silent morning at 4 A.M. Jane Harker awakened in the bedroom of her split-level home near Culpeper, Virginia, and listened with a sense of shock to her sleeping husband's labored breathing. In the darkness she felt him twitch and then stop breathing altogether for almost a minute. He ended this spell with a gasping rush of breath and a muffled moan, rolling to a new position and resuming his twitching.

'My God!' she muttered to herself. 'He's committing suicide.' And she reviewed the life her husband had been leading.

As an undergraduate at the University of Virginia, Tom Harker had played football and baseball and spent his summers as a hard-working counselor at a summer camp in New Hampshire. Several girls at Sweetbriar had been captivated by his manly behavior, and in the spring of 1955 one of them had invited him to a dance at the college. Unwisely, this girl had introduced him to Jane, and a vigorous courtship ensued.

After Jane had graduated from Sweetbriar they married, in June of 1957, and then moved to New York, where Tom was employed in a real estate firm. He worked ridiculous hours, and at high pressure, which resulted in his promotion.

Occasionally Jane would comment on the fact that he was growing quite thick about the waist, and she even suggested that he join an athletic club, but his reasoning was, 'I've got a game plan. We'll work like hell for a dozen years, then get us a farm down near Culpeper and live the good life.' In the meantime he continued to put on weight as a result of long lunches, longer cocktail hours and even longer business dinners.

Jane suggested that he take up golf, but he found this too demanding. 'Look,' he argued, 'to play golf I've got to leave the office at eleven, drive out to the club, get into my clothes, spend three or four hours, get showered, and drive home. It's too big an operation.'

His game plan worked. After fourteen diligent years he attained enough rank in his firm to land the job as its representative in Washington and the south, and with his first increased paycheck he made the down payment on a farm near Culpeper. It was a lovely spread of ninety-five rolling acres, with a small stream leading to a lake frequented by ducks and geese.

To reduce the mortgage, he worked harder than before, piling up commissions which impressed Jane. 'I thought it would take us twenty years to pay for this place,' she told Tom admiringly. 'It's even more fun than we imagined when you first told me your game plan.'

It was an enviable life. They had delightful neighbors, some of whom owned horses, and they made friends with people who held responsible jobs and who viewed life with reasonable perspectives. Virginia was, in this period, undergoing a political revolution, with Republicans winning offices that had been held for more than a hundred years by Democrats, and the Harkers worked enthusiastically for the change.

Tom said, 'My father would turn over in his grave if he knew that I was not only voting Republican but actually working for the party.' Jane headed one of the women's auxiliaries, and it was while working for the reelection of President Nixon in 1972 that she met a woman she liked immediately.

It was LouAnn Buford, married to an investment broker named Jack Buford. Fortunately, the two husbands got along well and for about a year the Harkers and the Bufords were inseparable. They went on picnics together, they drove out to Glacier National Park to see the wild parts of America, and played bridge frequently.

Jack Buford had attended Washington and Lee, where, like Tom Harker, he had played various sports. The two men threw a football now and then, coming in puffing to watch football or basketball on television. They knew the records of all the college and professional teams, for sports were important to them. One day Buford said, 'It's a shame we don't live in a city. I'd enjoy handball or squash. Something to keep in shape.'

Jane, hearing the conversation, asked, 'Why not golf?' and Buford gave the same reply her husband had, 'Takes too much time. But I'll tell you this, Jane. As soon as I get my branch office in Warrenton squared away, and the one in Charlottesville, I'm going to take it easy. Lots of horseback riding. And I'll take up golf.'

It perplexed Jane to see that she and LouAnn had stayed about the same weight they had been in college, whereas their two husbands had become quite paunchy, and she vaguely considered doing something about it. But these were the days when Tom Harker's firm was experiencing the uncertainty that swept all American business in the early Watergate days, and Tom was required to fly to New York and Chicago for emergency meetings.

He liked flying, liked the urgency of business confrontations. 'For me it's no trouble,' he told the Bufords one night. 'I jump into my Electra, drive easily to Dulles Airport and find myself anywhere in the United States within a few hours. I park the Electra at the airport and can be home again that night.'

But an important trip to Kansas City was interrupted by an urgent phone call. It was from his wife, and she was sobbing. 'You've got to come back right away. Jack Buford just dropped dead.'

He was only forty-seven, close to the apex of his career, and he had died in a space of four minutes. After the funeral Dr. Westlake, the cardiologist, told the Harkers, 'The trick is to postpone your first coronary till you're past the age of fifty-two. If you get one in your thirties, it's almost always fatal. If you get one in your forties, it's usually fatal. But if you can delay till your late fifties, you have a damned good chance of survival. And in your late sixties or seventies, it's much like a bad cold. Your chances for survival are excellent.'

'Why?' Jane asked. Suddenly she was vitally concerned with this problem.

'Well,' the doctor explained, 'in your thirties a coronary is a tremendous shock on a young heart. It's not prepared. It runs wild, and you're dead. Same way in your forties, but to a lesser degree. But by the time you're sixty, the heart is a beat-up old organ which has already suffered a lot of knocks. Some of its arteries have slowed down and it's had to set up alternate feed lines. If you have a coronary then . . . Well, just like Ed Gonzales. He had one hell of a blast in November, but he was sixty-six and his heart had already established alternate lines, so he was up and about within three weeks.'

'How do you establish those lines?' Jane asked.

'Exercise,' the doctor said.

'Is Tom too old to start exercising?'

'Never too old, if you observe simple precautions.'

Dr. Westlake explained what he meant by this—gradual approach, easy steps to hard tasks, never exhaust yourself—and Jane committed herself right then to seeing that her husband interrupted his frantic and hypertensive life with some sensible exercise.

But she was unable to get her husband's cooperation. Tom, who had been a really fine athlete in college, was now so preoccupied with other things which he deemed more important, he refused to establish any sensible and regular program. Under his wife's pressure he tried jogging, but that was a dreadful bore. He also tried some horseback riding, but without Jack Buford to accompany him, he did not keep it up.

What he really liked to do was sit in his Electra and speed over Virginia roads, enjoying the scenery with his wife, or fly to distant cities and meet exciting new problems, or spend a leisurely Saturday and Sunday watching his favorite teams on television. The years 1972, 1973 and 1974 were especially rewarding, for then the miraculous Washington Redskins stormed back into contention, and even went to the play-offs, and there was a constant sense of excitement in the air. At meetings men would interrupt to ask, 'Did you see what George Allen pulled in the second half against Philadelphia?'

Tom Harker was a hard-nosed Billy Kilmer man, once and for all. He had no patience with the sentimentalists who argued that Sonny Jurgensen should be used as the regular quarterback.

'Sure!' he would exclaim, his voice betraying tension. 'I can see using Sonny as a fireman. Bring him on in a crisis situation for a few throws. But a starting quarterback? Are you out of your mind?'

And then, in the latter part of 1974, Jane began to notice that her husband was not sleeping soundly, that his breathing was troubled, that he had begun visibly to sag. And he was drinking more than usual.

She watched him carefully, and even went so far as to consult Dr.

Westlake confidentially. He said, 'It's a wife's responsibility to see that her husband stays well.'

'What can I do? Hide the bottle?'

'Tom has no drinking problem!' Westlake snorted. 'If you ever saw a real drinking problem, you'd thank your stars for a husband like Tom. All he needs is less tension, more relaxation. And that's not my responsibility. It's yours.'

'But what can I do?'

'See that he gets some exercise.'

Again she spoke to her husband about this and again accomplished nothing. 'How many times do I have to tell you,' he snapped. 'I haven't time for golf. And jogging bores me to death. But I will cut down on my drinking. I was pretty fuzzy at the meeting Friday, and it scared me. I'd had three martinis, and I can't handle that many any more.' And so things drifted on, with Tom Harker headed directly toward a major coronary which would probably kill him off, as Jack Buford's had.

But on this night when his wife lay awake listening to his confused breathing, and when she saw with terrible clarity what could be its consequences, a new element entered ther lives.

'Tom!' she cried, shaking him. 'Wake up!'

It was easy for him to snap awake, for his sleep had been fitful. 'What's the matter? Fire?'

'No! It's you.'

'What's the matter with me?'

'Tom, you're killing yourself.'

'What do you mean?'

'You ought to listen to yourself. Your breathing. Your nervousness. Tom, you're going to die just like Jack Buford.'

'What in hell are you talking about?'

'Tom, I love you and I don't want to lose you.'

'Darling, it's . . .' He looked at his watch. 'Christ, it's four o'clock. Let me get some sleep.'

She turned out the light and soon her husband was again tossing in what he called sleep. She stayed awake, and by the time they rose she had her mind made up. At the breakfast table she handed down her ultimatum: 'Tom, you and I are going to start playing tennis.'

'What?'

'This afternoon, Tom Harker, you and I are taking our first lessons from the pro at the tennis club. No comment, please.' She rose, placed her right hand over his mouth, and said, 'You're the most precious thing in the world to me. And you're committing suicide. And soon I'll be a widow like LouAnn Buford. And I'm not ready for that.' She removed her hand from his lips and kissed him.

That afternoon the Harkers appeared at the tennis court in the new white outfits Jane had purchased from a sporting-goods store in Warrenton, and the pro, a young man who had played for Miami University, nodded approvingly as Tom Harker leaned easily into the basic strokes. With Jane he had more problems, for she was not a natural athlete like her husband, but the young pro saw that she had a determination which could be capitalized upon.

'You have all the natural rhythms,' he told Tom. 'I can see that you played various sports.'

This gratified Tom, but the coach continued, 'Yet I'll bet you a dollar that this young lady masters the game faster than you do.'

'My wife?' Harker asked incredulously.

'We'll see,' the coach said, and for the first month it looked as if his prediction could not possibly come true, for Jane was awkward. But she could run, and she had very quick reflexes, so that balls apparently hit past her were somehow reached, and returned.

'You're a born retriever,' the coach told her. 'You're stubborn and you're quick. You're going to love this game.'

At the end of three months the Harkers were a passable tennis partnership. Widowed LouAnn Buford had attracted the attention of a retired naval officer, a wiry man in his early sixties and a good tennis player. The four began to play doubles regularly, and although the naval officer was obviously better than any of the other three, Jane Harker was developing into a fierce retriever.

'I have the point put away,' the navy man complained one day, 'and your little tiger leaps over there and swats it back.'

When a local builder put up a year-round tennis building with six courts, the Harkers and their opponents took out memberships and played two days a week. Tom found himself hurrying back from Detroit or Chicago so as not to miss his regular doubles game, and at various meetings he would tell his associates, 'Since I took up tennis, I feel ten years younger,' and one of his older partners asked sardonically, 'Why is it, whenever someone does anything sensible he invariably feels ten years younger? Why not nine or eleven?'

But the person who was most pleased with Harker's rejuvenation was Dr. Westlake. He told Mrs. Harker, 'It's criminal the way young men can be so athletic in college, then drop all exercise for the rest of their lives. That's why they drop dead at thirty and forty. You got your boy started just in time. Congratulations!'

Tom Harker has discovered so much fun in tennis that he wonders why he delayed so long in taking it up. And he has been astonished at his wife's capacity to become a first-rate club player at age forty-one, when she had

had no previous athletic experience. He found that he positively liked mixed doubles, and told his wife, 'I hope LuAnn Buford marries her navy captain. It would be fun to have them permanently available.'

Playing vigorous tennis after a slow and proper start has almost certainly prolonged Harker's life. The credit, however, does not all go to tennis. His change in attitude, the diminution of tension, the loss of weight and a generally improved outlook on life would have ensured improvement even if tennis had not been involved, but his return to active participation enhanced his prospects.

Participation as a Business Asset

Morgan Forysthe sells advertising time on television shows, and his life in Hollywood and Los Angeles is hectic. He is a handsome thirty-eight-year-old former tackle at Southern Cal, which accounted for the rather good job he landed, and is aware that if he ever let himself go, he would tend toward fat. He therefore decided to join a country club, and sought one near the heart of the business area in which he works. He considers it a miracle that Hollywood has been able to retain golf links in the middle of the urban area, and to belong to any one would be a privilege.

His first choice was an extremely expensive club: $25,000 entrance fee, $900 each year thereafter for operating expenses, plus numerous fees and dining costs. Besides, it was one of those prestigious clubs in America that severely restricted its membership, and frowned on any member who tried to bring a Jew or black into the club. Bob Goldwater, brother of the Arizona senator, had been proposed for membership, but his sponsors were told, 'No Jews.' Goldwater responded, 'Since I'm only half Jewish, I'll promise to play only nine holes.'

Forsythe himself was not Jewish, but many of his best clients were, so this club was not practical. Actually, he might have had trouble gaining admission if he had applied, because, as a gentleman on the membership committee warned him, 'We permit no actors or theatrical people, either.' When Morgan pointed out that he was not an actor, the gentleman explained, 'Yes, but you do so much of your business with television types that sooner or later you'd want to entertain them with us, and we'd not like that.' Forsythe asked what about the cowboy actor who had been admitted, and the gentleman said, 'We screened seven of his films and concluded that under no possible circumstances could he be considered an actor.'

So Forsythe had turned his attention to his second choice, but for years this club had been exclusively for the great Jewish families of Hollywood —their riposte to the clubs that would admit no Jews—and it would have

COLLEGE OF
BUSINESS
ADMINISTRATION

B TOBEY

been difficult for Forsythe to join it, although now a few non-Jews were members. It was, in some ways, more expensive than the gentile clubs: $22,500 to join, $85 a month dues, very heavy costs at the bar and in the dining room.

The logical solution to Forsythe's problem was a well-regarded smaller club, convienient to Hollywood, cut by wandering streams and facing the hills at the edge of the city. The club excluded Jews and actors, but because expenses of running such an institution were high, it did welcome prosperous young businessmen like Forsythe, especially if they had played outstanding football at Southern Cal. The older men liked to golf with such youngsters, even if they did have Jewish and theatrical friends.

The club wasn't inexpensive. Forsythe bought a membership from an old Los Angeles banking family for $12,500. His monthly dues were $85 plus $15 for what was called 'the building fee.' As one of the membership committee told him, 'Best buy you ever made, that $15 monthly building fee. In 1971 we tore down the old clubhouse. It had been a stone church on this property and looked great, but no space. We spent two million three building our new mansion, and it's without question the finest clubhouse in America.'

Forsythe used the facilities a good deal. As he explained to his boss, who was picking up most of the tab, 'It's this way, J.D. Most of my customers are big executives. They work hard. They're entitled to those three-hour lunches if they wish, but since they're big-timers, they're also smart. They know they need that good old exercise a lot more than they need lunch. So for me golf is the answer.'

The tab for a foursome was high. One day Forsythe had to justify his expense account to J.D., and there it was:

Green fees 3 guests at $15 each	$45
Two golf carts for guests at $12 each	24
Caddy 4 of us at $5 each	20
Lunch	32
Drinks at bar	18
Locker room tips	7
Lost Top Flites, three	5
Massage, haircut, shoeshine	15

'I look at it this way, J.D.' Forsythe explained. 'If I can't take the really big shots, I'm just another time peddler. And if I don't sell advertising, you and I are both dead. One of my secrets is that I arrange my foursomes with such care. Only one client. Then I invite one of his friends who can boast about playing my club. Me and usually some other jock from Southern Cal or maybe a basketball player from UCLA.'

Like all the really good clubs in the Los Angeles area, this one has strict rules against members' using the club primarily as a place to entertain business clients, and Forsythe has to be careful not to abuse his privilege. On the other hand, the club needs income, so the officials look the other way when he circumvents the rule. He leads a good many California industrialists around the beautiful rolling fairways, and they love it.

He is adept at three styles of play: honest golf, customer's golf and gambler's golf. In the first, with his good coordination and a mastery of wood shots, he can regularly score in the upper 70s. In customer's golf he knows how to miss shots and make it look as if he were trying; he plays just well enough so that if the corporation president he is wooing shoots an 85, he trails with an 87. In gambler's golf he is one of the trickiest, sharpest men in the Los Angeles area, scoring anywhere from 73 to 93, but always just enough to win the big pots. The refinements of his play can best be observed when he tackles the par 5 thirteenth hole, bisected by a water-filled barranca in front of the green.

At honest golf he uses his new graphite-shaft driver, like the one Johnny Miller uses and for which he paid a cool $118. With it he lines out a tremendous drive, then uses his five iron to drop the ball just short of the barranca. With a nine iron he tries to lay the ball close to the pin for a chance at a birdie four. At customer's golf he still uses the graphite-shaft but holds back, so that his second shot will leave him well short of the barranca. Then, with his nine iron he slams the ball right in the drink for three. Lifting out is penalty four. A half-baked shot to the edge of the green leaves him with a chip and two putts and a triple bogey eight. But when playing gambler's golf for high stakes, he will hit a nice easy drive down the middle, play a safe second wood, somewhat short of the barranca, then pitch cautiously to the green for a sure five, trusting that his opponent will drift into the barranca and lose the hole.

He enjoys his club and is convinced it's worth every dollar he spends of his own money. But he was a little jolted last year when some of the older members of the club arranged for him to play at Pebble Beach in the Bing Crosby National Pro-Am. 'It was a great honor, sure, because several thousand amateurs from all over the country beg to get on the list of starters. So J.D. was rather pleased that one of his youngest men had made it. But the tab! $400 to enter. Stay at Pebble Beach Lodge, four nights at $115 per. Caddy $100. Food bill $180. Picking up the pros' bar tabs $116. Golf isn't exactly for the young man just out of college.'

Forsythe paid $600 for his clubs and the super-stylish bag in which he carries them, and his clothes cost another $700, but as he says, 'You're only young once, and you don't get invited twice to join the big time. For me, this is a sensible deal economically.'

He judges that the recreation he gets is just as valuable. 'It gets me out into the open. I refuse the carts and walk a brisk four to five miles twice a week. Playing golf encourages me to miss a couple of lunches a week, but maybe I make up for that by drinking extra martinis at the bar. But it's a huge plus, healthwise.'

As we shall see later, it's probably not so huge a plus as he thinks, but at thirty-eight Morgan Forsythe is in relatively good condition. He is only slightly overweight, he sleeps well, and he enjoys life. 'Many of the members don't use the dining room, but Marjorie and I find it a delightful place to entertain. We love that Thursday-night smorgasbord at $9.50 each. And the thick slabs of roast beef on Tuesdays at $5.95 can't be beat.'

All in all, his golf club is a logical solution to many of Forsythe's problems, and if the costs of belonging to such a club increase, so does his salary. And he knows that a goodly portion of that salary is earned because he belongs to a good golf club.

No matter what kind of golf Forsythe plays—honest, customer's, gambler's —he enjoys it. He likes competition and finds pleasure in manipulating things like golf games and his relationships to others. While it is true that almost any game he played would provide him with similar fun, golf seems tailored to his specific needs.

Because he has an easygoing nature, he is not subject to the emotional pressures which golf sometimes creates in hypertensive types. He can lose $40 on a Nassau and forget it by the time he's out of the shower. Golf gets him outdoors, in beautiful surroundings, and since he does not use a cart, does him a great deal of good. For the remainder of his life he can probably get all the exercise he wants from playing golf, but his life would be accelerated, and improved, if he could also learn to participate in some more demanding sport before he reaches forty-five.

The Mildest Participant

Forbes Easton is a Boston banker, sixty-one and president of an institution which handles many trusts for the elderly citizens of his community. He is an austere man, not given to smiles or idle chatter, and takes pride in wearing a vest and a three-button British-style jacket.

He works very hard forty-nine weeks of each year, eats sparingly so as to keep his weight to what it had been when he was at Harvard, and relaxes by working out twice a week at the small gymnasium maintained by his bank. He pulls a few weights, jogs a little, and rows on the simulated scull.

But his great delight comes during his vacation, for he is a fanatical fisherman and he loves equally both the thrill of searching out new areas to explore and returning to those famous waters which he has tried before. He will fly to any part of the world to test a trout stream, and in doing so, has compiled a short list of places that seem almost ideal.

First on his list is that splendid clear stream that flows out of Lake Taupo on the North Island of New Zealand. The Waikato it is called, and along its banks a famous fisherman named Alan Pye once maintained the Huka Lodge, where the foremost fishermen of the world assemble.

The trout in New Zealand are unbelievable. They were introduced from Canada and the western United States, and whereas in their home waters they grew to a size of three or four pounds, in New Zealand, where there are many flies and no predators, they grow to enormous size, twenty-seven pounds or even thirty. 'New Zealand,' Mr. Easton likes to explain in his dry, crisp manner, 'is the world's only truly virgin land of any size. The animals that inhabit the rest of the world never reached these two islands. So when deer and trout were introduced they prospered unbelievably. The government has to hire professional hunters to roam the hills and shoot down the excess deer. And the trout . . .' He often says that if a man cannot catch trout on Lake Taupo, he has no claim to be a fisherman.

But Mr. Easton has not been in New Zealand for some years. 'With the death of Alan Pye something great went out of Taupo,' he tells his friends. 'To sit in his lodge at night, after a good day's fishing, and compare notes with an English general or a German admiral or an Australian business leader was to know fishing at its best. Alas, it's gone now.'

His second preference is fishing for salmon on the island of Benbecula, in the Hebrides, off the western coast of Scotland. 'It's a legendary sort of island,' Mr. Easton says. 'Not a tree on it. The last outpost between Europe and America. It lies between North Uist and South Uist, and the strange thing about it is that at low tide there is a footpath to each of those neighboring islands, while at high tide the path is under twenty feet of water. People are drowned there when they miscalculate the coming of the tide.'

Banker Easton never tells the story himself, but his wife has quietly related to some of his close associates what happened on Benbecula during the salmon season of 1961. 'We had worked several streams on Benbecula with little result, when a guide said, "There's a fine stream on North Uist which is bound to have salmon," and he persuaded Forbes to walk over to the other island to try his luck. I remember standing at the edge of Benbecula as I watched my husband and the guide walk right out onto the sands which only a few hours before had been covered by the ocean. The footpath was several miles long, as I recall. Well, I returned to our hotel at Creagorry, and it was some hours later, maybe as many as ten, because I never understand about tides. Neither did the guide, because he had made a most awful mistake. And a young boy came running up: "Mrs. Easton. Your husband is trapped by the tide."

'Well, we jumped into the car and drove like fury to the north end of the island, and there we saw two boatmen rowing toward us, and they had Forbes and the guide perched on the back seat looking very foolish. A Benbecula woman who regularly scanned the ford to prevent just such accidents had seen that my husband and the guide were starting too late to come back safely, and she had alerted the boatmen.'

Only once did Forbes Easton, this very cautious Boston banker, confess what had happened. 'The guide suspected that we hadn't the time,' he told a fisherman during a trip to Alaska, 'but I was so elated by our catch of three salmon in North Uist that I said, "I'm a stout walker. There's plenty of time." You've heard what they say about the tide at Benbecula? It rushes in like a white horse. It was well above our waists when the boatmen rescued us.'

In spite of this misadventure, Forbes Easton often has returned to Benbecula during the salmon season, finding its austere landscape, with the Atlantic Ocean pounding on its western ramparts, much to his liking. His preference, however, in recent years, has been a curious, cold, swift-moving stream in western Alaska.

He first heard of the Kvichak River when he was stationed on Kodiak Island during World War II. Natives of Alaska told him repeatedly, 'There's one fine river north of here on the mainland. The Kvichak, running out of Iliamna Lake.'

Half a dozen times he tried to devise some way of getting north to the Kvichak, but the war drew him westward, and he never made it to this fisherman's paradise. Many years later, however, when a business acquaintance who had his own jet plane suggested that fishing in Alaska might be fun, Easton said, 'There's this river west of Anchorage that might prove to be rewarding,' and they had flown from Boston to Minneapolis to Edmonton to Anchorage, and then west to King Salmon, where they hired a one-engine local plane that flew them to the unlikely spot called Igiugig, where a flea-bitten Alaskan guide waited to show them the mysteries of the Kvichak.

It was one of the best fishing experiences Easton would encounter, a delightful change from the British tradition of either New Zealand or Scotland. The Kvichak was a rough, bitterly cold, turbulent river flowing out of a lake fed by glaciers, and the people who frequented it were as rough as the river. They were men who had lived with Eskimos, who had worked at the edge of the Arctic Ocean, who had spent their winters in Fairbanks, betting on when the ice would break up in the rivers.

They fished for forty-pound salmon and eighteen-pound trout, and they saw moose along the banks of the river, and wild fox, and the stories were salty and the card games endless. 'It's a primitive land,' Forbes Easton told his Boston friends. 'It's really like nothing else left on earth. And I want to go back.'

He did. His tales of the Kvichak were so compelling that several friends with their own jets wanted to try their luck with the huge salmon and trout, so that parties were organized at various times. 'But one thing. If you can't stand mosquitoes, stay out of Alaska,' Easton warned his Boston fishermen. One mosquito repellent after another was tried, with invariable failure. And then Easton discovered that if you went to the Kvichak in mid-October, the mosquitoes were gone and the trout were biting. So in recent years he has formed the habit of taking his vacation in October. Sometimes he meets snow. Always he encounters bitterly cold mornings, but the rest of the day is pleasant. And the trout are magnificent.

He wishes that Alaska were closer to Boston. 'But if it were,' he reasons, 'the place would be overcrowded. Anyone who gets to Igiugig has had to make a real effort, and maybe it's better that way.'

What he does, when the distance seems too great, is return to his first love, the water he fished as a boy with his father. In eastern Maine there is a chain of lakes set amid forests and connected by small swift-running streams. Fourth Machias does not sound inviting as a fishing area, but it contains a fighting supply of bass and eels, and pickerel and perch. The first and last are good eating; the second and third are considered by the Maine people as inedible scavengers and are thrown back.

As a boy, Forbes Easton had resented bitterly the actions of his father and the guide in making him throw back the eels and pickerel, for they were fun to catch, and fought much better than the bass. They were handsome, too, long and thin and much the way things living in the water should look. He determined therefore to try eating them the first chance he got, but when he went to a hidden area and cooked up a pickerel, he found it so hopelessly filled with bones that he had no opportunity to judge the taste.

Years later he discovered that the Japanese considered eel a major delicacy, but when he got to Japan as a member of one of President Eisenhower's commissions, he tasted Japanese smoked eel and found it too oily for his taste.

To leave Boston late in the day and fly to Princeton, the name of the little town closest to Fourth Machias, and to rise early next morning and go out upon this lonely and secluded lake to fish for bass and perch, accepting such eels and pickerel as came to his line, and to watch the eagles flying above is a joy that renews his youth.

'Horse racing may be the sport of kings,' he tells his associates at his Boston club, 'but fishing is the recreation of gentlemen.' He assures his wife that his fishing vacations have kept his mind clear, his senses alert, and his health in top condition. 'Of all the places we've gone,' he told her, 'I believe I've liked Lake Taupo in New Zealand best. That is, when Alan Pye was still living. But the place that makes my heart beat faster is Fourth Machias. I fished there as a boy.'

From Easton's own testimony, fishing has been a major joy of his life, and he is correct in attributing to it much of his sustained vigor. Throughout history certain men and women have found in this quiet sport recreation of inestimable value, and the high quality of writing devoted to fishing is a tribute to its values.

But I doubt that fishing contributes much to health. In fact, the constipation that usually results from inaction and an excess of heavy food probably offsets any possible contribution. I would judge that his regular visits to the bank gymnasium have done a lot more toward keeping Forbes Easton physically healthy than all his fishing. But of course, the outdoors made a contribution to his emotional health.

Fortunately, fishing has almost no public entertainment value, and as a fisherman who has tried most of the spots Banker Easton refers to, I hope it will always remain free from the pressure of competition. I have grave doubts that things like the deep-sea fishing contests held off the Kona Coast in Hawaii ought to be encouraged, but since the presence of spectators is not involved, for they can hardly go to sea to watch the fishermen, I would be willing to concede that little harm is done. The day's catch is measured and judged and prizes are awarded and everyone does a lot of drinking . . . on shore.

Therapeutic Participation

The directive was simple and easily understood. The base commander issued an order which read: 'Any officer or enlisted man in this outfit who is grossly overweight, as determined by the medical officer, will be separated from the service.'

When Major Rollins reported to the hospital for his examination the doctor said, 'Five feet, nine inches. With your body build you should weigh a hundred and sixty pounds. You're twenty-two pounds overweight and you have one month to lose ten pounds, six months to lose all twenty-two. If you don't, you know the penalty.'

Major Rollins recognized this threat as an invasion of his privacy, but he knew that he had to lose twenty-two pounds or get out of the army, and he had never found any other form of life that suited him better. He liked formal organization and knowing where he stood on the promotion table and being able to fit his otherwise chaotic life into an orderly process.

'How shall I go about it?' he asked.

'First, let me give you an EKG. Then stop eating so much.'

'What's an EKG?'

'An electrocardiogram. And if that proves out okay, as I'm sure it will, we'll start out on an exercise program.'

'I already play golf.'

'I said exercise,' the doctor replied.

The regimen he outlined consisted mainly of jogging, around the base and across the Texas countryside: 'One mile a day for two weeks, then two miles, then three miles; and after five weeks, four miles a day. Every day. Every week for six months.'

It was the hardest work Major Rollins had ever done. He was thirty-seven years old and in rather poor condition. True, he had played basketball in high school and had been on an intramural team at the University of Montana, but only to acquire his gymnasium credits. As soon as these were assured, he quit sports altogether and allowed himself to grow quite flabby.

At first it hadn't shown, for he was not inclined toward heaviness, but as he continued in his idleness and his devotion to army chow and the Thursday night freebies at the officers' club, he began to degenerate.

He always intended getting himself back in shape. 'I'm going on a diet one of these days,' he had said a score of times. And he had resolved to do some serious exercise. 'I think I'll take up handball.' But adult patterns in American life, even in the army, make it very easy to ignore physical well-being and rather difficult to preserve it.

He had told the doctor he played golf, and had this been strictly true he would have been in much better condition. Actually, he played at golf, in a desultory sort of way, four or five times a year. Those officers who really played the game, say twice a week, walking briskly over the four-and-a-half-mile San Antonio military course and cutting down on their food at least one day a week, kept in pretty good shape, and none of them were on the commandant's list of 'personnel grossly overweight.'

Major Rollins, who had protected his health in no way, was high on the list. So he jogged. In sweat suit and running shoes he bought from the Adidas dealer in San Antonio, he pushed himself around the track at the football field until the required mile had been covered. His legs ached, his stomach cramped, and he felt steady jolts of blood in his eyeballs, but on he went.

During the first week his weight showed no change, and he consulted the doctor about this. 'Perfectly normal. You've been hoarding water in your system. I could give you a pill to dislodge it, and you'd lose three or four quick pounds. But it's better to let the water drain off naturally. You come in at the end of next week, and you'll be surprised.'

So he continued jogging for the next week and did lose three pounds. During the next two weeks he doubled the length of his run and lost another two pounds. Then he shifted to three miles, and at the end of the month, showed a loss of ten pounds, as required.

He was pleased when the doctor showed him a copy of his report to the commanding officer: 'Major Rollins has disciplined himself admirably and has lost the proposed number of pounds. There is every reason to suppose that at the end of six months he will be in first-class condition.' At the next assembly the commanding officer congratulated him and added, 'There were others who couldn't discipline themselves to do it. They won't be here long.'

The next month began the sheer hell of jogging. Major Rollins was now up to four miles a day, and he ground them out faithfully, a kind of glaze settling over his eyes while a mechanical motion controlled his legs. He found that he had to put himself into a kind of trance in order to cover the four miles day after day. What was worse, he had reached a plateau in his weight loss and for two miserable weeks showed no drop when he climbed onto the scales.

He asked the doctor about this, and was told, 'Perfectly normal. Your body is adjusting to new conditions, and in another week you'll show a dramatic loss. Keep jogging.'

So on he jogged, and at the end of six months he weighed three pounds less than what the height-weight and body-build table recommended. He was elated and asked the doctor how he could maintain that level.

'Eat less. And if you can't find a game you like, keep on jogging.'

'I'll never jog again as long as I live,' Major Rollins said.

'Then take up handball, twice a week. Or golf. Or best of all, tennis. You can play that with your wife for the rest of your life.'

The major tried tennis, but he had so little skill that he felt embarrassed. He tried to make himself play golf twice a week, but the time required seemed excessive, and he dropped that game too. The base had several handball courts and he signed up for Monday and Thursday, and although he was no good at the game, he persevered. 'Anything's better than that lousy jogging,' he grunted when fellow officers asked him how he was doing.

And with his proper weight, and a better diet and fewer cigarettes, and fewer cocktails and regular exercise, he began to feel like a fresh, vigorous man.

From his interminable jogging Major Rollins derived no joy whatever. It was a cruel, punishing grind, but on one occasion he did happen to break the glaze over his eyes and saw a rather fine sunset. But the rest of the six months was drudgery. He was gratified when he came upon an article which warned older men against jogging because the steady hammering might dislodge their retinas. 'I knew I shouldn't have been jogging,' he shouted to his wife.

However, he later read a news release from Dr. Don Cooper, physical education specialist at Oklahoma State University, which said that over a four-year period involving a large number of middle-aged men, not one who had jogged faithfully had suffered a heart attack, whereas those who had not, experienced the predicted number. Major Rollins could have achieved similar results from almost any other type of serious exercise and dieting. Of course, participation in any demanding game would have been best of all.

As one who has jogged many weary miles I personally agree with Major Rollins that this is one of the world's dullest pastimes, but Dr. Cooper's data make the torture bearable. When I find myself in a place where tennis is unobtainable, I jog. I curse as I do so, but I jog.

The Social Participant

The happiest day in the life of Marvin Bates, shoestore operator, aged thirty-eight, came four years ago when a well-dressed gentleman entered his shop in Cheyenne, Wyoming, and said, 'Marvin, we've been watching you, and if you could manage to take out three hundred dollars' more advertising in our papers before September 15, I think you'd be invited on board the Treagle.'

Marvin had grown up in New Jersey, in the Passaic area, where he had been told a thousand times by his two uncles, 'Marvin, always remember that this town produced the greatest high school basketball team our country has ever known.' And they would relate the glories of those remarkable teams in the 1919–25 era which had won 159 straight games, whipping opponents from much larger cities and creating a legend that would never die.

There had been other good high school teams in subsequent years, notably in Indiana and Texas, but never any to equal Passaic, which had gone undefeated for so long a time. Marvin's uncles had not played on the team, but they had gone to Passaic High and had participated in the glory that had accrued to their city.

Marvin saw little grandeur in Passaic, a factory town with gloomy streets and a high school whose teams were now lucky to break even, let alone set records. So at the earliest chance he enlisted in the Air Force, convinced that he would never return to what he called 'that dump.'

At one point in his army service he was stationed at Francis E. Warren Air Force Base, and once he saw the Rocky Mountains and the plains and the clean attractiveness of nearby Cheyenne he decided that upon completion of his enlistment he was going to head right back. He subsequently served at Randolph Air Force Base near San Antonio and at Travis in California, but nothing he experienced in either of those favored states changed his mind. He was a Wyoming type.

So after his discharge he headed for the mountains, and the only job he could find was clerking in a shoestore. He did this for ten years, then bought out the owner. He liked the shoe business, especially in Wyoming, where he could sell everything from tennis shoes to high-heeled Texas boots worked in silver. He was an enthusiastic young man, married to a healthy Wyoming girl whose parents lived on a ranch west of Laramie, and he would have found his new life totally enjoyable except for one thing. He was never really accepted in Cheyenne.

Many former military people had decided, like Marvin Bates, to come back to this beautiful region after their service was completed, and the city was crowded with newcomers who stayed a while, then moved on. The local people could never determine which newcomers would stay and which would become disenchanted, so a natural reserve was practiced, and Marvin Bates suffered from it.

His boss had been no help. This man had come to Cheyenne after army duty in the area and had stayed only a dozen years, building a good shoe business, then selling it off to his clerk. The man had made no mark on Wyoming, nor it on him. Bates could well be the same kind of man, and he suffered from the indifference of his peers. For example, each autumn he saw the leaders of the community ride off on the Treagle, laughing and joking and drinking beer together, while he stayed home.

The Treagle was an amazing operation, a private train assembled each autumn to carry the leading citizens of Cheyenne to the opening football game played by the University of Wyoming at Laramie, some fifty miles to the west. It was an enchanting train, composed of golden cars that had once traveled the great railroads of the west, plus special Pullmans that had been used by Presidents.

It chugged into Cheyenne on Friday night before the big game and stood gallantly in the famous old station right in the heart of town, so that those fortunate enough to have been invited aboard the next day could say offhandedly to their friends, 'I'm riding the Treagle tomorrow,' and this stamped them as important citizens of the community.

The name was clever, the first part representing the *State Tribune,* the city's evening Republican newspaper, while the last half stood for the *Eagle,* the Democratic morning journal. Since both papers were owned by the same family, editors were given strict autonomy in running their respective dailies, so that Bernie Horton, the Democrat, would back one candidate for governor in the morning paper, while Jim Flinchum, the Republican, would back another in the evening.

Each summer representatives of the two papers would circulate through Cheyenne, advising this customer and that that he had been invited to ride the Treagle. Women, as was only proper in a western town, were not invited, although important women in the state were conveyed by large buses to the game. The Treagle was a man's affair, with a saloon car and free pretzels and memories of the old west. To be invited aboard was one of the best things that could happen to a citizen of Cheyenne.

Of course, certain citizens were invited whether they advertised in the two newspapers or not. Vibrant Teno Roncalio, the Democratic Congressman invariably elected from a predominantly Republican state, was always aboard, campaigning like mad. Since Wyoming was entitled to only one Congressman, Roncalio had to work like crazy through the entire state, and it was said that he knew more people in Wyoming than God. Senators Clifford Hansen and Gale McGee were usually aboard, as were the governor and the justices of the state supreme court. Jim Byrd, the black man who served as sheriff of Cheyenne, was sure to be aboard, as was the president of the Union Pacific, the outfit that put the train together. President William Carlson, of the university, was there praying under his breath for a victory, since football in Wyoming was almost more important than politics.

And each year out-of-state notables were invited, people like Curt Gowdy, who had started his career in Wyoming; Charley Halleck, Republican leader of the House for so many years; and Ted Kennedy, the Democratic luminary. Aboard the Treagle you could hobnob with everyone of importance in Wyoming, and with many of the leaders of the nation.

So when the advertising salesman informed Marvin Bates, a newcomer from New Jersey, that he was almost eligible for an invitation this year, he lost no time in upping his budget another $300; the papers ran his ad in a conspicuous space, so that he recovered the cost of the advertising in one big August sale.

Treagle Saturday was a glorious day that year, with a September snow on the hills and bright sun making the plains resplendent. Marvin boarded the train at eight and was no sooner aboard than he was greeted by Judge John Pickett, leading jurist of the state, who had come to Wyoming in 1941 to pitch for the Cheyenne Lobos. He had won so many games for them that leaders of the town asked him to stay, assuring him a bright future. 'Hello,

Marvin. Isn't this your first trip aboard the Treagle?' the judge asked.

'Yep.'

'We'll expect to see you from now on,' the judge said.

And it was that way all day. Men who had bought their shoes from Marvin Bates now accepted him as a leading merchant. They talked to him about today's game, and the prospects for this year's team, and of 1968, that glorious year when Wyoming went to New Orleans to play Louisiana State in the Sugar Bowl. Half the population had flown south to participate, and he began to sense the great pride these men had in their state, the overwhelming importance of football to them.

They spoke especially of the bad years, some time back, when a group of black football players wanted to wear armbands, or something like that, when they played Brigham Young, the Mormon school, because that religion downgraded blacks. There was a frightful stink. The coach had to fire all the blacks, threatening to disrupt the state until the governor intervened to back the football coach.

'We don't want no niggers telling us how to play football,' one of the men said, but to Marvin's surprise another replied, 'The blacks were right. They were bein' used as cannon fodder, and they had every right to protest.' The argument got nowhere, but one man sort of summed it up: 'Well, I can tell you this. Wyoming football is goin' nowhere till we do get a few good blacks like O.J. Simpson and Duane Thomas.'

Marvin Bates' life was refashioned by that day. He enjoyed the game so much, and the fraternity of men he had only vaguely known before, that he began to study football. His speech became peppered with sentences like, 'Defense is the name of the game,' and 'They sure came to play,' and 'When the going gets tough, the tough get going,' and 'A quitter never wins and a winner never quits,' and 'Way to hit, baby! Way to hit!'

He began to watch every football game on television and learned to distinguish between a down-and-out and a post pattern. For some reason, perhaps because he was not overly big himself, he became preoccupied with the cornerbacks, those indomitable men who ran backwards, slapping down passes and occasionally intercepting an errant pass to score an unexpected touchdown. But the cornerback he liked the best was Dick Anderson, the University of Colorado star who now performed for the world's champion Miami Dolphins. What a man he was! And what a game he had against Pittsburgh that Monday night when he scored two touchdowns on interceptions within the first few minutes. 'He came to play!' Marvin told his customers. 'That baby really came to play.'

And then came an unexpected development. Three of his customers had tickets to a Sunday game played in Denver between the professional Broncos and the Kansas City Chiefs. One couldn't go and asked Marvin if he'd like the ticket, and Marvin said, 'Sure, I'll buy it from you,' and the man said, 'No. It's yours. I enjoyed talking with you on the Treagle. You know your football.'

So Marvin and the other two men drove down to Denver, and for the first time, in real life, Marvin saw a professional game, and the magnificence of it quite staggered him. This was nothing like Wyoming versus Brigham Young. This was the classiest exhibition of super athletes he had ever witnessed, and from that moment on he was a Bronco fan.

Whenever he got the chance to see a Bronco game, he would arrange his weekend so that he could rise about six on Sunday morning, eat a skimpy breakfast, and leave Cheyenne at about seven. The ninety-six-mile drive down a straight superhighway would take about two hours; he could have done it faster, but the Colorado Highway Patrol kept two small planes with radar flying up and down the highway, spotting speeders and sending radio messages down to ground crews in fast automobiles.

In Denver he would head for Mile High Stadium to preempt a good parking space, then go to a lively restaurant for a real western breakfast of sourdough pancakes, sausage, two eggs, a wedge of cherry pie and two glasses of milk. It was while preparing himself thus for one of the games that he met two other men from Cheyenne. They recognized him from having been aboard the Treagle, and the three struck up a conversation which led to their getting tickets for all the Bronco home games and sharing one car.

Marvin became known in Cheyenne as 'The Bronco fan,' and when he managed to acquire an autographed photo of Floyd Little breaking a tackle on one of his touchdown runs, he posted it in his window.

Then, for a second time, his life altered radically. When the Broncos played a crucial game against the Oakland Raiders in California, he organized an excursion of sixteen Cheyenne businessmen, who flew to Denver to board a charter aircraft carrying the team's supporters to Oakland. His picture was in both the Cheyenne papers, and next year when the Treagle ran out to Laramie for the University of Wyoming game, he was a featured passenger. Numerous men stopped him to ask if they could join his club —it wasn't really a formal club—on the next flight to an away game, and he took down their names and said he'd see what he could do with the Bronco management.

The sad part of Marvin's conversion to professional football was that he lost interest in the college game. 'They don't really hit in college,' he explained to his customers. 'And yet, as a loyal son of Wyoming, I feel I ought to support the team.' He bought season tickets to the games at Laramie, because it was good business to do so, and he made his annual pilgrimage on the Treagle, but his heart was in Denver.

'Down there, they really come to play,' he said. 'And that's the name of the game. Desire is fire. If you don't hit 'em, you can't git 'em. Because when the going gets tough the tough get going.'

And when the Cheyenne newspapers made up a list of Wyoming's leading sportsmen, there was Curt Gowdy the broadcaster, and Lloyd Eaton the coach who had fired the black players, and Marvin Bates, the ardent Bronco supporter. He had never thrown a football in his life, nor shot a basket, nor rifled a throw from third to first, but under prevailing standards it was only natural for him to be ranked as a leading sportsman.

It galls me to classify sedentary spectators as sportsmen, but they are entitled to the designation. Marvin Bates certainly found more than mere enjoyment in football; it was the most comprehensive experience of his life, conferring both sanction and meaning.

His avid support of the Broncos had no positive effect on his health, nor any negative. One might suppose that his long drives to and from the games were debilitating, but a two-hundred-mile jaunt in Colorado is less demanding than a thirty-mile traffic fight in Massachusetts. And as with all similar sporting experiences, getting out into the open air and sunlight on a crisp day had its benefits.

Three of the examples I have cited—Herman Fly and baseball, the gamblers and horse racing, Marvin Bates and football—involved spectators, not participants. The contrasts which exist between these two categories will recur throughout this book, but it would be tedious to belabor each occurrence. Here are the summary considerations.

Every world culture that we know has provided some kind of spectator sports, and the tradition must have been productive or we would not have so many remnants of Greek and Roman coliseums. When I worked in large cities and found it easier to watch than to play, I discovered positive benefits. Watching as a member of a large, excited group was spiritually exhilarating. It was much better to be part of a crowd, sharing its enthusiasm, than to sit alone listening to the radio. When my team won I felt psychologically enlarged. The cost of this diversion was so reasonable that I always considered it a bargain. And the money I spent on tickets helped gifted young athletes to earn a congenial living.

The disadvantages of mere spectatorship are numerous and compelling. The health of the inactive watcher, whether in a stadium or before a television, suffers. He tends to accumulate tensions which are not discharged. While sitting and watching he contributes nothing to the common good, and does not do those constructive things he might otherwise have done. Passiveness in sports encourages passiveness in social life and in politics. The mere spectator never shares in the positive rewards of performance and competition. Watching tennis at age fifty is infinitely less productive than playing it. The mere spectator fails to develop whatever innate talents he has and cheats himself of sports' true joys.

III

Sports and Health

I have never seen a statement of philosophy issued by the physical education department of any school, college or university which failed to state that the promotion of good health was a major goal of its program, but I have observed many such programs in operation in which little regard was paid to the health of the general student body or even of the major participants. In sports there is almost as much empty philosophizing about health as there is about character-building.

I have said earlier that the cultivation of good health habits was my primary concern in evaluating any sports program, but I have never been confident enough of my own judgment to base my philosophy only upon my own observations or preferences. I have sought professional guidance for my thinking and expert support for my conclusions, and no document has influenced me more than the description of effective exercise enunciated by Thomas D. Wood back in 1924 in a summary he made for the National Education Association in conjunction with the American Medical Association:

BENEFITS RESULTING FROM EXERCISE

1. Circulation is increased throughout the entire body or through the part exercised. This circulatory activity increases carriage of food to the tissues, removal of wastes, distribution of the endocrine secretions, and equalization of the water and heat content of the body.

2. Big-muscle activity increases the demand for oxygen, and thus causes an increased respiratory activity, with the resulting increase in the rate of oxygenation of the blood, increased rate of elimination of the carbon dioxide, and increased

oxygen supply to the tissues. This increased respiratory activity is the result of the demands made by the exercise; and deep breathing without the bodily exercise will not have the same results. During increased activity the respiratory apparatus naturally responds by frequent and deep respirations.

3. Exercise stimulates the excretory system and increases the elimination of waste through kidneys, lungs, intestines and skin.

4. Digestion is improved and assimilation is accelerated by exercise. Digestion is not only a chemical but a muscular process. If the musculature of the alimentary canal is flaccid, digestion is retarded and impeded. Peristaltic movements are more vigorous when the muscle tone of the alimentary canal is good. Exercise is essential in keeping the muscles in good condition. The constipation resulting from sedentary life is in large part due to inadequate muscular activity.

5. Big-muscle activity stimulates growth, and for the growing child is absolutely essential.

6. The heart is strengthened by the exercise of the skeletal muscles of the body. The best-known way in which some types of weak heart can be made strong is by gradual and increasing amount of physical work of the skeletal muscles. Exercise for the person with a weak heart should be arranged by skilled specialists; it should not be prescribed by any untrained person.

7. The muscles of the body are directly developed by physical activity. This is of great importance for health as regards the muscles of the trunk; the abdominal muscles must be in good condition for the maintenance of the upright posture which is necessary for the best position and functioning of the abdominal and pelvic organs.

8. Rational exercise results in increased neural activity, and in neuromuscular control, which develops skill, accuracy, endurance, agility and strength.

Wood, Thomas D. *Health Education.* National Education Association.

Out of these principles should flow a nationally sponsored program conducive to the well-being and health of all citizens. This program would be twofold. To satisfy the public's hunger for sports entertainment, schools and colleges would choose a few exceptional athletes from among the student body and would field the most proficient teams possible. They would play rivals from other institutions, records would be kept, and champions crowned. Boys and girls who were far above average would move in orderly fashion from grammar school (or junior high school, if that nomenclature is used) to high school, and from high school to college, and from college to professional teams. There would be cheerleading opportunities and a band would be maintained. This branch of the program would be under the direction of the school's athletic department and would focus on developing skills and engaging in contests. This half of the program is operating rather well.

The second half would be less conspicuous but more important. It would provide exercise and playing experience for the vast majority of students who have no special athletic skills but who need the beneficial results of exercise just as much as the athletes do. Each student would also receive instruction in health practices, in diet, in the formulation of long-range health programs and in general hygiene. Special emphasis would be placed on those sports which could be used throughout a lifetime. This branch of the program would be under the direction of the school's physical education department and would focus on the future life of the individual. This half is poorly administered in most schools.

In an average high school of two thousand students, it is now easy for eighteen hundred to graduate without ever having contemplated the health problems they will be living with for the next half-century, and there is little chance that they will become familiar with exercise programs that would enable them to live longer and operate more effectively.

And even the fortunate two hundred with enough athletic ability to attract the attention of coaches leave school with little comprehension of how to maintain their personal health. Emphasis is almost solely upon competition and the perfecting of skills that will be rarely used after graduation. Participation is in those complicated team sports which provide minimal long-range health benefits. We conduct this segment of our public education as if lifelong concerns were an arcane secret about which nothing is known.

And while these fortunate two hundred are being undereducated insofar as health is concerned, the less fortunate eighteen hundred receive a really deficient health education. A winning team becomes a substitute for a general system of health education, and in the long run everyone suffers.

I see little practical hope that our educational system can be converted into an agency for the improvement of national health. Our school administrations, our athletic departments and even our physical education teachers are so indoctrinated with the concept of fielding semi-professional teams as the goal of education that attention to the health of the student body is impossible. The educators are not to blame; it is our society that demands a team first, health second. And it seems apparent that society will continue to make the same demand throughout the foreseeable future.

The critical question is this: Has our preoccupation with competitive games rather than with health produced American young people who are deficient in physical conditioning when compared with students in other nations?

In the spring of 1954 many Americans, including President Eisenhower, were shocked when Professor Hans Kraus of New York University published a paper in the *Research Quarterly* (Volume 25) entitled 'Minimum Muscular Fitness Tests in School Children.' Dr. Kraus, who became the energetic spokesman for the study, appeared in one forum after another to publicize his findings.

A battery of six simple tests of muscular fitness had been administered to 678 Austrian children between the ages of six and sixteen, 1,036 Italian, 1,156 Swiss and 4,264 American. Only 8 percent of the Italian children failed the test, with the other foreign countries reporting comparable scores, but 57.9 percent of the Americans failed. Of the Italian children, 8.5 percent failed one of the six tests; 80 percent of the American children failed at least one. Dr. Kraus said:

> The major difference between these two groups is the fact that European children do not have the 'benefit' of a highly mechanized society; they do not use cars, school buses, elevators or other labor-saving devices. They must walk everywhere—even to school, frequently a long distance. Their recreation is largely based on the active use of their bodies. In this country the children are generally conveyed in private cars or by bus, and they engage in recreation as spectators rather than as participants.

He said that the years ten through thirteen are critical so far as the loss of general fitness is concerned, but he was not hopeful that American educational patterns could do much to improve the health of children: 'It further appears that we are unable to alleviate the situation during the time the children are in elementary schools. They leave elementary school in very much the same condition as when they entered it—if anything, a little worse.'

When these national deficiencies were given wide publicity, authorities devised a simple, clever, easily administered battery of tests of physical fitness that were administered in the school year 1957–58 to 8,500 boys and girls aged ten through seventeen. After the test scores were tabulated, norms were established.

When the results were made public the findings were alarming. American children rated conspicuously lower than their counterparts in other countries. They were markedly deficient in upper-arm strength and shoulder development, and less agile in overall body movement. They had noticeably less endurance.

A kind of shock passed through the physical education departments of the country, because our children had demonstrably better foods available to them and in general a better system of health care. What could account for the inferior performance, especially when in Olympic competition, or any other kind, our top athletes performed as well as those of other countries and oftentimes much better?

The explanation was simple. Our educational system was stressing so heavily the public games played by a few semi-professional athletes posing as scholars that the general health of the student body was going unattended, and the tests proved this.

To the credit of the physical education people, when the test results were made public, they took action. Backed by school boards who were appalled at this proof of deficiency, the educators devised new types of training programs and placed new emphasis on physical fitness. In other words, they speedily initiated programs they should have been offering for the past half-century.

The results were so reassuring that in 1963 it was decided to administer the new tests to 9,200 children who had experienced the recommended training. When new norms were calculated, it was found that in 111 categories out of 112, there had been significant improvement. (That is, seven tests for boys in eight age groups, ten through seventeen, and the same number for girls for a total of 112. Only the softball throw for girls seventeen years old failed to produce an improved norm.)

Some of the improvements were notable. In the first test fourteen-year-old boys did about 44 sit-ups. Five years later fourteen-year-olds could do 70. It took fifteen-year-old girls 3:18 to run-walk 600 yards the first time, but only 2:50 the second. American children are not yet the equal of their European counterparts, but they are closing the gap.

Take, for example, a thirteen-year-old boy in the eighth grade, because this is where American young people begin to fall seriously behind their European counterparts. I shall list three figures. The first represents the 90th percentile performance, which means that the boy can do better than 89 percent of boys his age but is excelled by the top 10 percent. The second figure represents the 50th percentile, which means that half do more poorly, half do better. And the third figure represents the 10th percentile, which means that 90 percent do better and 9 percent do worse.

PERCENTILE NORMS FOR A
THIRTEEN-YEAR-OLD AMERICAN BOY

Test	90th	50th	10th
Pull-ups (also known as chinning)	9	3	0
Sit-ups	60	38	24
Shuttle (run and turn, 40 yards)	9.5 sec.	10.4 sec.	11.8 sec.
Standing broad jump	6'10"	5'9"	4'7"
50-yard dash	6.7 sec.	7.5 sec.	8.7 sec.
Softball throw	183'	140'	101'
600-yard run-walk	1:50	2:10	2:45

Youth Fitness Test Manual. National Education Association.

These performances seem respectable, but as soon as the new norms were announced, Howard G. Knuttgen, in Copenhagen, tested a mixed group of Danish children and showed that 70 percent of Danish boys and 86 percent of girls achieved scores better than the mean for Americans. (For example, out of a hundred twelve-year-old American girls, only fifty could do more than 32 sit-ups, but out of a hundred Danish girls, eighty-six could do more.)

In nations like Czechoslovakia and East Germany, which make a fetish of physical fitness, the levels would have been even higher. Knuttgen gave these three reasons for the superiority of the Danish children: 1) their children use bicycles instead of automobiles; 2) Danish schools emphasize sports requiring running and give instruction in gymnastics; 3) Danish adults participate in lifetime sports more than Americans do and this probably encourages their children to do likewise.

There is no reason why we should expect our schoolchildren to lead the world in the seven exercises of the test; a reasonable level of performance which enhances health should suffice, and I would guess that we are achieving that level in some of our schools, but not in many.

The question then arises as to what specific sports we should sponsor if we wish to attain the best results for the health of our nation. Here Criteria III (public entertainment) and II (health) are in competition, and the conflict can be resolved only by appeal to national priorities.

Criterion III argues that we must continue to provide the public with sports entertainment, and I agree. The American people will always demand that our schools, colleges and universities provide such exhibitions; will approve spending public money on stadiums for exhibition rather than on tennis courts for participation; and will demand that television bring into their homes the best sports entertainment available. I see no likelihood of change in this situation.

Criterion II, however, argues that at the same time we are emphasizing entertainment we should also be providing education at all levels in lifetime sports that will improve the health of the nation. Emphasis should be paid to those which promise maximum personal rewards and which can be utilized throughout a lifetime.

It is necessary, therefore, that the reader analyze all sports and games to which he is addicted, or accustomed, in order to judge their relative values. Not all sports return equal rewards, and some kind of comparison between them is essential.

To clarify my own thinking on this problem, I selected eleven widely varied sports drawn from various nations. I wanted as complete a coverage as possible, and I particularly wanted to include several types with which the average sports enthusiast might not be familiar. In short, I did not want the list to be parochial. When it was completed, and the criteria for using it specified, I circulated the questionnaire among several hundred men and women interested in sports and asked them to rate the eleven types as to the degree of physical demand imposed.

PHYSICAL DEMAND MADE BY CERTAIN SPORTS

Here is a list of eleven sports. Grade each one on a scale from 10, the most demanding physically, down to 1, the least demanding. You may, for example, grade three of the sports at 7 should you so wish, and none at either 10 or 1.

The following criteria should be used:
  Does this sport place a felt demand on heart and lungs?
  Does it require the repeated use of the big-body muscles?
  Does it induce substantial perspiration?
  Does participation require the athlete to be in top physical condition?

  • Baseball, 9-inning game
  • Basketball, 48-minute game
  • Bicycle race, Tour de France, 30 days
  • Football, 60-minute game
  • Golf, 18 holes
  • Ice hockey, 60-minute game
  • Jogging, 2 miles in 15 minutes
  • Marathon racing, 26 miles, 385 yards in 2 hours, 50 minutes
  • Prize fighting, 12 3-minute rounds
  • Soccer, 90-minute game
  • Tennis, singles, best of 5 sets, using tie-breaker

The results were interesting. Bear in mind that these figures represent the thinking of some of America's top athletes and sports directors, the real experts who have competed in many of the sports described.

COMPARATIVE DEMAND MADE BY ELEVEN SPORTS

Bicycle Race, Tour de France	10	Soccer	7
Marathon race	9	Tennis	6
Boxing	9	Jogging	5
Basketball	8	Baseball	3
Football	7	Golf	1
Ice hockey	7		

Certain notes are necessary. Several respondents wrote that in their opinion the one-day, ten-event decathlon was the most grueling sporting event ever devised, and that it should be rated 10-plus. When I circulated this opinion to others, they agreed. 'That was why we changed the event to cover two days,' one official explained.

It was also believed that the late-summer football training camp was a 10-plus. 'One of the toughest experiences an athlete can have,' several football players reported: 'Tape-up, morning and afternoon. Brutal practice, morning and afternoon. Wind sprints, morning and afternoon. I'd take my salt pills and vomit. I couldn't eat till about nine o'clock at night.' But even the most ardent football players agreed that with the two-platoon system, the game itself rated below basketball in sheer demand. Several respondents pointed out that in baseball the pitcher would rate at 5 or 6.

There was surprising agreement on the evaluations, except for ice hockey. Even among the participants of that game, opinions differed radically, and the score of 7 is an average rather than a consensus. Some felt that hockey was the most demanding of all games, what with sprinting back and forth, the sudden stops, the requirement of body control at all times, but others pointed out that since a team has three alternate lines, no one player has to exert himself at top speed for very long. All agreed, however, that the game was hell on teeth, and I met very few hockey players who had a full set of originals.

Judgments on tennis varied, but to a lesser degree; those who had not played the game rated it somewhat lower than shown. But all who had played it in stiff competition not only rated it high but also commended it as an excellent all-around conditioner. The judgment on golf was almost unanimous, but I must point out that the men and women I was interviewing tended to be younger than the average golfer and not yet ready for this slower but most exacting game. When they are older they may rate golf somewhat higher, but it would still stand at the bottom of the list. The judgment on baseball was also surprisingly uniform, with even those who had played the game professionally rating it at about 3.

And everyone insisted upon one point which I should like to emphasize. To perform at peak level in any sport or game—pentathlon, football, golf, bridge, chess—one must be in top physical condition. When I start to write a long novel, which for two years will place heavy demands on my attention, my brain power, my eyes and my imagination, I go into training as severe as the program I followed when I played basketball. I eat sparingly, drink large quantities of grapefruit juice, take a daily nap, exercise vigorously in the late afternoon, and get to bed by ten-thirty. If I did not follow this regimen, I would not possibly have the energy to face the tasks I set for myself. Therefore, the problem in this questionnaire is not 'Does super-golf require good conditioning?' Of course it does, just as super-bridge does. The question really is 'Which sports place the heaviest reasonable demand on the human body?' And here the variation is substantial.

Concurrent with the study reported above, I kept listing opinions on other sports. Rarely did someone I interviewed fail to remark that in my list of eleven I had overlooked certain sports that he was particularly interested in and on which he was qualified to have an opinion. I therefore put together a much larger list, which I offer herewith, apologizing in advance for its incompleteness and for the fact that it was compiled on a much narrower base than the preceding. However, it is valuable in reminding the reader that not all sports activity is of equal value, insofar as demand upon the big muscles, the lungs and the heart.

MASTER LIST OF SPORTS
RATED AS TO DEMAND ON MUSCLES, LUNGS, HEART

Archery	1	Hammer throw	5	Rodeo	3
Auto racing	3	Handball	8	Roller derby	3
Badminton	5	High jump	7	Roller-skating	2
Baseball	3	Hiking	2	Rowing	7
Basketball	8	Horseback riding	2	Rugby	7
Bicycling	4	Horse racing		Sailing	2
Billiards	1	harness	1	Scuba diving	3
Boating, small	2	flat	5	Shotput	2
Bobsledding	2	Horseshoe pitching	1	Skiing	5
Bocce	1	Hunting	2	Snowshoeing	6
Bowling	2	Hurdles	6	Soccer	7
Boxing	9	Hydroplane racing	1	Softball	2
Calisthenics	5	Ice hockey	7	Squash	7
Canoeing	3	Ice-skating	4	Street hockey	4
Casting	1	Jai alai	6	Surfing	4
Cliff-diving	2	Javelin	2	Swimming	6
Cricket	2	Jogging	5	Table tennis	2
Croquet	1	Judo	7	Tennis	6
Cross-country	6	Karate	5	Touch football	5
Dancing, social	1	Lacrosse	6	Tour de France	10
Dashes	7	Lawn bowling	1	Trampoline	6
Decathlon	10+	Long jump	4	Tug of war	4
Diving	2	Marathon	9	Volleyball	6
Dune-buggying	1	Motorcycling	2	Walking	1
Equestrianism	3	Mountain climbing	7	Water polo	7
Fencing	5	Paddleball	4	Water-skiing	1
Field hockey	6	Pentathlon	8	Weight-lifting	4
Fishing	1	Pole vault	5	Wrestling	8
Football	7	Polo	2	Wrist-wrestling	2
Frisbee	2	Relay racing	6	Yachting	1
Golf	1				
Gymnastics	6				

SYVERSON

A legitimate question arises when one studies these estimates. Are some activities with very low scores really sports? Or are they something else? This debate was launched when someone voiced his opinion that golfers did not qualify as athletes. I have heard considerable controversy on this point and find myself unhesitatingly on the side of the golfers. Apart from the fact just mentioned, that they had better be in topflight condition if they want to play topflight golf, I suspect that many of them could have excelled in other sports which place a greater demand on the body. In my opinion Arnold Palmer, Jack Nicklaus and Johnny Miller are athletes and good ones.

But I wonder about some other sports. For example, in the preceding chapter when Artemius Crandall, the superior black running back, looked over the roster of the Kansas City Chiefs, he saw only three players past the age of thirty, and those three were specialists. What would he have thought of harness racing, where Earle Avery was a leading driver at age seventy-five and Joe Hylan at age eighty. Obviously, if football and harness racing are both sports, they impose radically different demands.

As my study progressed I was careful to check it against previous evaluations, and it will be interesting to compare my findings with those of experts who had spent many years at their work. I shall summarize them briefly.

The first study of specific athletic exercises came in 1943, when researchers at Harvard University devised the beautifully simple but effective Harvard Step Test, in which the athlete to be tested is asked to step up and down a twenty-inch step thirty times a minute for five minutes. The subject's pulse rate is then taken three times during the first three and a half minutes following the exercise. A complicated formula is applied to the figures, and an index is arrived at—the higher the number, the quicker the subject's return to a normal pulse rate.

AN INDEX OF THE CAPACITY OF THE HEART TO RECOVER FROM THE EXERCISE OF THE HARVARD STEP TEST

Pentathlon	154	Volleyball	112
Basketball	128	Judo	111
Rowing	123	Hockey	106
Swimming	122	Track and field	105
Cycling	121	Fencing	96
Football	117	Weight lifting	95
Canoeing	115	Gymnastics	93
Boxing	115	Yachting	92
Wrestling	114	Equestrianism	86
Water Polo	112	Shooting	83

Reported by Thomas, Vaughan. *Science and Sport.*

The implications of this test are threefold. 1) The athlete with a high score has accustomed his heart to a heavy demand; therefore, it is less excited by any demand and able to return quickly to normal because it is in better condition. 2) It is good to have such a heart, and vigorous exercise is the way to get one. 3) A pentathlon performer engages in a sport that is markedly more demanding than target shooting. Notice also that according to these results, the demands made by basketball are greater than those made by football, which confirms my unscientific study.

Dr. Robert E. Johnson, of the department of physiology and biophysics at the University of Illinois attacked the same problem with different assumptions. He reasoned that the number of calories consumed in the performance of a given sport yields an index of the energy required. The more calories consumed, the more demanding the sport.

THE NUMBER OF CALORIES PER HOUR EXPENDED IN CERTAIN SPORTS

Running (10 mph)	900	Hill climbing (100 ft. per hr.)	490
Scull-rowing (race)	840	Water-skiing	480
Bicycling (13 mph)	660	Tennis	420
Squash and handball	600	Wood chopping or sawing	400
Skiing (10 mph)	600	Table tennis	360

Roller-skating	350	Lawn mowing (hand mower)	270
Volleyball	350	Lawn mowing (power mower)	250
Square-dancing	350	Golf	250
Horseback riding (trotting)	350	Canoeing (2½ mph)	230
Badminton	350	Gardening	220
Walking (3¾ mph)	300	Walking (2½ mph)	210
Swimming (¼ mph)	300	Bicycling (5½ mph)	210
Rowboating (2½ mph)	300		

Wilkinson, Bud. 'Our Guide to the Best Sports for Your Health.' *Today's Health* (May 1972).

In 1972 Dr. Lawrence A. Golding, of Kent State University, a leading expert on the physiology of exercise, achieved nationwide publicity when a reporter from a Cleveland newspaper asked him to rank various sports according to the degree of physical fitness required by participants. The question was not an improper one to put to Dr. Golding, for he had spent the past decades doing intensive work on coronary aftermaths, dehydration as a cause of serious injury to athletes, drug use by athletes, acclimatization for athletes moving from one altitude to another, and the personal training habits of champions.

As a consequence of such studies Dr. Golding gave it as his opinion that the various sports should be listed as follows insofar as demand upon the athlete's physical fitness was concerned: at the top, track; followed by swimming, cross-country skiing, soccer, ice hockey, basketball, football, tennis, baseball, golf; and at the bottom, bowling.

This report occasioned so much comment that Dr. Golding had to remind his questioners that his list represented merely his off-the-cuff estimate and was not based on any scientific evidence. In a letter to me he stated:

> It was my personal ranking based on my own experience in testing a great number of athletes and knowing what various sports demand physically from their participants. I am sure that the order could be changed slightly; however, I am confident that track and field participants, swimmers, cross-country skiers etc., are among the most cardiovascularly fit athletes . . . Unfortunately, no objective study was done, so I can't really send you the results of any particular testing.

Until such testing has been accomplished, Dr. Golding's list does bear the personal authority of an expert in the field.

Dr. Kenneth H. Cooper, author of the popular book on aerobics, did conduct experiments on the oxygen intake of athletes under stress, and his findings seem of great importance to me, because they were the first to yield a specific index of how hard the lungs are working (the higher the index number, the greater the oxygen utilization):

RELATIVE DEMANDS ON THE OXYGEN SYSTEM OF THE HUMAN BODY DURING
THIRTY MINUTES OF ACTIVE PARTICIPATION

Wrestling	12	Squash	4.5	Fencing	3
Rope-skipping	9	Basketball	4.5	Football	3
Boxing	*	Skiing	3	Volleyball	2
Rowing	5	Soccer	3	Skating	2
Hockey	4.5	Lacrosse	3	Baseball	*
Handball	4.5	Tennis	3	Golf	.5

*No test conducted, but sport estimated to be in this relative position.

Cooper, Kenneth H. *Aerobics.*

The implications of this study are crucial to the thesis of this book. 1) Forced heavy breathing, and thus the intake of large amounts of oxygen, encourages the heart to set up alternative feed lines, which may save a life in later years. 2) Such intake is the best way to combat emphysema, the degenerative disease of the lungs. 3) Jogging, here called running-walking, is, in my experience, the most miserable form of sport, but one of the most effective. If an individual can possibly do anything else, he or she should, but if nothing else is available—no gymnasium, no tennis court, no attractive open space—jogging in place for even five minutes before an open window can be a life-saver. I have a high regard for Exercycles, which I have used to good advantage. In China, I was impressed by the early-morning exhibitions of shadowboxing with which so many officials began their day. And I know men and women who have derived much good from isometric exercises at their desks.

One of the most interesting studies of energy expenditure is also one of the most scientific. Two Scottish scientists, John Durnin of Glasgow and Reginald Passmore of Edinburgh, started with the modest theory that 'a certain level of physical activity is required to maintain normal health and to prevent degenerative diseases, notably obesity and cardiac disease.' They then conducted their own experiments, and sought out reports of those conducted by others in an effort to determine the caloric expenditure per minute for the various sports. Unfortunately, since the investigators were British, they focused on sports native to their country and ignored certain major American sports, but their conclusions can be extrapolated.

ENERGY EXPENDITURES DURING RECREATIONS
EXPRESSED IN KCALS PER MINUTE

Archery	3.2 to 5.7	Boxing	9.0 to 14.4
Badminton	6.3	Canoeing	2.5 to 7.0
Basketball	9.0	Climbing	7.0 to 10.0
Billiards	2.7	Cricket	5.0 to 8.0
Bowls	4.1	Cross-country	10.6

Cycling, easy	4.0	Music playing	2.0 to 4.2
Cycling, Tour		Rowing	4.1 to 11.2
de France	20.0	Skiing, cross-	
Dancing	4.0 to 8.0	country	18.6
Fishing	4.0	Skiing, mixture	5.4 to 10.0
Gardening	2.7 to 8.6	Soccer	5.0 to 12.0
Golf	4.0 to 7.0	Squash	10.1 to 18.2
Gymnastics	2.5 to 12.0	Swimming	5.0 to 15.0
Hockey, field	8.7	Table tennis	3.6 to 5.2
Horse (walking)	3.0	Tennis	5.7 to 8.5
Horse (galloping)	10.0	Volleyball	3.5
Judo	14.6	Weight-lifting	8.2
Mowing lawn	9.1		

Durnin, J.V.G.A. and Passmore, R. *Energy, Work & Leisure.* Data reduced to tabular form by the author.

The chief pleasure to be derived from this study, however, comes in the uninhibited observations of the authors. *Cricket.* 'This is a sophisticated English game, which neither Scots nor Americans have the wit to understand.' *Croquet.* 'Success at the game requires skill, judgment and an active dislike of your opponent.' *Cycling.* 'The Tour de France, which lasts three weeks, must be one of the most arduous of sporting events.' *Fishing.* 'We are unable to appreciate the interest that thousands of English fishermen find in spending a cold winter day crouched on a little campstool by the side of a sluggish canal with their eyes fixed on a float. This appears to be a sedentary pastime.' *Football* (Soccer). 'Few boys play football after leaving school, and it is exceptional to continue to play after leaving the university. In our opinion many school and university authorities have placed too much emphasis on football. There are many other better forms of active recreation for boys and young men.' *Gardening.* 'Even those over eighty years can derive benefit from simple tasks in a garden.' *Field hockey.* 'Hockey is an excellent game to teach in schools. The best players in the world come from India and Pakistan, and these countries might well send a mission to provide technical aid to the underdeveloped U.S.A.' *Swimming.* 'This is perhaps the ideal form of exercise.'

I believe that the reader who has inspected these various summaries of research will have acquired a better understanding of where his preferred sport stands in relation to others, so far as physical demand is concerned, and this was my experience. But it was not until I had completed the above analyses that I received my biggest surprise. It came from a most unlikely source, the conductor of a symphony orchestra. I had attended a Saturday night concert of the New York Philharmonic, and at its conclusion I went to the Green Room to congratulate André Kostelanetz, who had conducted. 'I'm heading uptown to meet an interesting friend,' he told me. 'Care to come along?'

The friend turned out to be Dr. James Nicholas, the tall and handsome medical doctor who serves as orthopedist for the New York Jets, and when he learned of my interest in sports, he invited Kostelanetz and me to the Jets-Buffalo game the next day, when O.J. Simpson was expected to go over the 2,000-yard mark for rushing in a single season.

Sunday was a horrible day, with a December wind whipping snow across Shea Stadium and about half the ticket holders staying home to watch the game on television. Simpson was outstanding. Namath was desperate. Receivers had no chance of holding on to passes. And the day ended in a dismal fog, with everyone chilled to the bone and the Jets losers again.

After the game Dr. Nicholas took me down to the Jets' dressing room, where Weeb Ewbank was making a tearful and final farewell to coaching and where Joe Namath talked with me as he undressed at the close of this painful season. I was appalled at the massive knee braces he wore, and hefted them as he took them off.

'Twenty-five pounds,' he told me. I slipped them on and could scarcely move. Joe said that Dr. Nicholas had devised the braces and that they had kept him going. I said I couldn't conceive of playing a game like football in such armor, and Joe said, 'If you had knees like mine, you'd be lucky to find gear like that.'

It was at this point that Dr. Nicholas joined us, and when he saw my interest in the braces he surprised me by saying, 'I'm conducting a major study on the physical demand made by certain sports,' and with this we were off on a long discussion of our two studies. I was astonished that he had covered in such depth the very field I was interested in.

In succeeding weeks we compared notes and exchanged data. The figures I now offer are markedly superior to mine, for three reasons: they cover many more cases; they have been compiled by a trained expert; and he had at his disposal several trained interviewers and diagnosticians. I place considerably more reliance on Dr. Nicholas' figures than I do on my own.

Dr. Nicholas, known affectionately to football players whose knees he has saved as 'Nick the Knife,' identified twenty-one components of an athletic act, grouping them into three categories: neuromuscular-physical (endurance, reaction time); mental-psychometric (intelligence, alertness); environmental (playing conditions, equipment). He then applied these criteria to sixty-one different sports, covering eight on my list, to which I add four others which he rated high.

TWELVE SPORTS GRADED ON THE NICHOLAS CHART

Sport	Partial Score 13 Physical Factors	Total Score All 21 Factors
Prizefighting	37	51
Basketball	35	50
Football	36	56
Hockey	37	54
Soccer	32	44
Tennis	26	42
Baseball	27	44
Golf	23	39
Ballet	37	55
Fencing	35	49
Gymnastics	36	50
Judo	36	51

Dr. James A. Nicholas, M.D., *Sports Classification Chart,* 1975

The similarity of rankings between the Nicholas list and my own is striking. We both place football and basketball high. We both rank football and hockey about even. And we both place golf far to the rear. Here are the total scores for the other sports Dr. Nicholas cited:

FORTY-NINE SPORTS GRADED ON THE NICHOLAS CHART

Archery 28	Curling 36	Polo 50
Auto racing 45	Diving 45	Rodeo 49
Badminton 40	Equestrian 46	Racing 46
Ballroom dance 27	Field hockey 36	Rugby 52
Bicycling 36	Figure skating 41	Sailing 43
Big-game hunting 45	Fishing, deep-sea 33	Scuba diving 37
Billiards 27	Handball 37	Skiing 41
Bobsledding 39	Hiking 18	Snowmobiling 38
Bowling 29	Ice Follies 50	Surfing 50
Bridge 26	Jai alai 52	Swimming 39
Bullfighting 55	Jockey 52	Table tennis 34
Calisthenics 33	Karate 50	Tap dance 37
Canoeing 37	Lacrosse 38	Tumbling 45
Camping 23	Modern dance 28	Volleyball 44
Circus acts 48	Motorcycling 37	Water polo 44
Cricket 44	Mountain climbing 47	Yachting 46
	Paddleball 42	

Of special significance, I think, is the very high mark given by Nicholas to ballet. This is justified because he takes into consideration such intangibles as intelligence and creativity, which are not factors in my study and which do not represent actual physical demand. But his figures do emphasize a point I have recently made to college students who have asked me what courses they should take in order to become writers:

> If I had a daughter or son determined to be a writer—and by that I mean poet or dramatist or novelist or advertising writer—naturally I'd expect them to be competent in their own language and to know something about psychology and the history of what fine writers have accomplished in the past. But the two courses I'd make obligatory would be one in ceramics, so that you could feel form emerging from inchoate clay. I think this is very important, that you have a feeling for form and a sense of how it's achieved.
>
> And the second course would be eurhythmic dancing, so that you could feel within your own body the capacity that you have for movement and form and dramatic shifts in perspective. Of course, if you can't locate a class in such dancing, you might pick up the same sensations in a long game of basketball or tennis, where the ebb and flow of movement is pronounced. Or perhaps in any other sport requiring bold shifts of movement. What the artist requires is a sense of emerging form, a kinesthetic sense of what the human body is capable of. If you marry those sensory capacities to a first-rate brain, you have a good chance of becoming an artist.

I developed these conclusions many years ago but lacked confidence in setting them forth, for they seemed both peculiar and arbitrary. But when I read Johan Huizinga's masterful *Homo Ludens* (Man the Player of Games) I found that as early as 1938 he had expressed ideas far in advance of mine. Indeed, he envisioned most of life as a game, but it was George Leonard who expressed exactly my attitude in his poetic and learned discourse *The Ultimate Athlete:*

> Out of a lifetime of sports spectating, the moments that live for us are pure dance. We may forget league standings and final scores and even who won, but we can never forget certain dancelike movements . . . Perhaps it is actually this desire for the transcendant rather than for mere victory that keeps us locked to our television sets on those sunny afternoons when we ourselves might be out playing. Perhaps even the most avid team supporter, dispirited and surly after a defeat of 'his' team, has gained an unspoken understanding of the dance that will keep him coming back again and again, regardless of the final score . . .
>
> If only one subject were to be required in school, it should be, in my opinion, some form of dance—from nursery school through a Ph.D. I can't say that the dancer is the Ultimate Athlete. I am quite certain, however, that the Ultimate Athlete is a dancer.

I endorse the conclusions stated in that second paragraph. The exquisite moments I have known in sports have related more to the dance of the human figure than to anything else; the spiritual freedom I have often found in games has derived specifically from the dancing body seeking new forms and new releases.

A more important conclusion from these studies is that certain sports contribute less to general health than others. Golf, boating and fishing place so little demand upon the lungs and heart that many critics feel their practitioners should not be called athletes. The same deficiency can be charged against numerous similar activities. However, several cautionary judgments must be made.

Any activity whatever which takes a man or woman out of doors is healthful. Even if it involves no physical exertion—riding in a car through a pleasant landscape, for example—it is constructive if it provides a chance to breathe fresh air and an escape, however temporary, from customary tensions.

It is therefore a hundred times better to play golf than not to play it, with one precaution. If golf creates a greater tension than it releases, which is often the case, then the playing of golf could be a detriment rather than an asset. Since it involves no large-muscle exertion and since it places no demand upon heart or lungs, its positive virtues are limited.

The problem is quite different from that posed by tennis, for in the latter game one has a live opponent against whom one is contesting, and frustrations can be easily discharged, even if specific shots go astray. Also, at the height of tension one can smash the ball, run vigorously to the net, lunge sideways to retrieve a return, and in many other ways get rid of one's frustrations while working up a healthy sweat. The natural anger that the fierce competitor generates can be instantly discharged, which is not always the case in golf, where one often competes against oneself, against an impersonal par.

I know many men who would be better off not playing golf, because consistently they end the day in worse emotional shape than when they started, whereas had they been playing tennis or some similar sport with an attacking opponent, they might have ended the day exhausted emotionally as well as physically, which is a marvelous condition to be in occasionally. The professional golfer Billy Casper had these facts in mind when a friend assured him, 'Every time you go fishing, Billy, you add a day to your life,' to which Casper replied, 'Every time you play a round of competitive golf, a day is subtracted. It's a tie.'

A different kind of precaution applies to boating and fishing. I have done a great deal of each and have been much impressed by the fact that the great enemy of the boater or the fisherman is constipation, because one remains inactive for long periods of time. Yet one is in fresh air and the appetite flourishes. Especially in the company of good friends, one eats excessively and perhaps drinks too much, so that after a week one's health is apt to have deteriorated rather than improved.

I have noticed that the one sure way to determine whether a man is a real

SYVERSON

fisherman or boater is to note whether, when he unpacks his gear on the first afternoon, he has brought along a supply of dried prunes and fresh cabbage, the first to gnaw on during the idle moments, the second to make into cole slaw, which should be eaten at every meal, including breakfast.

But I repeat my first conclusion: anything that takes a human being out of doors and places him or her in contact with nature is bound to be beneficial. Strenuous sports not only do this; they also place heavy demands upon the system, and this is conducive to better health.

The health benefits derived from participation in sports seem obvious. Are there accompanying dangers?

Yes, and they are substantial. They divide into two groups, normal dangers to the young and special dangers to the old.

As to the young, Dr. Nicholas, who has specialized in this field and keeps national records, reports that each year sports in America are responsible for seventeen million accidents serious enough to require the attentions of a doctor. 'That's more casualties in one year than American troops suffered in all our wars put together,' he says. And six million of the accidents leave permanent results, but some are no more serious than a scar.

'Look at it this way,' he says. 'Suppose an epidemic swept this country and left six million children crippled, injured or with some residual scar or other effect. You'd say, "What a catastrophe!"

'Suppose I told you that in California there are two hundred and fifty people hurt every month just from motorcycle accidents. Permanent crippling to the hip. Some of them die. Suppose I told you that forty thousand people a year suffer crippled knees as a result of sport. How do those figures compare with twenty-five thousand polio victims, which we considered a catastrophe?'

Dr. Nicholas estimates that for young people under the age of fifteen who participate in the normal American sports, their parents can anticipate one accident each year for every three players. Some of the accidents can be fatal. Over many years I kept a running record of the number of deaths occurring each season which could be attributed to football. Few sports fans have bothered to notice, but each year in December one of the wire services issues a brief paragraph tabulating the number of football deaths for that year, and during the time I kept my records the number hovered around thirty-eight.

This meant that year after year, in all parts of the country, boys and young men were regularly being killed at the rate of thirty-eight a year, and no one seemed to care very much about the total. However, when a specific death occurred in a specific community, as had happened in my town when I was a boy, it created something of a scandal . . . for a brief period. But on the whole, our nation was prepared to accept a regular plague of deaths without protest.

For some years I kept a record of each reported death. In August and September an appalling number of young men died from heat prostration, some because their coaches honestly believed that intake of water during practice was injurious, others because their coaches thought that for a boy to require water was a sign of weakness. One cup of water, arriving at the right time, could have saved many lives over the span I studied, and the deprivation of this water was the consequence of ignorance.

In October and November the causes for death shifted away from heat prostration to those dreadful injuries of neck and spine, caused again by specific coaching procedures. It was considered gallant for a tackler to thrust his head into an on-charging halfback, or for the halfback to go head-down right at a would-be tackler. In either case, a neck could be snapped or a backbone fractured, and if death did not result, lifelong incapacitation did. There are many towns in this country which harbor some young man who is spending his life in a wheelchair as a result of improper instructions.

In the weeks that I was working on this chapter, the following cases drifted across my desk without my having made any special conscious effort to compile them:

• Kenton, Ohio. Mark Valentine, seventeen years old, a heavy lineman, dies after running two miles in under twelve minutes during a heat wave in mid-August.

• Chapel Hill, North Carolina. Bill Arnold, twenty years old, dies as a result of a heat stroke incurred while practicing football in early September.

• Honesdale, Pennsylvania. Walter Richard Wilkinson, seventeen years old, dies of exhaustion after a two-hour-and-fifteen-minute football practice in full uniform during a heat wave in early September.

• Dothan, Alabama. Jon Davis, fifteen years old, dies of a broken neck sustained in a tackling drill held in the gymnasium in mid-September.

• Harleton, Texas. Terry Ray Muse, sixteen years old, dies following his collapse while playing a football game in mid-September.

• Chicago, Illinois. Marco Cervantes, seventeen years old, dies from brain damage suffered while butting into a 200-pound linebacker in late October.

• Livingston, New Jersey. Bob Taratko, seventeen years old, dies following a pileup in a high school football game in early November.

• Wilkes Barre, Pennsylvania. Bobby McBride, twenty years old, dies from injuries received in a college football game in mid-November.

• Bakersfield, California. John Vaughn, sixteen years old, dies from head injuries received while tackling in a sandlot football game in mid-December.

The above data are inconclusive, because I gathered them at random. A more responsible summary appeared in 1971 in the *Encyclopedia of Sport Sciences and Medicine,* whose editors reported that in the period 1931–65 a total of 642 fatalities occurred which could be attributed specifically to football. Of these, 348 were high school players, 54 were college players, 72 were professionals and semi-professionals, plus one official who was struck fatally while refereeing.

In the most complete study yet made, the National Collegiate Athletic Association (NCAA) reported that in the period 1931–73 (excluding 1942, when no study was made) a total of 795 fatalities occurred which were attributable directly to football, plus another 384 relating indirectly. (The boy made it home, collapsed, but did not die till four days later.) The average per year was 28, proving that my figures were too high.

In the fall of 1974 one of the television networks carried a show relating to football injuries in high school, and made the documented statement that out of 100 boys who play the game in high school, 86 could expect to sustain at least one injury, and I reflected on what would happen in this country if high school physics had a record of killing 28 students every year and maiming in some degree 86 percent of all enrollees.

I think it obvious that physics would be eliminated as a subject, and within a very short time, for such a cost would be deemed excessive. But there is no cry to end football, nor will there be, because every society decides what it is willing to pay for its entertainment, and if football injuries and deaths do not markedly exceed the present rate, they will not be considered excessive.

Football has been so enshrined as a spectator sport, both in college and professionally, that it would be impossible for revisionists to alter it without protests of an almost revolutionary character. As long as the deadly violence does not accelerate, football is in no danger of discipline from without, and it is my own sad guess that deaths could triple or quadruple without causing much outcry. Football is the American form of violence, and whereas Spanish bullfighting is pretty despicable—one practitioner killed about every four years—and Mexican cockfighting abominable—no men ever killed—our violent sport is neither, because we have given it our moral sanction.

Steps to police the sport from within are being taken. Constant preaching by coaches has warned everyone within the ranks that dehydration on a hot field in August and September can cause death, and this particular cause of tragedy has diminished. Also, concerned specialists like Dr. Nicholas have worked imaginatively to provide equipment that remains protective to the wearer but causes less damage to the opponent. The rules committee has also done salutary work in outlawing tackling that involves grabbing the face mask, a tactic that used to snap necks. (Football is not our most lethal sport. Scuba diving, with relatively few participants, kills about 120 each year. Swimming, with enormous participation, accounts for about 600, but this figure includes accidents to people who were not intentionally in the water.)

But while football coaches strive to diminish the number of deaths, the general public appears to want an ever-rougher game. Newspapers extol a linebacker as 'a real animal,' and patrons exhort him to 'tear the quarterback's head off.' When a linebacker delivers a bone-crushing tackle, women throughout the stands scream, 'Way to hit, baby. Way to hit!' And recently when an NFL team acquired a tackle from the Canadian League, the player's coach said of him admiringly, 'They're getting a real gorilla.'

I would therefore expect the game to become rougher, with the rules committee endeavoring vainly to stem the carnage. Rough football is salable. It attracts the loyalties of wealthy older men who never played it themselves, and it seems destined to run its present course for at least another fifty years.

This is no new phenomenon. In 1905 in the relatively few colleges that played the game, 18 students were killed, but apologists pointed out that the manly sport killed at a rate of less than one in 50,000 players, and only one in 7,000 broke a limb. Another argued that 'the game does not profess to be a gentle, tame affair like a church social or an afternoon tea. I am sure a much greater harm, even loss of life, results from overstudy or dissipation.' And a speaker at the Harvard Club of Boston that year stated his belief that 'even death on the playground was cheap if it educated boys in the characteristics that had made the Anglo-Saxon race pre-eminent in history.' (Quoted in the *Yale Alumni Magazine* of November 1974. I would undertake to find in Oklahoma, Nebraska or Ohio many adherents of the game ready to advance similar arguments today.)

I would permit my son to play football in high school or college, even though I am aware of the dangers. This game has become so much a part of the American psyche, and it confers so much charisma on its participants, that I would not deny my son the right to take part, but I would not encourage him to do so.

I feel the same way about adolescents and motorcars. I am much impressed by the influence the automotive engine has on American life, and I would want my son to participate in its mystique, even though he might get into serious trouble with his car, or more likely, mine. But I would not allow him to own a motorcycle while he lived with me, and I would hope that he would not want one afterward, because the risk of injury is too great. I lived in Great Britain when the great motorcycle craze hit there, and one girl after another was swept off her pillion seat and under the wheels of oncoming trucks.

All sports, even croquet, involve risk. (I have known people in Hollywood suffering from some rather nasty mallet wounds not acquired by accident.) The prudent situation is that one risks a minimum of injury in order to gain a maximum advantage to one's health. I have always been willing to take sizable risks because my enjoyment of sports has been so rewarding. But there are limits, and if those who make the rules for sports do not maintain a cautious respect for those limits, I would hope that society would step in and perform that function for them.

In 1905 it was President Theodore Roosevelt who saved football by insisting from the White House that it be de-brutalized. As so often happens, his demand for reform led to the improvement of the game: the forward pass was legitimatized. Of the new game Roosevelt said admiringly, 'I disbelieve in seeing Harvard or any other college turn out mollycoddles instead of vigorous men. In any republic, courage is a prime necessity for the average citizen if he is to be a good citizen. Athletics are good, especially in their rougher forms, because they tend to develop such courage.'

For older people the danger from sports can be very real. For a man of forty-five who has been sedentary for the preceding two decades to engage suddenly in violent sport is suicidal. However, the vigorous program which I have been recommending can be followed by men in their seventies, provided they have continued active through the middle years of their lives.

I would not recommend to anyone recovering from a heart attack that he follow my strenuous tennis regimen, nor would I want someone fifty years old and in apparent good health to go out and play a quick thirty-six holes of golf on a hilly course if he had laid off all exercise for the past twenty years.

But even being a spectator at a thrilling game involves dangers, as Harvard University discovered when many of its elderly alumni suffered heart attacks at football games. Two cardiac units had to be installed at opposite sides of the stands, and were put to good use. (When a western friend heard of this he said, 'My God! A man who would drop dead at a Harvard-Yale game, he shouldn't even be allowed to watch Oklahoma-Nebraska on television!')

The strongest counterattack against physical exercise for older people to appear in recent years is contained in the medical best seller *Type A Behavior and Your Heart,* by Drs. Meyer Friedman and Ray H. Rosenman. The authors mount a frontal assault on exercise for anyone past thirty-five, and if any sedentary reader has been heckled by his wife or his friends to 'get up, get out, and do something,' this book will give him encouragement to persist in his lethargy.

Approximately 200,000 American men who had never experienced a single symptom of coronary heart disease died suddenly last year. From our own studies of scores of these cases, we have learned two facts. First, even if these men had no symptoms of heart disease before death, in each case postmortem studies revealed coronary artery disease of sufficient severity that a treadmill electrocardiogram may very well have shown its presence. Second, more than a third of these men died during or a few minutes after indulging in strenuous activity. In many cases, moreover, the men had been exercising strenuously, regularly, and for years prior to their demise.

What are these severe or strenuous exercises which we are cautioning every American past thirty-five years of age to avoid as if they were a plague? First on our blacklist is jogging. This miserable postcollegiate athletic travesty has already killed at least scores, possibly hundreds, of Americans. Jogging is a form of exercise in which man transforms himself into a machine. Chug-chug-chugging along, looking neither to the right nor left, panting, the 'man machine' chugs along. And what is 'its' goal? To see if 'it' can chug-chug faster today than yesterday. And what is 'its' only joy? The soothing miraculous feeling of relief when the chug-chugging is finished. If ever an exercise was custom-made for the attack-prone person, jogging is that exercise. Yes, some of our best friends are joggers!

Competitive handball, tennis singles, and squash rank next to jogging in potential lethality for the middle-aged American who plays these games— whether once a month or every day—without first having had his heart checked at least by the treadmill-electrocardiographic test (which, incidentally, is certainly not foolproof). And fully as dangerous as any of these violent sports may be speed ice-skating and playing touch football or basketball with your teen-aged sons, particularly after even a moderate-sized meal.

Friedman and Rosenman do recognize that moderate exercise can make a contribution to general well-being:

Of course, you might be tempted to ask why we bother to recommend even moderate exercise in view of our doubt about its efficacy in preventing coronary artery disease, and our belief in the evident danger of violent exercise. We would reply that man has always felt better physically and psychologically after indulging in bodily exercise . . . By moderate physical activity, we mean any form of exercise whose execution does not cause panting, excessive acceleration of your heartbeat (that is, above 120 beats per minute), or leave you unduly fatigued. Walking on the flat, up very gentle hills, up one flight of steps or down as many flights of steps as you wish, swimming (non-competitive), golfing, bicycling, tennis (but only doubles, and preferably mixed doubles), fishing, hunting (but not deer hunting at high altitudes or wading after fallen ducks), skeet shooting, horseshoe playing, croquet, billiards, and so forth, are the forms of exercise we recommend.

Anyone defending sports must sooner or later confront the popular belief that 'men who play vigorous sports in college die prematurely.' One rumor states that 'the men who rowed on the Harvard crew in 1922 all died in their forties.' Just the other night a leading educator asked me, 'Is it true that Big Ten football players and distance runners rarely live beyond their fifties?'

Three substantial and trustworthy studies have explored this question. In 1928 Louis I. Dublin, the widely known health statistician, reported in *Harper's* magazine on a study of 4,976 graduates of Harvard, Yale, Cornell and seven other colleges. He compared men who had won letters in sports with the standard life-expectancy figures contained in actuarial tables. He found that athletes enjoyed a 4.5 percent longevity edge over expected deaths. But as soon as these favorable figures were published, critics pointed out that Dublin was comparing college graduates, a favored lot, with run-of-the-mill citizens who had not had the advantage of wealth, superior family circumstances and above-average health services. 'Of course the college men would live longer whether they were athletes or not,' the critics argued. 'The real test would be college athletes versus college non-athletes.'

Dublin recognized the validity of this criticism; indeed, he had anticipated it, and in 1932 issued a more sophisticated analysis. He had gone back and studied 38,269 graduates of eight eastern colleges during the years 1870 to 1905. He compared men who had won letters in major sports with men who had been primarily scholars. The non-athletes lived 2.17 years longer than the athletes, and that remains the definitive study, although why the athletes tended to die earlier has been the subject of much subsequent discussion.

In 1956 Henry J. Montoye compared 628 varsity athletes at Michigan State University with 563 classmates who did not win letters. The athletes tended to die two years earlier than the non-athletes, age sixty-two versus sixty-four, but the numbers of participants covered by the study were not large enough to be statistically significant. Five years later Montoye updated his study and found that the seventy-seven new deaths that had occurred in that interval confirmed the earlier results. The athletes died two years earlier.

In 1970 Anthony Polednak and Albert Damon, of Harvard University, published in *Human Biology* an article entitled 'College Athletics, Longevity and Cause of Death' in which they not only provided an excellent review of all previous studies but also reported the results of an intensive study of 2,631 who attended Harvard between the years 1880–1912. The men were divided into three groups: major athletes (baseball, football, crew, etc.); minor athletes (fencing, golf, swimming, etc.); non-athletes (no record of having participated in formal intercollegiate sports.)

The conclusions were specific: 1) Non-athletes lived longer than athletes, but the difference was not statistically significant. 2) Minor athletes lived longer than major athletes or non-athletes, and here the difference was statistically significant. 3) The man with a stocky apelike build characteristic of most athletes (mesomorph) died markedly sooner than the tall, skinny man (ectomorph). The round, chubby man (endomorph) rated in between.

Polednak and Damon make many learned guesses as to causes. My own suspicion is that athletes tend to be of the body build that is most susceptible to early death, and that the cause of death is not athletics but the nature of the human being engaging in them.

The weakness of such studies is that they must deal with conditions that existed half a century ago. It could not be otherwise, for a study of longevity has no final validity until most of the participants are dead. (In the Harvard study, 90.9 percent had died.) I believe that athletes today have learned from experience to take better care of themselves and are living longer, but proof cannot be forthcoming until forty or fifty years from now.

There remains the problem of 'athlete's heart,' which popular legend claimed was so enlarged as to limit the life of the strenuous athlete to fifty-five years or less. Research does not substantiate such belief. R. Ackermann of Germany photographed the heart shadows of athletes who had been under severe stress, and reported, as others have since, that in such conditions the normal heart actually retreats in size; it is the weakened or diseased heart which enlarges. Professor H. Herxheimer, also of Germany, studied nearly five hundred champion athletes and found that their heart could be indicated by the following index numbers—the higher the number the larger the heart:

HEART SIZE IN ELEVEN TYPES OF ATHLETES

Tour de France cyclists	24.8	Middle-distance runners	18.1
Marathon runners	21.5	Weight lifters	17.6
Long-distance runners	20.5	Long-distance swimmers	16.4
Oarsmen	19.3	Sprinters	16.0
Boxers	18.9	Decathlon	15.7
	Short-distance cyclists	18.1	

Steinhaus, Arthur H., *Toward an Understanding of Health and Physical Education,* 1963. Herxheimer's fractions are converted into index numbers.

From this and parallel studies I conclude that training for endurance enlarges the heart, whereas training for short bursts of intense effort does not. The case of weight lifters illustrates this principle: they develop large muscles without enlarging the heart significantly, hence their index remains low, even though they are capable of enormous bursts of sudden energy.

But even if the heart is somewhat enlarged, does this mean premature death? Vaughan Thomas, in his study on stamina, concluded that the slightly enlarged heart was an asset rather than a liability:

> In the old ignorant past it was commonly observed that those who had led a strenuous athletic existence tended to develop enlarged hearts similar to some chronic invalids. This led to grave warnings about the bad effects training had upon the heart. We now know that in such invalids their heart muscle has been developed in order to compensate for a weakness elsewhere, or to overcome the heavier resistance provided by hardened arteries and such like. Provided the heart itself is normally healthy, then such development through graduated training programmes does nothing but good to the heart. Recent discoveries concerning training effects on the heart have shown, in fact, that there is an increase in the number of blood vessels serving the heart, and an enlargement of the coronary arteries, thus increasing the possible blood flow to the heart muscle.
>
> In addition, the capillaries interconnect in such a way as to provide alternative routes to almost any part of the muscle. Previously a blood clot which formed in any part of the heart's blood supply caused a large area of heart muscle to die. In a trained heart, however, the area of muscle affected would be very much smaller. Those fortunate individuals 'suffering' from athletic heart can feel great confidence in their ability to withstand cardiac stress.

Thomas, Vaughan. *Science and Sport*

On balance, I conclude that sports, conducted reasonably, produce more health benefits to both young and old than they do dangers. However, I must admit that I know many men and women who live perfectly satisfactory lives without ever moving an unnecessary muscle. They stay alert; they achieve their allotted longevity; through television they appear to enjoy sports as much as anyone else; and they keep on performing their jobs with distinction. They are a minority, but they exist.

I would cite as prototype a gentleman in his sixties, tall and lean, who works hard at a demanding job. He commutes to the city, walks slowly from the railroad station to his office, eats sparingly at lunch and does not smoke. He never exercises, in the ordinary sense of this word, but he loves nature and lives in harmony with it. He rakes leaves occasionally, does some mild gardening, walks his dog, and moves indoors when anyone mentions tennis. He remains in better health than many of his more vigorous friends.

I am not, however, much impressed by obese publicity-seekers who proclaim, 'Whenever I feel the need for exercise, I lie down till it goes away.' Or, 'The only exercise I ever do is reaching out for a second martini.' Or,

'The only exercise I get is serving as pallbearer at the funerals of my friends who exercise.'

These are witty statements, but I have observed that most of the men who make them die prematurely.

I defend sports as a means of obtaining exercise pleasurably. I am more impressed with sports as a developer of health than as a developer of character, and I want to see them prosper for health reasons, because I know of no other human activity which so well serves that purpose.

IV

Children and Sports

When my interest in automotive sports was at a height, and I was traveling to various tracks to watch the leading figures, a friend grabbed my arm as I was talking with Mark Donohue—the chubby-faced marvel who would be killed within the year—and said, 'Why are you traveling so far from home? You have one of the most interesting tracks right in Doylestown.'

I could not credit these words, for I thought I knew my hometown and I'd never heard of a racing track, but he made a date with me for the next Friday night and drove me to a small field near the shopping center, and there introduced me to a new world.

The track was one-eighth of a mile in circumference, its turns lined with bales of hay. Eight tall poles held bright lights and four loudspeakers, even though the area was so small that a strong-voiced man could have been heard if he used a megaphone. I would learn later in the evening that the loudspeakers were an essential part of racing.

As we approached the track entrance I saw several large vans attached as trailers to touring cars. The most interesting was painted with red and white stars and bore the proud legend: *The Fighting Rigbys. America's Best.*

When we reached the track itself a woman pointed to a grandstand on whose plank boarding we were invited to sit, and for the first time in my life I saw minicars circling the dirt raceway at high speed. They were being driven by young boys, nine or ten years old, I thought, and one of the drivers was first rate.

He wore a red scarf and a sign on his car which proclaimed him to be the Red Baron. He liked to weave in and out, and cut rivals off at the turns.

He wore a helmet, leather gloves and a leather jacket, and he was at nine or ten a much better driver than I had ever been. I noted especially that he was ruthless in riding his opponents down and forcing them into the bales of hay. He was obviously destined to be a big-league driver when he grew up, for he had all the moves.

And then something happened, or someone said something, that made me wonder about the age of that boy. I turned to the two women sitting next to me and asked, 'How old is that kid?'

'You mean the Red Baron?'

'Yes.'

'He's my son,' the woman said proudly. 'He's one of the Fighting Rigbys.'

'I saw your trailer outside. Very impressive. Where you from?'

'North Jersey.'

'What you doing down this way?'

'Where there's cups to be won, we go,' she said, pointing to a table where six silver cups waited to be handed to the victors that night.

'How old is your son?' I asked.

'Five,' she said. And I looked at the speed demons as they whirred around the track, and things fell into place.

These drivers were five years old! And the reason the Red Baron was able to push so many of them into the bales of hay was that he was already a long-time professional, coached by a dedicated mother and father, while the others were terrified beginners barely able to keep their cars on the track.

'Look at him go!' the mother shouted. 'Keep hittin' 'em, Roger!' And on he sped, in his leather outfit and large helmet.

When the race ended the announcer cried ecstatically, 'Now watch as he takes his triumphal turn! Here he comes, the Red Baron, undefeated in eleven races and our new champion!' The little boy was handed a checkered flag, which he held aloft in his right hand as he made a solo turn of the track. And over the loudspeakers the announcer kept roaring for applause to mark his progress.

I spent most of that night talking with Mrs. Rigby. She had two boys and a girl in competition and she expected each of them to win a cup. 'We brought three cars with us, each specially tuned for its own driver.'

'What do they cost?'

'We use a special Japanese quarter-horsepower engine. Our cars cost about eighteen hundred dollars each, but with 'em we win.'

She told me the family was buying a fourth car next week. 'That's why we needed the larger trailer. My husband and his brother painted it last week. Looks pretty snazzy, eh?'

I told her it was outstanding, the one I noticed first when I drove in. As

I talked I became aware of a young child sitting beyond the two women, a little girl staring intently at the racing, and it began to dawn on me, if I can use that word to describe something which occurred at night, that the Rigbys were buying their fourth minicar for this baby.

'How old is she?' I asked.

'Fleurette? She's four.'

'And the new car's for her?'

'Yes. You gotta start 'em young. Already she could beat most of the boys you saw in that last race.'

I turned my attention to Fleurette, a very pretty blond pigtailed little child. She could barely speak in sentences, but when her older brother Victor revved his car up for the nine-year-old race, she became excited. 'Give it to 'em, Vic,' she shouted.

He did. So did Flora Mae, the twelve-year-old girl. That night the Rigbys won three silver cups, and the announcer called their names so often that at the end he went into a rhapsody about this remarkable family who showed the rest of us how it ought to be done. He called for Mr. Rigby, a salesman in his late thirties, to step forward as an example of a devoted father who really looked after his kids, and I saw that Mr. Rigby was the tall, thin man who had been so active in the pits, adjusting carburetors and coaching his children when to make their big moves as the races progressed. He was the most important single person at the track that night, except perhaps for the tireless announcer, who kept up a drum-roll of chatter, telling the audience what it could see for itself.

'The announcer seems to talk a lot,' I said to Mrs. Rigby.

'It wouldn't be a race without him,' she said. 'Very dull, just the cars whizzing around.' And it occurred to me that in an age of radio and television the audience had lost the capacity to see an event unaided; we needed to be told what was happening, what its significance was, how it compared with other like happenings. Birmingham fans had told me that they enjoyed University of Alabama games more if they switched on the television image, turned down the volume to nothing and listened to the radio broadcast of Doug Layton over Station WERC. 'He gives you more words,' a devotee told me. 'He explains better just what's happenin' down there on the field, and you feel more intimate.'

At four years of age Fleurette Rigby would enter this exciting world of minicar racing. She would be driving a gasoline engine that could make better than twenty-two miles an hour, and she would be competing with families who had spent between $900 and $1,900 for their cars. Few of the $900 cars would win, because the more costly the car, the more delicately balanced its carburetors, the better its performance. And there would be few boys and girls of five capable of taking on this little demon.

'Her brothers and her sister train her every day,' Mrs. Rigby told me. 'Right now she's big-time.'

I was appalled to think that this baby had already entered professional sports, and I was brooding as to the implications of this fact when the drivers of the midget cars began to assemble at the middle of the field.

The announcer raised the decibels as he told us, 'Tonight we bid farewell to one of the most gracious competitors we have ever had on this track. Miss Julie Jackson had her sixteenth birthday last week, and she's no longer eligible. Miss Julie, we bid you a fond farewell.'

Into the ring her father and mother lugged a huge birthday cake, which they cut into many slices. The Red Baron grabbed his, ate it in two gulps, and went back to his car, but the other children in their leather outfits clustered about long-legged Julie Jackson and shook her hands and kissed her and told her how much they had enjoyed competing against her.

'She was a real winner, folks,' the announcer bellowed. 'She was a credit to her sex, and there was many a boy who ate her dust as she reached for the checkered flag. She was a real champion, folks.' Some women near me were crying, for Julie had been a terror on the track.

'And now, her last ride, folks. Let's hear a great big hand for a great big champion!'

Julie put on her helmet, climbed into the car her father wheeled out for her, and started a culminating turn around the track while the other kids munched her birthday cake. As she passed the starting line an official reached out and handed her the checkered flag. Driving at maximum speed, she slid into the curves, holding her flag aloft, and the spectators cheered as the announcer droned on with his incessant and metallic spiel.

I leaned over to ask Fleurette Rigby if she intended to be a champion one day, but she merely looked up at me with baby eyes and asked, 'Huh?'

In this unexpected way I was introduced to the jungle world of juvenile sports competition. Because I wanted to understand the system at its best, and see it with everything in its favor, I sought out an old-time college champion, a distinguished former athlete named Joe Tomlin. I remembered him as a big, amiable guy who had played a formidable game of football and who had loved the game so much that upon graduation he had cast about for some way to remain associated with it. He hit upon the bright idea of organizing the Pop Warner Junior League Football, named after the much-loved coach of the Carlisle Indians. He became its champion and its czar, and achieved a remarkable success in establishing leagues across the country.

Through the years I had followed Joe's restrained promotional activities and approved of the solid manner in which he constructed his empire. A good scholar himself, he had postulated an unusual scoring system for determining his champions:

> The evaluation formula takes into consideration a team's scholastic as well as its football record. Scholastically each player's average is converted into a numerical point value. The player point values are then added and divided by the total number of players on the roster to determine the point average of the team. This scholastic average is then added to the point value of the team's won-tied-lost record. The result is then divided by two to determine the final point standing of the teams.

Tomlin conceded that under this system, which many tough-minded coaches ridiculed, it would be possible for a team with an 8–1 record and high grades in school to win the championship from a team with a perfect won-lost record but poor grades. 'But this almost never happens,' Joe says. 'The best team on the field is usually the best team in the classroom, too.'

I began attending Junior League football games on Friday nights and found them to be pretty much as Tomlin described them in his literature:

> The general objective of Pop Warner Junior League Football is to inspire youth, regardless of race, creed or national origin, to practice the ideals of sportsmanship, scholarship and physical fitness as reflected in the life of the late Pop Warner. The specific objectives of the program are to familiarize all boys with the fundamentals of football, to provide an opportunity to play the game in a supervised, organized and safety-oriented manner, and to keep the welfare of participants free of any adult ambition and personal glory.

Note the last clause. Youth leagues have been severely criticized because of the misbehavior of parents. Tomlin was determined to keep his free of this aberration, and because football does not depend upon an umpire's calling every ball and strike, it lends itself less to parental fury than baseball. At any rate, in the games I saw, the kids played and not the parents, but I was told later by one of the coaches that 'Moms can be hell on wheels if you don't play their kids.'

But even in this favorable atmosphere certain questions began to arise. The teams I watched were divided into seven categories, according to age and weight: Tinytot, Junior Peewee, Peewee, Junior Midget, Midget, Junior Bantam and Bantam. The Tinytots could be eight, nine or ten and weigh no more than sixty-nine pounds. The Bantams could be thirteen, fourteen, fifteen or sixteen and weigh no more than a hundred and fifty-six pounds. Each team had to be fully suited, with complete gear, and I wondered if boys of eight, weighing forty pounds, were really ready for heavy contact sport. I think football should be delayed till age eleven.

My apprehension certainly did not bother them. Nor their parents. I remember attending one Tinytot game and sitting near a group of mothers.

When one of the eight-year-olds made a flying tackle, 'Just like on television,' one of the women said, the others shouted, 'Way to hit, Tommy! Way to hit!'

I was told that the league had wanted to adopt the sensible rule that whenever a team got ahead by sixteen points, all its substitutes had to be put into the line-up so as to give the trailing team a chance to catch up. 'But we couldn't enforce the rule. Mothers especially wanted their gifted sons to play the whole game and score the maximum number of points.'

'Why?' I asked.

'If a Tinytot shows real skill as a backfield runner or a receiving end, he may get some kind of special treatment in junior high.'

'What kind of special treatment could he possibly get?'

'Oh, his family could be invited to move into a better house in another district and pay no rent. Where they had a top team. And there he'd attract the attention of the high schools in the region, and he might be invited to join the best team there. And after that, a full college scholarship. These kids are playing for gold, and their parents know it.'

On the other hand, the rules are well conceived to protect the youngsters. Spearing—driving one's helmeted head into a fallen player—is forbidden. Coaches are not allowed to send their overweight players to steam rooms, or put them in rubber suits, or administer diuretics to reduce water content

of the body in order to help them make weight. Footballs of a smaller size are used by the youngest teams. Time of quarters is reduced for the younger players. And Tinytots are not permitted to play post-season bowl games. (Junior Peewees, aged eight through ten, may compete in bowl games if they are held within 150 miles of home.)

From its inception, Junior League football has made a special effort to win the support of mothers, aware that opposition from that quarter would doom the program. Early in the prospectus governing the system, tribute is paid to women:

> Pop Warner Football is a family activity. The women of Pop Warner families also take an active part in the program. The mothers staff Pop Warner women's clubs and handle concession stands at ball games. They also take part in fund-raising drives and other related activities, while young sisters of Pop Warner players form cheerleaders, twirlers and pompon groups. Parents should be encouraged to enjoy their son's participation and allow him to enjoy it. Both will be richer for the experience.

This accounts for a phenomenon which struck me whenever I attended a Junior League game. In addition to the little boys dressed in full gear, each team had a cheering corps consisting of little girls dressed in grown-up cheerleader costumes. They were known as cheerleader-mascots and they maintained a steady chant throughout the game, waving their pompons 'Just like on television,' the woman in front of me said. And girls who did especially well could compete for the national title of L'il Miss Pop Warner, who would reign for one year, complete with a court of three princesses chosen from the runners-up. In 1973 Kathi Kerr—of the Scottsdale, Arizona, Cowboys—did not win the competition, but she did gain honorable mention for her original cheer.

> Hea you guys we're rootin' for you!
> Let's give a cheer for the Gold and Blue!
> There goes the whistle. It's time to begin.
> You've won before. You can do it agin!
> Don't take it easy or nice and slow.
> Get on out there and GO, GO, GO!

The speaker at the national banquet that year was Spiro Agnew, and he paid high tribute to the lessons that could be learned in Junior League football:

> Football as we know it is a uniquely American game, emphasizing some of the finest aspects of our national character. We are a competitive people, and it is the spirit of competition which has made our economic system the envy of the world. It's the competitive spirit among the young that causes excellence in adult life . . . There's an extra dimension in the life of any city that finds a truly great major-league athletic team, and thanks to George Allen and his Redskins, Washington has people that just walk a bit taller these days.

Junior League football certainly sponsored competition. It printed badges containing yells to encourage the team's rooters, and some of them got right down to the nitty-gritty:

Slay the Aces	Massacre the Braves
Scalp the Apaches	Crush the Chiefs
Batter the Bantams	Mangle the Matadors
Destroy the Blue Devils	Stomp the Moccasins

After a steady diet of this from age eight through sixteen, it would seem that the boys could only escalate to machine-gunning the opposition high school, atom-bombing Notre Dame and hydrogen-bombing the Dallas Cowboys.

A real effort was made to inculcate a spirit of sportsmanship, but I noticed that it required forty-two pages of closely printed rules to keep the leagues orderly, with a group of twelve intricate procedures for conducting a hearing when rules were broken:

1. The tribunal should, where possible, seek the help and guidance of a lawyer.

5. The chairman of the tribunal should provide for the preparation of a reasonably complete and accurate hearing transcript.

12. Provisions should be made to allow parties to request a rehearing in appropriate circumstances.

When I asked why such legalistic precautions were necessary to govern a game played by eight-year olds, I was told by a parent, 'It ain't the eight-year-olds we're worried about. It's the boys ready to move into big-time stuff in high school. Their rights got to be protected.'

The official Junior League huddle prayer, 'to be said with boys on one knee, helmet in hand, prior to the start of any game,' was composed by a Catholic priest, a rabbi and a Protestant clergyman, the last being Norman Vincent Peale. It reads:

> Grant us the strength, Dear Lord, to play
> This game with all our might,
> And while we're doing it we pray
> You'll keep us in Your sight;
> That we may never say or do
> A thing that gives offense to You.

Under Joe Tomlin's severe and conservative guidance, Junior League football has escaped the cynical attention poured on Little League baseball in recent years. The baseball league, through a series of unfortunate actions on the field and decisions in the front office, has garnered much unfavorable publicity, most of it deserved. Three differences exist between young people's baseball and football: baseball is played in the summer, with maximum attendance by parents who all too often give vivid examples of foolish deportment; although football is now more popular than baseball, the latter is still considered the national game around which loyalties still cling—only Little League baseball operates under a federal charter granted by Congress and signed into law by President Lyndon B. Johnson in 1964; and everyone from the President to the Cardinal to the head of Rotary has for the past half-century assured us that in baseball young Americans learn the finest of the American virtues. When baseball turns sour, or when it displays unsportsmanlike conduct, the very foundations of our society are endangered, at least in the minds of moralists who like to write about such things.

But as I did with Junior League football, I should like to present Little League baseball in its most favorable light, and there is no better way to do this than to recommend to any parent with young children a remarkable book by Al Rosen, who set numerous batting records while playing third base for the Cleveland Indians from 1947 to 1956. One point to remember is that Rosen was a tough competitor, a real take-charge guy, and that he writes from a background of the sternest competition.

The book is *Baseball and Your Boy*. (If Rosen were writing it now he would call it "Baseball and Your Girl and Boy," for he proves himself to be a sensible man, able to adjust to new situations.) It presents the best arguments I have ever read for youthful athletics, and it does so with a perception that is refreshing. If all Little League teams were coached the way Al Rosen coached his, there would be no complaints. You will catch his philosophy from a series of quotes:

> . . . In teaching all phases of fielding to the beginner, one factor should be kept in mind. The objective is not that the boys be taught to make plays like major leaguers. The manager wants them to make plays like Little Leaguers.

> . . . I cannot think of a single legitimate excuse for having a Little League pitcher throwing curve balls. The kindest explanation would be to blame managerial ignorance. Certainly, it would be a more damning charge to accuse him of wanting to win so badly he would risk serious injury to a youngster's arm. Youngsters should not throw curve balls until the growth centers of their arms are fused. This does not occur until age fourteen or fifteen.

> . . . On occasion the manager has the right to seek out a father and lodge a strong protest. For example, one father whose boy was pitching kept shouting the instruction, 'Stick it in his ear!' baseball's traditional challenge to hit the batter in the head. This sort of thing is inexcusable in a boys' league. A manager is ducking his responsibility if he does not tell the father so.

> . . . There is satisfaction in knowing you have pushed yourself to the limits of your ability, even if the rewards are modest . . . I will not be remembered as one of the great third basemen, but I am happy with what is listed in the record book under my name. I am satisfied that I did what I could with what was given me.

Rosen's book is short but sagacious. It is also tough. He makes a profound point about sports when he tells parents:

> The youngster will get his lessons in democracy-in-action from other sources. Organized sports are not democratic nor should they be. They teach respect for authority, discipline, and the individual's role in a group activity. The manager's job is to make the decisions and he does not poll an electorate.

Rosen's overall view of Little League, in which he coached his own sons for several seasons, is that it is a child's activity supervised by adults, and that the best results are obtained when understanding and supportive parents hand their boys into the charge of an enthusiastic and self-disciplined manager who knows what he's doing. The tension that must normally exist between the father and the coach is never far from Rosen's mind, and he usually sides with the father *if* the father can control himself and allow his son to progress at his own speed.

The goal of the game is to have fun within a structured activity, at a level of performance appropriate to the age of the participants, and if this goal were honored in the conduct of Little League baseball, there could be no objection. But the reality of Little League competition has been so perverted that Al Rosen's idealism makes him seem naïve. Any manager in the leagues I know who conducted himself the way Rosen recommends would be out on his ear within two weeks. The aim of the game is to win, and if in order to win your pitcher has got to throw curves three days a week, let him throw curves, and when his arm is ruined, find yourself a new pitcher.

It is with a sense of sadness that I recommend Rosen's book, for I realize that in doing so I must seem as naïve as he. He speaks of the sport as I have known it; he is the kind of sportsman I have sought out and enjoyed.

The reality of Little League is told in one of the basic books recommended in Chapter I. Martin Ralbovsky's *Destiny's Darlings* tells the story of the Schenectady Little League team that won the world's championship in 1954. The author had grown up in the city and worked there as a sportswriter before moving on to *The New York Times*. Twenty years after the glory days, he travels about America to interview nine of the boy champions, asking them to assess what winning the championship had meant to them. He closes his book with a perceptive interrogation of Mike Maietta, the manager whose iron will and stern control led the boys to their memorable victory.

And it was memorable. Ralbovsky begins his book with a list of eleven flamboyant consequences of the championship. This group of twelve-year-old boys rode in convertibles at the head of a parade through the city; they received keys to the city; they attended fifteen banquets at which they were given bicycles, radios, watches and clothing; they attended a World Series game in New York; one of their members threw out the first ball to open the Series, and was described on nationwide radio as doing so; one of the players made a series of tapes for national radio; the team appeared on the Dave Garroway *Today* television show; one of the players appeared on the Perry Como show; the team rode in convertibles through a manufacturing plant, waving to workers; the players were photographed in color for *Collier's;* and they were the subject of a long article in *Sports Illustrated.*

They were given, in short, the all-American build-up, with motorcycle cops screaming ahead of them wherever they went and banquet speakers exuding heroic images. 'You are destiny's darlings,' they were told, and as I read the hyperbole thrust upon them, I am surprised at the dignity with which they handled the inflated nonsense.

Twenty years later Ralbovsky is visiting them, seeing them as men who will soon be entering middle age, and he listens as they reminisce about the days of their grandeur. They return again and again to certain incidents, so that the reader observes the old days from various angles and becomes familiar with the men's memories. They are repetitious, like chatter in a barbershop, and the shocking message they convey is that this early taste of glory was mostly ashes:

Pete Fennicks, the only black player: 'My life didn't change a bit. My mother, she still worked all the time, and my father, he still worked all the time, and we still didn't have nothin' . . . You know, I got the key to the city from the mayor at city hall; you know how many doors that key opened in twenty years? None. Not a single stinkin' door.'

Jimmy Barbieri, the team captain and star center fielder, who threw out the first ball in the real World Series: 'The kids in the American Division were saying they would cream us . . . I can remember right then and there acquiring this killer instinct: we're gonna go out there and destroy them; not beat them, destroy them. We did; it was twenty-three to nothing. The rest of that summer I had this killer instinct, that I didn't want to win, I wanted to destroy. I remember going into those games with this feeling of kill, kill, kill.'

Bill Masucci, the winning pitcher: 'I pitched that whole series with an elbow that hurt so bad I could hardly stand it.' I asked Bill Masucci if that sore arm stayed with him awhile, or did it disappear in the hysteria over a world championship? Bill Masucci glanced over at a window, which was covered by a white lace curtain. 'I can't throw a baseball from here to the street now.'

Johnny Palmer, the left fielder: 'But what happened after that, winning the world championship and all, I have mixed feelings about that experience. I don't know if it was good or bad. Sure, we won and that was good; but we were used, we were exploited, we didn't even win the championship on our own—Mike Maietta won it for us. It would mean a lot more to me today if I knew that we kids had won it on our own, but we didn't. I sometimes feel that Mike could have taken any fourteen kids from that league and done the same thing; he was the general, and we were a bunch of privates.'

Mike Maietta, the demon manager: 'So we're playing this team from Montreal, and the manager has obviously told his team to wipe us out; they're running into my first baseman and taking out my second baseman, and barreling over my catcher; their pitcher is throwing at my kids' heads. It was the first time that any of my kids had seen the bad side of baseball. They thought you won games by outplaying the other teams; they didn't know you could win games by scaring the other teams half to death. If you're gonna win in Little League tournaments, you gotta have tough kids, kids who would give it right back and not be scared off.'

Captain Jimmy Barbieri again: 'I think back on it now, and I'd have to say that Mike wanted to win the world championship for himself, for his own glory, and not for any experience that it might have given to us. We were pawns on the chessboard, and he made all the moves.'

Coach Maietta, reflecting on the poor material he has to work with in 1974 as contrasted with his great team of 1954: 'My heart goes out to these kids. I carry a lot of them who are lousy ballplayers, kids I would have gotten rid of right away in the old days. But if I had fourteen kids who were half as good as those kids I had in '54, I'd have a fighting chance. I'd play the game for them, and they'd do all right.'

I'll say this. If Al Rosen, the Most Valuable Player in 1953, were to take his Little League team to Schenectady to play one coached by tough old Mike Maietta, whose players might not be so good but who would know how to cut for the jugular, Al Rosen would get clobbered.

The scandals that overtook Little League baseball were twofold. Parents with ordinary common sense began looking with a critical eye at what was happening to their sons. They started going to games and saw the paranoia, the coaches screaming at twelve-year-olds, fathers belting their sons for striking out, little boys ruining their arms trying to pitch like big leaguers before their bone ends hardened. They saw mothers behaving insanely, and boys falling into despair because of an error for which their parents abused them.

And they began to write articles in newspapers and magazines, questioning the philosophy that underlay such performances. Little League was attacked because of its danger to health, its damage to a boy's psychiatric base, and its encouragement of preposterous behavior on the part of parents and coaches. I became aware of the criticism very early, perhaps ten years ago, and have collected the attacks, some of which I thought were as hysterical as the abuses they were condemning. But when these were laid aside, there remained a body of substantial criticism.

Representative of the best is a detailed study conducted by Dr. Jonathan Brower, assistant professor of sociology at California State University, Fullerton. He spent ten months following 28 different teams in playground leagues, getting to know managers, parents and 350 players while taking notes at 70 games. During a visit I made to his home, he told me some of his findings:

> Laws exist to protect children at work and school, but their 'play' as governed by adults goes unchecked. Playground ball is a pressure-packed thing for boys. For good athletes it may be fun. At least they can tolerate it, but for boys who are not good athletes and who try to please their managers and parents, it's a matter of tension.
>
> Parents get too caught up in the win ethic. One father proudly told a friend, 'My kid doesn't care about sportsmanship. He says winning is what's important.' This thirst for victory and its accompanying competitiveness was far

stronger among managers and coaches than players. The kids would offer help to other teams. Adult leaders frowned on this interteam cooperation because they did not want assistance given to those whom they might later be fighting for the league championship.

To compound matters, there was no opportunity for boys to voice complaints of any kind to the grownups who controlled the team. Kids who wanted to play knew that they had to listen and follow orders issued by managers and coaches who often assumed a Vince Lombardian authoritarian manner. Hot summer days left players parched, but folklore and the suffer ethic encouraged most managers and coaches to caution, Don't drink during games! Just rinse your mouth out! Several managers felt this advice was ridiculous and told their colleagues so, but to no avail. The majority of the men had been conditioned to swallow the old myth that the intake of fluids during physical exercise is harmful.

One of the most poignant moments during my study took place at the awards' night ceremony. Only one manager spoke of the fun that his team had, and this only as a parenthetical aside. All the other managers' comments focused on their won-lost records and their chances of improvement for the coming year.

Dr. Brower did concede that during his long summer he did meet a few coaches who seemed almost ideal. They were gentle, understanding, empathetic, and invariably they were good sports. 'They were truly nice guys. But unfortunately, they always finished last.'

Dr. Brower concluded with one important value judgment: he doubted that athletics build character. The boys he watched going through the summer program were no better off than the ones who didn't, and some were worse off. His final conclusion was that the units of fun provided by playground baseball were fewer than the negative units of tension it produced.

On one point I have been persuaded by the testimony of professional athletes. More than a score have told me that they would not permit their sons to enter Little League competition until rather advanced ages. They said there was a strong likelihood that rigorous competition so early would destroy a boy's enthusiasm for sports in general and certainly would kill any interest he might have in baseball.

It is important to understand what these knowledgeable men are saying and what they are not saying. They are not against competition; in their day some were fierce competitors. They are not against rugged games for boys; they want their sons to engage in the rough-and-tumble of childhood sports. But they are against highly structured leagues run by hypertensive adults, urged on by overenthusiastic fathers and mothers.

Joey Jay, the first Little Leaguer to make it to the majors—pitcher for the Braves, Reds, Phils—recalls, 'Our team went all the way to the 1948 Little League World Series and our shortstop had his picture in *Life* magazine. By the time that boy entered high school, he had lost all interest in baseball. Parents interfere too much with Little League players. Even those who don't interfere find it difficult to conceal their disappointment when their sons have a bad day.'

Robin Roberts, the Philadelphia pitcher who compiled a pretty fair record, is even stronger in his criticism:

> I have four sons and when my wife asked me about Little League, I told her, 'No way in the world.' And most professional athletes feel that way about kids under fourteen. If you try to make it serious before they're physically able to handle what they're doing, you run into all sorts of problems.
>
> Generally in the Little League you're up against a good pitcher who throws like hell. What does the coach say? Get a walk. Isn't that a beautiful way to learn how to hit? For four years you stand up there looking for a walk.
>
> Baseball at that age should be a softball thrown overhand where a boy can hit fifteen times a game, with no walks and strike-outs. They should be running and sliding into bases. The score should be 42–38. That's what sports should be for kids that age.
>
> I certainly would never let my boys enter a league where they'd be throwing curves at eight or nine years old. And I wouldn't want them all steamed up, heading for a pennant play-off at eleven, or a World Series at twelve. My father encouraged me to take it easy, and at eighteen I had an arm prepared for the strain of real pitching.

Mike Marshall, workhorse of the Dodger pitching staff, has his B.A. and M.A. from Michigan State and is close to his Ph.D. in kinesiology, the study of human anatomical movement. He is opposed to youngsters' taking baseball too seriously and recommends radical alterations in current procedures. 1) Two outs to constitute an inning. 2) All players to switch positions every inning. 3) No boy or girl below the age of fifteen to pitch more than two innings a week. 4) Plus any additional steps to minimize the emotionalism involved in the overemphasis on winning.

What makes Marshall's arguments compelling is that while working on his doctorate he has taken x-rays which prove that elbows can be permanently damaged by excessive youthful pitching. He explains his own career: 'As a kid I never pitched. The others were too much better. So they ruined their arms, but when I reached eighteen I had a good arm and was ready to go.'

Orthopedists from various parts of the country have begun to issue warnings against premature overexertion. Dr. Nicholas Gianestras of Cincinnati believes that it constitutes a serious health hazard. Others are joining Marshall in recommending that no youthful hurler be allowed to pitch more than two innings if under the age of thirteen, nor more than three below the age of fifteen. And all advise that the curve ball be outlawed prior to age fifteen.

Anyone who has studied this problem can predict what future orthopedists will be recommending. Dr. Thomas E. Shaffer of Columbus, Ohio, says, 'We just don't teach boys and girls the right sports in schools, the ones they will enjoy during their adult lives.' He commends archery, bowling, golf, skating, tennis, swimming, boating. It is ironic, and a consequence of our adult attitudes, that the two sports on which we have spent the most effort and money for young boys are the two which they will not be able to use in adult life: football and baseball.

The second area in which Little League got into trouble was its refusal to accept gracefully the dictate of a New Jersey official that girls must be allowed to play if public recreation areas were used or public support solicited. The bumbling response of the Little League officials became a source of national merriment and will be discussed in Chapter V.

The most notorious scandal, however, erupted when Little League wrestled futilely with the problem of Taiwan. In 1939 a group of public-spirited amateurs assembled in Williamsport, Pennsylvania, to hatch a program that would encourage boys to play baseball during summer vacations. Every precaution would be taken to prevent injury and ensure good sportsmanship. In the following years millions of boys would participate in Little League, and in one follow-up study of 750,000 participants, only two percent had suffered any kind of injury, mostly trivial raspberries or dislocated fingers.

The apex of this developmental period came about 1954, when the boys from Schenectady were winning their world championship. After that, things began to get a little sticky. Baseball for boys became so popular that thirty-one countries sponsored Little Leagues, and some of the better ones started coming to Williamsport for the world championships. Many Americans can remember the thrill that swept our country when a gallant bunch of kids from Monterrey, Mexico, won in 1956. Of course, our enthusiasm waned a bit when they won again in 1957. And when the Japanese picked up a couple of crowns in 1967 and 1968, we became downright hostile.

But the blockbuster came in 1969 when a dedicated team of young men from Chiang Kai-shek's Taiwan appeared at Williamsport with a new definition of what boyhood baseball could be. They were lean, lithe, superbly trained, and the high school teachers who coached them had taught them all the nuances of big-league play. The teachers had learned from American coaches sent to Taiwan in the aftermath of the war, and from reading 'inside baseball' books supplied by our government.

What admirable learners they were! Their teams were masterpieces. The Chinese boys could field without error, run like Formosan deer, and hit the ball without striking out. Most of all, they could pitch.

Once they became acclimatized to the diamond at Williamsport they proved tough to beat. In 1969 they won all the marbles. In 1970 they lost their opener to Nicaragua, 3–2. The 1971 series was a runaway for Taiwan, as was the 1972. But in 1973 the slim little fellows from Taiwan really unleashed their power.

In the opening game they faced a team of sons of United States military personnel stationed in Germany, and the Taiwan pitcher hurled a perfect game, 18–0, which meant that not one American reached base. In the second game against Tampa, Florida, the Chinese pitcher threw another no-hitter, 27–0. And in the big championship game against Tucson, Arizona, the Chinese pitcher tossed yet another no-hitter, 12–0. Score at the end of three games; Taiwan 57 runs, America 0 runs; Taiwan 43 hits, America 0 hits.

The only logical explanation was that the Taiwan players were cheating. No bunch of Chinese could come here and beat American boys at our national game by a combined score of 57–0. So an investigating committee was secretly slipped into Taiwan to see what these almond-eyed little devils were up to.

If Taiwan was cheating, it had to be done in one of three ways: the Chinese could be lying about the ages of their boys; or the boys could be a team of all-island all-stars rather than an ordinary team from one area with a population of under 15,000; or it could be coached by professionals. Even the most cursory investigation satisfied the sleuths that none of these offenses had occurred.

The Taiwanese were meticulous about the ages of their boys, the rigorous island identity system helping in this respect. The teams they had been sending to America were from population areas of under 15,000 and not all-star aggregations. Indeed, many locals believed that one year the best team did not go to America, and one wonders what the scores might have been had a better team come. And no professionals were coaching, for the very good reason that Taiwan had almost no professionals. Our spies did criticize the fact that paid schoolteachers coached the teams instead of amateur volunteers, but this could be corrected.

With some apprehension the Little League people awaited the 1974 championships. The Americans prayed that some United States team would pull itself together and at least score a run, even if it couldn't win. And the wiser heads among the Taiwanese hoped that their team would lose for a change, just to make the Americans breathe more easily, but at the same time they knew that the entire island back home was counting on another world championship in the one sport they dominated. It was a fateful tournament.

In the first game Taiwan met New Haven, Connecticut, and beat them 16–0. The Williamsport people began to groan, sensing that they were about to witness a replay of preceding years.

In the second game Taiwan went up against Tallmadge, Ohio, and scored another shutout, 11–0. The combined scores since America had last scored a run against the Chinese was 90–0.

But in the championship game the American team finally put it all together. The players from Red Bluff, California, actually shoved one run across the plate, but Taiwan won, 12–1. In nine games over three years the combined score was Taiwan 120, America 2.

The American officials knew what had to be done, but not how to do it. In a maladroit performance, Peter J. McGovern, board chairman of Little League, announced bluntly, and without explanation, that henceforth the world championship would be decided in an abbreviated tournament comprising only the four United States regional champions.

The Taiwanese were crushed. 'We are suffering from a strange phenomenon,' an official said. 'We are too good.' The chairman of the Taiwanese Baseball Association was restrained when he said, 'A world series with only American teams participating can hardly be a world series.'

And then the roof fell in. Everyone who had been accumulating suspicions about Little League jumped in with acid editorials or cynical letters to the editor. Rarely has an American sporting body taken such a unanimous lambasting. Some very funny lines were written, the best being, 'If you can't beat 'em, ban 'em,' and much of the fatuousness of American sports was reviewed, especially the overemphasis on winning.

The Little League directors took a bum rap. The international competition had been getting way out of hand. The Taiwanese, and other nations, enjoyed a climate that permitted baseball games the year round. They were pouring into their leagues a degree of national intensity that we could not match, nor would want to match if we could. They were able to muster a degree of support unknown in America; and asking American boys of twelve to compete with Taiwanese who were concentrating on baseball and nothing else was like asking boys from snowbound Maine to compete in tennis against boys from sunny California.

The overemphasis had to be stopped. In fact, it should have been stopped after the 1954 world series, as we have seen. It is unfortunate that Taiwan had to be the team on which the onus fell, and I believe the operation could have been carried out more gracefully. But I support the basic decision of de-emphasizing the hysteria.

I do not think the Little League action bespeaks our unwillingness to face the fact that players of other nations can sometimes play our national games better than we. After all, our big-league baseball teams might have to fold if Spanish-speaking players were not allowed to play, and it is quite possible that an all-star team of Caribbean, Mexican and Venezuelan players might annihilate a team of only white Americans. European-style field-goal kickers tend to be better than the American product, and our university tennis teams are happy to have Latin-American stars matriculate. I do not believe we are overly chauvinistic. Let those Taiwanese no-hit pitchers mature— if they haven't already ruined their arms—and if they're as good then as they are now, there will be a place for them on any big-league team they choose to play for.

No, the problem lies with taking twelve-year-old sports too seriously. It does the grownup no good and the child actual harm. It is an aberration that should be corrected. Little League does not need to be abolished, but its excesses must be curtailed.*

I have already commented on the ridiculousness of having a twelve-point arbitration procedure, including lawyers, appeals and reversals to settle disputes in football games played by eight-year-olds. This cannot possibly be for the protection of the children; it can only be for the gratification of adults who are sponsoring the children.

Baseball has its equivalent. In Hempstead, New York, a Mrs. Joan Leite, mother of a nine-year-old Little Leaguer, had a disagreement with her son's forty-two-year-old manager. The mother, feeling that her son's rights had been abused, insisted that the manager be fired. He was, whereupon he took the case to the state's Supreme Court, demanding that he be reinstated.

Recently a more insidious abuse has become common. Little League rules specifically state that teams must be composed of boys who live within a specified homogeneous area, but cases are surfacing in which overzealous coaches have roamed far afield to recruit talented youngsters to play for them. There have even been cases in which coaches have persuaded parents actually to move into their districts, so that a nine-year-old star can bolster the home team.

*On December 30, 1975, Peter McGovern, Little League president who had taken the abuse when Taiwan was outlawed, announced that the ban against foreign teams had been lifted. By a vote of 12–1 directors of the league decided to reissue invitations, making the competition once more a real world series. This was probably a mistake, but McGovern did make certain stipulations: the foreign teams could not practice all year long; they must abide by the rule governing maximum population of the area from which the team is chosen; and they must adhere to the principle that 'the important thing isn't to win but to have fun.' Tell that not to Taiwan but to Destiny's Darlings up in Schenectady, or to the American coaches preparing for next year's series!

If recruiting is encouraged with nine-year olds, it will obviously escalate to junior high school and then to high school. We shall have, across the nation, the hideous farce that now operates when colleges recruit in high schools.

Philadelphia has been riven by two notorious cases. In the first, a junior-high-school boy named Gene Banks, already six-foot-six and with a deadly eye, was living with his father in a house which placed him in a high school that accomplished little in sports. By moving into his mother's house, in a different district, he made himself eligible to play for West Philadelphia High, one of the traditional basketball powers in the city. Coaches of the competing schools were goaded into issuing statements, reporters escalated the argument into a first-class brawl, and citizens caught an inside glimpse of school power plays. At one high school which was luring topnotch junior-high prospects into its boundaries, the faculty and student body issued a protest stating that their school was being misused, but since the coach was producing a winner with his imported talent, nothing could be done. At the same time, the coach of a district which was losing all its best players complained that some dozen who were legally his boys were starring on competing teams, and he wondered how his school could continue fielding a decent team if his best players were continually stolen from him.

The second case was a classic and should be studied, because schools across the country will be facing the problems it poses. Eddie Olsen, sports-writer for the *Philadelphia Inquirer,* received an anonymous note from a trouble-making taxpayer living in Abington, a choice suburb to the north. The note charged that Abington sports officials were recruiting so many basketball players from the center of Philadelphia, that boys legally entitled to attend the school had to remain on the bench, unable to play.

The newspaper focused on the case of Richard Wright, whose mother and father lived in the city in an area which required him to attend a ghetto school. He was five-foot-nine and known as 'a quicksilver guard with a hot eye for the basket,' and somehow or other he heard of Abington, where life was good and where quicksilver guards were appreciated.

He therefore moved to Abington, left his parents, and allowed an uncle to adopt him legally. As a basketball player he proved to be even better than reported and was mainly responsible for Abington's state championship.

The Abington coach, Jim Wilkinson, explained to the press:

> I guess his mom and dad were concerned, and I only heard this in the court-room when he had to go through legal adoption, why he left Philadelphia, he said he had to take a different route every day to school, he had to go through five gang territories and he didn't think it was a good place to go to school.
> Now when I first met Richard and he told me he was coming to school, I

complained to him. I said, 'Richard, we'd love to have you but you can't play basketball unless you're legally adopted.' When he found out that, he checked, and his aunt and uncle were willing to do that and his mom and dad too, so that was it. I never in any way, shape or form asked Richard Wright to come to Abington. It was his decision.

Four other instances in which inner-city boys transferred to Abington and played basketball caused so much discussion that specific legal steps, including a court adjudication, became necessary. Athletic director Raymond Coleman said in retrospect, 'Last year I carried guardianship papers with me wherever I went through the whole season to prove it was legal.' Norman Schmid, principal at Abington, defends his school resolutely:

> Some persons chose to parlay these different circumstances into a mass of circumstantial evidence that Abington High School engages in recruiting. Nothing could be further from the truth. In no case did the high school or its personnel seek out the student. In all cases the school immediately notified the PIAA District Committee and abided by its ruling on the student's athletic eligibility. Neither the school nor its staff engages in recruiting.

Two other cases which reached the courts are instructive. In Tuscaloosa, Alabama, the local high school had a chance to win the state football championship, but its hopes were destroyed when a rival team discovered that Elbert Williams, the star Tuscaloosa running back, was nineteen years old, and they produced records from the state Bureau of Vital Statistics to prove it.

Since anyone over the age of eighteen was ineligible, the Alabama High School Athletic Association had no recourse but to order Tuscaloosa to forfeit a game, pay a $250 fine, and accept probation for one year. And that should have been the end of the case, except that thirteen of the Tuscaloosa players, quarterbacked by adult partisans of their team, stormed into court, filed suit against the state athletic association, and demanded that Circuit Court Judge Fred Nicol issue a mandamus directing the Bureau of Vital Statistics to issue a new birth certificate to Elbert Williams proving him to be not nineteen but only eighteen, which would make him eligible, reverse the forfeit, and restore Tuscaloosa to the championship play-offs.

The argument of the boys was ingenious: since Elbert Williams' mother had had fourteen children, it seemed likely that she might have become confused regarding the birthday of her son, the running back. The judge issued the mandamus and the State of Alabama was required to alter its records so that a boy could play in a crucial game and a school pursue its championship.

Belatedly common sense came into the picture. State officials pointed out that if Alabama birth certificates could be revised at the whim of a high school football team, all insurance policies, social security payments and retirement funds would be in jeopardy. Supporters of Tuscaloosa argued that this was not too high a price to pay for a really good running back, but state leaders felt that the integrity of the state's records had to be preserved, and the mandamus was vacated. Once again an Alabama birth certificate meant what it said.

In Kent, Ohio, a fascinating case developed. A boy athlete from an outlying district was advised by his friends that if he could somehow transfer his place of residence from the minor district in which he lived, and which had no good coaches, to the big high school in Kent, which had excellent ones, he would have a better chance of attracting attention and winning a scholarship to college.

The boy left his parents and went to live with an uncle who had established residence in the Kent district. The association governing Ohio school athletics challenged his eligibility on the sensible grounds that this was clearly an evasion of the state rules about residence and eligibility. The boy was told that he was ineligible to play for Kent and that he must go back to his rightful home, where his eligibility would be restored.

This seemed an admirable ruling, just and clear-cut, but the people who wanted to see him play in Kent advised him to take his case to court, and there a most interesting situation developed. The boy was eighteen, eligible to vote in national elections, and to deprive him of the right to take up residence where he wanted was a denial of his civil rights. The case did not reach a final adjudication. The judge appears to have let the Ohio High School Athletic Association know that if the case were carried to a conclusion, he would have to rule in favor of the boy, and this would upset all existing laws and rules governing interacademic sport. Rather than see their whole disciplinary structure destroyed, the state body wisely decided to drop their opposition against this one boy and allow him to live where he wished and to play for whom he wished.

The gravamen of the case was twofold. First, governing bodies can no longer tell eighteen-year-old voters where they must live. Second, the possibility that a boy, through his athletic prowess, may gain a college scholarship and later a contract for hundreds of thousands of dollars with a professional team is a property interest which may not lightly be abused; an eighteen-year-old boy is free to move to whatever school can best advance his economic interests. American sports are going to discover a lot of new horizons in the future, and this case indicates where some of them are going to be.

My friend Robert Casey, Auditor General of Pennsylvania, turned up a cute trick the other day. In the course of his investigations into various aspects of education, he found that Mount Carmel Area School District,

did have five tough New York playground types who might give the average college team a good tussle, they really had no chance against a disciplined, tall team like Kentucky, which had won its semi-final against Duke, 83–79.

Well, the final, played on Saturday night at College Park in Maryland, was a revelation. White Kentucky ran onto the court tall and beautifully coached and impressive in their pre-game drills. The Texas Western blacks straggled on, a bunch of loose-jointed ragamuffins ready for a brawl; they seemed hopelessly outclassed.

When the whistles blew, and the game began, the big men from Kentucky started moving the ball in their accustomed way, with precision and polish, and against an ordinary team they would have prevailed, but Texas Western was in no way ordinary. It was a gang of furious young men who had come to wrestle the ball away, flood the forecourt with shooters, and keep throwing the basketball toward the basket until it went in.

Within a few minutes Kentucky was demoralized by this swarm of gang-busters, and I remember telling the men beside me at the bar of the local Maennerchor, 'If Kentucky doesn't stomp on those little bastards, this is going to be a rout.' Kentucky tried to stomp, but by the time their heels hit the floor, the El Paso gang was far down the court on another fast break. Texas Western won, 72–65, and the following year Kentucky started recruiting blacks.

But this popular victory was not the real story of the 1966 play-offs. Later in 1967 stories began circulating to the effect that of the seven blacks who had won the championship for El Paso, only a few had stayed in college after the tournament; the others had no intention of coming back for a degree. Since this seemed a classic case of a university recruiting blacks, using them, and then tossing them aside when their eligibility was exhausted, considerable interest was evidenced, and in its issue of July 15, 1968, *Sports Illustrated* blew the whistle.

In an eye-opener five-part series of articles on black athletes in America, Jack Olsen provided the first in-depth look at a scandalous situation, and the highlight of his report dealt with the situation at El Paso, with special emphasis on the championship basketball team. The rumors I had been hearing were confirmed. The blacks who had been imported from New York had been treated as poorly paid gladiators, and of the seven black champions—no whites got into the final game—none had graduated. To maintain their eligibility, they had been encouraged to take Mickey Mouse courses of no possible substance which enabled them to get B grades but which did not count toward graduation credits in their major fields. They had not been allowed to take those difficult real courses which would have enabled them to earn degrees in physical education, and without such degrees they could not become coaches in black high schools.

And while still eligible they had not been treated well. They had no social privileges, were threatened with loss of their scholarships if they dated white or Mexican girls—there were no black girls—and were discriminated against in every particular. Several were married but their wives could not get jobs; they could not pick up extra money under the table the way white players did; they were used as cynically as one could imagine, and when their utility was ended, they were thrown aside to make place for a new batch.

The El Paso story is one of the most wretched in the history of American sports. I have merely alluded to the disgraceful details so well presented in the Olsen series, and anyone interested in the fundamentals of the problem should consult his article. In reflecting upon the El Paso incident, I have often thought how much luckier the white players were under Coach Adolph Rupp. He looked after his players; they had a shot at a real education; and they were secure within the traditions of their university, their community and their state. They may have lost the play-off, but they were winners in every other respect, and their black opponents from El Paso were losers.

It was from such beginnings that I started my study of black athletes, and wherever I looked, they were enjoying conspicuous success. In 1947 professional baseball had had room for only one black player, Jackie Robinson, but by 1970 the percentage had risen to 25. Over a span of twenty-two seasons a black has been chosen sixteen times as the most valuable player in the National League. Pittsburgh saw nothing wrong in fielding a totally black team in the closing days of a recent season, and the all-star baseball teams average about 36 percent blacks.

Professional football saw an equal growth in black players. As late as 1957 the combined rosters showed only 14 percent blacks; by 1971 the figure was 32 percent. One year all the Rookie-of-the-Year awards went to blacks; another year 44 percent of the All-Star team was black. Gradually all the important statistical records are falling into the hands of black players, and a heavy percentage of the superstars are black.

But it has been basketball which has shown the most conspicuous explosion of black talent. When the National Basketball Association was reorganized in its present form, only 5 percent of the players were black; by 1971 over 54 percent were. The most valuable player has been black twelve times in thirteen years; in one series of all-star games, 63 percent of the players were black, as were most of the superstars. In the old days, before blacks were totally accepted in professional basketball, the rule was, 'You start two blacks at home, three on the road, and five when you're eighteen points behind.' Now it is not uncommon to see a starting line-up with five black stars, and at the end of each season the all-league team is dominated by blacks.

In college the same improvement has been made. All the major teams recruit black athletes extensively, and the path to a college education, all expenses paid, is easier for a black now than ever before. No university could presume to stay in the big time if it discriminated against blacks, and even in the Southeastern Conference, last bastion of white supremacy, in schools like Mississippi, Louisiana State and Alabama the linemen and backfield starters are apt to be black. Bear Bryant, who led the way in accepting black players when the south reluctantly decided to accept them, has said, 'At Alabama we don't have any black players, or any white ones for that matter—we just have players. I don't care if they're green if they can play.' Even the University of Texas, which had no blacks during the years when the branch at El Paso was winning national championships with them, has succumbed and now depends upon black stars for much of its power. As a matter of fact, the superior black athlete probably has an easier time in the south than in the desolate north, for in the south he has a black community near the college and a social life in which he can participate. He is therefore not sequestered, as he might be if he played in certain northern areas where there are few blacks either in school or in the community.

In other sports, too, the black has been making his mark. Althea Gibson and Arthur Ashe have won the major championships in tennis; Lee Elder has finally cracked the hitherto restricted Masters; and a dozen great track and field performers have dominated our Olympic teams. In the future there will be many black hockey players in the NHL, whether the conservative patrons like it or not, and it would seem that there never was a time more favorable for the black athlete.

And yet, when one studies the basic literature on this subject, and talks late at night with blacks, he finds this supposed Garden of Eden overrun with reptiles. The white reader who wants to acquaint himself quickly with problems of which he has not been aware should read the book by Dr. Harry Edwards listed in the opening chapter, *The Revolt of the Black Athlete*. Or he should study the eminently sane report of the black faculty members who assembled the complaints of black athletes in the Big Ten, one of our best conferences and one which should have been alert to this problem decades ago, but which was almost as discriminatory as the south. It can be found in *Integrated Education* (May 1972). And finally, for a bitter attack on the manner in which white educational institutions use black athletes and discard them, nothing so far is more succinct than a remarkable document prepared by Dr. Henry P. Organ, a member of the Board of Directors of Nairobi Schools. It appears in *The Nairobi Schools Digest* (April 1974). If the serious student can read only one publication on this subject, I would recommend this, because of its uncompromising determination to look at the subject with a cold, fresh eye.

Finally, there is a series of outstanding interviews and studies made by Dr. Roscoe C. Brown, Jr., dealing with the impact of athletics on the black community. The gist of his position is summarized in an interview given *The New York Times* on April 16, 1972, but I have been privileged to see an unpublished report he made for the American Council on Education which spells out his basic philosophy. I hope this will be published and widely read.

From these and similar sources I should like to present the thinking of many men and women who are deeply disturbed by the idolization of sports which dominates black communities. We had better listen to these criticisms, for if present imbalances are allowed to continue and perhaps intensify, we are headed for trouble.

Black salvation through sport is an enervating myth. What actually happens is that a few superstars win spectacular contracts, almost always inflated in the press. They usually detach themselves from the black community from which they sprang, return no social good to that community, and leave it worse off than it was. And they themselves too often wind up with nothing to show for their years of prowess, for they do not win the good jobs that accrue to the white superstars.

Obsession with sports is destructive of black youth. Blinded by the dazzling temporary success of a few black stars, the ghetto boy dreams only of success in sports. His chances for ultimate stardom are not great; in the meantime he has destroyed whatever chances he had for becoming a good doctor, or engineer, or social expert. More black talent is aborted on the ghetto playground than can be calculated, leaving the black community impoverished.

The damage starts in junior high school and is compounded in high school. It is downright shameful to contemplate the number of potentially gifted black boys whose entire education is perverted in junior high school, where overenthusiastic coaches start them on the downward course of athletic specialization, indifference to scholastic accomplishment, and dedication to a dream that can never be realized. For a few years of adolescent glory, the black boy surrenders his chance for a lifetime of meaningful participation in the community.

Acceptance of a college athletic scholarship may be the first step to a truncated career. If the college intends to use the black athlete merely as a performer, while accepting no responsibility for his education, the chances are really great that he will terminate his college career without an education, without a job, and without adequate preparation for any. The young black might be much better off rejecting the scholarship, enrolling like an honest student, finding a job washing dishes in some all-night restaurant, and winding up with a degree in accounting. At present the chances of his playing four years of college football or basketball and graduating are not good. And if he does manage to graduate, it will often be with a mangled, second-rate degree that qualifies him for nothing.

When Artemius Crandall ended his high school football career and was preparing to graduate, eighty-seven institutions of higher learning sent emissaries offering him scholarships that would pay all expenses plus spending money for four years of college training in such subjects as calculus, economics, history, chemistry and literature. At that stage his educational competency was as follows:

He did not know the multiplication table, had no concept of its significance, could not even have made a guess as to what 8×7 was, and would have been astounded to learn that 7×8 yielded the same result as 8×7. He had never read a book; indeed, he had never once been in any house that had a book other than an unopened Bible. He was not illiterate, for he could read the sports pages of the local newspapers and understand what the writers were saying about him in their enthusiastic articles, but he comprehended few of the big words. He had no concept of history, no familiarity with any science, had never attended a laboratory session and did not know what a poem was. If strict standards were applied, he had the education of a normal third-grader, and yet he was a bright, intelligent young man with a fine character.

How had such an abortion of the educational process been permitted? Because at every stage of his career he had been recognized as a marvelous potential athlete and pushed ahead. From the seventh grade on he had rarely attended class yet he had received top grades. In his junior and senior years he got straight A's in subjects whose classes he attended one day in five and in which he did no work at all. In order to make him eligible for top scholarships, an adoring faculty twice gave him A's in classes for which he was not even enrolled.

What in hell were eighty-seven universities doing, offering scholarships which, if he could have accepted them all, would have totaled more than two million dollars? One coach said, 'Artemius is no less prepared than many of the boys we already take. With a tutor to write his papers and see that he attends at least some of his classes, we'll get him passing grades. And that's all that counts.' Another said, with some perspicacity, 'He's a damned sight better human material than most of the crumbums we have to do business with. He has character, and you'll be amazed at what that kid will learn in a good college.'

Thousands of boys not much better prepared than Artemius Crandall receive full academic scholarships year after year. The only explanation can be that my Criterion III—universities must provide public entertainment —supersedes all other considerations. Few colleges or conferences are blameless in this strange perversion of the educational process, and any who might seek to terminate such abuses would find themselves besieged by their alumni, who would argue that a boy doesn't need too much book learning. It is not corrupt coaches who haul such boys to the academic doors; it is the general public who insist upon it.

The statistical possibility of landing a paying job in professional sports is bleak. Every young black who is starting his career on the ghetto playing fields should bear in mind these probabilities. In a typical year there will be 200,000 schoolboy seniors eager to win basketball scholarships at some college, but since there are only 1,243 colleges playing the game, the scholarships available cannot exceed 12,000. Four years later the colleges will be graduating about 5,700 seniors, most of them hoping for a professional contract. But there are only 25 professional teams, and they draft somewhere around 200 players each year, but they actually offer contracts to only a portion of that number. About 55 college seniors will land salaried berths with the pros, but of them only about six will earn starting positions. The chances for the average high school hotshot are not alluring, and that is why thoughtful black social critics deplore the emphasis given to basketball in black mythology. The odds against the young would-be athlete are somewhat worse than those which face the would-be actor or novelist, and over the long haul the rewards are more meager.

I first became aware of the tragedy involved in ended careers when I stood along the sidelines at a professional football camp with two scouts who had recruited the young men I had been watching over the past week. Now came the cutting time, and one of the scouts pointed to three young blacks, attractive, well-behaved rookies whom everyone liked, and said, 'Tonight they come to the end of the trail. Tomorrow they wake up to reality.'

When I asked what that meant, the other scout explained, 'They're being cut. The end of the line. And I'm afraid they're not good enough to land a job anywhere else as free agents.'

'That happens to a lot of us, in other ways,' I said.

'Not quite,' the scout said. 'Those three young men have not had an honest day's experience since the seventh grade. They've been passed along as football heroes. Grade school, high school, college, everywhere they were handed grades. Tomorrow they wake up to the fact that they have no job, no degree, no education, no prospects.' I thought that since he had helped draft the young men for one last fling at a corrupt system, he was being cynical about their departure. Not at all. He told me, 'It breaks your heart to see dreams vanish this way. I'm not going to be here tonight. I can't stand watching.'

At the end of his professional career, even the successful black player faces unusual difficulties. Each year those who have been retired because of age or illness must start their lives over, and with lesser advantages than those pertaining to white veterans. The conspicuous case of the black who becomes a television sports announcer must not obscure the hundreds of cases of men who are left adrift. If they have ability and strong character, they can catch hold of something rewarding; if they have no special ability, their lives are apt to be frustrating, and no collection of headlines will help them attain the position they might have had if they had pursued an honest education instead of the spurious athletic route. Bob Love, black basketball star with the Chicago Bulls, made an interesting point:

> Sure the college scouts and coaches are wrong for exploiting the athletes. But many of the athletes are guilty also for letting themselves be used. Most of those who end up with nothing are brothers, too. That's why I'm glad I went to a black college, Southern University at Baton Rouge, because they generally work harder to help the athletes get an education and learn a skill. They are interested in you as a man and not just an athlete.

Even the highly successful black athlete runs the risk of establishing himself as a destructive behavior-pattern for younger blacks who cannot hope to emulate him. This may be the greatest problem of all. If the entire black community surrenders itself to the dream of a life in sports, while the white community is aspiring to a full-fledged body of options, the black community not only restricts itself to one of the most ephemeral life goals, but it denigrates itself, limits its talented youth, and appears juvenile in the eyes of others. It is as if a large portion of the black community had consciously set for itself the goal of providing gladiators for the white arenas, and that seems immoral.

Too often the publicized salaries are illusory or even fake. Closer inspection needs to be given this tricky subject. Let's take the best aspect first. A great superstar like Wilt Chamberlain, Kareem Abdul-Jabbar or Henry Aaron who can remain a professional for many years, drawing a top salary most of that time, can earn and save a good deal of money (but rather less than a man of equal talents in business or creativity might earn over the same span of years). It would be reasonable for any young black to dream of being a Willie Mays or a Jim Brown or a Bill Russell, for these extraordinary men had not only the approbation of an entire society but also a financial success which should keep them solvent for the rest of their lives. (Again, I would not trade their income, substantial as it was, for what a man of equal talents might have made in management or music or merchandising.)

But when one comes to the overnight sensation who signs a contract for 'a million dollars, guaranteed,' I would always want to inspect the details. The agreement may call for five years of services, with so many conditional clauses that the young man has little chance of ever fulfilling them. There are deductions for agents' fees and lawyers' fees and proliferating expenses. There are cancellation clauses. And in the end I suspect that what the young man is getting is less than half a million dollars, over five years. Prorated over a working lifetime, that's no great bargain.

Two points should be considered. From what I know of intricate contracts in varied fields, I am satisfied that the athlete who hauls down one of the much-publicized deals would probably be much better off, weighing a whole lifetime, if he had played games for fun, renounced a professional career, and prepared himself for a profession which would assure him a constantly growing income from ages twenty-six through seventy. Look at the figures. The athlete picks up his one big contract, pays excessive expenses, lives beyond his means, and faces life at thirty-four forcibly retired from his sport and without a job that pays substantially. He becomes a bartender at the American Legion and his life income will be that first $500,000 plus little more. The trained man, on the other hand, works forty-five years at an average salary of $30,000—or perhaps much, much more—and his life's earnings are $1,350,000 plus an honored place in his community. The advantage is so strongly in favor of the constant earner, and by such a large margin, that one must conclude that the athlete was victimized. He was short-changed.

My second point is perhaps more important. I will grant that perhaps the young athlete had no other skill to sell, so that his contract, unsatisfactory in principle, may have been quite good for him personally. I will also grant that as a professional athlete he will have known a sense of glory that the non-athlete can never know, which would justify him in deeming the bargain a good one. But I do object most strenuously to having rather mediocre deals held up to a whole segment of society as the best a young man can shoot for. It is destructive to have a generation of black youths daydreaming about becoming the next Moses Malone, jumping right from high school to the pros 'for a cool two million.' Malone will be lucky if he gets his hands on two million and even luckier if he can save any of it.

Sports are the opiate of the black masses, and must be evaluated more realistically. Here we reach one of the most difficult intellectual concepts in this entire field. I see no hope whatever for diminishing the obsession so many blacks have with sports. It is illogical for me to preach that black boys in the ghetto should build alternate hero-figures when Walt Frazier's dazzling presence is so compelling, and I suspect that even thoughtful parents will prove powerless in trying to alter those childhood images. But an effort is being made; many black critics sense the destructiveness of sports within the black community far better than I, and they are beginning to be heard.

Dr. Brown, whose forthcoming book will be entitled *The Black Gladia-*

tor: Challenge to an American Myth, warns the black community: 'Black youngsters pour their time and energy into sport, they're deluded and seduced by the athletic flesh market, used and discarded. Most of them never get a pro contract, and most of them don't graduate from college. So they're left without the skills needed for servicing and enriching the community. That's the rip-off.'

Carl Rowan, the black columnist, has said that so far as black youth were concerned, American sports are 'the great corrupter.' He added, 'The great athletic exploiters don't care what a big, tall boy's intellectual potential is. They are out after flesh, muscle, brawn, reflexes, during whatever period that young man can perform. What happens to the kid over the long haul is of no consequence to the recruiters, agents, coaches, team owners. Witness the sickening fact that the flesh peddlers have already moved down into *junior* high school with their under-the-table offers of cash, cars or whatever else is required to lock up a talented athlete.'

One of the most perceptive essays I've read on this subject was written by a black columnist of the *Chicago Sun-Times.* Lacy Banks had to have more than his share of courage to write in this manner while working in a city with a large black population:

> Top-name athletes will get lots of scratch, big cars, luxury cribs, women and swimming pools of champagne. What I have to say is for the others. Most of you will fall short of making a pro team or signing a rich guaranteed contract. Your only settlement will be a multi-year pact of gloom. A great portion of you will suffer disappointment, unemployment, anxiety and even psychosis. Many will be minus a degree or viable vocation to show for your four or five years of college, and you will be relegated to common laborers' working jobs you don't like—jobs relatively demeaning to the superstar image you enjoyed during your heyday in sports. You will be a has-been and your most popular pastime may become standing around ghetto pool halls and taverns talking about your old jump shot. . . . It's no harm to work and hope for a successful career as a professional athlete. But make peace with the fact that it's a long-shot possibility. Don't bank everything on such a dream, no matter how good you are. You may be blinding yourself from other talents you possess. . . . Take soul singer Curtis Mayfield's advice in an educational sense and *Check out your mind. Check out your mind.*

It remained for Dr. Organ to issue the ultimate in warnings: 'I believe that schools operating in Black Communities, and most especially Black colleges and universities, should abolish varsity athletics until obsession with organized sports by the youth of the Black Community is minimized, if not completely arrested.' Since this is not practical, he makes two interesting recommendations: that each student be limited to participation in one sport, on the grounds that scholastic development is almost impossible if the child is participating in three or four sports a year; and that students be limited to two years of varsity sport in high school. 'Some Black students participate in three or four sports each year, every year, from the sixth grade all the way through college. This is entirely too much.' He concludes with a bitter recommendation: 'The soundest option for the Black Community appears to be a massive exodus from varsity and professional athletics. This should be done for several generations, or for whatever period of time is required for the Black Community to achieve a reasonable standard of living. Organized sports have been a trap for black youth, from which few recover. The Black Community is more in need of teachers, not coaches; more in need of proper nutrition, not drugs; more in need of health scientists than center fielders; more in need of economists and business administrators than pivot men.'

Let's look at four of the early examples of rebellion against the stereotypes governing black athletes. In the months prior to the 1968 Olympics in Mexico City there was a rumbling among black track and field athletes in all parts of the nation. It centered, however, at San Jose State University, California, where the black sociology professor Dr. Edwards was drumming up support for a boycott of the Olympics by all black American athletes. His argument was forthright and calculated to be effective: blacks were being asked to perform abroad to bring international acclaim to a nation which spurned them at home. 'A system of athletic slavery,' he called it.

A storm of public discussion followed his launching of the boycott; sportswriters condemned this attempt to drag athletics down to the cheap level of protest, and sentimentalists pointed out that a gesture like this was the very antithesis of the Olympic spirit. Dr. Edwards remained obdurate, however, and argued that the blacks had been subservient long enough. Now they must act.

Dr. Edwards' neighbors joined the debate. They shot his two dogs, dissected the bodies, and dumped the pieces on his front porch. He received telephoned death threats constantly, and surreptitious bribes amounting to more than $125,000 were offered if the blacks would call off their boycott.

The proposed boycott failed, which was probably a good thing, but it certainly shook up the establishment. And it engineered two propaganda triumphs: Lew Alcindor (later Abdul-Jabbar), the world's best amateur basketball player, said that the arguments in favor of the boycott were so convincing that he preferred not to represent the United States; and when Tommie Smith and John Carlos finished first and third in the two-hundred-meter dash, instead of standing at attention on the victory stand like good citizens when 'The Star-Spangled Banner' was played, they turned in a circle, giving the raised-fist symbol of the black liberation movement.

The reader should try to recall his or her reactions to that inflammatory moment. I was appalled at the effrontery and approved when the United States Olympic Committee suspended the pair and gave them forty-eight hours to leave Mexico City, but that was before I began looking seriously into the condition of the black athlete.

How far my education has come! When Bill Russell declined the honor of being inducted into the Basketball Hall of Fame, as a consequence of the long years he and other black players had suffered discrimination at the hands of white coaches, owners and public, I applauded. I did so because Russell had been a constant, courageous advocate of social justice; when he was the supreme professional athlete in the United States, sharing world honors perhaps with another black, Pelé of Brazil, he could have shied away from racial confrontations, but he never did. Soft-spoken, never aggressive with his views, always the gentleman, he nevertheless persisted in his basic philosophy, and when a man does that he builds his own Hall of Fame, which in Russell's case is even larger than the more popular one he rejected. Abdul-Jabbar and Russell have been model athletes in that they were able to keep their game and their humanity in tandem.

On Thursday, October 16, 1969, the University of Wyoming Cowboys had a full head of steam on their way to another football conference championship and a high national rating. They had already won four straight games and seemed certain to extend their streak against Brigham Young on Saturday and San Jose State the following week.

But on Friday, October 17, everything went to hell, and when the day was over, Wyoming hopes lay in shambles. What had happened was that fourteen black football players, imported into all-white Laramie as paid athletes, had tied black bands about their left arms and walked as a group into the office of head coach Lloyd Eaton, a crew-cut, tough disciplinarian who had always promulgated one clearly understood rule for his players: they could not participate in any demonstrations. The job of a football player, in Eaton's book, was to play football, and any side rumpus like civil rights or anti-Vietnam protests was a distraction which might damage the player's capacity to play.

The fourteen black players had come peacefully seeking permission to wear black armbands in their game against Brigham Young University, a Mormon school. Mormonism, explained the blacks, discriminates against blacks and will not allow them to progress to the priesthood, which all other male Mormons are supposed to attain. (Some blacks spread the malicious rumor that Mormons preached that blacks are descendants of the devil; this was a libel. Mormonism teaches that blacks are descended from Cain, who slew his brother Abel, and are thus ineligible for the priesthood. Blacks are

*'Give me Wilt Chamberlain's height, Muhammad Ali's strength,
O.J. Simpson's speed, Arthur Ashe's ground strokes . . .'*

free to attend Brigham Young, but few do. In Provo, where the university is located, of the 36,000 residents, there was recently only one black family.)

We know that the fourteen black athletes entered Coach Eaton's office. What happened next is unclear. The blacks say they requested permission to wear the armbands on their uniforms the next day when they lined up against Brigham Young; Coach Eaton says they demanded the right. The blacks say Eaton took one look at them, smelled defiance, and fired the lot from his championship football team; Coach Eaton says he listened patiently for ten minutes as they presented their petition, then realized that he had rebellion on his hands and informed them quietly that they were no longer members of his team.

The ensuing fracas practically tore Wyoming apart. The faculty senate voted 37–1 to ask the athletic department to rescind the dismissal and impose instead a temporary suspension, but the community, which had always resented the intrusion of the big-city blacks into their peaceful cowboy town, insisted that the blacks be run out. And when seven faculty members threatened to resign unless the blacks were reinstated, the Touchdown Club offered to raise money to pay their fares out of the state.

The university board of trustees met from seven o'clock Friday night till five o'clock Saturday morning trying to bring some order into the situation, and finally they agreed to back Coach Eaton all the way. I arrived accidentally on the scene a few weeks later and found bumper stickers across the state proclaiming the driver's undying faith in Coach Eaton. Friends told me that at the height of the trouble, bands of armed men drove about the streets of Laramie ready to shoot the place up if blacks caused any trouble; word had been passed that two thousand Black Panthers armed to the teeth were descending on Laramie from points like Chicago and San Francisco, determined to capture the town.

Finally, the case went to the courts and struggled along with recriminations and countercharges. State officials in Wyoming held firm; the blacks had scandalized the university by openly challenging the dictates of Coach Eaton, and their testimony was persuasive. In 1972 the Tenth Circuit Court of Appeals, sitting in Denver, ruled that the university had been within its rights when it dismissed the fourteen blacks and that they had no further recourse, since none of their civil rights had been infringed.

When the Cowboys, without their black stars, pulverized Brigham Young 40–7 for their fifth straight victory, then walloped San Jose State 16–7, there was jubilation across Wyoming. 'We can go all the way, even without our niggers,' ranchers throughout the state rejoiced. 'Gettin' rid of them will turn out to be a blessin'.' Not so. Without its blacks, Wyoming lost seven straight games, finishing 6–4 in 1969 and 1–9 in 1970. In succeeding years the ardent Wyoming fans watched as their football and basketball teams wallowed in despair. Unable to recruit top black talent, the Cowboys compiled dismal records, and in 1974, the year Marvin Bates took his third trip on the Treagle from Cheyenne to Laramie, the football team won only two games while losing nine to opponents they once beat with ease. In 1975 they had the same record.

Wyoming is a state I cherish, one of the truly distinctive areas of the United States, and its university has a proud history. I am distressed that football, which should be a unifying experience, has been the cause of such a fracture. In 1968, when the Cowboys went to New Orleans to play in the Sugar Bowl against LSU, it was said, without too much exaggeration, 'that half the state flew south for the game.' In New Orleans they still say with fond memories, 'We never had a bunch of better spenders than that Wyoming crowd. Wish they'd come south again.' I should think that within another two or three years Wyoming might be a pretty good place for a black athlete; the redneck ranchers will have learned by then what the Southeastern Conference learned earlier, that you can't field a first-class football team without black players.

The third confrontation was more to my liking, because it was intellectual, orderly and responsible. In early 1972 blacks at Michigan State University, athletes and faculty alike, decided to compile a document that would inform Wayne Duke, Big Ten Athletic Commissioner, of the actual state of affairs in his conference. Drafting a preliminary paper listing griev-ances, they circulated it among the other Big Ten schools, soliciting their counsel. Finally, three black faculty members from Michigan State, Robert Green, Joseph McMillan and Thomas Gunnings, drafted the final report, using scholarly procedures and non-inflammatory language:

> . . . Of the black student athletes in the study, 100 percent reported that their coaches expected them to remain eligible, but only 7 percent reported that their coaches expected them to receive their degrees. Seventy percent reported that their white coaches and professors and white students expected them to be weak academically.

> . . . Black athletes from several Big Ten schools commented that severe punish-ment was meted out for missing practice, yet no real concern was exhibited when classes were missed.

> . . . At one university 156 letter winners in football, basketball, wrestling and track were observed from their freshman year in 1960 through November of 1970. Of the 113 whites, 82.3 percent had graduated; of the 43 blacks, only 46.5 percent had done so.

> . . . Those black athletes who were admitted to one university with only a marginal chance of academic success, according to the Big Ten Prediction Table, had about as good a record of graduating as the black athletes who entered with satisfactory prediction scores.

> . . . Black athletes also commented that recruiters make them think they are going to the university to get an education and that athletics is a secondary concern. By their junior year, many feel that the reverse is actually true.

The report then made a series of recommendations to Commissioner Duke. Black officials should be hired for every sporting event. Departments of physical education should hire a reasonable quota of black assistant coaches, secretaries, trainers, medical personnel, publicity people and custo-dial help. Big Ten schools should see to it that black athletes get a fair share of jobs dispensed by the athletic department. And black counselors, outside the athletic department, should be responsible for the educational progress of black athletes.

The report ended with a mournful judgment: 'The patterns of racial discrimination both overt and covert, institutional and individual, found in the larger society are reflected in and perpetuated in athletics in the United States.'

(In view of my low opinion of cheerleading as an occupation for women, I must in fairness report that in the Michigan State confrontation, and in scores of others throughout the United States, one of the principal protests of the male black athlete is: 'Complaint 7. MSU has never elected a black cheerleader.' The men feel, and understandably so, that if American society considers the cheerleader the highest position to which a co-ed can aspire, it is unfair to deny admission to that Valhalla to black Valkyries.)

Three special problems have fascinated all imaginative observers who have speculated upon the problems of the black athlete, and I should now like to summarize each briefly. The first is sex, a harsh, constant reality for which there seems to be no adequate solution. Stated bluntly, the problem is this. A university in the north, with no history of ever having accepted black students and with none in residence, suddenly decides to 'go big time,' send its recruiters into city ghettos, and hire a group of black gladiators. These young men are super-virile types, at the precise age when sexual pressures and longings are greatest, and they are brought into this sterile setting, where every coach they meet, every advisor, every faculty member cautions them that they must never, no, never, date a white girl.

The literature is jammed with case histories of exactly what coaches have told their black importees. For a good summary see Jack Olsen's second article in his series in *Sports Illustrated* (July 8, 1968). From a score of horror stories the one that seemed saddest to me was a trivial thing that sprinter Harold Busby of UCLA's championship track team recalled. 'The first three finishers in each event were to be kissed by the queen and trophied at a victory stand. This was fine as long as it was the mile or the pole vault. But when Charlie Green won the hundred, Jim Hines finished second, and I was third, the girl wouldn't even shake our hands.'

The black athlete, cut off from black society of any kind, is supposed to spend four of his most virile years playing games for his university, and sitting alone in a room, forbidden to speak to any female. If he dares to do so, the whole weight of the athletic establishment falls on him; he is castigated verbally, threatened with the loss of his scholarship, demoted by his professors in class, and denied a starting position on the team where he is probably the best player of the lot.

Prior to the big final trouble at Wyoming one of the football players had made overtures toward dating a white girl, and word got to her cowboy brothers, who organized a posse to 'gun down the nigger if he makes another move.'

It seems to me immoral for a university to import black athletes into a situation where there are few black co-eds and almost no blacks in the surrounding community and then to demand that the athletes refrain from social contact of any kind with what young women are available. And if it isn't immoral, it's ridiculous.

The second problem concerns stacking, the procedure whereby a coach who wants some blacks on his team but not too many, because his rich white alumni might complain, channels all his blacks into two or three positions commonly reserved for them, so that they can compete against one another rather than land one of the more important positions reserved for white players.

The so-called 'white positions' in football are quarterback, center and the two inside running guards on offense, it being held that whites, with their supposed superior intelligence and capacity to react to unfolding situations, will handle those jobs better than flighty and irresponsible blacks. On defense it is the linebacker, who must ebb and flow with the play as it develops, who has to be white.

In baseball the 'white positions' are those down-the-middle slots which control the movement of the game and especially the execution of the double play. Catcher, shortstop and second base are critical, and folk wisdom demands that whites, with their supposed superior mental adaptability, handle these spots.

Once this assumption of white intellectual superiority is accepted, it becomes logical to direct blacks away from those positions where intelligence is required and into those where fleetness of foot, muscular agility and capacity for quick turns in flight, characteristics that blacks are supposed to have, are an asset.

For several decades I had heard rumors of stacking and dismissed them. But recently several teams of investigators have applied computer analysis to football and baseball rosters, coming up with startling results. John Loy and Joseph Elvogue in 'Racial Segregation in American Sport,' *International Review of Sport Sociology* (1970), provide the best summary. In an article crammed with philosophical implications, they advance the theory that blacks, because of the social prejudices of white managers and owners, are channeled into those peripheral positions on the field where they will have least contact with their teammates and least influence upon the intricate development of the game. In a computer analysis of all the teams in professional football, they found that the central positions of close contact and generalship—quarterbacks, centers, guards on offense—were 96 percent white, whereas the peripheral positions where contact was not constant and generalship not required—cornerbacks on defense—were 77 percent black. They analyzed each position and found without question that certain ones were reserved for certain colors. Thus linebackers, who play a central role on defense, were 92 percent white, while halfbacks, who play off to one side on offense, were 62 percent black.

In baseball the situation was the same. In the three crucial down-the-middle slots where intelligence and quick response to fluid situations were prized, 91 percent of the players were white. In the outfield, far from responsibility for central decisions, 49 percent of the players were black, and if the figures had been broken down into right field and left, the really isolated positions, as contrasted to center field, where more judgment is required, the discrepancy would probably have been even greater.

Left or right field in baseball, cornerback in football, these are the ideal spots for black players according to present thinking, and it is probable that many intelligent college blacks, aware of the stacking that faces them, specialize in these positions, knowing that they will have a better chance to land one. Thus discrimination feeds upon itself.

There is a contradiction in the philosophy of stacking which defeats me. Why would an athletic department spend thousands of dollars recruiting the best black players, traveling to all corners of America to do so, and then not use the men at their maximum capacity? Why would a coach recruit eleven superior blacks and then turn them all into cornerbacks competing against one another? The only answer is that they do. It is quite probable that no basketball team in any American college or university ever plays all its best players, because if the coach did so, his team would be all black, and the white alumni would not stand for it. Furthermore, we know from many accounts that institutions like Notre Dame and Texas recruit some ten times the number of football players who will actually be able to play.

I remember one Notre Dame alumnus in the coal regions of Pennsylvania who told me, 'I went to South Bend all fired up. I'd been all-Scholastic quarterback. Tore my conference apart. Sixty schools wanted me. But I wanted the best, so I chose Notre Dame. I came on as a real hotshot, and at the first practice the coach has all us freshmen together and I see that among that mob I'm the runt. He reads off the first team, and I'm not on it. "Well," I mumble to myself, "I still have this great record. I'll accept second team." So then he reads off the second team, and I'm still missing. And the third and the fourth. I'm on the eleventh team, but by that time they've run out of footballs. So we have to practice with a helmet. Here I am, the hottest thing ever to come out of the coal regions, and I'm forward passing a helmet. Right then I understood what big time meant.'

The final topic is one that merits the closest attention, for it is bound to recur; it engenders the fiercest partisanship; and it is deeply ingrained in American folklore. *Is the black athlete different physically and psychologically from the white?* Translated into its simplest terms, is Archie Bunker right when he says of the black football player, 'Them jungle bunnies can run faster than any white man'?

This popular subject for barroom debate was given a rational structure in *Sports Illustrated* (January 18, 1971), when Martin Kane, then a senior editor, advanced the theory that there were indeed substantive differences between the young black man and his white competitor. Reviewing all known existing studies, Kane offered these tentative conclusions:

. . . Blacks tend to have longer limbs, smaller calfs, less fat and narrower hips than whites, and this combination gives the black athlete a superior agility.

. . . Whites have substantially greater lung capacity than blacks.

. . . Blacks have marked superiority in hyperextensibility, or capacity for double-jointedness and general looseness of joints. This may be because they tend to have more tendon and less muscle.

. . . This point is subjective, and not measurable, but many observers who have worked closely with both black and white athletes contend that the former have a superior capacity to relax under pressure.

. . . One researcher points out that all living things from tropical climates tend to have longer limbs, which aids them in dissipating heat. Blacks share this characteristic.

. . . Black infants are able to control their heads and muscles much sooner than white babies.

. . . Perhaps because of physical inheritance, no black has ever been a swimming champion or even a near-champion.

. . . And finally, the most contentious theory of all: centuries of slavery placed a premium on the superior physical specimen and weeded out the weakling, so that in time the black genetic structure became superior. Two black athletes have been outspoken supporters of this theory. Calvin Hill, the great Yale-Dallas running back, says, 'I have a theory about why so many sports stars are black. I think it boils down to the survival of the fittest. Think of what the African slaves were forced to endure in this country merely to survive. Well, black athletes are their descendants. They are the offspring of those who are physically tough enough to survive.' Lee Evans, Olympic champion in the 400 meters, says, 'We were bred for it. Certainly the black people who survived in the slave ships must have contained a high proportion of the strongest. Then, on the plantations, a strong black man was mated with a strong black woman. We were simply bred for physical qualities.'

The publication of this daring article, containing so much unsupported speculation, created a storm of discussion and hopeful refutation, which was understandable, because if the article was correct in its suppositions, then the black athlete, and indeed the whole black race, was a thing apart, and society would be justified in treating blacks differently from the way it treated whites.

It fell to Dr. Edwards to lead the fight against Martin Kane, and he did so in a series of beautifully reasoned articles reminiscent of the nineteenth century when the world's top scientists were arguing in measured prose the strengths and defects of Darwinism. I recommend Edwards' argumentation most warmly, but in doing so I am not presuming to pass judgment on its conclusions. I am commending only the rigorousness of his approach;

indeed, I think that both Edwards and Kane have served us well in bringing this inflated topic down to the level of reasonable debate.

I have read three different versions of Edwards' thesis; the best appears in his book *Sociology of Sport,* but a good summary appears also in *Psychology Today* (November 1973). Edwards breaks Kane's arguments into three broad categories, which he proceeds to rebut.

Do blacks have athletic superiority because of race-linked physical characteristics? Edwards denies this totally. He argues that no researcher cited by Kane studied a random sample of the black population and that to extrapolate from the small samples studied is unacceptable. He also doubts the existence of a clearly defined race, white or black. He finds many more differences between black athletes than between black versus white, and asks the rhetorical question, 'What physical characteristics does Wilt Chamberlain have in common with Al Attles?' He is scornful of Kane's attempt to rationalize discrepancies in this theory by pointing out that 'the Kenyan Keino and the Ethiopian Bikila have black skin but many white features.' He questions the theory that blacks living in equatorial regions developed long limbs in order to dissipate heat by citing the fact that pygmies, without elongated limbs, live in close proximity to the spidery Watusi, and prosper. He concludes with a strong paragraph which reminds the reader that simply because a difference is ascertainable it is not necessarily causative.

Is black athletic superiority caused by race-linked psychological factors? Edwards argues that 'racial character' was disposed of by scholars decades ago. He questions the scholarly competence of a bunch of coaches to decide that black athletes are happy-go-lucky. He cites recent studies by Thomas Tutko and Bruce Ogilvie to the effect that when it really matters, black athletes, because of the pressures on them, are less happy-go-lucky than whites. He concludes with the observation that if the black athlete has any psychological advantage it is because the white athlete has psyched himself to think so. 'The "white race" thus becomes the chief victim of its own myth.'

Did racially specific historical occurrences create a superior black athletic ability? Edwards seeks to rebut the slave arguments of Calvin Hill and Lee Evans by pointing out that so far as the history of slavery is known, the slaves who survived best were not the hulking brutes but the shrewd ones. He is on stronger ground when he argues that the black race can hardly be pure, considering the amount of miscegenation that took place. And he is strongest when he points out that it required more than physical superiority for a Bill Russell or a Gayle Sayers to excel.

Edwards then proceeds to a discussion of the dangers of the Kane theory. He says that if blacks are superior only because of a racial physical endowment, it is not illogical to reserve the thinking positions in football for the whites, since they may be presumed to have excelled for intellectual as well as physical reasons. An inevitable consequence of the theory would be that if blacks are physically superior, then they must be intellectually inferior. 'So, if in the affirmation of black identity Afro-Americans should accept the myth of racially innate black physical superiority in any realm, they could be inadvertently recognizing and accepting an ideology which has been used in part as justification for black slavery, segregation and general oppression. For, in the final analysis, the argument of black physical superiority over whites is a potentially racist ideology.'

I have spent many years of my life contemplating this problem of racial differences as I worked in the world's major xenophobic countries: South Africa, Australia, the Arab lands, Israel, Japan, Spain and the United States. I have listened patiently to arguments on racial superiorities and inferiorities, but nothing I have encountered has had a more profound impact on my thinking than an ingenious study conducted at Harvard many years ago. A budding sociologist simply checked on what men had appeared in Boston prize fights over a hundred-year period. At first all the fighters bore sturdy English names, for the ring was the traditional avenue of escalation for underprivileged English workmen without an education. But after the English became well established, and any workman could find a good paying job, the fighters all became Irish. It was Kid this and Kid that. But now the theory broke down, for when the Irish gained a social and economic foothold they should have exited from the ring, but they did not. The Irish names still continued, until the researcher looked a little more deeply into the matter and found that the new cycle of Irish fighters were really European Jewish immigrants, who had adopted Irish names to profit from their popularity in the preceding cycle. In real life Battling Johnny Kilrain the Second was apt to be Hyman Finkel.

After some time Jewish fighters were free to fight under their real names, and for some years they dominated the Boston rings, but one should not be surprised to find that they quickly established themselves in the community and no longer had need of pugilism as their escape route. Next came the French immigrants, and at long last the black fighters.

With a little practice, one could look at the Boston newspapers of any given era, and by seeing who was fighting whom, determine where the various immigrant groups were on the social ladder. Men fought in the Boston rings not because they wanted to, but because that was the only way out. And to a large extent that truism still governs sports.

I remember the bitterness with which one professional-football scout told me, 'So help me God, I'll never again draft a football player from Stanford. You scout 'em, talk with 'em, keep records on 'em, and remind yourself that John Brodie and Jim Plunkett graduated from Stanford and made it big. You advise your team to draft 'em high. But after you waste a high draft choice on 'em, the Stanford kid suddenly realizes that he'd be a damned fool to waste a bunch of years playing professional football when he can move right into a good firm or profession. We've drafted three, and we didn't get a damned one of 'em. From now on, it's Grambling for me. Those guys need the money. They'll report.'

Jesse Owens may have summed it up accurately when he said, 'There is no difference between the races. If the black athlete has been better than his white counterpart, it's because he's hungrier—he wants it more.'

My thinking on such matters was fortified by my study of Jewish history. From ancient days the inner councils of Judaism taught that athletics and soldiering were lower forms of social activity and not to be encouraged. Ancient literature is filled with references on the subject, and as a consequence, the world has always had fewer Jewish athletes of note than their proportion of the population would warrant, and fewer military leaders too.

But when Israel became a self-governing state, it began to produce soldiers at will, and athletes. In the United States we have had far fewer Jewish athletes than one might have anticipated, but here, too, the tradition is changing.

I suspect that any group of people on earth has about the same percentage of skilled physical specimens as any other. It is the customs of society that determine whether or not the young men of any one group seek excellence in athletics as a primary mode of expression. Blacks dominate in many areas of American sports not because they are racially superior but because for generations sports have been the one area in which they had a chance to excel. I know of few young white boys in the north whose dream of excellence is to excel in sports, although there are still many in the south. But there must be thousands of black youths who have no other aspiration, especially those tall enough to play basketball.

It will be interesting to see what happens if soccer becomes fashionable in the United States. Then superior size will not be an advantage, and I suppose that our experience will be much like the rest of the world's. There will be a few marvelous black players like Eusebio of Portugal (via Mozambique) and Pelé of Brazil. But there will be an equal number of outstanding whites, like Johan Cruyff of Holland, Gerhard Müller of Germany, Dino Zoff of Italy and George Best of England.

The life of the black in sports cannot be understood unless one knows about the Rucker, for this summer tournament played in Harlem by famed professionals, college stars and playground phenoms is the essence of black basketball. It was started as an informal pickup operation in 1946 by Holcombe Rucker, a young teacher who wanted to keep ghetto kids out of the alleys. When Rucker died prematurely of cancer in 1955 it was converted into a cherished institution. When Lew Alcindor, at the height of his fame, gave a press conference in New York, someone asked 'Where's the Rucker being played this summer?' and without hesitation Lew gave the address.

Three books report on the Rucker in loving detail. The Connie Hawkins story noted in Chapter I is good. Pete Axthelm's *The City Game,* available in paperback, is better. And best of all is a novel by Jay Neugeboren, *The Big Man,* which depicts a case similar to Hawkins'. In his novel, one of the best so far written about black sports, Neugeboren casually suggests that during the notorious basketball scandals of 1951 officials at Catholic colleges were able to persuade city officials to hush up the participation of their schools, while the obloquy fell on the Jewish schools and particularly on the blacks.

These books are filled with gripping passages about the unheralded black stars who dominated playground games without landing college scholarships or professional contracts. By common consent, the greatest one-on-one player ever to operate in New York was Earl Manigault. Axthelm describes one of his moves:

> For a few minutes Earl seemed to move slowly, feeling his way, getting himself ready. Then he got the ball on a fast break. Harper, who was six-feet-six, and Val Reed, who was six-feet-eight, got back quickly to defend. You wouldn't have given Earl a chance to score. Then he accelerated, changing his step suddenly. And at the foul line he went into the air. Harper and Reed went up too, and between them, the two big men completely surrounded the rim. But Earl just kept going higher, and finally he two-hand dunked the ball over both of them. For a split second there was complete silence, and then the crowd exploded. They were cheering so loud that they stopped the game for five minutes. Five minutes. That was Earl Manigault.

Axthelm then goes on to relate how this iridescent star fell into ghetto ways, leaving behind only legend and heartache.

My favorite was a young man I never saw but about whom I heard many stories when I was doing research on this chapter. He was known simply as Helicopter, as fine a defense artist as Manigault was a one-on-oner. Axthelm tells of how Jay Vaughn, a local hotshot, had his confrontation:

> I said to myself, 'Well, fine, I'll try him,' and I went out there one-on-one with Helicopter. Well, it was a disastrous thing. I tried lay-ups, jump shots, hooks. And everything I threw up, he blocked. The word had gone out that Helicopter was there, and a crowd was gathering and I said to myself, 'You got to do something. You're getting humiliated.' But the harder I tried, the more he shoved the ball down into my face. I went home and thought about that game for a long time. Like a lot of other young athletes, I had been put in my place.

It is from such endless playground competition against the Rucker stars like Chamberlain and Alcindor and Helicopter and Manigault that the city blacks learn their profession. After spending ten hours a day, year after year, at such schooling it is little wonder that they excel; the white boy from a small town who plays the game casually cannot expect to perfect his moves the way the city black who practices against Helicopter and Manigault can. But there is a bitterness about the play. Robert Bownes, a black assistant coach at Hunter College, explains the black player's attitude toward the NCAA ban on dunking (jamming the ball through the basket from above):

> The rule wasn't put in to stop seven-footers (like Alcindor). It was put in to stop the six-foot-two brothers who could dazzle the crowd and embarrass much bigger white kids by dunking. The white establishment has an uncomfortable feeling that blacks are dominating too many areas of sports. So they're setting up all kinds of restrictions and barriers. Everyone knows that dunking is a trademark of great playground black athletes. And so they took it away. It's as simple as that.

A similar protest was launched after the Rose Bowl game in 1975, which Ohio State lost primarily because its brilliant defensive back, Neal Colzie, spiked the ball after having intercepted a USC pass and running the ball back to the nine-yard line, where a touchdown would have been probable. The referee penalized Colzie for the spike, and Ohio State got the ball on the 24-yard line, from where it failed to score. Southern Cal, reprieved, won the game in the last minute, 18–17. Spiking (slamming the ball exuberantly to the ground after an unexpected gain), like dancing into the payoff zone, is a playground tradition of black players, and Bownes is probably correct in believing that it irritates the white establishment, which has outlawed spiking and may soon outlaw the victory dance. The black is free to participate in white sports, but he damned well better conduct himself like a white man.

I have not dealt adequately with the problems of other minorities in sport, especially men from minority groups. I think it extraordinary that so few American Indians have won a major place. Jim Thorpe, Chief Bender, Pepper Martin are remembered, but not many more. Hawaiians have done rather well in sending a series of fine football players to western colleges, and certainly Duke Kahanamoku was a major figure in swimming. Laura Blears Ching is a world surfing champion. The Chicano and Filipino, because of their diminutive size, have not excelled in basketball or football, but Jim Plunkett and Roman Gabriel are fine quarterbacks. If soccer becomes a popular sport, I would expect the Chicanos to excel. But it has been in horse racing and baseball that they have begun to dominate. A large number of good jockeys are Latins—in 1963, two of the top ten; in 1974, the top four money winners—while an all-star team of Chicano baseball players could take on all comers. It is quite commendable how baseball, which fought blacks so long, adjusted so easily to accommodate Venezolanos and Puerto Ricans who could speak no English. One of the truly funny sequences in a sports film occurred in *Bang the Drum Slowly* when Vince Gardenia, playing the bumble-tongued manager is delivering a locker-room exhortation with an involved metaphor while the translator for the Chicanos attempts to translate it into meaningful Spanish; his students respond with open-mouthed astonishment at the gibberish their coach is talking. Several ballplayers have assured me that this was the truest scene in that fine movie of baseball life.

When black athletes began to make substantial gains in college and professional sports, a degree of resentment became inevitable, but the white backlash has not been discussed openly because of its ugly implications. I happened to be involved peripherally in a classic instance. When Philadelphia had a world-beater basketball team, featuring outstanding stars like Wilt Chamberlain, Billy Cunningham and Hal Greer, I was surprised and in a sense hurt to find it playing in the new Spectrum to small audiences of four and five thousand. That city had a robust basketball tradition, with many championships in its background plus some of the most exciting college basketball in the country at the Big-Five barnburners played at the Palestra. So the sparse attendance at the 76ers was a mystery.

Especially since the newly founded hockey team—the Flyers, a pitiful gang going nowhere—was packing in 17,007 paid customers game after game. Subterranean rumors began to circulate and I started a one-man investigation of just what was happening.

It was simple. Big-time sports in big-time arenas are supported primarily by upper-well-to-do families who live in the suburbs, and these people, by their own confessions to me, had grown tired of driving into Philadelphia to see a professional basketball team that was primarily black, and to hear black stars on other teams making what my friends called 'derisive and provocative statements about race.' Also, there was some fear that the audience at the basketball game might erupt into violence, either within the Spectrum or on the parking lot. There was thus an unannounced boycott of professional basketball, while college basketball, which retained a racial mix more acceptable to the suburbs, continued to prosper.

The suburbanite could drive into the city to see a hockey game played by all-white Canadians, and patronized by an almost all-white audience, and enjoy himself in what he termed security (and in what he did not openly acknowledge, a sense of racial superiority). Here are a few quotations gathered during my study.

'Jabbar can make all the cracks he wants, but not on my money. I've seen my last basketball game.'

'I know nothing about hockey, and neither does my wife, but it's a pleasure to go to their games. It's on a whole different level.'

'It costs me a bundle of dough to attend a sporting event in the city. Baby-sitter, drive in, dinner for four, parking, tickets. I don't intend to lay out that dough to be insulted by some black agitator or get mugged on the way home.'

'Sports have been the salvation of characters like Bill Russell and now they bite the hand that feeds them. They won't bite mine any more.'

'Sure, there are just as many blacks in football, and I attend every Eagles game. But the football field is a long distance away from my seat, and the players are encased in armor, and it would take a good spy to detect whether a man is black or white. But in basketball you sit right on the playing floor and the men are almost undressed and their blackness hits you right in the face.'

'Blacks comprise twelve percent of our population. Now you know, Michener, how I fought to help them gain their fair share of jobs and teaching positions and everything else. They're entitled to twelve percent. But not to eighty percent, or a hundred percent, which is what they want in basketball. From here on out it's their game, not mine.'

The chasm has widened. In 1974 I went to a 76er basketball game and what I saw depressed me. Now I'll admit that in 1972–73 they had the worst team in the league, maybe the worst team in the history of any sport, but now they weren't so bad. It was a sparse crowd, if you want to call 1,385 spectators a crowd, with many blacks in the audience. But when the Flyers hockey team played in the same arena a few nights later, there was hardly breathing room with 17,007 in attendance, and I saw not one black specta- tor.* I suppose this de facto segregation will continue for a few more years, then diminish. When the present period of tension subsides nationally I expect to see suburbanites coming back to basketball and blacks turning to hockey, both as players and as spectators. In the meantime the double boycott is deplorable. Anything that can be done to diminish it should be.

The goal of American sports must be to provide every man or woman an equitable opportunity to develop his or her skills to maximum capacity.

*Such reasoning about the 76ers received a reversal at the opening of the 1975 season. When the team came up with three black superstars—George McGinniss from the Indiana Pacers (ABA), Joe Bryant, a LaSalle college hardship dropout, and Darryl Dawkins, a sensational eighteen-year-old high school player from Florida—the Spectrum was filled to overflowing, and a cynic observed, 'We're not against black players. We're against black players who lose.'

Arbitrary limitations because of sex or race are offensive and must be extirpated.

If I were a young minority boy or girl with athletic talent, I would compete furiously in high school to win a college scholarship, but when I got to college I would insist upon an honest education.

If I proved to be exceptional in college, I would strive for a professional contract, and ask for as high a wage as I could command, but while I played I would be careful to acquire skills which would enable me to earn a decent living when I had to retire. I would want my owners to help me find a job, as they help white players.

And above all, I would not allow myself to be made a pattern for less-gifted minority youth to mimic. I would level with them, warn them, and try to show them that there are hundreds of jobs which offer a more productive lifetime experience than sports.

VII

Colleges and Universities

This chapter deals mainly with football and basketball, because those are the areas in which our academic institutions face their most pressing moral and financial problems, and in which, during a time of financial stringency, they cannot escape making certain value judgments. I shall be speaking a good deal about money, for which I apologize, but money is at the root of the commercialism that has overtaken certain schools. And I shall not be speaking much about track and field, swimming, baseball or women's sports, for which I also apologize, because they are not beset by the problems of outrageous recruiting.

Research began four years ago when I belatedly joined a dinner party at which a spirited conversation was under way. The party took place in a state which I shall call Jefferson. It was not in New England, nor was it New York either, for schools in those areas had long since given up big-time football; its characteristics are drawn from seven or eight representative states.

The men talking so spiritedly were doctors, lawyers and successful businessmen. Each had attended some fine university—Michigan, Stanford, Harvard or Jefferson itself—and all had doctorates or the equivalent.

They were discussing the military strategy of one of history's principal leaders, and from the reverence in which they held him I judged that it must be either Hannibal or Julius Caesar, for his command of tactics was outstanding. But then someone spoke of him as if he had been living within the past decades when his statesmanship was supreme, and I knew then that they were talking of either De Gaulle or Churchill. Finally I could control myself no longer, so I burst into their intense conversation to ask, 'Of whom are you speaking?' And a doctor turned to me and snapped impatiently, 'Honest John Taggart, of course.' He was the football coach at Jefferson, the man we have already seen in Chapter II jetting into that small Texas city to recruit Artemius Crandall.

In the conversation that followed, and in the months that I was to know these men, I discovered that nothing in their lives, not even their families, was bigger than Jefferson football; when the season came around they flew to the away games and knew the stadiums of the United States. They arranged scholarships for likely halfbacks, contributed regularly to the university's athletic fund, made special donations to help build a $680,000 press box at the stadium, and found their cultural and spiritual life within the athletic framework of a university which most of them had not attended.

The more I investigated Jefferson the more apparent it became that this state and its university epitomized the current intercollegiate scene. Attendance at the stadium was growing, but the budget faced increasing trouble. Basketball prospered, but minor sports were threatened with elimination. Recruiting of players from city playgrounds far removed from the state continued, but few of them had any right to be in an institution devoted to learning. And the hysteria with which the citizens of Jefferson idolized their teams was representative of general American attitudes.

In the rest of this book I shall be using two special terminologies. Instead of repeating the cumbersome 'colleges and universities,' I shall often use the word *schools*. This has wide acceptance in sportswriting and is most useful; I was tempted to use only the word *college*, but it has come to mean the small institution; Pomona is a college; the University of Texas with its thousands of students is not. I tried also *academic institutions*, which is accurate but which sounds terribly antiseptic or correctional. *Schools* is a useful solution. To my shame, I shall have to use repeatedly those horrible phrases *'big time'* and *'going big time'* to describe the antics of schools that seek to enter the semi-professional ranks, often with inadequate resources. I shall not use these phrases in quotation marks, but the reader can imagine the marks and my distaste.

The University of Jefferson is located, thank God say the faculty, some one hundred and eighty miles southwest of the capital, Franklin City. It is not a land-grant university, but it has always been the political darling of the state legislature and receives copious public funds. It is the socially elite institution, not only of Jefferson but of several surrounding states as well, and the doctor or politician who wishes to succeed in this region has a leg up the ladder if he has gone to Jefferson. If he also played on the football team, he is assured of a high position within his profession.

For the first fifty years of this century Jefferson participated in a tripartite athletic rivalry with Jefferson State, the land-grant agricultural college, and St. Jude's, the Catholic school in Franklin City. In basketball St. Jude's was often able to beat Jefferson, and in baseball Jeff State usually triumphed, but in football, which was what counted, Jefferson claimed the title. The three schools were also in a regional conference of seven schools, and Jefferson regularly won that championship too.

It is important to remember, however, that it was the competition among the three Jefferson schools that really mattered, and a losing season in the conference could be salvaged for either St. Jude's or Jeff State if in the closing days they managed to defeat Jefferson. Some of the notable football games in American collegiate history were played between these schools; it was difficult, in those years, to find a ticket, and from 1899 through 1950 there was never an empty seat in any of the stadiums when they met.

But starting in 1950, with the arrival of Honest John Taggart at Jefferson, things began to change. 'We're going to go really big time,' Taggart announced, but this could be done only if the alumni chipped in with financial help. Taggart then developed an amazing scouting network manned by some hundred and fifty Jefferson graduates who proselytized high school prospects across the nation; he also cultivated faculty members who would allow the athletic department to run its affairs in its own manner and who would give high marks to athletes who needed them. His prize in this regard was Dr. Mary Armbruster, in astronomy, who marked on what she herself called 'the A-B-C system. A for athletes, B for boys, C for co-eds.'

In 1951 Honest John had a winning team, 10–1, and with the leverage this provided he dropped the first shoe. He proposed that Jefferson quit the piddling conference it was in and move into one of the big-time conferences that had an opening. The next year he insisted that Jefferson remove Jeff State and St. Jude's from its schedule. He had no problem with the Catholic school, for as we shall shortly see, it was getting fed up with the 48–0 beatings the new Jefferson University was administering, but with Jeff State the situation was quite different.

It was vital that Jeff State keep Jefferson on its schedule; its whole athletic program would face disastrous consequences if this one big money-maker were lost. But Honest John was adamant. 'You can't have a big-time team with a small-time schedule,' he pointed out, and Jeff State was dropped.

As we saw in Chapter V, Honest John soon had his big-time budget up to $3,900,000, which he controlled more completely than any governor of the state had ever controlled his. In fact, the nearly half a million dollars which Taggart received from his Boosters' Club, car pool and Beef Boys was his to dispose of as he wished, as were the various special funds he solicited from ardent businessmen, like the fund for building the new press box and the one for covering a practice field with Astroturf 'so that the boys will be accustomed to it in their regular games.'

The $680,000 for the press box was an interesting story. In late May one year Taggart told the Rotary Club in Franklin City, 'I say it's a disgrace for a state like Jefferson to go really big time and then to seat reporters from *The New York Times* and *Sports Illustrated* in a strictly third-rate press box. It demeans everything our boys try to do on the field, and it cheapens the national reputation of our state.'

By the first of July, Taggart had collected more than half a million dollars, with assurances that he could have whatever more he might need. Labor unions set aside overtime requirements, and materials were hauled in free by trucking concerns, so that the press box could be dedicated in mid-September at the opening game against Oklahoma. It was mentioned favorably in newspapers throughout America, a magnificent structure which allowed the sportswriter to sit in comfort during six home games each year. It also contained luxury boxes assigned to those who had contributed over $50,000, and these also were used six times a year, but the favorable impression created by the new quarters encouraged Honest John Taggart to announce proudly, 'Now Jefferson is really big time, and the entire state can be proud.'

When the press box was finished, Honest John decided the time was ripe for a move he had long contemplated: erecting a lavish dormitory for his football players. He explained the project to legislators and potential donors: 'No coach can exercise control over his team unless the members live together. I want my boys to be insulated against the ugly pressures that develop in your normal university. I want to know what my boys are doing twenty-four hours a day. What they're eating, what pills they're taking, what their mental habits are.' His arguments were so reasonable that he was quickly given $1,450,000 to build what cynics christened The Taggart Hilton, an athletic dormitory so resplendent that the young men who lived in it for four years would rarely ever in the remaining years of their lives occupy any hotel room half so grandiose: a special kitchen, a bowling alley, a billiard room, half a dozen television sets, a weight room, a sauna, a magnificently appointed infirmary, and not a single bookcase. Here the footballers lived in splendid isolation, protected from ideas or challenging bull sessions or any student who might be reading *The National Review* or *Harper's*. Other students dubbed this gilded prison 'Hall of the Primates . . . where we keep the animals.' When Coach Taggart heard this calumny he growled, 'The students who say that are the same radicals who spit on our flag.'

Taggart was skilled in collecting money. But he always spent it with an eye as to what it could accomplish for his team. As we saw in Chapter II, he was able to recruit vigorously, for he had the cash to travel to distant towns and to take some enticing offers to the high school players he found there. In this he was aided by the wealthy men of his state, for they provided him with a fleet of five private jets which he and his coaches could use throughout the year.

Not even Taggart could have afforded the air travel he piled up if he had had to pay commercial rates. To operate a Lear jet for one hour, with its two professional pilots, costs about $800, beyond the cost of the airplane itself, which was one million dollars. Taggart and his staff flew about four hundred hours during a recruiting season, which would have cost the university $320,000, but Honest John received this free from his supporters, who found delight in helping him fashion a big-time power.

As a consequence of his money and his jets, if a likely prospect appeared on a high school team in the Pennsylvania coal regions, Taggart could compete nose-to-nose with Notre Dame, Alabama, Pitt or even Penn State. Because Jefferson was somewhat removed from the centers of population, and because Taggart had learned that it was wise to keep in touch with each prospect at least once each week, his phone bill ran over $47,000 a year, but it was money well spent, for he kept enlisting some of the best boys in the country, and they kept earning Jefferson huge sums.

To help him, Taggart had a staff of fourteen additional coaches, three trainers, two medical doctors, three equipment managers, four press agents and two traveling secretaries. A cynical newsman from the college paper once wrote: 'At Saturday's game our side had fifteen coaches in action, theirs had fourteen. On the field there were six top officials in black-and-white stripes, four lesser men to handle the lines, and two men to indicate yardage on the far side. That's forty-one grown men to supervise the play of twenty-two boys. Was something out of balance?'

Taggart's great strength lay, however, neither in recruiting nor in coaching, but in the personal assistance he was able to give the boys he brought to the campus. Each year he would recruit some ninety freshmen, even though he knew that he would ultimately find places for no more than sixteen or seventeen. He signed up the extras, he told his associates, 'so that Woody and Bear and Ara can't get their hands on them.' At all the big-time schools one soon learned that the games were really played not between the universities and not between the players, but between the coaches, for the players came and left, but the coaches continued. When Michigan faced Ohio State in a game which would decide the championship and a trip to the Rose Bowl, the signs at the motels read:

> Will the Roses go
> To Woody or Bo?

And later on when Alabama played Jefferson, bumper stickers throughout the state said:

> Honest John will dare
> To tackle the Bear.

Taggart had to be aware that he was the team, and not the boys, but he did all within his power to build their egos, keep them a happy group, and find them jobs when they left. When he read Gary Shaw's book about how useless members of the University of Texas squad were terrorized until they voluntarily surrendered their scholarships, which could then be passed along to more likely prospects, he was appalled. Never in his life had he driven a boy off his squad merely to save the few dollars of a scholarship; after he had identified among the ninety incoming freshmen the twenty or so that Jefferson could use, he took each of the others aside and laid the facts before him. 'Son,' he would say, assuming his avuncular poor-folks voice, 'you just ain't gonna make this team, and I know that's a grievous disappointment. But I'll tell you what I'm gonna do. You're gonna keep your scholarship for as long as you want it, and you can suit up every day and learn the plays on the B squad and scrimmage 'em against the varsity. And once a year, I promise you, I'm gonna take you to Oklahoma or Penn State or even Notre Dame, and we'll have Lewie send your picture back to your hometown paper provin' that you're a real football player. And you got all the privileges of a first-squad man, because I got boundless admiration for a boy who'll stick it out, because a winner never quits and a quitter never wins.

'On the other hand, son, if you should want to relinquish your scholarship right now, and let me use it for some other aspirin' boy down in Arkansas or North Carolina, I would be most proud to have it, because I could put it to good use. And in return I'll find you a job that'll pay you just as much, and you'll have your whole day free to crack books the way your momma wanted you to.'

Taggart maintained a happy squad, for he delivered on his promises. With the aid of enthusiastic alumni, and businessmen who had no connection with the university, and doctors and lawyers like the ones I had met, he paid his athletes well, finding them automobiles, jobs for their wives, summer employment for themselves, and tutors to write their papers for them. He was especially adept at handling black players from impoverished homes, for he had been a poor boy himself and knew the anxieties that accompanied that doleful estate. Frankness and honesty were the keys to his success with blacks: 'Carter, I just plain and simple can't find your wife a job in this prejudiced town, at least not one I'd allow her to take. But Mrs. Bannister—her husband owns Western United, the food chain—she under-

stands the problem, and if your wife wants to baby-sit once a week for Mrs. Bannister's daughter, who has three rambunctious kids, he'll pay your wife one hundred dollars an hour, and I advise you to take it and keep your mouth shut.'

Taggart's salary was $37,000 a year; it could have been much higher, but he said, 'It would be improper for me to earn more than the president of the university. If you want to raise my salary, raise his first.' He had a radio show on Sunday mornings and a state-wide television show on Sunday nights; his sponsor was Western United; his incidental income $113,000. He spoke frequently at business gatherings for a fee of $4,000, and admiring men in the community who appreciated what he was doing for their state saw to it that he invested his money profitably in a score of different ventures guaranteed to succeed. He was worth, conservatively calculated, close to $2,000,000.

It had been suggested numerous times that he run for the United States Senate—on the Republican ticket, of course—and impartial observers estimated that he would win, but he declined. 'I already got me one of the great jobs in America. Goddammit, I enjoy recruitin'. I enjoy flyin' into some small town in Texas or the Pennsylvania coal fields and goin' up to some door and knockin' and thinkin' as I listen for footsteps, "John Taggart, you old sombitch, you're bringin' destiny to this doorstep." And I can't wait to see who opens the door, and if it's the mother, which I always hope it is, I tell her, "Ma'am, I'm here to see if I can borrow your son for a few years and help him become a man." Because when you got the womenfolk on your side, you got a powerful agency for good.'

In a strictly profit-and-loss judgment, Jefferson had a gold mine in Honest John, and the state knew it. The stadium was always filled, and if his team appeared on national television twice a year, and then went to a bowl game, the university would have additional income of nearly a million dollars. Curiously, Taggart was not pleased with this aspect of his regime. 'The rich get richer, and the poor get poorer,' he complained frequently. 'You look at all our conferences. Ohio State and Michigan on top, followed by the eight dwarfs. I am desperately afraid the bottom teams in all our conferences will have to quit playin' big-time football. How long can they go one and ten and still collect the necessary funds? I'm not happy to see all the money comin' my way.'

He often cited the statements of two coaches as representing his thinking. Darrell Royal of Texas had said, 'The big schools should govern themselves according to their own needs. I don't want to be told what to do by Hofstra.' Taggart did not want Haverford and Colorado College and Pomona laying down the rules for Jefferson, whose problems were infinitely more complex.

And Frank Broyles of Arkansas had come close to the truth when he warned, 'The superpowers should combine in a super-league.' Taggart could see this coming. Notre Dame, Michigan, Ohio State, USC, Penn State, Alabama, Texas, Oklahoma, Nebraska, Arkansas, Jefferson and perhaps a dozen others, playing among themselves, dividing the television profits and allowing schools like Harvard and Iowa and Washington State and Vanderbilt to play at a much lower level without the headaches of big-time football, or a big-time budget. And then the little schools like Williams and Tufts and Augustana and Reed playing one-platoon informal games, or even touch.

'We big ones have a national responsibility,' Taggart often said. 'The nation looks to us for leadership. The boys of this country dream of comin' to our schools. We set the moral standards for the nation, and if we diminished football, it would be a national catastrophe, for it's on our fields that the character of this nation is built. I know of nothin' in American life more significant and worthy than hard, honest football played between equals, and if you bother to look at the television ratings, you'll find most Americans agree.'

As a consequence of his outstanding record in conference and bowl games, Taggart became a popular speaker at football clinics and banquets, and his best quotes became a portrait of the successful coach:

> . . . Victory is the natural estate of the self-respectin' man. Victory over poverty through hard work. Victory over enemies through justifiable war. Victory over ridiculous ideas at the ballot box. And victory over death through religion. I do not care to associate with men who are prepared to accept defeat.

> . . . When a boy steps on my football field he knows that I am the boss. No long hair. No mustaches. No alcohol except beer when we celebrate a victory. No drugs, by God, no drugs. And a decent sense of respect toward authority. In return he is assured of my loyalty. I see that he keeps his scholarship, that he gets the money he needs in an emergency, that silly traffic tickets are taken care of, that his name keeps out of the papers if he gets into some minor trouble. And I do my damnedest, night and day, to see that he keeps up his grades and that he graduates. At last count 87 percent of my boys got their degrees, oftentimes in six years, but they got 'em.

> . . . Three times Jefferson has ranked number one nationally, and we'd have had it twice more except that I had to suspend our all-American quarterback in 1968 and our defensive captain in 1972 right before our big games. I never hesitated one minute. They broke the rules. They were out. Every boy who plays for me knows that the application of our rules is relentless. They are on this team to obey, to be self-respectin' men, and to win their victories through the only way God allows a man to win anything, through discipline.

> . . . I sort of get sick to my stomach when some faculty committee issues a statement that my boys should be scholars first and athletes second. Any

self-respectin' man with his head screwed on right must realize that football consumes so much of a boy's time, fall, winter, spring and summer, that he simply ain't got time to be a scholar too. If we didn't have a supply of snap courses, and cooperatin' professors who know the score, ain't no way my boys could stay in school. We hire them to play football, and we pay them well to do it, and it's only after their eligibility is used up that they got time to be scholars.

. . . The job of a real woman is to support and console her man while he fights for victory. No self-respectin' woman would bother with this Women's Lib stuff. And as for playin' on the same team with boys, that's plain revoltin'. Archery and field hockey, that's what a self-respectin' co-ed would want, and that's what they're gonna get.

. . . What am I proudest of during my reign at Jefferson? This may astonish you, but it isn't the three national championships. Nor my twenty-nine superstars who are now playin' in the NFL bringin' honor to this state. No. Believe it or not, it's this press box we're sittin' in. You ever see the old one? What a shambles. I felt ashamed when the big-time sportswriters from *The New York Times* and *Sports Illustrated* used to come out here and climb those rickety stairs. So one Thursday at Rotary, I said, 'Jefferson ought to go first class. If we're really big time, let's be big time.' And within five weeks I had me $500,000 for a press box of which this state could be proud. I taught a whole state to go first class.

The success of Honest John Taggart and his Jefferson team came partly at the expense of Jeff State, for when he broke up the old conference one year and dropped Jeff State from his schedule the next, the agricultural school was left in disarray. Its big money-making game was gone; its ability to compete for local football players was destroyed, and its position in the affections of the state threatened.

Under the lash of energetic alumni it fled to a disastrous solution. 'We'll go big time, too,' one of the wealthy alumni said, and he bulldozed a plan whereby Jeff State would build its own massive stadium, seating 55,000 and with a press box at least equal to the one at Jefferson. But when the stadium was finished, at an unpaid cost of $8,000,000, the drab Jeff State team could not begin to fill it even one day a year, let alone six.

The great concrete hole in the ground became a suppurating abscess; student fees had to be raised to $48 a semester, the bulk of the money going to pay off the interest on the bonded indebtedness. Year after year, playing mediocre opponents, Jeff State compiled records of 2–9 and even 0–11. And as the teams deteriorated, coaches were fired, often with accompanying scandal, and new coaches found it impossible to recruit players who would improve the won-lost record.

Then ugly jokes began to proliferate. There had always been bad blood between Jefferson, the gentlemen's school, and State, the farmers' outpost, and in the old days there had occasionally been riots, as in 1922 when Jefferson had an unbeaten season going into the last game against a badly underdog State. The farmers had won a miraculous victory, to celebrate which they burned down a Jefferson dormitory. It was then that the jokes began.

'It's lucky Jeff State didn't end the season number one, because they wouldn't know how many fingers to hold up.'

'When the astronauts brought rocks back from the moon they sent samples to all the great universities in the country for analysis, but when they got to Jeff State they had no more moon rocks left, so they sent a boy out to a pasture to pick up some, and after six months of intense study the Jeff State lab sent back this report: "We found no traces of precious metals and no signs of vulcanism, but we can state without fear of successful contradiction that the cow really did jump over the moon." '

'This town was invaded by rats, so they mobilized the Jeff State ROTC to fight them off, and at the end of the campaign the commanding officer reported, "Rats repulsed. Our losses minimal but significant. Three of our men lost hand-to-hand combats with enemy soldiers. Two of our men defected to their side. And three of our junior officers married members of the enemy's female brigade." '

While absorbing such constant abuse, Jeff State was transforming itself into a major scientific center, one of the best of its kind in America. Since it was repeatedly selected by the federal government to conduct major research in foodstuffs, river movements, ecology, building materials and pest control, it not only received huge grants which allowed it to erect a chain of splendid laboratories, but it also stood rather closer to the problems of our national life than the more detached university at Jefferson. Its professors headed significant research committees and served on presidential inquiries. One of its young men was seriously considered for a Nobel Prize as a result of his work on air pollution, and it was expected that he would get it at some future date.

Because of its burgeoning reputation, graduates of Jeff State found it rather easier to land good jobs than did the graduates of the university, but in spite of such accomplishments, State continued to be held in low esteem by the general public because its football team performed so poorly.

Then a curious thing happened, one that had occurred in other American states. Legislators elected by the state's cities were usually graduates of Jefferson University; Jeff State produced the legislators from rural areas, and there were always more of the latter than the former. So the question of football was moved off the playing fields and into the legislature, with both houses of the Jefferson governing body spending days and even weeks debating whether or not Jefferson University should be compelled by law to play Jefferson State in football.

The legislators split into factions; every bill that came before them was determined not on its merits but, rather, on its impact on the football question. At one point the rural legislators actually passed a bill terminating all funds and perquisites for Jefferson until such time as it placed Jeff State on its schedule, but this frivolity was challenged by Honest John Taggart, who appeared at a public hearing to state, in funereal tones, 'The one thing that the great state of Jefferson has to be proud of is its football team. We are really big time, and sportswriters across this nation speak of us with respect. I warn you that if you force us to move backward in our schedulin', if you force us to relinquish the hard-won position we have attained, you will set this whole state back a hundred years.'

The bill was vetoed by the governor, but at the risk of his political career; rural legislators swore that from that day he could count on them for no support, and they advised their constituents that henceforth the governor was a man to be destroyed; they predicted that at the next election he would be thrown out of office.

In the meantime, State's pathetic football team staggered on to one dismal season after another, led by one ineffective coach after another, and with two or three good players recruited from the Pennsylvania coal fields but unable to accomplish much because they had no teammates who knew what big-time football really entailed. Jeff State became a classic case of a fine university being dragged down unnecessarily by an ineffective athletic policy.

Why didn't State just quit football and rid itself of this heavy incubus? On frequent occasions the faculty raised this question, but those who did were quietly threatened with dismissal at the best or lynching at the worst. Startled alumni swore that State would rise again. Legislators insisted that the honor of State would one day be restored. And citizens of the area, who had no association with the school except that their tax dollars helped support it, agreed that it would be shameful for a potentially great school like State to abandon football.

'The stadium's already there,' they reasoned. 'What would we do with it?' So the travesty continued. State, with a yearly athletic budget of $1,063,000, was determined to compete with Jefferson, which had $3,900,000 in cash plus the use of five Lear jets.

St. Jude's, a church college that had to balance its budget or go out of business, handled its athletic problems rather more sensibly. In the late 1940s when it became apparent that The Saints would never be able to keep up with Jefferson University in football, or with Jeff State in its ability to get funds from the legislature, the priests who ran the school convened their advisors and a group of hard-nosed alumni in a three-day planning session. Spelling out the fiscal facts, Father Sylvester said, 'Gentlemen, it's either find an additional million and a half dollars each year for ten years or drop football. There is no middle ground even worth discussing.'

Those were rather sharp alternatives, and the advisors concluded, 'It looks like we have only one choice.'

But a wise priest, who had followed the experiences of other Catholic schools, said, 'I'm content that we drop football, but as we do so, let's pick up basketball. '

So the decision was made, but not publicized. St. Jude's continued football until all its scholarship boys had graduated, then announced on January 1, 1954, that it was forthwith discontinuing that sport on the intercollegiate level.

An explosion followed. Alumni, who understood the financial impossibility of continuing, supported Father Sylvester, and so did the student body, but the media jumped on him as if he had profaned the Vatican. Repeatedly, the newspapers accused him of having betrayed the honor of St. Jude's, of having cut at the heart of a noble institution.

On the 1928 team St. Jude's had produced a prodigious tackle, Ev Poroba, who had gained permanent local fame as the school's only all-American. Reporters now sought him out and wrote doleful stories about how Ev felt that his old school had lost its sense of honor, and one cartoonist showed him brooding at the side of a cemetery where the fame and dignity of his college lay buried.

But the Jesuit fathers who ran St. Jude's were not foolish men; they had no intention of being booby-trapped by either the football coach, who deplored the decision, or Ev Poroba, who continued to lament. At the start of the basketball season they presented a team with two towering blacks they had recruited in New York, and with these excellent players the Saints proceeded to mop up the Missouri Valley, then, moving into the Atlantic Coast conference, to throw scares into teams like Duke, Maryland and the North Carolina geniuses.

In the years that followed, St. Jude's became one of the real basketball powers. There are few men in this country of more undeviating purpose than a devout Jesuit who has discovered a black high school star six-feet-ten who can average twenty-three points a game and eleven rebounds. And if the young giant happens to be attending a Catholic high school in New York, which many do, the recruiting becomes a subtle art, with unexpected complications developing from all sides.

For one-eighth of the budget St. Jude's had once spent on a less than mediocre football team of fifty-two expensively uniformed players, it now

'54–0! What the hell do they do with my alumni dues?'

had close to a national champion in basketball, with sixteen players dressed in shorts and sneakers. And where the athletic department had been losing $265,000 a year, it was now showing a profit of $145,000.

But if Father Sylvester had ever thought that getting out of the football racket and into basketball would somehow relieve him of ugly pressures, he was soon enlightened as to the facts. In football, which is a game of mass movement, no one player can of himself turn a college team around, not even the greatest star. A stellar fullback can do only so much if his offensive line is weak; and when the defense plays he is not even on the field. Many teams with four great running backs find themselves losing by scores of 28–23 and 37–32.

But in basketball one real star can mean the difference, because he plays both offense and defense, and he is one of only five players, not one of twenty-six as in football (eleven offense, eleven defense, two kickers, two run-back specialists). And if a new contender like St. Jude's is lucky enough to land two superstars, they find themselves in immediate contention for the national crown.

However, the competition for such superstars is brutal, and St. Jude's found itself spending as much money to land one basketball player as it used to spend to recruit six football players. As Father Sylvester told his board, 'I do believe that if in a high school game tomorrow afternoon a six-foot-ten basketball player suddenly broke loose and showed himself to be a potential superstar, with thirty points and fifteen rebounds, by Friday night Frank McGuire would have heard about him in South Carolina, and Digger Phelps at Notre Dame, and Dick Harter out in Oregon. We're all after the same twelve or thirteen great ones, and our little college competes with Marquette and Bradley and Villanova and Creighton. Mark my words, if our Catholic schools continue to fight for black players the way we do, we'll convert the whole black race to Catholicism, which may turn out to be the answer.'

Various questions have to be asked about the St. Jude's approach. Last year I visited the $7,000,000 palestra in which the team plays and found it an athletic paradise, something that Kublai Khan might have devised. There were unobstructed seats for 15,400 spectators and a perfect playing surface, but what enchanted me were the locker rooms. The floors were covered with carpeting, even the room for the showers, and the basketball players, when they undressed after a game, simply left their duds on the carpet. Uniformed attendants moved in, picked up the suits, and conveyed them to the laundromat next to the shower. On and on it went, with whipcord blazers and three pairs of shoes for each player, donated by enthusiastic merchants; cars for all the players, on loan from an agency; mounted police protecting them when they moved back to their training dormitory; and adulation unbounded. What surprised me was that all this expenditure was for sixteen young men out of a student body of eleven thousand.

'When the rule came in allowing us to play freshmen,' explained the coach, 'we had no further need for a freshman team, so we dropped it. And with the emphasis we were putting on our varsity, we couldn't afford a junior varsity, so we dropped that too. We identify the best sixteen and spend all our efforts on them. Now if a boy comes to us on scholarship, and we see that he can't cut the mustard, why, we take him aside and say, "Look, Eddie, or Tom or whatever his name is. You were real great in high school, but you just aren't going to make it here at St. Jude's. Look at the men ahead of you. Look at the great freshmen who'll always be better than you are. But if you want to stay with basketball, you can help me run the locker room, or the publicity office, or help with practice, or whatever." '

St. Jude's runs its entire basketball program, involving a $7,000,000 palestra and a yearly budget of about $650,000, for just sixteen players.

But such a program can pay off. In recent years two unknown schools, starting from scratch, have exploded into the big time. Austin Peay, a new university in Tennessee, named after a local politician, recruited just one superstar from the asphalt courts of Brooklyn, Fly Williams, and overnight Peay became national news, with Fly standing second in national scoring at 29.9 points a game.

Oral Roberts, in Tulsa, enjoyed an even more spectacular rise. A religious school founded by the famous faith healer, it boasted a topflight campus costing $40,000,000, plus a healthy endowment and a basketball-social center costing $5,500,000. From the moment of opening, Reverend Roberts knew what he wanted. He has said, 'I believe that athletics has a mission to bring people to God, and a great university like ours must have a team. Football is too expensive and it requires the university to find too many star players. Basketball is simpler. We'll specialize in basketball.'

And he did. Combing the south, he came up with a first group of really fine players who, in their first two years among the small colleges, went 21–5 and 27–4 while running up enormous scores. He decided to enter the major-college division, where he had the same spectacular success. He then started recruiting nationwide, attracting a handful of first-rate players who took the school to the NCAA play-offs and the NIT in New York. When I wrote this they were in the semi-finals of the latter tournament, having defeated teams that looked on paper to be much more powerful than they.

Oral Roberts—the minister, that is, not the school—uses extraordinary devices to lure spectators into the coliseums when his university plays. When they came into Madison Square Garden in December 1971 to participate in a doubleheader, he sent 55,957 letters to his followers in the metropolitan area, pleading with them to attend the game:

> Like everything else at Oral Roberts, athletics is part of our Christian witness. The players on our basketball team are all Christian boys. When we received this invitation to play in Madison Square Garden, we felt led of the Lord to make it an opportunity of witness.

Records of the game in which Oral Roberts defeated Hofstra 83–74, after having been down by five at the half, show that only 7,286 paying customers appeared, and more than three-quarters of these came to see the other teams. Disappointed though he may have been, after the game Reverend Roberts assembled some 750 of his followers in the rotunda of the Garden and assured them that 'this was a victory for God, not for basketball.'

From studying such programs in football and basketball I have developed certain convictions as to how an average American college or university ought to structure its athletic program, but before I make any prescription I must share with the reader my personal predilections, so that he will be better able to assess what I am about to propose.

First, the United States is the only nation in the world, so far as I know, which demands that its schools like Harvard, Ohio State and Claremont assume responsibility for providing the public with sports entertainment. Ours is a unique system which has no historical sanction or application elsewhere. It would be unthinkable for the University of Bologna, a most ancient and honorable school, to provide scholarships to illiterate soccer players so that they could entertain the other cities of northern Italy, and it would be equally preposterous for either the Sorbonne or Oxford to do so in their countries. Our system is an American phenomenon, a historical accident which developed from the exciting football games played by Yale and Harvard and to a lesser extent Princeton and certain other schools during the closing years of the nineteenth century. If we had had at that time professional teams which provided public football entertainment, we might not have placed the burden on our schools. But we had no professional teams, so our schools were handed the job.

Second, if an ideal American educational system were being launched afresh, few would want to saddle it with the responsibility for public sports entertainment. I certainly would not. But since, by a quirk of history, it is so saddled, the tradition has become ingrained and I see not the remotest chance of altering it. I therefore approve of continuing it, so long as certain safeguards are installed. Categorically, I believe that our schools must continue to offer sports entertainment, even though comparable institutions throughout the rest of the world are excused from doing so.

Third, I see nothing wrong in having a college or a university provide training for the young man or woman who wants to devote his adult life to sports. My reasoning is twofold: 1) American society has ordained that sports shall be a major aspect of our national life, with major attention, major financial support and major coverage in the media. How possibly can a major aspect of life be ignored by our schools? 2) If it is permissible to train young musicians and actors in our universities, and endow munificent departments to do so, why is it not equally legitimate to train young athletes, and endow them with a stadium?

Fourth, because our schools have volunteered to serve as unpaid training grounds for future professionals, and because some of the lucky schools with good sports reputations can earn a good deal of money from the semi-professional football and basketball teams they operate, the temptation to recruit young men skilled at games but totally unfitted for academic work is overpowering. We must seriously ask if such behavior is legitimate for an academic institution. There are honorable answers, and I know some of them, but if we do not face this matter forthrightly, we are going to run into trouble. I could fill the rest of this chapter with hilarious stories of recruiting mishaps, but I no longer find them amusing.

The first of the two men who impressed me with their insights regarding these problems was Don Canham, the charismatic former track coach and businessman who was selected some years ago to guide athletic affairs at the University of Michigan. I spent part of two days with him in November 1973, just prior to the dramatic game with Ohio State that would determine which team would go to the Rose Bowl.

'I'm so excited about this damned game, I don't think I'll be able to stay and watch it,' he told me. 'I'll put in an appearance at the stadium and then duck out. Because this game means everything to us.'

'Under Big Ten rules,' I asked, 'isn't it really immaterial whether you go to the Rose Bowl or not? Don't you get your share of the gate whether you play or not?'

'Technically correct, but you miss the important point,' he said, rising and walking about his office near the hockey rink that had been recently built in the old Yost Field House. 'The Big Ten earns about one million dollars from the Rose Bowl, and each of our ten teams shares the split. We get about one hundred thousand. So it's not the money that counts. It's that public exposure the visiting coach gets on television.'

'Is television that important?'

'It's everything. Ohio State went out last year. Woody Hayes was all over the screen, pre-game, middle of the game, post-game. Very quiet. Very gentlemanly. Saying all the right things. I could visualize families in every small town telling their boys, "That's the kind of coach you ought to have, son." If he goes back this year, and appears on television again, we might have to stop recruiting in certain areas.

'Look, I have an enormous hole in the ground out there. Seats 105,500. And it's my job to keep it filled.' He showed me a copy of the radical advertisement he had been running in national magazines. 'How to Mix Business with Pleasure . . . Try Michigan Football.' It was a classy Madison Avenue pitch to businessmen in all parts of America to do their business entertaining at a Michigan game: 'Tailgate picnics . . . the nation's top marching band . . . every seat excellent . . . a unique way to entertain . . . Michigan has won three Big Ten titles in the last four years . . . send me your ticket needs and I will personally attend to them.' While ticket sales at some Big Ten schools were declining, Michigan's were growing.

But Canham was not resting on his laurels. 'If we don't win tomorrow, and get Bo Schembechler on national TV, we're in trouble. Because when you recruit, the basics you can offer a boy are little better than what the other guy can offer. But if you can go into the family kitchen and say, "Son, if you come to Michigan, you'll be on national TV. Your family can sit right here and see you. On national TV." '

He paused, then said confidentially, 'You take . . .' (and he named a team which I will not disclose). 'How can they possibly compete with Ohio State or us? They're never on TV. They never make a bowl trip. What can they promise the boy in high school? That's why, the way things are now, the rich get richer and the poor get poorer.'

I rattled off the names of eight teams which stood near the bottom of their various conferences. 'Can they possibly survive?'

'I have the gravest doubts. Take . . .' (and he specified a team I knew to be in trouble). 'How can they expect their state legislature to keep pouring money down their rat hole? Three years in a row 1–10, except once it was 0–11. They can't possibly recruit if the boy they're talking to knows these figures. And I'll tell you this. You let Ohio State dominate the next two or three Rose Bowls, with Woody Hayes on national TV saying all the proper things, and we'll have a rough time recruiting too . . . 105,500 spectators or not. Because today's player wants national exposure, hopes to land a professional contract—and TV's the only way to do it.'

But when I asked if conferences like the Big Ten or the Southeastern might have to disband, he said, 'Never! Because any club in either of the conferences you named has the capacity to rise from the ashes. Look at the records,' and he showed me a table giving the finishing positions of the Big Ten from 1960 through 1972 (I have added 1973–75) and this showed graphically the ebb and flow of success during that period. In that span every school except Northwestern had won the title at least once.

THE BIG TEN—FINAL STANDINGS, 1960–1975

	60	61	62	63	64	65	66	67	68	69	70	71	72	73	74	75
Illinois	5	10	8	1	4	5	3	5	8	10	10	3	6	4	5	3
Indiana	10	9	9	10	10	9	9	1*	5	5	10	9	6	10	10	10
Iowa	1*	7	5	8	10	10	10	10	5	5	4	10	9	10	7	7
Michigan	5	6	10	5	1	7	3	5	2	1*	2	1	1*	1*	1*	2
Michigan State	4	3	5	2	6	1	1	5	7	9	5	3	4	4	3	3
Minnesota	1*	2	2	9	4	3	5	1*	3	4	7	6	5	3	7	8
Northwestern	5	7	3	5	7	6	7	8	8	5	2	2	10	4	7	9
Ohio State	3	1	3	2	2	2	6	4	1	1*	1	3	1*	1*	1*	1
Purdue	5	4	5	4	3	3	2	1*	3	3	8	6	3	4	6	3
Wisconsin	9	5	1	5	7	7	7	10	10	5	5	6	8	8	4	6

*Tied for first place

I pointed to the poor records of Iowa, Indiana and Wisconsin, and asked if they might be forced to withdraw.

'Not so,' Canham protested. 'Any one of them could turn it around in a couple of years.' But I doubted the possibility, given the financial and publicity advantages Ohio State and Michigan enjoyed. 'The Big Two and the Eight Dwarfs' was the way cynics were referring to the conference.

Then Canham showed me a rough of his budget for 1973–74. 'We'll handle about four million dollars. We'll spend about four million, one hundred thousand, with some seven hundred thousand going to grants-in-aid to student athletes.'

'How much goes to servicing debt on past expenditures?'

'About two hundred thousand dollars. And another two hundred thousand for improving our facilities with things like Tartan Turf for the stadium and a new running track.'

I asked how much income he got from television and he had the figures: 'Well over two hundred thousand dollars plus another hundred thousand from the Rose Bowl, even though we didn't go last year.'

And so it went, the fiscal report of a brilliant man who knew that he could keep his system viable only by excessive advertising of a constantly winning team. 'That's why the game tomorrow is so crucial,' he said. 'We've got to win. We've simply got to win. To keep our image before the national audience.'

As you may remember, the game that year (1973) was a tingler. Ohio State rushed to a 10–0 lead at the half, and it should have been more like 28–0 if Woody Hayes had used his talent properly. I could visualize Don Canham at home, his head in his hands, dreading the second half.

But at the whistle Michigan sprang to life and kicked Ohio State all around the stadium. Quickly they tied the game at 10–10, and then put on two magnificent drives, each of which ended in a missed field goal. The game was a draw but Michigan clearly was the better team.

By all the rules of logic and precedent Michigan should have been selected to represent the Big Ten in the Rose Bowl against Southern California; Ohio State had gone the preceding year; Michigan had been superior in the tie game; and it would do well in California. However, in one of the closing plays Michigan's stellar quarterback, Dennis Franklin, had suffered a damaged throwing arm when an Ohio State player tackled him needlessly. The athletic directors of the Big Ten, who then had responsibility for selecting the conference representative when two teams tied for first, held a poorly disciplined phone discussion Saturday night and Sunday morning, and decided that Michigan without quarterback Franklin was too great a risk. Anxious to pick up any extra publicity, they selected Ohio State, and Woody Hayes was on national television again.

In 1974 Michigan and Ohio State again played for the championship, and this time Woody won by the score of 12–10. So for the third straight year he dominated the New Year's Day television channels, and Michigan's problem of recruiting worsened.

It was perverse. Over a period of three years Don Canham's Michigan had compiled the best record in the nation, 30–2–1, and had probably been one of the top two or three teams if not the top, yet by the fall of the cards it had appeared in not one bowl game.

At various times I kept asking Canham three questions which perplex football people today. 'Should the Big Ten drop its restrictive rule which allows only one representative to play in a Bowl Game each year?' Canham says yes, the present rule, which also operates in the Pacific Eight Conference, prevents the best teams from competing. Michigan is strongly of the opinion that it has been discriminated against in this regard. It should have been in three bowl games, with attendant financial and publicity returns. (In 1975 the Big Ten altered its rules, allowing second-place Michigan to play Oklahoma in the Orange Bowl.)

'Is Frank Broyles of Arkansas right when he suggests that the various conferences break up, with the top teams from all parts of the country joining with the major independents to form a super-league?' Canham, in late 1973, rejected this proposal, but the expert manner in which he discussed it satisfied me that he has at least contemplated the possibility. He said that he could see no advantage to a super-league in which the Michigans, Ohio States and Notre Dames competed against themselves. He rather preferred the present system of a mixed schedule, but when I pointed out that teams like Oklahoma were massacring their opponents, because they played so many patsies whom they should not be playing, he said that this could be corrected by more realistic scheduling. But it seemed to me that every correction he suggested could better be made by establishing a super-league, and that before too many years passed, he would become an advocate.

'Why is the Big Eight consistently the best conference in the nation?' Canham bristled at this heresy, to which I was a convert, and stoutly denied it, affirming his faith in the true religion, the Big Ten. My points were manifold: that this western league which comprised Oklahoma, Oklahoma State, Kansas, Kansas State, Iowa State, Missouri, Colorado and Nebraska was better balanced than the others, with the bottom teams always capable of knocking off the top; that for long stretches it produced the national champion, or at least the realistic one; that it appeared to present a better brand of play; that it yearly sent at least half of its members to bowl games; that it sent more graduates into the professional ranks; etc. etc. One by one he knocked down my arguments. The Big Eight awarded more full scholarships. Its rules were so flexible that all its teams could garner bowl money if invitations were extended. (In one year, five of eight did.) And it dominated its geographic area. At the end of Canham's spirited rebuttal I got the impression that the Big Ten represented class, while the Big Eight were the parvenus, and I will admit that he shook some of my preconceptions. Regarding the defense of standards, the Big Ten is still a majestic conference; regarding scoring power I'd still take the Big Eight, and if one hundred interconference games were scheduled involving all the teams over a span of years, I would expect the Big Eight to prevail by about 70–30.

If I were president of either a Big Ten or a Big Eight university, I'd want Don Canham as my athletic director. He's young; he's sharp; he sees the total picture as well as anyone; and he's innovative. He has that great hole in the ground which seats 105,500 people, and he keeps it more or less filled while operating under the strict rules of one of America's top universities. I am not sure that Canham could do the same at Iowa or South Carolina or Washington State, but he'd certainly give it a try. In the meantime, Michigan, with its multiple championships in all sports, is a mecca in the university scene.

The second man on whom I relied for guidance came to my attention by accident, and a most fortunate one it was. I had spoken on cultural matters to a gathering of college presidents, and afterwards they asked me if there was anything they might do to reciprocate, and I surprised them by saying that I'd like to talk with some of them about athletic programs at their schools. So they convened an informal breakfast meeting at which Stephen Horn of Long Beach gave the details of his sad experience when one of his coaches ran wild, got Long Beach put on probation, cost his players a chance at a title, and then moved on to a better job. Bud Davis, of Idaho State, related an even sadder story. When Colorado won the Big Eight championship in 1961 and went to the Orange Bowl, grotesque irregularities were uncovered, and its popular coach had to be fired. In an inexplicable move, the football-crazy university appointed as his successor Davis, the alumni director, who would lead his team to such triumphs as Iowa State 57–Colorado 19, Oklahoma 62–Colorado 0 and Missouri 57–Colorado 0. Says Davis, 'When we played Missouri, we could get only twenty-five able-bodied players on the plane, and when we landed at Columbia only twenty-three were brave enough to get off.'

The student body, having anticipated the horrendous season that lay ahead, had groaned when Davis' appointment was announced, and that night they hanged him in effigy, 'the only coach in American collegiate history,' says Davis, 'who was hanged *before* the season started. Somebody in that crowd was clairvoyant.'

The presidents had brought with them a man I did not know, either in fact or reputation, and he turned out to be the gem of the morning. He was a tall, well-groomed scholar with a deceptive Irish brogue that could have been a New England heritage, an obvious love of sports and a genial approach to the follies of this world. He was George H. Hanford, executive vice-president of the influential College Entrance Examination Board of Princeton. For the past six months he had been on leave, conducting a preliminary study for the American Council on Education to determine whether it should launch a full-scale investigation of college and university athletics similar to the famous report issued by the Carnegie Foundation in 1929. His findings, published in a mimeographed edition of a few copies, were titled *An Inquiry into the Need for and Feasibility of a National Study of Intercollegiate Athletics.* In other words, Hanford had been applying his considerable intelligence to all the questions dealt with in this chapter.

He did not provide answers. His *Inquiry* was merely an outline of the complexity of intercollegiate sports; scores of enticing topics could have been developed into chapter length, but Hanford merely said, 'Here is something worth looking into.' What he provided was an outline of contemporary problems under headings such as these:

Sports in society today	Commercialism in college athletics
Amateur versus professional	Professional sports and the media
Alumni attitudes	Competitive excesses
Minorities	Economics
Women	Sports and education
The counterculture	Moral issues
Congressional attitudes	Sports and human rights

I was particularly interested in one section which reflected his reaction to my Criterion III: *Sports have an obligation to provide public entertainment.* Hanford tackles this presumption in a section titled 'Intercollegiate Athletics as Entertainment.'

> There is no doubt that big-time college sports programs are in fact in the entertainment business whether they like it or not . . . It is on the issue of whether they should be in the business in the first place that opinions differ. Those who argue against the proposition do so mainly on the philosophical ground that public entertainment is neither traditionally nor properly a function of higher education, period. Those who support the proposition do so on essentially three grounds. First, like it or not, the institutions have assumed a responsibility which they cannot now abdicate. The second ground is economic. Even though college sports may not pay for themselves, they provide a focus for alumni, taxpayer and legislator attention which has an indirect payoff in general financial support for the institution. The third argument is philosophical and rests on the logic that colleges and universities have traditionally and properly been providing entertainment of many kinds over the years. They see inconsistency in the logic of those who find lectures, concerts, recitals and plays acceptable but disapprove of football. They find intercollegiate sports, big-time and low-profile, less corrupting *on the whole* than some other features of higher education. And they call attention to the desirability of an institution's cultivating a variety of constituencies for economic support and that big-time sports in particular attract such support. The inquiry found validity in the arguments of both camps and suggests that the issue for consideration in a national study is related not to sports entertainment as entertainment but to sports entertainment as big business.

I was gratified to find that Hanford's concern with the problem was much the same as mine; he was not, however, willing to accept as an axiom my belief that collegiate sports were obligated to provide entertainment.

In every area Hanford pinpointed the hot issues; in each he indicated how a national survey ought to proceed, if one were authorized by the Council. His slim report should be published for the national audience; it is available to experts and no one should make major decisions in this field without consulting it.

In some ways, the best part of the report is the voluminous Appendices, A through I, which give the basic data from which Hanford worked. These are remarkable documents, well worth detailed study. Only one hundred copies of the Appendices were mimeographed, and I suppose the supply has long been exhausted, but they should be available in major study centers. I list the subject matter:

A: Alvarez, Carlos, a law student at Duke University: Current litigation involving intercollegiate athletics.

B: Atwell, Robert H., president of Pitzer College: Financial problems of intercollegiate athletics.

C: Beasley, Jerry, doctoral candidate at Stanford: State politics of intercollegiate athletics.

D: Brown, Roscoe C., Jr., Director of the Institute of Afro-American Affairs, New York University, assisted by six experts: The black athlete.

E: Froomkin, Joseph, head of a firm specializing in the analysis of public questions: General factors influencing sports in the post-secondary field.

F: Ireland, Bernard P., director of admissions at Columbia College: New circumstances influencing the conduct of intercollegiate sports since the Carnegie Study of 1929.

G: Lowi, Theodore J., professor of political science at Cornell: Campus, society and the place of amateur sports.

H: McKeown, Mary, doctor of education, University of Illinois: Women in intercollegiate athletics.

I: Springer, Felix, doctoral candidate at Columbia University: The experience of senior colleges that have discontinued football.

Anyone offering a course in Sports in American Society, and there are many such courses being given today, could well use these two documents as syllabi, for Hanford lays out the problem, and the Appendices provide the study data.

It is quite obvious that intercollegiate football and basketball, as now played, are semi-professional sports in most schools and professional in others. This should be publicly acknowledged; I see nothing to be gained by denying it and much to be lost. My concern is therefore how best to administer a professional entertainment program within the normal guidelines that now operate, and I would wish to hear no complaint that 'Things oughtn't to be this way in a self-respecting institution of higher learning,' because they are that way and our society intends that they remain that way. We are faced with a *fait accompli,* but we can administer it somewhat better than we are now doing.

Our colleges and universities should divide themselves into four groups, with the understanding that a school might elect to be in Group One for certain sports and Group Two or Three in others. The decision would be left to the school, but once it was made, the school would place itself under the jurisdiction of the group it has chosen.

Group One would consist of those schools who wished to compete in a super-league, with all its television contracts, bowl games and national publicity. In these schools, perhaps thirty-six in number, players would be paid a salary for performing, and I would think they might therefore want to be unionized, as are the members of dance bands which play at college festivals. To bring some order into recruiting, which might otherwise become even more vicious than it is now, I would propose a national draft of the best five hundred high school football players, and the best three hundred basketball players. Group One schools would assemble at some neutral point, or conduct the draft by telephone as the pros do, and would select in reverse order of last year's standings. I grant that this would tend to diminish the perpetual superiority of football teams like Notre Dame, Oklahoma and USC, for they could no longer pick off the prize apples, as they now do, but it might produce a larger crop of first-class teams and save the sport for all of them.

It would be practical, I think, for the super-teams to pool their recruiting resources and support one master group of scouts who would tour the high schools and send back reports which would be computerized for all to see. This works in the pros, and we are speaking now of a junior pro league, so I believe it would work there too. This would not prevent Ohio State from maintaining its select group of super-scouts reporting personally to Woody Hayes, but it would enable the lower teams in the standings to draft wisely and thus improve their chances.

If such a draft is not initiated, I see no alternative but to continue the present insane procedure which led some two hundred and fifty colleges and universities to compete for one black high school boy who could not possibly have understood any college class, and for several of them to send highly paid coaches to live in his small town during the latter part of the season, so as to apply daily pressure on him to register at their schools. The excellent series of articles on recruiting assembled by reporters from *The New York Times* and published in their issues starting on Sunday, March 10, 1974, outlined the lengths to which high school players were being corrupted by college scouts, and since then the situation has worsened.

For some years the NCAA had a sensible, if complicated, rule that no institution of higher learning ought to enroll a boy who could not read or write at the college level. The experts devised a list of criteria—school records, scores on generalized tests, predictability scores—which were to be applied to all applicants, and if the young man showed that he could not possibly maintain a 1.6 average in college, which is about a D, he should not be considered college material. Anyone with a good fourth-grade education should have been able to bust the system for a 1.6, but it was appalling how many would-be professional athletes could not.

Various scandals arose when extra-eager coaches at either the high school or college level altered grades to enable their athletes to pass the 1.6 barrier, and so much pressure was put on college coaches to play ineligible men and thus risk reprimand that the NCAA junked the 1.6 and substituted a 2.0 rule which took all the onus off the college and placed it on the high school. Now all that is required is for the high school, even the weakest in the nation, to certify that a boy has averaged 2.0 during his high school career, and he is entitled to play in college!

The chicanery that such a rule encourages is scandalous. Not only do many high schools grant a 2.0 average if a warm body appears in class without slugging the teacher, but those who do try to maintain standards will now be under extreme pressure to grant a promising athlete any grade he requires to bring his average up to 2.0, whether he attends class or not. Bill Hunt, who rides shotgun for the NCAA, told *The New York Times:*

> Violations of these academic rules are definitely on the increase. You have the high school figuring out what it takes to get a 2.0 for the boy and then giving such a grade where needed. We've had boys go into their senior year with a 1.7 average and get a 3.0 average in their senior year so they have a 2.0 for high school. Sometimes he hasn't even attended classes in his senior year. If we'd made the rule a 2.5 needed average, they'd have given the athletes 2.5 averages.

Deplorable conditions have been allowed to proliferate. Numerous cases have surfaced in which high school faculties have given honest grades showing that students in their classes have not come even close to passing, only to have athletic departments falsify official transcripts so that young athletes turn up with A's and B's where they originally had D's and F's. I have six such cases on my desk as I write.

Various fly-by-night outfits have taken the next logical step. For a fee they will print up a fake transcript of a school that never existed and award grades that would win a boy a scholarship to Harvard.

But the operation which represented the ultimate in athletic professionalism was a college athletic placement service operating out of suburban New York. This flourishing agency undertook to find a scholarship for any likely high school athlete, and to charge only 10 percent of whatever the scholarship paid. It landed more than five hundred scholarships. Before the agency was launched, the owner cleared his plans with the NCAA, which gave approval, but when they saw how big it was becoming, and when they appreciated the cynicism it was engendering, they petitioned the court to issue a cease-and-desist order on the grounds that it might encourage professionalism in college athletics! I can understand why our nation, in time of war, might seek to uncover citizens who speak exotic languages, and I can even understand why the AMA might pay an agency to locate good prospects for advanced medical training, but it baffles me as to why our colleges should need help to find athletes to whom they can give large scholarships.

A scandal of nationwide proportions threatens to break over the athletic establishment, and the way to avoid it is to make playing for the super-league a strictly professional affair, with no emphasis on academic suitability. Let the boy be drafted in an orderly procedure without regard to his academic ability; let him be offered a decent salary with the opportunity of acquiring a degree if he wants one and has the capacity to do the work, and then let him move on to the professionals in accordance with the rules of their draft.

Nothing I have been saying must be interpreted as a charge that all high school athletes are deficient academically. The best are equipped to succeed in any American university, or European either. Let's take the specific cases of Bill Bradley, Jerry Lucas, O.J. Simpson and Calvin Hill. The two white basketball players were intellectual stars at first-rate institutions, and could have been straight-A students wherever they had wished to enroll. The two black football players were equally intelligent, two sophisticated young men who would have been an adornment wherever they went, whether they played football or not.

The majority of athletes I have known fall into this category. The other day I ran into Ron Johnson, stellar running back for the New York Giants. I wanted to talk with him about football; he wanted to talk with me about my book on Spain. In the Dolphin locker room I started to interview Dick Anderson, their star defensive back from Colorado, and he wanted to interview me about a novel I'd written on his state. The athletes I've been associating with during the past three or four years were all-American brains, capable of any achievement, and no system needs to be devised to protect them. If, under the plan I advocate, they were to be drafted by Michigan, they could easily handle the Michigan academics.

But there is another group, and a most numerous one, composed of young athletes physically able to play for any college but mentally prepared for nothing more advanced than the fourth grade. It is these who must be protected. And the place to start is at the beginning of college. These young men must not be deluded into believing they are going to get an education. They are going to play for money in a supervised system, and if they have the will, they can gain an education free on the side. But the one will have little relationship with the other.

A major objection to a high school draft is that it would constitute peonage, because it would force young men to attend colleges they did not themselves elect. This is a substantial accusation, and it can also be made against the present draft of college seniors onto professional teams they might not have chosen. But today, if the college star wants to play with the professionals, he must abide by their rules and play as drafted. If the high school graduate wants to play for one of the university super-teams he must abide by their draft. If he prefers total freedom of choice, and many bright boys would, he can ignore the draft and enroll in some good school not a member of the super-league. Such young men will have made a conscious choice to forgo the publicity that would accrue to them at a football school and the possible professional contract that might ensue. Freedom of choice would be protected, but at a price. To continue the present frenetic system of recruiting demeans everyone. Read what many coaches have testified to as the humiliation of recruiting arrogant boys who should never be in college in the first place. An orderly draft would restore dignity to a profession that thrives on dignity.

How could such a super-league be created? The NCAA is aware of the necessity for such a change and has proposed that the best of the 136 teams now playing Division One football be reorganized into a Division One-A. The following would be eligible: all teams in the seven major conferences—Atlantic Coast, Southeast, Big Ten, Southwest, Big Eight, Western Athletic, Pacific Eight—plus seventeen proved independents like Notre Dame, Penn State, West Virginia and Pittsburgh. The new division would contain 76 schools; the remaining 60 would spend less money on their teams, issue fewer scholarships, and compete as at present. This is not at all what I had in mind. Throwing together all the teams in the present conferences would merely prolong present imbalances. Of the 76 proposed members, at least 40 could not field major teams; we would merely have a new name with all the old problems. I would much prefer a hard-nosed super-league based on reality, and we do not begin to have 76 schools who could qualify for that.

My Group Two would be comprised of the 136 present teams in Division One, less the 36 superpowers. It would contain many famous universities that wished to remain in conferences, play major schedules with teams of their own caliber, and distribute scholarships to athletes of promise but not skilled enough to be hired by schools in Group One. This group, which would comprise the lower two-thirds of all the present conferences plus some of the better independents, forms the heart of my proposal, and it is essential that it establish sensible rules which will be adopted by all competitors and enforced rigorously by a paid staff of supervisors and investigators. I had better not list the teams I would nominate for Group Two, lest they have aspirations to Group One, but they would form the solid backbone of the system.

Since this group would encompass many of the greatest schools in America, it might well be that some blue-chip athletes qualified for Group One would prefer to enroll at the best schools in Group Two, where they could not only play before large audiences but get an education too. Therefore, the essential requirement of this group would be that it give scholarships only for need, that it make no under-the-table payments, and that its athletes be expected to graduate. Concessions would be made as to ensuring a boy's progress toward a degree, as I shall outline in a moment, but none insofar as academic achievement was concerned.

The reader undoubtedly has grasped that this group would operate pretty much as intercollegiate competition now does, with the powerhouses moved upstairs. Since our present system is riddled with contradiction and corruption, why should we expect some new version of it to be any better? Frankly, I am not confident that our schools can find the intelligence to administer the program I visualize; it may be that we have been so contaminated by the past three or four decades that deescalation to a sensible program is impossible. In basketball particularly, Group Two might quickly be invaded by operators who were buying students, falsifying transcripts, and running semi-professional teams of the same old type. To be number one in a conference whose three top teams had moved into Group One would still be enticing, and to gain this honor, coaches would still wheel and deal. On the other hand, I have met so many splendid men and women in college athletics, leaders of such wisdom and charity, I retain a hope that they might gain ascendancy and run a sensible program, especially if competition with the powerhouses of Group One were eliminated. But the danger would still be basketball, where obtaining only one great player could still mean a championship.

Group Three would consist of those schools that wish to provide a full schedule of two-platoon intercollegiate football, but without the burden of athletic scholarships, overstaffed coaching departments and heavy stadium expense. Admission would be charged for their games.

Group Four would consist of all remaining schools that wish to provide football as recreation for their students, but not the expensive two-platoon kind. No admission would be charged to their games.

It is important, I have always believed, for teams in Groups Three and Four to play against outside competitors. Therefore, I am strongly in favor of regularly scheduled intercollegiate contests, and I am not much impressed by the various informal and club teams I have watched. I think there is a positive good, both emotional and mental, in traveling to a foreign field and engaging in a game against strangers, and I would hate to see this advantage of intercollegiate sport lost, for it is educative, challenging, exciting and productive of lifelong friendships.

HOW AMERICA'S 695 COLLEGES AND UNIVERSITIES
MIGHT DIVIDE THEMSELVES INTO THE
FOUR GROUPS

Group	Number in Football	Number in Basketball	Total Athletic Budget
Group One, hires would-be professional players, appears on television, in bowl games and play-offs	48	110	$2,000,000–5,000,000
Group Two, plays at the level of the fourth and fifth teams in conferences as they exist today	250	260	$1,000,000–2,000,000
Group Three, plays deemphasized two-platoon football and non-recruited basketball	182	175	Under $1,000,000
Group Four, plays one-platoon football without heavy coaching, and local and intramural basketball	215	150	No income from spectators. Substantial activity fees

The number of schools in Group One for football may be too low; I have seen studies which claim that as many as 124 schools are playing big-time football, and perhaps that many aspire to do so, but I doubt if they make it. However, since any school with the money, the coaching and the recruiting can insert itself into the big time if it wants to, there could be up to a hundred schools in this category. My preference would be to restrict membership to the thirty-six proved powers.

Many of the benefits available in this four-tier plan will depend upon sensible but minor changes. In Groups One and Two no paid player or player on a scholarship should be allowed to take more than one academic course during the season when his sport is being emphasized. The testimony of former players is overwhelming that no young man can go all-out for a serious football or basketball team and carry a full load of studies; therefore, a realistic solution would be to limit the professional to one course, which would keep him in touch with the academic community in a way that permitted some success. To require him to take three or four serious courses, as is attempted now, is ridiculous; worse, it is damaging, since it corrupts the academic process at the same time it initiates the player into a sense of academic failure. Alabama's Bear Bryant has had some salty things to say on this problem:

I used to go along with the idea that football players on scholarship were 'student-athletes,' which is what the NCAA calls them. Meaning a student first, an athlete second. We were kidding ourselves, trying to make it more palatable to the academicians. We don't have to say that and we shouldn't. At the level we play, the boy is really an athlete first and a student second.

Should the paid athlete wish to avoid course work altogether, he would be free to do so, but the great majority would want to be studying something and they should be encouraged. In this system, the paid athlete could graduate from college at the end of five years. If he attended summer school and took an extra course in the semesters when he was not competing in athletics, he could still graduate in four years. We must also consider the case of the occasional genius who could play big-time football and pass his regular four courses at the same time; there are not many such and some kind of exception might have to be made for them, but in general the one-course rule would prove both sensible and practical.

How can we best protect the right of the young semi-professional athlete to gain an education, assuming he wants one? Any scholarship in any group ought to remain viable for five years. Let the athlete devote his fall to football, or his winter to basketball, without regard to piling up credits toward a degree. But when his eligibility is over, let him enjoy a fifth year of study, tuition and board free, to complete his degree. This rule should be initiated right now, regardless of whether the four-group plan is adopted or not. To use an athlete for four years and then chuck him aside with no degree is contemptible.

Now, if the young man turns out to be a superior athlete, and if at the end of his college eligibility he is drafted into professional ranks, his leaving college with an unfinished degree is his decision and the college drops any responsibility at that time. But even so, I would like to see a system whereby the professional is always encouraged to return to his college, either in the off-season or after his professional career has ended, and pick up his missing credits. Therefore, tuition should remain free for a period of fourteen years after departure from college; I choose this length of time to cover the longest typical professional career, and I believe many athletes would avail themselves of the opportunity thus to finish their education. (Once they join the professionals, they pay for their own room and board; only the tuition remains free.)

I now come to a crucial provision, and to comprehend it the reader must consider two main types of professional sports. Baseball and hockey matured in years before the sports were well established in colleges, which meant that the professionals could not depend upon colleges to train the young men they would require in the future. Professional baseball and hockey had to develop well-regulated and costly minor leagues in which aspirants could learn their trade, and it was the cultivation of these minor leagues that enabled the two sports to flourish.

Professional football and basketball, on the other hand, did not mature until long after colleges had developed highly skilled teams. When professional leagues did materialize, they could depend upon the colleges to provide them with an assured supply of trained young men eager to play for pay. Professional football and basketball were thus excused from the financial obligation of maintaining minor leagues.

To put it bluntly, baseball and hockey were self-sustaining; football and basketball were like cuckoos, depositing their eggs in the nests of others and accepting no financial responsibility for either the rearing or the training of the beginning players on whom their very existence depended. The American educational system has been called upon to provide enormously expensive training programs so that professional teams could prosper without putting up any money.

Chancellor Maurice B. Mitchell of the University of Denver, which dropped football to become a big-time hockey power, has been especially vocal on this issue. I have heard him fulminate several times:

> Our universities train professional athletes at a dead loss. We give them scholarships, large helpings of the best food, medical care, the finest coaching. And what do we get back? Not even thanks. The professional owner uses our product with no obligation but with enormous profits. The universities ought to rebel against this unfair exploitation.

James Armstrong, in his capacity as member of the Orange Bowl Committee, has many contacts with universities, and he agrees that under present conditions they are being ill-used:

> I think we should institute a program, right now, whereby any professional team which drafts a player out of a university is obligated to reimburse that university for the full cost of the player's education, coaching and health services. In addition, the professional team should hand over to the university a percentage of any bonus paid the young man, but here I'd establish a top limit of, say, $5,000.

Chancellor Mitchell suggests a practical refinement:

> Colleges should state that they'll give no more athletic scholarships . . . only loans, and then if the athlete goes into business or law school or medicine, when he graduates you tear up the loan. But if he goes into professional sports because of what you've done for him, you don't tear up the paper, and he owes you that money. We might even institute a check-off system, with the professional team sending us our money direct from his pay check.

Since most baseball and hockey players reach the pros without passing through college, they would be exempt from this rule; but any who did attend on athletic scholarships would be subjected to it. If an athlete had attended two or even three schools, the income from the pros could be prorated.

Even if a given university elected to participate in Group One with an openly professional team or in Group Two with a semi-professional one, it would be obligated to provide a full program of amateur athletics for the entire student body. The professional teams perform in the stadium, the amateur teams on the practice fields. The indefensible situation that prevails at St. Jude's, where the entire basketball program focuses on only sixteen young men with a gigantic palestra reserved for their use alone, would no longer be tolerated.

For Groups One and Two, I tend to favor the accounting system followed at Michigan, where the athletic department has a separate budget, separately controlled, and this receives funds for public entertainment and disburses them for that, without heavy faculty interference. Health programs, which loom so large in my thinking, should be paid for by the general fund of the university, as should intramural programs of games for fun. Let the professional offering be conducted professionally.

If Group One were assembled, with proper rules—and this may be closer at hand than some think; economics and television combined will hasten the day—there would be agitation for an end-of-year play-off for the national championship, comparable to the one now conducted so successfully in basketball. Originally I favored this, because I have a Germanic-type mind which likes to see loose ends tied up, and it offended me to watch the slap-happy manner in which the bowl games were arranged, with rarely a clear-cut match-up of the two top challengers. It seemed to me that it would be simple to arrange schedules so that eliminations could begin by mid-November, with the quarter-finals going to various bowls in early December, the semi-finals to other bowls at Christmas, and the finals, with play-offs for third place, in still other bowls on New Year's. (The finals would be shifted year by year from one of the four major bowls to the next.)

Penn State's Joe Paterno, who is rapidly becoming the philosopher of the coaching profession, is strongly in favor of such a national play-off. 'Look what the system has done for the pros. There's interest right down to the final week. Look, we're supposed to be academic institutions. You mean we can't sit down and figure out a workable play-off system for college football? I think it's important for our game that we do.'

I do not think it right for a television network which has a contract for a particular bowl game to inflate that confrontation into a play-off to decide the national championship, as ABC did in the fall of 1973 when it decided

—and stated so on the air interminably—that the game between Alabama and Notre Dame in the Sugar Bowl would decide who was number one. True, the two teams had unbeaten records, so that the claim was not ridiculous, but in actuality they were not the first two teams in the nation; they were more likely the fourth and fifth best teams, behind Oklahoma, Michigan and Ohio State.

I also objected to that delightful little racket a bunch of southern gentlemen had rigged up whereby it was they who ran every bowl but the Rose Bowl, dispensing each year some $5,000,000. They saw to it that southern schools were regularly selected; in one year five SEC teams appeared, drawing down a neat $3,700,000 for their conference. The southerners had a good thing going for their cities, their stadiums and their athletic departments, and I wanted schools in other regions to be cut in for a fair share of the gravy.

Finally, I suspected that a good deal of loose money might be floating around for the benefit of everyone but the schools involved, and I wanted a stricter accounting so that a larger share of the profits could accrue to education.

I now confess that I was wrong. I see no advantage in establishing a system which leads to one uncontested champion. We have too much of that thing in America. A motion picture cannot be a modest success; it must be an all-time grosser. A book cannot be well received by knowledgeable people; it's a failure unless it's an all-time best seller. Girls cannot play tennis; they must become champions of this county or that state.

We have a play-off in basketball primarily because a scheduling of twenty-seven games throws up natural area champions, and in the play-offs a team has little difficulty in playing one game Thursday night and another Saturday afternoon. But I am not sure we have gained much by the basketball system, and I fear that if we attempted to mimic it in football, we might lose a great deal. The sloppy manner in which the bowl match-ups are made leads to a lot of frivolity, and at the end of the day almost any team can claim the national championship. Who is offended by such nonsense? A mania for neatness should not become an excuse for forcing things into unnatural postures. I now find that I prefer the present system, because it allows Penn State to claim the national championship each year, with some validity, whereas in a play-off it might not even make the quarter-finals.

There remains, I admit, a question of propriety. Should we continue to allow a bunch of southern sporting types to run the bowl system, and perhaps the national play-offs? And is it reasonable to siphon so much of the football dollar into the hands of athletic directors of southern schools?

I have been attending bowl games for some time now, and I think they are best evaluated as part of the grandiose nonsense of American life. They do no good and very little harm. They are a diversion without much consequence, and they liven the end-of-year festivities. The players do not take them too seriously, and neither should we. For example, the 1974 game between Texas and Auburn at the Gator Bowl in Jacksonville was a disgrace insofar as football was concerned, since the Texas players obviously did not want to bother with a post-season game that meant nothing. I was appalled at their performance and wondered what had overtaken them. A friend told me that after the game he had talked with various Texas players, and they told him, 'It was all a crock of shit. Where can we get some beer?'

I was privileged to work rather intimately with the group of Miami sportsmen who operated the Orange Bowl. The committee in charge of selecting the two teams could have been composed of lineal descendants of Cesare Borgia, Blackbeard the Pirate and Jack the Ripper. They knew every trick in the book and had but one objective: to scuttle the Sugar and Cotton Bowls by getting their bids in first.

Selecting the right teams was an operation so intricate that I could not follow the various divagations. Out of respect for the Orange Bowl people I had better use pseudonyms here, but they told me, 'You've got to steer clear of teams like the Dynamiters and the Exterminators. They compile good records, and they play good ball, but they bring almost no supporters to the game, and those that do come sit on their pocketbooks. They don't spend a goddamned nickel, that crowd.' To my astonishment, I found that two other teams I had always judged favorably, Gesundheit and Fare-Thee-Well, were also duds. 'They come down here the day before the game, refuse to engage in pre-game publicity, don't play well, and bring no supporters into town.'

'Who do you like?' I asked.

'Nebraska. Their supporters fly down like a swarm of locusts. They spend money like they were printing it in their basement. And they always put up a good game. Wyoming only came once, but it was super. Oklahoma's good. But maybe Notre Dame is the best. Real class.'

I noticed that the Orange Bowl crowd was not afraid to spend money. They flew in scads of sportsmen from all over the country. For the big parade the night before the game they had three dozen marching clubs, a score of topnotch bands and enough floats to fill the streets of Miami. For the half-time ceremonies they had an incredible nine hundred performers, including clowns, dancers, trumpeters, unicyclists and a monstrous pyramid containing three dozen acrobats. This was gaudiness supreme, and everyone loved it.

I think it best if we not apply reason to bowl games. My wife, a Japanese-American who spent her formative years in California, may have summed it all up when she said of the Rose Bowl: 'It was glorious! Those wonderful floats! Each one decorated with millions of flowers and beautiful girls! The Japanese gardeners would stay up all night fixing the flowers just so, and we kids would help. And when day came, and you saw that glorious thing going down the boulevard with the flowers that you had tended so carefully . . . It was something, I tell you. Something you never forget.'

'What did you think of the football game?' I asked.

'Football? We all went home and went to bed. Dead tired from fixing the flowers.'

While in Miami savoring the delectable nonsense of the Orange Bowl, I had an opportunity to look into a problem which is causing considerable heartache nationally. I attended three football games played by the University of Miami, once one of the real powers in intercollegiate play. The opponents were among the best attractions in the country—Notre Dame, Alabama, Florida State—and on each occasion the vast Orange Bowl was less than half filled. The teams rattled around in cavernous silence, as mournful an exhibition of indifference as I have seen.

"What's happened to Miami?' I asked friends of the school, and they put me in touch with James Bollings, a businessman serving as vice-chairman of the board of trustees and a stalwart supporter of college football:

> You know our history. Energetic, wonderful school. Very young. Filled with the brightest ideas. You folks up north used to call us Swimming Pool U, but we had a lot more going for us than that. Topnotch professors. Fine tennis. A breathtaking football team. We played them all, still do. Texas, Oklahoma, Notre Dame. We had 75,000 in the stands, maybe 80,000 for Notre Dame. In our success and enthusiasm we helped finance building the Orange Bowl, then volunteered to pay a whopping 17.5 percent of the gate as rent. But we were still making money.
>
> Then the professional Dolphins came to town, and although at first their team wasn't very good, we could feel a ripple passing through the community. Our attendance began to falter. Then the Dolphins imported Don Shula, one of this country's great coaches, the Dolphins caught fire with Csonka, Kiick and Warfield and our average attendance dropped to 16,000.

In response to my direct questioning, Bollings refused to concede that Miami University might soon have to drop football, but he did admit that no university could indefinitely absorb the heavy financial losses which accrue if its team has to compete head-on with a successful professional team. Shortly after our interview the University of Tampa, across the peninsula, announced that with the granting of a new professional franchise to that city, there was no way that college football could continue. Tampa was dropping the game.

So I made a list of the thirty-six college teams most often nominated as members of the so-called super-league, and only one was located in a city which sponsored a professional team. Run down the list: Oklahoma, Nebraska, Penn State, Notre Dame, Ohio State, Arkansas, Texas, Michigan, Missouri, Tennessee, Louisiana State, Alabama, Auburn. They all play in safe locations that offer no professional competition. The one exception is Southern California, which competes with the Rams, but Los Angeles is in many ways a special city, and there are even those who argue that it is not a city at all and is therefore not governed by ordinary laws.

The borderline case is one which should be followed most carefully. The University of Colorado is not actually in Denver and therefore not in direct competition with the Broncos, but Boulder is not far away and I fear that the future of Colorado football could be in jeopardy. If it survives, there would be hope for other schools similarly located; if it collapses, a shudder will pass through collegiate ranks.

Another case to watch is Georgia Tech, located in Atlanta, and therefore in competition with the Falcons. It is trying desperately to rejuvenate its program and return to big-time scheduling. It has hired a charismatic new coach with a good record, Pepper Rodgers, and I have heard fervent prayers that it succeed. Certain things are in its favor: it has a great tradition; it has always been supported by the Atlanta community; and there is some doubt that the Falcons, after their recent deportment, are entitled to be called professionals. At any rate, Colorado and Georgia Tech are the litmus papers for collegiate football.

In all the other big cities—Boston, New York, Philadelphia, Chicago, Detroit, San Francisco—college football has withered and, to a degree, college basketball as well. It is very doubtful that either will revive, because the professional game attracts those very people of the middle class who, while they did not attend the local college or any other, used to support it at the turnstiles. There is simply no reason why a workman in Philadelphia should attend a University of Pennsylvania game at Franklin Field when he can see real football at Veterans Stadium, where the Eagles play.

If this reasoning is correct, then the proposed collegiate super-league is best seen as a junior professional league restricted to those areas of small population which the real professionals do not wish to invade. Believe me, once the professionals decide to place teams in Birmingham and South Bend and Columbus, the university teams in those areas are in trouble.

Wherever I went in the big cities, or close to them, I found this same mournful tale. Two-platoon football, with its squads of sixty players and costly uniforms and proliferation of coaches and scholarship funds, was in trouble. And so was basketball. It no longer attracts crowds in New York. I attended a pair of superlative doubleheaders at Madison Square Garden, which used to be crowded on such occasions. The teams I saw were attractive: South Carolina and Southern California as visitors, Fordham and Seton Hall to attract local supporters. The attendance was about 4,000 in an arena which a few hours later seated 19,588 for a Knicks game. In cities like Chicago, Cleveland and Detroit the situation is worse.

Philadelphia was the exception. Through the most adroit publicity and intelligent scheduling, the Big Five—three fine Catholic schools, St. Joe's, LaSalle, Villanova; one Ivy League, Pennsylvania; and one Jewish-black, Temple—put on some of the wildest college games on record, using Pennsylvania's old Palestra. We were told endlessly that 'Big Five basketball is the best in the nation,' and we believed. This was a kind of high-class brainwashing, like the movies in Mexico; at every show a card flashes on the screen stating *'Como México no hay otro'* (Like Mexico there is no other), and after a while that becomes accepted truth. When friends in other cities asked me, 'If Big Five is tops, why were your teams eliminated in the first round of the NCAA last year?' I explain, 'We got bad breaks in the draw.' For the past eighteen years Big Five teams have gotten bad breaks in the draw; they've usually been eliminated early; but loyal Philadelphians like me still believe they play the best basketball in the country.

But now even the Big Five is feeling the pinch of professional competition. Attendance is down. Enthusiasm has waned. The 1974 Christmas tournament was a bust. Philadelphia, the hotbed of sports, was beginning to show itself unwilling to support basketball when so many new professional sports like hockey, lacrosse, soccer and tennis competed for attention. In 1976 one superb doubleheader featuring four contenders drew 1281 spectators.

In football, because of the way television money is distributed, the less-advantaged schools have diminished chances of survival. In 1974–75, for example, Penn State picked up over $1,150,000 in television and bowl money: $158,000 for their game with Maryland; $243,000 for their night game with Pitt; $243,000 for their game with Stanford; and $508,000 for their Cotton Bowl game with Baylor. But nearby Villanova, at one time as strong as Penn State, got nothing. And this disparity not only existed everywhere; it threatened to get worse.

It's not television's fault. Why should ABC or CBS bother with a game like Villanova-Temple when it could get Oklahoma-Nebraska? What fan in his right mind, even if he lived within the shadow of Villanova, would not prefer seeing the two leaders? So the big teams will split the $18,000,000 which television and radio yearly distribute, and the medium teams will get nothing.

The Villanova story is a horror. One autumn afternoon in 1973 those in charge of the university's destiny convened to discuss the alternatives: either give up intercollegiate football altogether, or go big time! That a university could sensibly pose two such extremes, the second involving millions of dollars and complete restructuring of programs, was itself remarkable.

Common sense dictated that football be dropped; the budget demanded it and many strong Catholic colleges had demonstrated that it could be handled without loss of prestige. But a group of nostalgic alumni would not permit it; they'd finance one last shot. Promises were made; funds that did not exist and never would exist were earmarked; Lou Ferry, the respected old coach, was summarily fired; Chip Bender, a dynamic promoter, was given unusual powers as athletic director; and Villanova was off to the majors.

Immediately Bender got in touch with schools already on the Villanova schedule and informed them unilaterally that their games were canceled to make way for big-time opponents. Thus West Chester, a traditional rival and formerly a teachers college, was told that it would be dropped so that Houston, a rising powerhouse, could be scheduled, which would bring in $100,000, Bender said. Wisconsin was lined up, and Boston College and Maryland and powerful Colorado. For future seasons there was talk of Ohio State and maybe even Notre Dame. Villanova would rise again!

Then things began to come unstuck. The new athletic director had found just the coach he wanted in Jim Weaver, who had a good record as a tactician and a reputation as a character-builder. He was hired with considerable hoopla, but he was on campus only briefly when he saw that the promises so glibly made by the alumni the preceding autumn were never going to be fulfilled. Instead of the five-year contract he had been offered, he got a one-year job. Instead of unlimited funds, he got barely enough to keep the program going. Instead of scores of talented boys ready to move onto the first team, he had trouble getting scholarship funds for a few possibles.

So on June 7, three months before the triumphal season was to begin, Coach Weaver secretly found himself a better job and signed a contract to coach at nearby Clarion State the next year, where they weren't going big time but where they did keep promises. Announcement of his retiring would be kept secret until the football season was over, and he would do his best to salvage something for Villanova but his heart would be elsewhere.

I have spoken earlier of Bud Davis, the coach who was hanged in effigy before the season began; now we have Jim Weaver, who quit before spring practice had ended.

The Villanova players, unaware of desertion by their new coach, performed valiantly in their first four games, defeating Massachusetts, Toledo, Idaho; losing to Richmond by one point. But then they faced the real powers, and absorbed five crushing losses: Tampa 47–8; Houston 35–0; Boston College 55–7; Delaware 49–7; Maryland 41–0.

The worst was yet to come. In early November 1974, in the middle of the season, someone squealed about the secret contract; Coach Weaver had to confess that he had quit the team before the season began; he was fired on the spot and his team captain, Chuck Dreisbach, reported that in dealing with the team 'Coach Weaver had always stressed the necessity for honesty.'

After its brief taste of big-time glory, Villanova went back to its old coach, Lou Ferry, the respected one; a new schedule; and a proposal that it play teams of its own caliber whose campuses could be reached by bus rather than jet plane. There was even talk that it might try to persuade West Chester to return.

At the same time that I was attending bowl games and following the ups and downs of big-time collegiate sports, I was meeting with those quiet and dedicated men and women who supervised the programs in the smaller colleges. I had the good luck to know Lew Elverson, the football coach at Swarthmore, whose teams had a ten-year record of something like 8–88, and he was taking the year off, a victim of shell shock no doubt, to survey several score of the better small colleges in the east to determine what they were doing or ought to be doing.

He told me, 'It's heartening. I see some of the most intelligent decisions being made. With support from faculty, student body and alumni.'

'For instance?'

'Well, the way they're responding to the football problem. I've been to quite a few small colleges which used to attempt a full schedule of intercollegiate two-platoon football. And how many boys reported for the squad? Twenty-three. They didn't even have enough for scrimmage. If one lineman got hurt, they had no substitute. And by the time the season was half over they had maybe seventeen or eighteen men. That couldn't continue for long.'

'What are they doing?'

'They're dropping two-platoon, for one thing. They're shifting to club football, but they schedule games with other colleges, so the boys get the benefit of intercollegiate contacts. It works moderately well.'

'Does a general evaluation take place at the time they're questioning football?'

'You better believe it. Everywhere I go men and women are sitting down to do some hard thinking. New programs. New allocation of budgets. New ways to achieve old targets. Colleges like those in the New England Small College Athletic Conference are making some very sensible decisions which may show the way to others.'

'I don't know that conference. Who's in it?'

'Eleven like-minded schools that are close enough to each other to make travel easy.' He consulted a piece of paper and read off the list; it sounded like the *Who's Who* of eastern colleges: 'Amherst, Hamilton, Union, Bates, Middlebury, Wesleyan, Bowdoin, Trinity, Colby, Tufts, Williams.'

'Interesting,' I said. 'I've been on every campus except Hamilton. Where is it?'

'Central New York.'

'At Hamilton?'

'No. Colgate's at Hamilton. Hamilton's at Clinton.'

'I thought the harness track was at Clinton.'

'No. It's at Vernon.'

We were beginning to sound like Abbott and Costello, so I broke the impasse. 'Would Hamilton be a good place to visit?'

'One of the best. They have a lively athletic director up there, man named Gene Long. He'd be glad to talk.'

So later, on my way to the Vernon race track, I stopped off for two days to visit Hamilton, a college founded in 1793 when Baron Von Steuben laid the cornerstone. It prospered, with an endowment of $30,000,000, a favorable teacher-student ratio and a reputation for solid scholarship. Originally a men's college, it had in 1968 admitted women to a sister college, Kirkland, and now served as a prototype for the best in small American colleges. Its present enrollment, including Kirkland, is 1,570, and all know of the school's remarkable tradition: 'Of our first five hundred students back in the 1800s, three became United States senators, fourteen were congressmen, three were federal judges, nine were state supreme court judges, two were ambassadors, nine were college presidents, and four were national leaders of their respective religious denominations.'

One of the school's current assets was Gene Long, a dynamo who had been a long-distance runner in college. Supported by the general faculty, he initiated a program for all incoming men. It was in parts and seemed to me exactly what I would sponsor if I were president of a small college. 1) Do 12 push-ups, 30 squat jumps, 3 chin-ups using front grip, and run 400 yards in 80 seconds. 2) If those requirements seemed too precise and physical-education-dominated, the student could elect to run one and a half miles in 12 minutes. (I told Long, 'That seems too fast,' but he said, 'Not at all. Any freshman in reasonable condition ought to handle that.') 3) In the winter he must demonstrate his proficiency in swimming, and if he cannot, into the pool for him. 4) In order to encourage lifetime sports, he must exhibit moderate proficiency in either golf or tennis, and if he can play neither, he must take instruction in the one of his choice.

These requirements seem reasonable. Many students, I am sure, would protest, but I really wonder if a young man is ready for hard intellectual work if his body is in such poor shape that he cannot pass such tests. And if he is in delinquent shape, should he not be quickly improved so that he forms health habits which will sustain him throughout his life? I would like to see a program such as this in operation everywhere.

If the incoming freshman passes his tests, and most do, he is free to choose from a complete program of eleven intercollegiate sports, plus three formal clubs in sailing, skiing and squash. Or he can elect to participate in a lively intramural program, which about 75 percent of the student body does. A recent questionnaire seeking student opinion on the program showed these results:

REACTIONS OF HAMILTON STUDENTS TO THE
COLLEGE ATHLETIC PROGRAM

Requirement	Too Much Emphasis	Not Enough Emphasis	About Right Emphasis
Physical Education	77	56	149
Intramural Program	9	103	167
Intercollegiate Program	26	122	127

	I Approve	I Disapprove	I am Undecided
Initial testing for General Physical Fitness	137	102	44
More Opportunity for Co-ed Sports	160	71	46

Thanks to a generous alumni, Hamilton had one of the first indoor hockey rinks, and this has always been a major sport; the present coach, an ex-marine, has been on the job for twenty-five years. Football presents a special problem, for barely enough men come out to field a proper team with the necessary depth. One of the most poignant comments I heard during all of my research came from Gene Long: 'We're one of those colleges whose alumni remember us principally on Sunday mornings when they run down the left-hand alphabetical listing of Saturday's games in *The New York Times.* If we've won, they can find us. If we've lost, they have to scatter through the right-hand column to see who beat us and by how much. One important alum told me, "Just once I'd like to find Hamilton in the alphabetical listing." '

Many small colleges, in the present financial stringency, will have to quit two-platoon football; they will have no option. At schools like Hamilton, where there is a well-rounded program, reasonable alternatives will be found: Schedules with other small schools. Trips by bus rather than plane. No more putting up at the swankiest motel. No more purchasing uniforms for sixty and seventy players. No more coaching staffs with seven and eight men. But good, sound programs, perhaps of one-platoon teams, perhaps on an informal home-and-home basis to provide some spark to the competition.

And some colleges may have to drop football altogether. If they do, what will be the consequences? A good deal of legend has grown up in answer to this question, and at one time I accepted most of it. For example, I remember when St. Jude's discontinued its football program; the predictions were pretty dire, and I always thought the college had escaped only because it shifted quickly to basketball, whose successful teams took away the sting.

I believed that if a college or a university dared to drop football, it would lose alumni support, meet with bitter criticism from the state legislature, suffer a drop in student enrollment, and generally hit the downward toboggan. But now we have an objective study of just what does happen. Felix Springer's Appendix I to the Hanford report grapples with this question: 'What actually happened to those 151 senior colleges who gave up football in the years 1939–74, with particular attention to alumni support, legislative reaction, maintenance of school spirit and diversion of attention to other sports?'

Springer's list contains many minor institutions whose names would not be readily recognized, but also many colleges of distinction, some of which had once been football powers:

1939	DePaul	1955	Fordham
1940	Chicago	1961	Denver
	St. Joseph's		
1942	LaSalle	1963	Hardin-Simmons
1943	Manhattan	1965	Detroit
1951	Niagara	1967	George Washington
	St. Mary's		
1953	New York University	1971	Bradley
	Santa Clara		
1954	Washington and Lee	1972	Haverford
	Case		
		1973	Drexel

Even from this small sampling, one can see the concentration of schools from the eastern seaboard where preoccupation with football has sharply diminished in the last four decades. Here are Springer's findings.

First, one must keep in mind the circumstances that led to the discontinuation, and almost always the major consideration was money. The average school was pumping some $250,000 to $500,000 a year into a program that was providing no championships, few winners and little student participation.

Second, almost every school that quit had a won-lost average below .500; students, alumni and the paying public were losing interest in such a drab performance. Numerous respondents said that if their students had continued to support the team, it would have been continued, but that without student support, there was really no reason for continuation.

Third, an obviously faltering football program led alumni and the general public to question the ability of the school's administration to carry on its other affairs respectably. Thus the football program was not only of itself negative but it was also casting the whole reputation of the school in a negative light.

Fourth, those schools which felt themselves forced to surrender a once big-time program often said that they did so because of their situation in a large urban area which brought in successful professional teams which preempted public support.

Fifth, to compete successfully against the professionals would require at least $1,500,000 a year for many years, and even this would not ensure success. Football had simply priced itself out of existence.

Sixth, at least one school dropped football because of scandalous behavior on the part of the athletic department in illegal recruiting.

What were the consequences of quitting? To an astonishing degree, no visible consequence at all, except that the dropping often served as a catalyst for improving the rest of the athletic program. Alumni giving did *not* drop. Alumni did *not* sever connections with their schools. Student applications for entrance did *not* diminish. And state legislatures did *not* cut yearly grants. In fact, businessmen and legislators alike tended to agree that when the school stopped pouring money down the football rathole it gave evidence of managerial responsibility; its reputation was enhanced rather than damaged. Springer notes that many schools launched successful fund-raising drives coincident with dropping football, as if having done so were evidence of the school's determination to improve its general posture.

A major consequence is one I have alluded to indirectly in discussing St. Jude's. The better Catholic colleges were able to shift from big-time football directly into big-time basketball, and to make considerable money while doing so. Other colleges tried to do the same, but with less success. The differential might be that the Catholic schools had homogeneous student bodies accustomed to big-time sports, and they were able to shift their loyalties to basketball, or that Catholic schools were apt to be located in cities, where basketball was a popular sport.

Springer is not enthusiastic about club football and intramural leagues as a substitute for a big-time varsity. He says such programs start enthusiastically, then peter out after the originating body of students departs. There is a real advantage in intercollegiate competition.

On the moral side, almost every college or university that dropped football announced that it would honor athletic scholarships through the athlete's year of graduation; most of the recipients had dreams of a professional career and shifted immediately to some other school. And among the few who did stay in school with a full scholarship but no obligation to play, not one said that he appreciated this opportunity to study. All felt they had been cheated of a chance to play professional ball.

Finally, throughout all the schools there seemed to be an undercurrent of relief that they were through with the scholarship racket, the athletic dormitories, the necessity of providing tutoring for boys unable to meet ordinary scholastic requirements. But as I have previously indicated, the Catholic schools that freed themselves of the football burden quickly found themselves saddled with a basketball albatross, because, unfortunately, basketball players tend to be even more poorly qualified than football players.

But the bottom line of Springer's report is that nothing happened. If the school took pains to keep its alumni and its surrounding community informed, if it explained the financial problem, if it carefully spelled out its reasoning to its student body, everyone accepted the conclusion as inevitable. Obviously this does not mean that Notre Dame would be free to drop football tomorrow, or Alabama, or Texas; they could not cite any reasons that would be persuasive, and if good reasons were found, they would not be accepted by either their local constituency or their national fans. Such schools are obligated to provide nationwide entertainment and they would be delinquent if they sought to avoid this responsibility. But the average institution, if it persuades its followers that it is in a position of financial suicide, can do pretty much as it wishes, especially if it argues that by so doing, the school's financial and educational postures will be improved.

During my research on these lugubrious topics I tried never to lose sight of the fact that sports should be fun, and I occupied my spare moments with the pleasant diversion of trying to determine where in America the college football fans were craziest; in other words, where was the nut capital of the nation?

I visited eight universities in some depth, and could logically have voted for any one. Michigan seemed a special case, a center of academic excellence much like Juvenal's ideal of a sound mind in a sound body. Year after year they produced absolutely topflight teams, only to see the gonfalons awarded to others; to sustain heroic partisanship after such disappointments required fortitude, and the Michigan fanatics had it.

I lived for a while near the University of Colorado, whose fans will believe anything. They attend games in that marvelous stadium set against the Rockies, and through each October assure each other, 'We're number one,' and even in late November they keep saying the same thing, when they ought to know better.

To attend a game at Notre Dame, staying at the college inn a short distance from the stadium, and to watch the medieval mania that settles upon the institution as game time approaches is to see football at its best. If a stranger to this country could attend only one football game to inform himself as to what the game was all about, it should be at Notre Dame. Fans here must be the most loyal in America, but the exalted reputation of their school prevents them from becoming quite as nutty as those attached to competing schools.

I grew up inside the sphere of Penn State influence and had participated in its maniacal partisanship. This university serves a gracious purpose in keeping alive in the northeast the tradition of big-time football: a frosty day, a long ride through rural Pennsylvania, the little mountain town with no industry except the university, the Nittany hills in bright fall colors, tailgate parties, some with a selection of hot dishes cooked on Coleman stoves, and a well-coached team rolling up its next victory. Those are pleasant memories. And I find innocent amusement in the way a Penn State fan can watch his team face one real opponent and ten teams called East Podunk State Teachers and then claim that once again Penn State is national champion. The hickory trees in the coal region produce some great football nuts.

I had known Ohio State University rather intimately and had often expressed wonder at the hysteria which gripped the city of Columbus during football season. In the spring of 1970, in a town east of Columbus, some beer-drinking students at Kent State University caused minor damage along saloon row and later, in frustration over the war in Vietnam, had burned the ROTC building. Ohio officials, who recognized rebellion when they saw it, summoned armed guardsmen, who subsequently shot and killed four students. In November of that year Woody Hayes led Ohio State to a glorious 20–9 victory over Michigan, and the students fairly tore Columbus apart, causing substantial damage to property and considerable risk to life, but the same Ohio officials saw no need to call out the guard, because to show such high-spirited support of the football team was not only understandable; it was laudable proof of good citizenship.

And one would have to rate Texas high. To see a football game in Austin with the Lone Star hoop-la, the stadium filled with fans screaming 'Hook 'em, Horns,' the team roaring down the field, the gigantic band playing marches, and the whirly-girly majorettes performing is, as the announcers say, 'something else.' The band is a state treasure, and the wealthy rancher who supports it a state hero, because in Texas they take football seriously. When the chancellor of the vast system had to fire the president recently, the only reason announced was that the latter had not been judicious in whom he invited to sit in the university box at the football games. The State of Texas could confer no higher accolade, and this courtesy ought to be dispensed with an eye to keeping legislators happy.

But as my comparisons continued, the competition began to focus on two sites: Nebraska and Alabama—and to my chagrin I found that I lacked character. Whichever state I visited last seemed the winner.

I flew out to Nebraska to watch as an entire state went bananas over football. Ranchers rode in from three hundred miles away, dressed all in red, they and their wives, and they painted the town the same color. At two in the afternoon on a Saturday the stadium was a pulsating red mass. Once I stopped at a town in the remote southwest corner of the state, and the local bank had purchased a monstrous billboard to proclaim 'Go Big Red.' I took the trouble to stop by the bank and ask why a business four hundred miles from the university would be so excited about football, and the banker said, 'Our clients take it for granted that we're solvent. But if they suspected for even one minute that we were not sound where Big Red is concerned, they'd drive us out of business.'

I also heard about Reverend Kenneth McDonald, 'as fine a clergyman as you'd want to meet, but he was called to a church in Michigan, where he can't attend Nebraska games and has to listen to his parishioners praise Michigan football as if it was first class. So the Reverend builds himself a Big Red Shrine with portraits of Nebraska's greats, and on game days he sits there and meditates.' I asked if his Michigan parishioners interpreted this as an act of disloyalty, and my informant said, 'No, they realize that religion requires a man to be faithful to what he believes.'

One morning with my motel breakfast a copy of the *Omaha World-Herald* appeared, featuring a full-page color spread showing the home of Mr. and Mrs. V. Russel Swanson, and everything on the ground floor, including carpets, furniture, wallpaper, decorations and a three-wall bulletin board dominating the living room was a shattering red, including Mr. and Mrs. Swanson, two attractive people in their mid-forties, who during the football season dress only in red. As the newspaper proudly explained, 'The Swansons not only go all-out for Big Red in decorating but they fly a "Number One" flag in their yard on game Saturdays.'

I was so bedazzled by the article that I got in touch with Swanson, and he made these points:

> ... The resurgence of Nebraska began when the university hired a new coach, Bob Devaney. A local radio announcer coined the jingle which became our state song:

> Get off your fanny
> And help Bob Devaney.

. . . Nebraska football provides a plan for every pocketbook. The Extra Point Club can be joined for one dollar on up, and for five dollars you get the coaches' printed comments following each game. The Touchdown Club costs twenty-five dollars or up, and a hundred dollars gets you a parking space. The Husker Educational Award rate is a thousand dollars and the Husker Beef Club contributes steers for the football training table. A two-thousand-dollar contribution to the press box carries the right to purchase tickets for the enclosed seating.

. . . We love to wear red and are expected to wear it. Our family has red in all weights of coats, all lengths of dresses, shirts, sports coats, slacks, jackets, shoes, boots, lined boots, hats, caps, scarfs, sweaters, shorts, ties, gloves, mittens, socks, watches, pins, bracelets, earrings, buttons. One cartoon showed a manufacturer who said, 'If it won't sell, paint it red and send it to Nebraska.'

. . . Our fans are so rabid that if the weather report on Monday warns of possible storms, fans from the western part of the state hurry to Lincoln early in the week so as not to miss the game.

. . . Fans in other states think that football fever strikes the nation from late summer to midwinter, but in Nebraska we follow it longer. We expect news coverage from August practice, through the fall season, including bowl practice in December and the bowl game in January. The balance of January and February are ugh. We look at the line-ups in March, follow spring practice in April and attend the spring Red-White squad game in May. Somehow we manage through June, but pro football with some former Big Red players starts in July, which carries us back to August practice.

. . . You might say that our big breakthrough came when we discovered that we could buy a bright-red bathroom with a Go Big Red toilet seat to sort of set the scene.

The Swansons sent me color photographs of their bathroom and I decided on the spot, 'Nebraska must surely be the football capital of the world.'

But then I went to Alabama, where the first eleven people I met—businessmen, professors, housewives—took me aside to assure me confidentially that 'Bear Bryant is the greatest man this state has ever produced.' I wondered why they should be so insistent, until Alf Van Hoose, one of the best sportswriters in America, confided, 'They're afraid of writers. Jim Murray and that smart-aleck columnist from Georgia have said ugly things about the Bear, but let me tell you this, Michener, when you get to know him you're going to find that he's even better than we say. This man is simply the greatest.' Wherever I went I heard that Bryant was a demigod, a man with such unusual powers that they defied ordinary description, and when I had a chance to test the reality against the fable, I found that what Van Hoose had said was correct. I doubt if there is any sports figure in America who comes close to dominating his community the way Bear

Bryant dominates Alabama. When David Mathews, the bright young president of the University of Alabama, was chosen by President Ford to join the Cabinet in Washington as head of Health, Education and Welfare, a wire service phoned the university for a photograph, and the girl in the office sent back a shot of Bear Bryant. When she was reprimanded for her mistake, she asked, 'It's Bear's university, isn't it?' So I concluded that whereas people in Nebraska liked football, they didn't really put their heart into it the way those fans in Alabama did.

But in late December as I was about to start writing this book, I was invited back to Nebraska to speak at the university and a little thing happened which turned the scales. I was seated next to the chancellor, a wise and witty man who explained that in his state football was the total mania for several understandable reasons. 'We did win the national championship twice, and that delighted everyone. Secondly, Nebraska is almost unique in that we have no second university to divert attention. Even Oklahoma has Oklahoma State, a very strong school. Colorado, Alabama, Kansas. You name them. Their loyalties are divided, but not us. If you live within the confines of this state, you're a Nebraska fan. And thirdly, we have no competition from any professional teams. We are football.' A cynic sitting on my other side whispered, 'He leaves out the fact that the State of Nebraska has no opera, no drama, no symphony, no exalted social life and not much intellectual life. In this state if you don't go for football, you're a pariah.' As I pondered this, he added, 'And it's the same throughout the Big Eight. Our football is good because we haven't anything else. And if you look at it honestly, that holds true for Ohio State and Arkansas and Penn State and Texas and Auburn and all the powers. They support football because their towns don't offer anything else.' But then I heard the clincher. It was a merchandising feat described by a man who sat opposite me. He said, 'This friend of mine is cleaning up. He's invented something that's selling like mint juleps in the Sahara. It's a gadget that you fix to the wall in your bathroom. It dispenses bright-red toilet paper, and each sheet is imprinted with the slogan "Go Big Red," which under the circumstances is rather appropriate, don't you think? But what makes this gadget superlative is that it also contains a transistor radio pre-tuned to the Nebraska broadcast, so that if you should be called away unexpectedly from the television, you wouldn't have to miss a single play.' Eat your heart out, Alabama!

But it wasn't as simple as that, because the next month I was invited to attend inductions to the Alabama Sports Hall of Fame, and I saw this state in its off-football season, and the passion with which it praised its ancient heroes. As they came to the podium, these great baseball players, and golfers, and racetrack drivers evoked empathies I had never witnessed before. They were the grain and fiber of Alabama, more important than politicians and bankers, and finally the old-time football players came forward, the deeply revered predecessors to the Namaths and the Stablers, and these men were living gods. In the course of the festivities Bear Bryant had occasion to announce that if Alabama went to a bowl game next New Year's, 'and we will, because since 1962 we've gone to fourteen of 'em and we don't intend to stop now. Well, if we go, I'm gonna invite every livin' member of our 1926 team which beat Washington in the Rose Bowl to attend as guest of the university, and if the college won't pay the freight, I will.' There was a hush, then Pooley Hubert, architect of that first win, Alabama 20–Washington 19, rose and tried to express his thanks, but his voice choked. He was very tall, a powerful fullback in his day, and he tried again as the audience leaned forward. Finally he blurted out, 'Bear, you the greatest sonofabitch ever been born.' The crowd roared its ratification of this judicial opinion, and the woman seated next to me on the dais, widow of the quarterback Bryant preferred, Pat Trammell, whispered, 'You know, he really is the greatest,' and without any thought of further reconsideration of my vote, I had to decide that any state which would express such affection for a curmudgeon coach who had failed to win once in eight straight bowl games had to be the looniest football center of them all.

But when I reported this conclusion to some men in a New York bar, one of them leaned over, grabbed me by the arm, and said in a rich western voice, 'Son, if you ain't been to Norman, Oklahoma, you ain't even entitled to an opinion.' I was so impressed by his fervor that I promised to visit Oklahoma if an opportunity ever arose.

At the start of the 1975 football season I was working in Denver, and a Tulsa tycoon offered to fly me to Norman to see some real football, so I went. The first Oklahoma fan I met set a high standard for partisanship. He was Earl Wells, oil magnate from Henrietta, Oklahoma, who told me, 'The doctors said it was a matter of life and death. Open-heart surgery immediately. I told them, "Hold on! I've got to be able to walk up four flights of stadium steps on the opening day of football season." They said, "No way," so I said, "Then no operation." And they said, "Then you'll die." So we compromised. They'd operate and I'd come to this game. When they warned me that if I did I might drop dead, I told them, "If I'm gonna die, let me die doin' what I love most in this world. Watchin' Oklahoma football." And here I am!'

The first woman devotee I met was Earl's equal. Betty Eick, a tall, lovely woman told me, 'When we were first married my husband worked out a scheme by which we could each sell a pint of our blood and pick up enough money to see the Oklahoma-Texas game. He said that in a marriage it was important to get started right where fundamentals were concerned.'

Most instructive of all, I had two long sessions with Barry Switzer, the razor-sharp, tense, knowing coach who volunteered to answer any question I cared to throw at him: 'We ought to institute a new conference immediately. At the end of this year. Made up of those universities who demonstrate a serious commitment to real football. Call it Division One-A. Keep it under the supervision of the NCAA. Clear-cut eligibility rules and a staff to enforce them. Employ as many coaches as you need. Provide a substantial number of full scholarships for the income sports of football and basketball. Eighty other scholarships for minor sports, to be allocated as the university prefers. Oklahoma would apply many to wrestling; Indiana to swimming. A realignment of the conferences as they exist today. And don't call us a super-conference. We're not super. We just want to associate ourselves with other schools like us who have a commitment to excellence.'

At his press conference following the game Switzer told a host of reporters from small Oklahoma towns, 'I wasn't pleased with today's performance. We played very spotty ball that first quarter. Sat back and allowed Oregon to carry the fight to us. Couldn't spring our runners free. We've got to look at the game films to see what happened to our kicking. We've got to do better.' Score of this disappointing game: Oklahoma 62–Oregon 7.*

When I had finished visiting schools and digesting reports, I tried to summarize my personal feelings about college sport, and found myself coming back to a letter which George Hanford had sent me at the conclusion of his similar study:

> I do not side with those who claim that the negative effects of unethical practices in intercollegiate athletics outweigh the positive values. There is an infection, and because it could spread, something needs to be done to control it. On balance, however, I believe that there is much more that is healthy about intercollegiate athletics than is sick.
>
> I side with James Coleman, the University of Chicago sociologist, who told me that he had observed that many of the successful people he had encountered —individuals in business, the professions, education and the like—turned out, on specific inquiry, to have participated in sports. Like Coleman, I am inclined to ascribe some measure of their success to the lessons learned and the values developed on the playing field—lessons and values that have something to do with coping with success and failure, with the benefits of practice and persistence, and of teamwork and cooperation, and with the joys of physical well-being and healthful recreation.

*Switzer had a right to be apprehensive. A brilliant coach, he had already sensed that this team might be rather mediocre by Oklahoma standards. After the Oregon massacre it barely eked out several cliff-hanging wins, suffered a shattering defeat, but in the Orange Bowl, Oklahoma defeated Michigan, 14–6, winding up with the national championship.

VIII

The Athlete

When I originally outlined this book I had plans for twelve chapters, and this was not among them. A sobering experience forced its inclusion.

Within the space of a week I had social contacts with eight top athletes; three of them had been close personal friends of many years; the other five were outstanding professionals with national reputations. My friends were an interesting lot, men about my own age with whom I played tennis regularly.

Ham Place, a successful cartoonist who had invented a new way to make animated cartoons for television, had won a number eight national ranking as a tennis player at Ohio State. Pete Richards, a hundred and seventy pounds of gristle, had been one of the first professional football players for the old Frankford Yellow Jackets. And Barney Berlinger had been not only a great track and field star at the University of Pennsylvania, but also a member of our Olympic team in 1928.

The five professionals were younger. Robin Roberts had won 286 games while pitching primarily for the Phillies. Hal Greer had played more professional basketball games than any other player in history, 1,122, primarily for the Philadelphia 76ers. Chuck Bednarik, that granite monolith, had been the last professional football player to go sixty minutes on both offense and defense, for the Philadelphia Eagles. He was all-American all-Everything. Don Budge had won every championship in tennis and was the last American man to win back-to-back titles at Wimbledon in 1937–38. And recently I had entered into a business agreement with Don Meredith, the Dallas quarterback, to purchase a local radio station in hopes of upgrading it.

The sobering experience was this. One afternoon as I left a meeting with Roberts, Greer and Bednarik it suddenly occurred to me that these superlative men, plus the other five I had been meeting, had been forced to retire from their athletic careers at an age when I, in my profession, had yet to write word one. Their public lives had ended before mine began. In their middle thirties these gifted men had reached the climax of their fame; they had scintillated for a decade, then been required to find other occupation; I had stumbled into a career at which I could work till eighty, if I lived that long.

It was then that I began to speculate on what kind of person the athlete is, and to compare him with other talented performers. Chuck Bednarik, a man of herculean talent, had blazed across the sports pages for a few brilliant years; Henry Fonda, a man of comparable gifts, could flourish as an actor during four decades or five. Hal Greer, a model of consistency and cautious self-preservation, had been through at forty, while David Rockefeller, the same kind of person, had just begun his illustrious banking career at that age.

There was another aspect. The newspapers were filled at this time with accounts of former athletic greats who had fallen on bad times and were ending their days in misery. A book of considerable literary merit had appeared, showing how the members of one of baseball's finest teams had withered away. On Broadway a stunning drama depicted the moral erosion and physical downfall of a high school basketball team. And all these accounts derived their sense of tragedy from the fact that the athletes involved had known their moments of greatness so early and had spent so many bitter years in decline.

At this juncture I came upon a book whose author had analyzed this phenomenon as expressed in American fiction: Wiley Lee Umphlett, *The Sporting Myth and the American Experience.* The author, after reviewing a score of creative works focusing on athletes, reaches various conclusions, three of which are relevant to the present discussion. He says that American fiction presents young athletes who are: 1) anti-urban in their basic mind-sets and always longing for a return to a simpler life closer to nature; 2) anti-feminine and incapable of coping with women; and 3) victims of a prolonged juvenilism, clinging to memories of youthful glory and rarely attaining enough maturity to grapple with adult problems.

> The fact that success in athletics does not always mean success in business or life provides Philip Roth in *Goodbye, Columbus* and Irwin Shaw in 'The Eighty-Yard Run' with a convenient means for satirical expression. We discover that Roth's Ron Patimkin and Shaw's Christian Darling as ex-college athletes are unable to involve themselves with the realities of life. Instead, they continue to live in the idealized world of 'the game'; consequently their lives exemplify still another theme in modern literature—the search for maturity.

Like a child, he cannot see himself clearly in relationship to his environment, and in this so-called innocent state is compelled to relate everything to his own ego-centered world. The result is lack of self-awareness and a failure in communication, not only in marriage but in social dealings as well. The only real world for him is, and always will be, we recognize, the world of the game. As early as F. Scott Fitzgerald's portrait of Tom Buchanan in *The Great Gatsby* (1925), we are given an important clue to the reason for such an outlook. Tom as an all-American football player at Yale is described as 'one of those men who reach such an acute limited excellence at twenty-one that everything afterward savors of anticlimax.' For the star athlete nothing in life can ever again approach the significance of the lost world of the Big Game.

I wish there were space to discuss each of the works Umphlett cites; he is especially perceptive in dealing with William Faulkner's 'The Bear' and Bernard Malamud's *The Natural,* but I must concentrate on the four examples which focus on prolonged adolescence and the harking back to days of glory.

The archetypal story is Irwin Shaw's 'The Eighty-Yard Run.' Christian Darling, a one-time college hero, returns fifteen years later to the scene of his triumph. Because of his football accomplishments he has married the daughter of a rich alumnus and now stands in the shadows of the stadium, trying to understand why he has lost her. In a haunting scene he dashes once more down the field, re-creating his eighty-yard run, the high point of his life, and discovers to his embarrassment that college lovers have been watching him. 'I—once played here,' he tells them. Shaw is brutal in his summary of his hero's character:

> He had practiced the wrong thing, perhaps. He hadn't practiced for 1929 and New York City and a girl who would turn into a woman. Somewhere, he thought, there must have been a point where she moved up to me, was even with me a moment, when I could have held her hand, if I'd known, held tight, gone with her. Well, he'd never known. Here he was on a playing field that was fifteen years away and his wife was in another city having dinner with another and better man, speaking with him a different, new language, a language nobody had ever taught him.

Ernest Hemingway's 'The Short and Happy Life of Francis Macomber' is the classic depiction of the stupid, unfeeling sportsman who stumbles and fumbles his way into adult life, only to be gunned down at last by a wife who despises him. I know of few portraits more cruel. John Cheever's story 'O Youth and Beauty!' translates the Macomber situation into a suburban situation in which the fatuous and intolerable ex-college athlete is gunned down by his wife.

Philip Roth's *Goodbye, Columbus* deals with the basic athletic situation, but comically. Ron Patimkin, not the major character in the novel but brother to the girl who will date the hero, had been a hotshot basketball player at Ohio State but is now a would-be adult, dreaming vacuously of his glory days. He delights in listening to a long-playing record summarizing the sounds of his senior year: 'And here comes Ron Patimkin, dribbling out. Ron, number eleven, from Short Hills, New Jersey. Big Ron's last game and it'll be some time before Buckeye fans forget him . . .' But, as Ron's business-minded father observes, his son doesn't even know how to unload a truck.

The character study which best bridges the two shores of realism and ridicule is John Updike's *Rabbit, Run,* in which the unforgettable Rabbit Angstrom, once a basketball hero in the coal towns of Pennsylvania, tries vainly to find a secure place for himself in adult society. He cannot unravel his relationships with his wife, or with the bar girl he has made pregnant; he cannot resolve his interior conflict between his longing for a free open space, symbolized by his flight south, and his actual life in the northern urban sprawl in which he is trapped; nor can he reconcile his religious beliefs. He can do only one thing: run furiously as he had once run during the closing minutes of basketball games. He is an engaging man, in spite of his confusions, and a tragic one because of his refusal to grow up. He is a significant figure in modern American fiction, and in numerous college classes he is presented as the standard American athlete.

After the preceding works had become popular, a play came along which summarized them all; indeed, it seemed to have been written to accomplish just this and will undoubtedly stand for some time as the culminating statement because it attacks the problem so relentlessly yet with such appealing humor.

That Championship Season, by Jason Miller, won the Pulitzer Prize for 1973, plus all the other prizes that year. It is a tightly constructed, one-set, five-character play covering the events of one evening in the home of a Pennsylvania high school basketball coach. It is reunion night for the team which twenty-five years before had won the state championship, and four of the five heroes from that historic quintet have come back to meet with the coach who led them to victory.

The four ex-champions disclose themselves to be a sorry lot. Phil Romano, now mayor of the city, is a characterless cuckold, willing to engage in any nefarious behavior if it will ensure his reelection. George Sikowski, the big Polish guard, has become a millionaire, a fearfully hollow man ready to destroy the countryside for a few extra bucks. The two Daley brothers who held the team together have become a pitiful pair: Tom, the elder, is a whining, masochistic schoolteacher maneuvering to attain a minor promotion for which he is not qualified; James, the younger, is a marvelously drawn alcoholic to whom the comic lines are given so that he can laugh at himself as his life staggers into chaos.

The central character, the coach, is a fiercely bigoted man who recites from memory Teddy Roosevelt's flamboyant statement about being in the middle of the fight. He preaches sportsmanship and practices the most virulent anti-Semitism. He parades old virtues and launches a character assassination. Steeped in hatred and disappointment—for he has never subsequently had a championship season and has been fired for maltreating his players—he is invited, at the end of the play, to watch the NBA finals on color television, but he says he won't bother: 'It's not a white man's game any more.'

This bleak and very funny drama deserved the many prizes it won, for it is a cogent statement on a recurring American theme which Umphlett identified: the falling away of the dream, the incapacity of the athlete to adjust to adult life. I recommend it to anyone interested in American sports, and if one finds no chance to see it in the theater, it is a drama that reads almost as well as it plays.

And then in rapid-fire order I came upon one statistic after another which supported the thesis that sports are an ascent to greatness followed by a sickening drop to oblivion:

• S. Kirson Weinberg and Henry Arond compiled an analysis of what happened to ninety former boxing champions, each of whom had earned more than $100,000 in years when that amount of money was substantial and when there were few taxes. They now worked in taverns, or as unskilled laborers, or as ticket-takers at movie houses, or as bookies, or as janitors, or as helpers around gas stations, or as men walking race horses. Not one had a substantial job.

• Bill Murray, of Duke University, made a study of nine hundred young men who had signed contracts with professional baseball teams before graduating from high school. About twenty actually made it to the big leagues, but only five stayed there for the required five years that would qualify them for a pension. And only a handful were able to get a college degree. The rest . . . Murray didn't say, but we can imagine them working beside the former boxers in beer halls and in the digging of ditches.

• Eddie Arroyo, the jockey, told Studs Terkel that flat racing must be the most dangerous of all sports in view of the large number of jockeys killed at the track: 'I'd say the casualty rate is three, four times higher than any other sport. Last year we had nine race-track deaths, quite a few broken backs, quite a few paralyzed. A real close friend of mine, he's paralyzed. Three days after I fell, he fell. Just a normal accident. We all expected him to get up and walk away. He's paralyzed from the waist down. It's been a

year and some months. Gettin' money out of those people—track owners
—is like tryin' to squeeze a lemon dry.'

• John Paisios, a psychologist, explained why his consulting firm decided
to specialize in helping professional athletes adjust to adult life after their
playing days were over: 'They find that they have been living through a
period of enforced adolescence. For years they are both pampered and
bossed like rich little children. Consequently, they often find it difficult to
make decisions about themselves, because they really don't know who they
are. This comes down especially hard on the nameless guy in the line when
he reaches the twilight of his career.'

• Statistics were released showing that the average career of a professional football player is three years, which means two things: they retire
before thirty; and the majority of college seniors who are chosen in the NFL
draft each winter, to the accompaniment of approving headlines in local
papers, will not last in the big time long enough to earn a pension.

Depressed by such thoughts, I read again that magnificent summary of
the problem written years ago by the English poet A.E. Housman in his
collection *A Shropshire Lad*. Unquestionably the finest poem ever written
about sports, better than Homer's lines on Ajax or John Updike's well-
regarded poem 'Ex-Basketball Player,' it tells of a village athlete who won
a great championship and then died prematurely. I have always thought
that the opening stanza, which I have recited to myself through the years,
is the best evocation I know of sports:

> The time you won your town the race
> We chaired you through the market-place;
> Man and boy stood cheering by,
> And home we brought you shoulder-high.

Now those who carried him through the town in that early triumph bear
his casket shoulder-high, and the poet makes this wry observation:

> Smart lad, to slip betimes away
> From fields where glory does not stay
> And early though the laurel grows
> It withers quicker than the rose.

And then comes the other stanza that I have recited to myself so often. The
lines are heartbreaking in their simplicity and truth, the epitome of all the
stories I have mentioned and the play:

> Now you will not swell the rout
> Of lads that wore their honours out,
> Runners whom renown outran
> And the name died before the man.

A few years ago an American writer produced a work of the same philosophical gravity as Housman's threnody. Roger Kahn's *The Boys of Summer* is more than a book about athletes—in this case the Brooklyn Dodgers of their heroic years—it is also a work of high purpose and poetic accomplishment. It has been called the finest American book on sports, for it is both a re-creation of a heroic age and a tragic statement about the young men who provided the heroism. I commend it without qualification; spectators will find their appreciation of sport intensified; participants will be forced to reconsider their values.

What Kahn has done in this book is recollect what it was like to be an avid Dodger fan in the 1950s and then, by a miraculous stroke of luck, to become a baseball writer for the *New York Herald Tribune* at twenty-four, covering his heroes during some of their finest campaigns. But when he has done this, and done it very well with a superior prose style, he moves his book onto an entirely different emotional level by seeking out, almost twenty years later, his former heroes to see how they have adjusted to their post-heroic years. He tells, in singing paragraphs filled with emotional overtones, what happens to the boys of summer when they are forced to become the men of winter.

Perhaps by accident, perhaps because Kahn intended it that way, the team he chose to write about provided an unusual amount of drama, both in summer and winter. Jackie Robinson broke the color barrier; then watched his son stagger into confusion and tragedy; then died prematurely. Roy Campanella played it more cool; his accusers said he Uncle Tommed it; we know for certain that he made himself into one of our greatest catchers, then jammed a rented automobile into a telephone pole, to spend the rest of his life immobilized in a wheelchair. Carl Furillo was one of the most daring outfielders baseball has produced; Kahn finds him an embittered right-wing hard-hat. Billy Cox was a fabled glove; Kahn discovers him serving beer in an American Legion bar.

It is a tender account of how men play games for a brief season, then spend the remainder of their lives listening as strangers drop by their tables to tell them, 'I saw you once . . .' I am reminded of that noble painting by Nicholas Poussin in the Louvre in which the shepherds try to decipher the lines on an ancient tomb left standing in Arcady; there had been days of grandeur, of this there could be no doubt, but now the memorial cannot even be deciphered.

This is the literary tradition in America regarding sports, and in the years ahead each of us will read a dozen new accounts of young studs who tore the town apart in high school and made love to all the pretty girls, went on to college with bundles of illegal money and all the pretty girls, graduated into the professionals with absolutely oodles of money and even more pretty girls, and then, at the age of thirty-two, watched in dismay as the world crumbled and they lost their money, and were deserted by the pretty girls, and ended their lives in despair.

But at this low point I began to look soberly at the hard evidence about me. I have known some sixty major athletes moderately well. The earliest was Domingo Ortega, the Spanish bullfighter who revolutionized his art and performed at the head of his profession for an unheard-of thirty years. The most recent was Taiho, a Japanese sumo wrestler who dominated his sport as no other contemporary athlete has ever dominated his. Taiho's incredible record would have been equaled if Babe Ruth had hit ninety home runs in one year, or Jim Brown had piled up four thousand yards in a single season. In between I have known racing-car drivers, tennis players, deep-sea divers, soccer players and champions in the popular American sports.

And of these sixty athletes, not one has conformed to the myth. Without exception, mine knew considerable fame before the age of thirty and they have conducted themselves with modest distinction after the age of forty. Let's look at the performance of the seven men I mentioned earlier.

Robin Roberts, whom I once described as my ideal athlete because of the way he reared back and slammed in his high hard one and to hell with the consequences, left baseball with an honorable chain of records, and then became a Philadelphia businessman with a delightful, outspoken wife and four sons. He made himself into a civic leader, a patron of the zoological gardens, a member of the board running a distinguished private school, and a coach of young boys.

Hal Greer, graduate of a small college in West Virginia, earned a great deal of money in basketball and saved much of it. After a career longer than the average—because he kept in such keen physical shape—he tried vainly to become a coach, at which I judge he would have been superior, and then resumed private life with dignity and success.

Chuck Bednarik, the man who walks like a gorilla, after compiling records in every aspect of his sport, also tried unsuccessfully to land a job as a coach, or a front-office man, or a publicity hand, or, as he says, 'damned near anything in football'—but had to acknowledge that it wasn't going to happen, and so became a very successful salesman for a company selling concrete. With an unusually beautiful wife and a batch of well-behaved kids, he has adjusted to adult life as well as most of my friends and discharges his aggressions easily by cursing publicly any one connected with the Philadelphia Eagles. 'I gave them a championship and they gave me nothin',' he growls, and he is not exaggerating, for in the waning moments of the 1960 title game with Vince Lombardi's Green Bay Packers, Bednarik pulled a play which saved the championship for Philadelphia. His team was ahead,

17–13, but Green Bay had the ball and quarterback Bart Starr was master-minding a drive which seemed certain to produce the game-winning touch-down. But on what should have been the next-to-last play of the game, with Jim Taylor, the Green Bay fullback, almost free, Bednarik slammed him to the ground with a ferocious tackle, and then so twined his arms and legs about the fallen man that the referee could not untangle them before the clock ran out. Chuck says, 'If I'd allowed him to get up, and they'd a had one more play, and with the way Starr was throwin' that ball, Green Bay woulda' won for sure. So Taylor kept tryin' to bite at my hands and was screamin', "Get offen me, you slob!" But I kept my stranglehold, and by the time the referee untangled us the whistle had blown endin' the game and we had the championship.' Of course he is peeved that he has been unable to find a job in football. Of course a writer could legitimately depict him as a failure who went around trying to relive his days of glamour. But that would not be the whole truth. Bednarik is a giant with giant resentments but also with a giant capacity to live a good life. 'I never go into a man's office talkin' football. I go there to sell him concrete. Now, if when the deal's done he wants to talk about my days at Penn or with the Eagles, be my guest.'

In some ways Ham Place, the cartoonist, is the most remarkable athlete of the lot. Now in his seventies, he is still a championship tennis player, a man almost impossible to defeat. Not long ago the number one and number two players from a Big Ten school were vacationing in our area and wanted a workout to keep their game in shape; they felt they had a good chance of landing the Big Ten championship. Friends told them that there was a fellow who had a court and some good shots, so they called Ham and he called me. When the collegians saw us they sort of gasped; they needed a slam-bang workout and here were two old ducks. 'Should we split up?' they asked solicitously, but Ham said, 'No, we'll try to give you a little competi-tion.' It's always interesting to see a young man hit a tennis ball with all his might, only to have it come floating back. He tries to wallop it even harder, and again it comes back. On his third try there is a slight sign of desperation, and pretty soon you can see the look of bewilderment in his eye. We won the first set 6–3 and the second 6–2, solely because Ham Place, over seventy, has some of the trickiest, meanest shots in the game. He hits no ball without a plan for the next three probable shots, the last of which will be a put-away for him. Like the other men of whom I·speak, he is happily married, with a son and a respected place in his community.

Pete Richards, the old-time professional footballer, is the most compact bundle of aggressions I have ever known. In college he won nine letters, and every game was Armageddon. On the Frankford Yellow Jackets he tore opponents to shreds, and after his playing days were over he operated in the retail business the same way. He retired a wealthy man with a fine family and a murderous determination to win at handball, or golf, or tennis.

Barney Berlinger is something special, a super-athlete now in his sixties. He was registered to enter Swarthmore the year following me, but his father wisely judged that he would have a better chance to graduate if he brushed up his math and English in a good prep school, so late in the summer Mr. Berlinger drove his son out to Mercersburg, where Dr. William Mann Irvine, the gruff headmaster, gave the father a lecture: 'You can't expect to come into a first-class school this late in the season and find a vacancy for your boy. Now you get out of here.' But then Barney sidled into the office, six feet tall, handsomely proportioned, clear-eyed and Dr. Irvine asked, 'Do you play football?' and Barney nodded. 'Well,' the good doctor mused, and then a bright idea struck him. Mercersburg was track-crazy and usually the interscholastic champion. 'Would a big fellow like you possibly know anything about track?' Irvine asked, and Barney said, 'I pole vault twelve-feet-six,' a tremendous height for that time. Dr. Irvine leaped from his chair with the good news: 'Son, we just found a vacancy.' The following year at the national interscholastic championships Barney, who could also run, jump and shot-put, scored more points by himself than the nearest competing team. He continued as an outstanding athlete at Penn and competed in the 1928 Olympics under the legendary coach Lawson Robertson, who said glumly as Finland and Sweden won the gold medals, 'Barney, there's two kinds of runners, human beings and Scandinavians.'

Barney went hunting one day with a friend and remembers remonstrating against the man's taking along a sixteen-year-old boy who hadn't handled a gun too often. 'The man said, "My boy's smart. He'll get by all right," but I was apprehensive, and for some reason I went back and put on a second vest, a leather one, and sure enough just a short while later I go into a swamp to flush some birds, the boy gets excited and fires a full blast right into the middle of my back. It knocked me into the water, and I remember thinking, "What a hell of a way to die! Shot in the back by a kid! And when I knew it was going to happen." Well, I fought against passing out, but I could feel the blood gushing out of my back and my mouth and they rushed me into the hospital and the surgeon said, "That leather vest saved your life. It's incredible you could have taken such a blast and lived." ' The medics cut twenty-five lead pellets out of his back, but by then it was so chopped up they decided to leave the other 210 in place along his backbone and in his lungs. So now when we play tennis, Barney sometimes has to twist his back until the score of lead pellets pressing on his backbone readjust themselves and relieve the pressure on his nerves.

Don Meredith is a special case. One of the most charismatic football players, he came from a small Texas high school, made all-American at

SMU and starred as the controversial quarterback for the Dallas Cowboys. From there he went to ABC-TV, where he attained fame as the honest country humorist contrasted to the snide city slicker Howard Cosell. From there he moved up, he says, to NBC and a career in both TV and the movies. At Meredith's departure from the Monday night phantasmagoria, Mr. Cosell widely reported that the program would not be hurt by his absence, and even intimated that he, Cosell, was pleased that he would no longer have to cover for the Texas hillbilly, but when Meredith quit, he left a conspicuous hole and his absence damaged the program considerably. For his retirement he purchased an old farm not far from where I live. The nearest settlement is the two-house village of Elephant, and he is now known as the squire of that community. If he conforms to the prototype of the American sporting myth, the delayed adolescent who falls from fame and broods about it, he has masked his character well. He seems to me a well-adjusted, happily married, irreverent type who loves to kid himself and the pomposities of others. He handles himself well, is not on the dole, and gives every indication of being able to maintain his complex and satisfying adult life.

In some ways the most reassuring adjustment has been made by tall, red-headed Donald Budge. Long retired from active competition, and with a cellarful of silver trinkets to prove that at one time or another he held every major title, he coaches tennis at Tres Vidas in Acapulco during the winter and at a posh tennis camp along the Delaware River in summer. Married to a beautiful and rowdy girl who takes neither herself nor her famous husband overseriously, Budge adjusts easily to whatever situation he finds himself in, tells great stories on himself, keeps in top condition, and graces any party he attends. I once spent fourteen straight lunches and dinners with him and found him more interesting and relaxing at the end than at the beginning. The good part about Budge's life is that he has been able to make his living in the sport he played with such distinction. We should all be so lucky.

I could continue in this manner, analyzing each of my sixty athletes, but their stories would become repetitious. As youths they knew extraordinary adulation. As relatively young men they had to surrender their places in the sun. Most of them married intelligent and beautiful women; each found himself a good job. They had children, most of whom have turned out well, and they filled places of significance in their society. Most reminisce about their golden days, and those who do not are forced to do so by strangers who love sports. Invariably, in my reasoned judgment, they have handled their adult lives well.

Of Umphlett's three mythic characteristics—an anti-urban mind-set, an inability to deal with women, an infinitely prolonged adolescence—my men certainly escaped the last two. They dated campus queens, and sometimes jet-set dazzlers, but they married stable girls and stayed married to them. They remained youthful in spirit and performance but could not be accused of clinging to a delayed adolescence; most of them attained a maturity far above average.

Umphlett's first generalization, however, did apply to them. They did prefer country life, and many of them, like Don Meredith and Barney Berlinger, went to some pains to ensure themselves of homes in the country where they could hunt and ride horses and run their dogs. But whether this implies that they were afraid of the city's duplicity and sought instead the safe simplicity of rural life, I cannot say. Surely, if preferring country life is a sign of deficiency, more than half our adult population would have to be so stigmatized.

One athlete epitomizes for me the rebuttal of the Umphlett thesis. He is not a friend, but during some research work I was doing in Florida, I kept hearing about him—an unusual man who typified so much of what I was then thinking about—that one morning I sought him out.

He was Billy Vessels, Oklahoma 1949–53, all-American running back and winner of the 1952 Heisman Trophy. He was a rugged man, well groomed, smiling, in his forties. He spoke forcefully and with a precise command of English, but his charm lay in the unpretentiousness with which he recalled old days.

'Let's get one thing straight,' he told me as soon as he discerned the trend of my questioning. 'On my last day in football I said to myself, "All this hoop-la never happened. It was a dream, and my real life starts tomorrow." So I put it aside for twenty years. Absolutely. I didn't get my job through football. And I didn't meet my wife there. And I certainly didn't find my life style in the locker room. I am not a child of football.'

'What happened at the end of twenty years?'

'I was voted into the Hall of Fame. All my old friends from Oklahoma and the professional team in Baltimore, they all crowded into New York and it was a mighty experience. Extremely warm, and at that late date I began to reflect on what sports had meant to me.'

'Like what?'

'Like Bud Wilkinson, at Oklahoma. He enlarged my horizons enormously. He made me a whole new man.' He stopped as if afraid that I might be writing down the wrong things. 'You've got to understand this, and it's difficult to understand, what with the nonsense they're talking about the great dictatorial coaches. But under Wilkinson we had more fun than any other team I've known. The only way I can say it is that he was a man of greatness, and he inspired his players to be the same.'

'What happened to your teammates?'

'Well, I'm sure that some of them must have turned out only average, or even failures. And for them I feel real pity. But when I think of my team I think of Eddie Crowder, who became a fine coach at Colorado. And Buck McPhail, who is with the big Levi Strauss clothing outfit in California. Or Buddy Leake, who's a permanent member of the Million Dollar Round Table in his insurance business. Or Harry Moore, who just sold his oil firm for more than three million. Or the three guys who are now doctors in Oklahoma City. Or the dentists and the educators and businessmen. We weren't world-beaters, Michener, but under Bud Wilkinson we were encouraged to become the best men possible.'

'What have you been doing?'

'You know, a little professional football in Canada. Darrell Royal was my coach. Two years in the artillery. A little pro ball in Baltimore, but already the monsters were moving in and I was too light. So at age twenty-six I put it all behind me. That's when I made that little speech I told you about. Came to Miami. Met a man named Robert Mackle. He didn't even know I'd played football. Never heard of the Heisman Trophy. And I started in real estate and worked like hell year after year.'

In 1968, when Robert Mackle's daughter Barbara was kidnapped and buried alive for eighty-three horrible hours, the family required someone of good reputation and nerves of steel to negotiate with the kidnappers and handle the ransom money. They chose Billy Vessels—he did not tell me this —and for several agonizing days he gambled for the girl's life. With extraordinary self-control he brought the negotiations to a successful conclusion and helped save Barbara from her living grave.

'Luck,' Vessels says of his life. 'Television came along just as I came along. In 1952 the year's big feature would be Oklahoma at Notre Dame, a week or so before balloting for the Heisman Trophy. National television. Big excitement. And we lose 27–21.'

'What was so lucky about that?'

'I broke loose for three touchdowns. Best game I ever had. And all on camera. Without that I doubt if many people in states like New York or Pennsylvania would have heard of me. With it, I was the Oklahoma boy who made good. Pure luck.' One might say that Billy Vessels was the mirror image of Irwin Shaw's Christian Darling, who made one eighty-yard run in the darkness and never recovered. Vessels made three of them in television spotlights and then forgot them, to build an acceptable adult life.

How does one reconcile such reality with the established myth? First, it is necessary to determine if each advocate is using honest data. John Updike in writing *Rabbit, Run* and Jason Miller in constructing his play *That Championship Season* were dealing with real situations as they observed them in the sports-mad coal regions of Pennsylvania. Young men did dedicate their whole lives to basketball and they did fail to mature into reasonable adults. Roger Kahn did observe at firsthand the tragic decline of those resplendent Brooklyn boys. And from research I have done I could list perhaps a hundred miserable cases of young men whose lives had halted abruptly at eighteen or twenty-six or thirty-two when the cheering stopped. Every small town has its quota of athletic failures, every city playground its wasted heroes who put on their basketball shoes for one last taste of glory.

So the negative side is using honest data. What about the other? Billy Vessels says that the majority of his Oklahoma team members achieved pretty good lives. I have said that of the sixty topflight athletes I have known personally, all have performed well as adults. Randy L. Jesick, in a study which has become famous, has analyzed what happened to every member of the University of Pittsburgh 1963 football squad which went 9–1 against the top competition in the nation, finishing third in the polls. This was a hard-nosed club, coached by super-tough John Michelosen, and what were the players doing ten years later?

Of the seventy-one players on the roster, sixty-six had graduated and an amazing thirty-three had stayed on to earn graduate or professional degrees. There were three doctors, fifteen dentists, five lawyers, seven educators, two ministers and twenty-eight in advanced positions in industry. Jesick does not give specifics on the failures; but they could not have been numerous.

He does, however, give the starting line-up of the team—one platoon in those days and all white—and of the eleven men, each landed a good job. He concludes his report with a sentence that must have given him considerable satisfaction: 'They were winners in the game of football, and now they're winners in the game of life.'

Stanford University, which is rather difficult to get into and even harder to get out of with a degree, made a similar study of its athletes who played during the academic year 1969–70 and found that taking 223 young men who participated in the five major sports—baseball, basketball, football, swimming and track—88.3 percent graduated, which is a remarkable achievement, especially since only 82.5 percent of the total student body did so. (Of the fourteen basketball players, all graduated; of the sixty-one football players, fifty-six did, with one likely to do so later.) Father Edmund Joyce, athletic director at Notre Dame has sent me a letter in which he states that '99 percent of our athletes graduate,' and Frank Howard, the outstanding Clemson coach told me, 'Over a coaching lifetime of thirty-nine years I had only two boys of which I am not proud. All the rest went on to make something of themselves.'

Michigan State, on the other hand, has released figures which show that only 51 percent of its athletic-scholarship men graduated with their classes, including an appalling 20 percent of the basketball players, which fortifies my earlier argument that a great many basketball players are in college who shouldn't conceivably be there, except for their ability to snag rebounds. (Of course, some of those who failed to graduate with their classes might trail along later, which supports my argument that all athletic scholarships should henceforth be awarded for five years.)

I think we must concede that the evidence in favor of the athlete is respectable, and we can now try to reconcile these conflicting points of view.

Some high school athletes are shamefully misled and waste their lives, especially blacks. Some college players pursue a dream they can never attain and are self-condemned to a life of protracted adolescence. Some professionals play out their years, fail to earn a pension, and never recover from the shock of subsiding back into the faceless mass.

But many young men and women engage in athletics, acquire a temporary inflated sense of their ability and worth, then have some sense kicked into them and proceed to live perfectly satisfactory lives. They are not scarred; they are not driven to perpetual adolescence; the boys are not afraid of girls and vice versa; and in the vast majority of cases they receive far more good from athletics than they receive harm.

It is possible that books about athletes are most often written by frustrated young intellectuals who *hope* that the agencies of moral compensation see to it that the superjocks whom they have watched so enviously in school and college fall on their faces in later life. The books tend to be written by people who have not themselves participated in games and to whom the fatuous idolatry granted sports heroes is ridiculous or even offensive. They have watched athletes gaining favors from misguided high school faculties and unwarranted scholarships from colleges, and they begin to visualize the day when the young studs who have enjoyed these prerogatives lose them and have to face real life. They want the beautiful girls to abandon them. They want the structured lives to fall apart. They want life to correct its manifest injustices, and they write stories in which these corrections take place.

The archetype of writer I am describing must be James Thurber, a man tormented by insecurities and blessed with one of the most mordant pens of our time. Blinded in one eye by a freak sports accident, he had to sit by and watch the heroes parade past, especially at Ohio State—which Philip Roth's monumentally silly basketball player also attended—and out of this frustration came the description of Bolenciecwcz, the lineman that *Time* has called 'the quintessential dumb jock.'

> In order to be eligible to play it was necessary for him to keep up in his studies, a very difficult matter, for while he was not dumber than an ox, he was not any smarter.

Even Shakespeare indulged in this kind of abuse, and possibly for the same reason. In *King Lear,* Act 1, Scene IV, line 86, this confrontation takes place between the king, the infamous Oswald, and Kent, loyal servant to the king:

> *Lear.* Do you bandy looks with me, you rascal? *(Striking him.)*
> *Oswald.* I'll not be strucken, my lord.
> *Kent (Tripping up his heels.)* Nor tripped neither, you base *football player.
> *Lear.* I thank thee, fellow. Thou serv'st me, and I'll love thee.

In a footnote to describe *football,* some cave-chested editor who loved the library better than the playing field has added this gloss:

> **football* (a low game played by idle boys to the scandal of sensible men)

Literature is filled with similar snide attacks on sports, but one night as I was reciting some of them, a wise librarian drew my attention to a sardonic little poem in which the comic versifier Morris Bishop distills in a few lines, as poets often do, what I had been thinking. 'Settling Some Old Football Scores' he calls his poem and it is written from the envious point of view of 'a small dark wiry person' who in his youth has had to sit in the library and watch the football heroes go past. His animosity reveals itself in the first stanza:

> This is the football hero's moment of fame.
> Glory is his, though erstwhile he may have shunned it.
> In hall and street he hears the crying of his name.
> By youth and maiden, alumnus and radio pundit.

In the next two stanzas Bishop relates how the hero's fame is revered in newspapers, in maiden's dreams and in the cinema. But! 'In literature his fame has reached its minima.' In Broadway plays the football hero is shown to be a downright dummy and in serious fiction a barbarian. And then in the last two verses Bishop's inferiority-ridden scholar gets his revenge:

> We read of him telling victories won of yore,
> We see him vainly pursue fame's fleeting bubble;
> The maid he adores is certain to leave him for
> A small dark wiry person, the author's double!

O football hero! Now while a million throats
  Acclaim thy glorious deeds, just set this much down:
A small dark wiry person is taking notes.
  Literature will make the ultimate touchdown.

I first became aware of the peculiar life a great athlete lives, when in the fall of 1960 John Kennedy was running for President and discovered that his regular supporters were finding it impossible to force newspaper coverage in certain strongly Republican states. A glamour plane was put together, with a variety of movie stars, intellectuals like Arthur Schlesinger, Jr., and some of the Kennedy girls. We flew into eleven states, I recall, held meetings, and by dint of ingenious publicity devices, managed to pry a few headlines from a reluctant press.

One member of our troupe accounted for most of our success. It was Stan Musial, who held a special place in the hearts of baseball fans across the country. I lived with him for the better part of two weeks and witnessed the awe and love in which he was held. I remember especially one dark, windy night as we landed at a small Nebraska airport well after dusk. In the shadows we saw several hundred silent ranchers awaiting us, dark shadows against the night sky.

A lone floodlight was switched on, and as I approached them I could see the stern anticipation with which they waited. 'Jeff Chandler!' the excited announcer yelled, but no one responded. 'Arthur Schlesinger, Pulitzer Prize historian,' but no one responded. 'Angie Dickinson,' as lovely then as now, but no one cheered. 'Ethel Kennedy, a great woman in her own right!' but no Republican cheers for her.

Then Stan Musial appeared, and before the announcer could name him, a low rumble rose from the crowd, and men pressed forward, dragging their boys with them, and one man shouted, 'It's Stan the Man!' And a great cry rose from the night, and Musial walked into the glare, a tall, straight man in his late thirties, an authentic American folk hero, and the men fell back to let him pass.

As we disappeared into a waiting car I heard one rancher say to his son, 'For the rest of your life, Claude, you can tell people about this night. You saw Stan Musial.' (Of the eleven states in which Musial campaigned, Kennedy lost every one.)

It was that way with Domingo Ortega, the bullfighter. I saw him not long ago, in his seventies, a dignified caballero with white hair and that incessant retinue of men and women who longed to be near him. I spent the evening with Taiho when he retired from the sumo ring, and hundreds stood along the streets and at the windows of the restaurant, longing to see him. It was the same with Joe DiMaggio when I knew him briefly, and it is that way now with Robin Roberts, Chuck Bednarik and Don Meredith.

The athlete lives in a world the rest of us can scarcely imagine. That any survive to live reasonably decent lives is a miracle. What kind of man or woman is fitted for this crucible?

Obviously, to play basketball requires superior height, to play football demands superior weight, to be a jockey requires a minimum weight. To perform well in any sport demands some degree of superior coordination, so the physical component is always critical. But studies are emerging which show that athletes also tend to be superior in intelligence. Some of these studies depend upon class grades and must be suspect, since as we have seen, high school and college teachers are often either tempted or bullied into awarding grades that are not earned; but there are other more substantial studies which do not depend upon subjective grades, and these, too, support the claim that athletes tend to be somewhat more intelligent than the general run of the school, college or adult population. I have found this to be true; James Thurber's Bolenciecwcz can still be found on most campuses, but he is far less common than he used to be.

Other studies show that athletes tend to be better adjusted socially. They have more friends, exert more social leadership, are forces for stability, and are objects of admiration. James Coleman found that the athlete had three times as many friends as the non-athlete, and Richard Rehberg, who has done the major work in this field, concludes:

> Contrary to the belief that athletics is detrimental to scholastic performance and educational expectations, the evidence we have reviewed appears to support the belief that interscholastic athletics is conducive not only to higher scholastic performance but to higher educational expectations as well. (That is, sport encourages high school boys to continue their education.)

Rehberg suggests that the athlete's superior experience stems from five conditions: 1) he belongs to the achievement-oriented crowd; 2) he develops achievement values which steer him toward further education; 3) he maintains a positive self-image; 4) he realizes that others expect him to do well in his classes; 5) he is supported by encouragement from his family and faculty, and receives superior counseling. With this kind of supportive system, athletics has every chance to exert a constructive influence, and parents are well advised to encourage their children to share in an experience which can produce so much good.

Some studies are emerging which show that athletes are slightly more tense, more subject to depression, more insecure emotionally than the non-athlete, but these usually relate to intense game-competition situations. The Harvard Psychiatric Service has reported that more non-athletes than athletes seek its help, but that when an athlete does report, he usually has several grinding problems, whereas the non-athlete usually has but one, and it less pressing. Also, the athlete rarely seeks help of his own volition:

> For many athletes, physical activity, rather than talking things out, appears to offer a means of expressing feelings and aggressions. Perhaps this substitution of action for words contributes to the seeming reluctance of athletes to come to a service that requires that they articulate their feelings.

Some years ago the San Diego Chargers of the NFL hired a psychiatrist in hope that he could tell the management things about football players that they did not already know, thus giving San Diego an edge over other teams. In a delightful report published in *Saturday Review* (October 5, 1974), Dr. Arnold Mandell, the shrink in question, tells his findings. The most significant was that each position, offensive and defensive, had its peculiar requirements, and the men who filled those positions conformed to patterns:

> I quickly learned what many Sunday widows already realized—that football is not a game but a religion, a metaphysical island of fundamental truth in a highly verbal, disguised society, a throwback of 30,000 generations of anthropological time.
>
> After only a few weeks I rushed to Coach Svare with my first systematic insight. 'Harland,' I said, 'I think I can tell whether a player is on offense or defense just by looking at his locker. The offensive players keep their lockers clean and orderly, but the lockers of the defensive men are a mess. In fact, the better the defensive player, the bigger the mess.'

And he proceeds to state why—offensive players seek an orderly world, with every man doing his assigned job, while defensive players like to wreck established offense, act on the spur of the moment and make unexpected tackles—but it is his analysis of the psychological requirements of each individual position which is most instructive. I have often daydreamed of being a cornerback and making flashy interceptions, but when I read the prescription for this hypochondriac position I realized that I would go stark batty trying to fill it. (While Mandell was revealing his hidden truths the Chargers compiled a 6–22 record.)

The most intriguing study I came upon was written not by a psychologist or an athletic philosopher, but by a geographer, John F. Rooney, of Oklahoma State University. He said in effect: 'Let us study the young men with football talent the way a geographic economist approaches a cargo of gold ore. Where was it mined? Where is it being sent for processing? Who will be the ultimate user?' He used as data the rosters of 136 major college teams over a period of six years, covering 14,500 players in all.

Rooney's conclusions are striking. They appear in three places, *The Geographical Review* (October 1969); Rooney's book *A Geography of American Sport;* and as a chapter in the excellent anthology *Sport and the Social Order* by Donald Ball and John Loy, which I shall be referring to several times. Rooney proves that a city like New York, with its crowded areas and inadequate playing space, produces 'at the incredibly low rate of only 13 percent of the national norm.' Philadelphia, Boston, San Francisco and St. Louis are almost as bad. But the suburbs of these same cities, where there is space for gridirons, produce more than the average. 'The counties around New York City operate at a rate fifteen times greater than the city.' So do the suburbs of Boston, Los Angeles and San Francisco. But it is in his analysis of the fifty states that his most interesting figures appear:

ORIGIN OF FOOTBALL PLAYERS ON 136 MAJOR-COLLEGE TEAMS
EXPRESSED AS A PER CAPITA INDEX NUMBER
(Norm: Alabama, Massachusetts, Florida = 1.03)

Rank	State	Index	Rank	State	Index
1.	Ohio	1.74	9.	Oklahoma	1.30
2.	Texas	1.68	10.	West Virginia	1.29
3.	Utah	1.67	45.	Maryland	.57
4.	Delaware	1.60	46.	Wisconsin	.56
5.	Mississippi	1.57	46.	Indiana	.56
6.	New Hampshire	1.51	48.	Missouri	.49
7.	Pennsylvania	1.47	49.	New York	.47
8.	Kansas	1.31	50.	South Dakota	.20

Rooney, John F., *A Geography of American Sport.*

Which states provide the greatest per capita percentage of players for the professional teams? Mississippi 2.94; Louisiana 2.44; Texas 2.11; Alabama 1.74; and Georgia 1.40, which data provide support for my earlier argument that it is young people from less advantaged areas who look to professional sports as a way of life. You do not find young people of promise from the advantaged states like Wisconsin, Iowa, Connecticut and Oregon bothering with professional sports. They don't have to.

Rooney's study, an extensive one filled with graphs and instructive maps, offers other data which one should discuss at length; I found most interesting his identification of certain areas in which the high schools produced football players for export:

COUNTIES THAT RANK HIGH IN OUTPUT OF COLLEGE FOOTBALL PLAYERS

Rank	County	Major Cities	Number of Players	Per Capita Rate
Counties ranking high in both total number and per capita comparison				
1.	Jefferson, Ohio	Steubenville	37	4.66
2.	Beaver, Pa.	Aliquippa	66	3.99
3.	Potter, Texas	Amarillo	33	3.57
4.	Harrison, Miss.	Biloxi, Gulfport	32	3.35
5.	Galveston, Texas	Galveston, Texas City	37	3.30
6.	Westmoreland, Pa.	Monessen, Jeannette, Latrobe, Irwin	91	3.23
7.	Washington, Pa.	Washington	54	3.11
8.	Fayette, Pa.	Uniontown	41	3.03
9.	Lucas, Ohio	Toledo	109	2.81
10.	Trumbull, Ohio	Warren	43	2.58
11.	Allegheny, Pa.	Pittsburgh	333	2.56
12.	Hillsborough, N.H.	Manchester, Nashua	35	2.46
Counties ranking high in per capita comparision only				
1.	Morgan, Utah	Morgan	6	26.48
2.	Rockwall, Texas	Rockwall	7	14.91
3.	Young, Texas	Graham, Newcastle, Olney	14	10.15
4.	Jones, Miss.	Laurel, Ellisville	8	7.40
5.	Simpson, Miss.	Mendenhall, Magee	11	6.90
6.	Burleson, Texas	Caldwell, Somerville	6	6.88
7.	Hutchinson, Texas	Borger, Phillips	17	6.15
8.	Transylvania, N.C.	Brevard	8	6.10
9.	Moore, Texas	Dumas, Sunroy	7	6.00
10.	Andrews, Texas	Andrews	6	5.58
11.	Victoria, Texas	Victoria	20	5.38

Idem.

Steubenville, Ohio, and Aliquippa, Pennsylvania, the two leaders in per capita rate, are some twenty-five miles apart. In fact, seven of the twelve leading counties are located in the steel region of western Pennsylvania and eastern Ohio. The belt that stretches from Johnstown, Pennsylvania, through the Pittsburgh region, across the panhandle of West Virginia, and via Youngstown to Cleveland accounted for 1,250 ball players, representing a production 2.5 times the national average. Thus from an area with a population of slightly more than six million came nearly 9 percent of the nation's major-college recruits, and they go anywhere to play.

Rooney also addresses himself to the problem that agitated me: 'Where is the hotbed of collegiate football?' He comes up with a statistical answer

—ignoring the emotional factors that impressed me so strongly—and shows that certain states support college and university teams far out of proportion to their population:

EMPHASIS ON MAJOR-COLLEGE FOOTBALL BY STATES
EXPRESSED AS A PER CAPITA INDEX NUMBER
(Norm: Connecticut 1.04)

Rank	State	No. of Teams	Index	Rank	State	No. of Teams	Index
1.	Utah	4	5.94	18.	Oklahoma	3	1.71
2.	New Hampshire	2	4.36	22.	Texas	10	1.38
3.	Wyoming	1	4.01	25.	Ohio	9	1.23
4.	Idaho	2	3.98	29.	Nebraska	1	0.94
5.	Vermont	1	3.39	35.	Alabama	2	0.81
6.	Rhode Island	2	3.08	41.	Michigan	3	0.51
7.	Arizona	3	3.05	45.	Wisconsin	1	0.34
8.	Delaware	1	2.97	46.	Missouri	1	0.31

(Alaska, Hawaii, Nevada, South Dakota had no major football teams at the time of the study and ranked 47 through 50.)

Idem.

One final item: Pennsylvania produced 1,333 high school players in this study, and 78 percent had to emigrate out of the state in order to find a college in which to play. Texas produced 1,290 players, and 82 percent of them found a college in Texas which wanted them.

Rooney gives similar breakdowns for other sports, and those for basketball contain some surprises. The city of New York does not lead the nation in supplying hotshot high school players for export; Philadelphia does. In the per capita production, Utah leads, possibly because Mormons emphasize physical well-being, but as the following table shows, Utah is such a basketball-crazy state, with four major teams in a sparsely populated area, that it has to import sixty-one players, seven more than it produces at home (53 percent of total). New Jersey, on the other hand, produces many fine basketball players, but because it is the state with the fewest colleges per capita, most of its stars have to emigrate if they want to play (86 percent). North Carolina and Maryland, whose teams have dominated eastern play for some years, produce so few players from within their states that their championship teams have to be recruited mainly from the north. In fact, no southern state produces anywhere near its projected quota, and whole teams in some of the southern conferences have to be lured south by attractive scholarships.

WHERE 161 MAJOR COLLEGES FIND THEIR BASKETBALL PLAYERS
SURPLUS STATES, LEFT COLUMN; DEFICIT STATES, RIGHT COLUMN

	Players Produced	Percent Exported	Percent Exported		Players Produced	Imported	Percent Imported
New Jersey	201	172	86	Texas	214	96	31
Indiana	234	173	74	Virginia	72	75	51
Illinois	359	233	65	Utah	54	61	53
Kentucky	163	100	61	North Carolina	73	101	58
Pennsylvania	310	184	59	Maryland	18	49	73
New York	354	177	50	New Hampshire	15	45	75
Ohio	303	128	42	South Carolina	19	82	81
California	392	119	30	Rhode Island	8	52	87

Idem.

A principal characteristic of serious athletes is that they can absorb pain much better than the average person. They may become hypochondriacal about it, and overly body-conscious, but they can withstand a level of pain that is startling. When I had the opportunity of attending a training camp run by one of the top NFL teams, I was prepared for everything I saw: the long drills, the intense dedication of the coaches, the skull sessions, the endless hours watching film, the huge helpings at the training table—everything, that is, except the obvious pain these men had to withstand.

I spent long hours in the taping room, watching as the trainers slapped on miles of adhesive, and it occurred to me that every one of these players bore with him some damage from previous seasons or some heavily discolored bruises from yesterday's drill. One speedy young black from a small southern college had on his right arm a lump bigger than a good-sized lemon; morning and afternoon the trainer applied special protective gear to absorb shocks which might land in its vicinity. Finally I asked what the lump was.

'Calcium deposit,' the lineman said.

'How come?'

'Gettin' hit day after day when I slam into the other guy.'

I moved the huge hard mass and could see him wince. 'What'll you do about it?'

'At the end of the season, get it cut out.'

'And in the meantime?'

'Live with it. What else?'

When I speak of the new athlete, I am afraid that many of the old clichés about sportsmanship have to be discarded. I was raised on that sentimental but moving stanza from Sir Henry Newbolt's 'Vitaï Lampada.' It tells of the fledgling cricketer at a boys' school in England who goes to bat at the end of a crucial game, exhorted by his team captain to do his absolute best to score the runs that will give his side victory:

> THERE'S a breathless hush in the Close to-night—
> Ten to make and the match to win—
> A bumping pitch and a blinding light,
> An hour to play and the last man in.
> And it's not for the sake of a ribboned coat,
> Or the selfish hope of a season's fame,
> But his Captain's hand on his shoulder smote—
> 'Play up! play up! and play the game!'

A disturbing group of studies shows that 'varsity lettermen and subsidized athletes score lower on sportsmanship measurements than do non-participants.' This is important, because if the ideals I learned from Newbolt and others are valuable, and I think they are, then it is the non-athlete who best upholds them and it is the athlete who knows that sentimental talk about sportsmanship is for the birds. Vince Lombardi's dictate about winning is a much more relevant precept than Newbolt's command to play the game.

We are back to the question of sport and character. Thomas Tutko has summarized the arguments in an article which has received both condemnation and support: 'Sport: If You Want to Build Character, Try Something Else.' And if players and coaches and owners persist in signing contracts and then breaking them whenever a slightly better offer comes along, sports are going to get such a dirty reputation that honest people who consider themselves bound by their word will find them distasteful and shun them.

I am beguiled by some of the nonsense that surrounds the athlete, and I am surprised that he emerges as reasonably sane as he does. Take, for one ridiculous example, this business of all-American. It would seem to me that any reasonably gifted young man would aspire to this high accolade. I would if I had the talent, and in the old days when Walter Camp picked the eleven top players in the country the designation meant something.

But today the process of naming an all-American team has degenerated into sheer burlesque and if any young man has enough talent to slip on a uniform, he stands a good chance of becoming an all-American something or other. I have noted this progression:

• At the beginning of every season the athletic department of each school identifies the player its publicity department is going to back for that year's all-American. (Big universities sometimes nominate two or three.) A publicity brochure is then printed up, often in four colors, proclaiming 'Tech State's all-American!' I have as I write a handful of these announcements and I have followed the results of six or seven of them through the season. Never, but never, is the local press allowed to refer to the nominee as anything but 'Tech State's all-American,' even though no outside agency has yet confirmed this august title. Since some 695 colleges and universities play football, it is obvious that before the season begins we already have nearly one thousand self-proclaimed all-Americans.

• At the end of the season, if even one newspaper or radio station or magazine or television station names a man to its all-American team, he is forever confirmed. Since a modern all-American football team consists of at least twenty-six players instead of the pristine eleven, it is quite possible that as many as four or five hundred men will be designated and will spend the rest of their lives in their hometowns as all-Americans, even though the origin of the title may have been only the local East Cup Cake *Bugle.*

• If even two papers, of whatever size, name the young man, he becomes the 'Consensus All-American' invariably spelled *concensus.*

• If more than two nominate him, he becomes 'Everybody's All-American.'

• And the other day I saw a real winner referred to as an 'all-American all-American.' I judge there are about three hundred of these each year. On the opening pages of this chapter I referred to Chuck Bednarik as an 'all-American all-Everything' because the mere phrase all-American was so depreciated as to be meaningless.

This nonsense has been carried to its apex by an enterprising firm that publishes a yearly book, with photographs, of 'our high school all-Americans.' To gain entry the young athlete simply sends in his picture and fifteen dollars; then he appears with some four or five hundred other stellar athletes of all-American fame. The lid was blown off this scheme by a newspaper which as a gag submitted the name of a cheerleader, who was promptly designated an all-American fullback. When the paper queried the publishers, they replied, 'Who's being hurt?' I had exactly that feeling when I looked at the most recent publicity brochure to reach my desk: 'John Jones, Our all-American!' The fine print disclosed that John had indeed been nominated, by one press association, as one of ninety honorable mentions!

Murray Kempton, in a long review of seven different books on sports, headed his cynical witty comment with the eye-catching title 'Jock-Sniffing,' referring to those men and women who, like me, have always respected athletes and enjoyed being in their presence. One glorious summer I toured in the wake of Domingo Ortega through the bullrings of Spain, and thirty-five years later wrote about Spain as a consequence of what I saw that year. I did the same with a remarkable troupe of bullfighters in Mexico. I attended all the sumo fights of Taiho that I could, and through two heart-breaking years I sat weekly in Fenway Park as the Red Sox with Ted Williams tried vainly to outlast the New York Yankees with Joe DiMaggio.

I have taken sports seriously, and those who play them, too. I was fortunate to have worked with one of America's premier publishers, Bennett Cerf, who was an admirable man to whom I still feel indebted. It always bothered him as to why we could not be better friends, because he knew I respected him. He raised the subject several times, and I finally had to tell him, 'I could never feel really close to anyone who rooted for the Yankees.' As a sportsman, he understood. For me, any year was a success if the Yankees lost, and I have been somewhat frustrated in recent seasons when the Yankees finished really low in the standings. I like it better when they remain in contention through August and collapse in late September. It lends a nice touch to autumn.

I would never admit that I was only a jock-sniffer, for I could handle myself reasonably well in whatever sport I tried, but I do confess that I have enjoyed talking with athletes. The most impressive I've seen in recent years is Ken Dryden, goalie for the Montreal Canadiens. Tall, above average in looks, unusually intelligent and street-smart, he could represent the prototype of the new athlete, the Bill Bradleys, the John Havliceks, the O.J. Simpsons. I interrupted a Canadien practice to ask if he could drop by my hotel for a short interview; then I got lost in that underground maze which is the pride of Montreal, and was shamefully late. I supposed that Dryden would have been long since gone, but there he was, seated on the floor outside my door, reading a law book.

'The maze,' I said apologetically.

'Few unravel it.' He laughed, and we went down to the bar, where we both had ginger ale.

He saw life clearly and knew that hockey was merely a gate-opener, a thrilling adventure for the early years. He'd even had the guts to drop out for a whole year to complete his law degree and ultimately he would shift to some productive activity like law or politics or business management. He must have an I.Q. of more than 180, and his superlative athletic competence has been proved many times over, for he is one of the best goalies in the business and has led his team to a championship.

There are many young men and women around today like Ken Dryden and Billy Vessels and Robin Roberts—to name three examples from three radically different sports—and we can hope that there will be a constant supply forthcoming. I wish that the 'small dark wiry persons' who write about athletes so disparagingly would just once build their fiction around a character like Ken Dryden.

And yet, being a writer myself, if I were to attempt a novel on this theme, even though I know what I would do about the commendable athletes who survive, I would base it on Jimmy Foxx. The drama of his life was so compelling and its denouement so tragic that I would not be able to avoid it.

James Emory Foxx was born on a farm near Sudlersville on the eastern shore of Maryland in 1907. Since this was the same year in which I was born, I followed his meteoric career with special interest, comparing my drab accomplishments with his resplendent ones. When I started work on this chapter, one of the first things I did was make a wintry pilgrimage to Sudlersville, a small crossroads country town.

I went to the bank and asked the vice-president, 'Is there anyone around here who remembers Jimmy Foxx?' and he replied, 'We all do. But the barber over there knew him best.'

Fortunately, the barber turned out to be a Ring Lardner type. His shop stood next to the house, now torn down, in which Jimmy had lived during his years of fame. 'Since you're interested,' he said, 'I'll give you a real Jimmy Foxx haircut,' and as he did he shared his many recollections.

'He was a big boy, huge square face, square shoulders, square arms. At fourteen he was knockin' balls right out of our little field, and Home Run Frank Baker managin' the Easton team in the Eastern Shore League heard of him and he come up to watch this boy slam homers and Frank said, "He'll hit more'n I ever did."

'Jimmy musta been fifteen or maybe sixteen when he started playin' for Easton, and down there he hit the ball so far the whole eastern shore was talkin' about him. When Jimmy was eighteen Baker told Connie Mack, because you see, Easton was a farm club for the A's which made Foxx legally their property already. Any rate, at eighteen this big country boy with the mighty shoulders was a big leaguer and he picked up right where he left off at Easton.'

I told the barber I remembered those first years. I was still in high school when this amazing natural athlete hit the big time, and the echoes reverberated for years. Fifty-eight home runs in one year. Hits that won World Series games. Champion of everything, with a batting average as good as the best. I must have watched this huge, square-faced boy play a hundred games, always with distinction, and he remained my favorite, the same age as I.

'But he was always a drinker,' the barber told me as he clipped away. 'And he wasted his money somethin' shameful. I saw in the paper where he earned maybe $250,000 and held on to practically none. A party? An automobile ride to the next town for some pool-shooting? A little hell-raisin' for any purpose? You could always count on Jimmy in the good years when he had the money.'

At thirty-eight the good years ended and I lost track of Foxx. I heard vaguely that he was in California, then in Florida, then mixed up in some land deal somewhere. He returned to my consciousness one night in 1956 in a peculiar way. Barney Berlinger, now president of a company making precision gears, told me after dinner, 'Strangest thing happened today. I was out on the street near our shop and who do I see but Jimmy Foxx! Same old square face and happy smile, but very much overweight, very much the bum, his eyes barely able to focus. He recognized me and said, "Remember me, Barney? The good times we used to have?"

'Did I remember? As a boy Jimmy had been not only a good baseball player but a great track star too. In spite of his bulk he could run like a deer. Held the Maryland title for the hundred-yard dash and the two-twenty. Just after he signed his first big contract with the A's he picked me up one day to go down to the eastern shore for a meet. We drove at eighty miles an hour in his convertible and he kept firing a .45 revolver at telephone poles. Lew Krause was in a second car, an old one, trying to keep up with us but falling farther behind, so Jimmy pulled over and waited for him to catch up. Then we drove together into the center of Dover, and Jimmy went into the showroom of a Studebaker dealer and bought a new car right off the floor. Flashing a big roll of bills, he paid the man on the spot and told Krause, "Now maybe you can keep up," and we roared south, with him firing his .45 at the telephone poles.

'We laughed about the old days and finally Jimmy said, "Barney, I'm desperate for a job. Anything you could possibly do for me?"

'So I took him into our plant and as soon as the men saw him they stopped work and crowded around, and everyone said, "Jimmy, you were the greatest," and they talked about the time he hit one of Lefty Gomez' best pitches so far and so hard that it broke one of the seats in the top row of the left-field stands at Yankee Stadium.

'And all the time Jimmy was sucking in his gut and telling one man after another, "I could get in shape again. I could lose a little weight and handle most anything you wanted to throw at me." And he told everyone, "I'm a little ashamed that I've allowed myself to get out of shape, but I could sweat off a little weight and be right back in there." There was no job that he could handle.'

In midwinter, 1958, when Jimmy was fifty years old, the sports pages of the country carried a dismal story. Boston sportswriters wanted someone for their winter banquet and naturally they thought of Old Double X, who had played at Fenway Park for many good years, but when they wrote to him they discovered, through one of his three teenage children, that the Foxx family was living in a shack, with no money. The father was dead broke and able to eat only because his eighteen-year-old son had dropped out of school and found a small job.

Well, there's nothing more sentimental than a sports fan, and soon the phones were ringing in newspaper offices everywhere. Roscoe McGowen wrote:

Old Double X has been double-crossed by time and fate. But Jimmy is about to rebound from misfortune's blows. The story that he was 'flat broke' has brought such a flood of offers of jobs that Foxx is overwhelmed.

'I just want a job,' said Jimmy. 'I want to be able to take care of my wife and three children. Baseball? Yes, I'd like a job in baseball. Sure, I'm broke. I've been pretty much broke for ten years. Oh, I've had a few jobs here and there, but nothing much.'

But now the job offers were rolling in! I took the trouble to find out what these munificent offers actually were. Jimmy Silin, his former manager who must have earned a small fortune off Jimmy, sent him four hundred dollars. Someone sent a small check to a radio station in Bridgeport, Connecticut. An old-time friend said he had nothing definite but he thought he might be able to find Jimmy a speaking job here or there. He would be welcomed at a sportsman's show. There might be a job in Spokane. All this for a man fifty years old with a wife and three hungry kids. You could have collected the whole nebulous bundle and it wouldn't have totaled a thousand real dollars.

At age fifty-nine the huge man died, and his obituaries carried two interesting items. Shortly before Foxx's death, Willie Mays had hit the home run which enabled him to pass Foxx, who had stood second in the home-run derby at 534. 'I hope Mays goes on to break Ruth's record,' Foxx said generously. 'They always said only left-handers could hit the long ball. They even teach right-handed youngsters to bat left-handed.' The second item was that Foxx had quit baseball one year before he would have become eligible for a pension.

As I was about to leave Sudlersville the man at the general store told me, 'While you were getting your haircut I told Mrs. . . .' and he used a name I had better not repeat, 'that you were in town asking questions about Jimmy Foxx and she said she'd be glad to see you, because she knew him well.'

I walked down to her neat frame house and introduced myself. She invited me in and sat me in a needlepoint chair protected by an antimacassar. 'I'm seventy-four,' she said primly but with a certain excitement, 'and I knew Jimmy all his life. He was a mean-spirited person, never did anything for his family while he had lots of money, then sponged off of them after he went broke. When his father died, and he was in Florida, he didn't have carfare home and we had to take up a collection right here in Sudlersville and wire it to him so that he could attend his father's funeral. Imagine, a grown man with children who couldn't even manage things well enough to attend a family funeral.'

The Jimmy Foxx story would make an excellent book, but if I wrote it I would be guilty of the same error into which Roger Kahn fell when he wrote about the Dodgers of the early 1950s. I have said how much I admire that beautifully written baseball story, but I am not blind to its inherent defect: Kahn stresses the fact that baseball heroes retire and lead lives of frustration, ignoring the fact that all professions produce men and women who end their lives in despair. I would like to write a book about the men who graduated from the Harvard School of Business full of hope, only to end their lives in prison or in grim failure, or about the young people who know one season of success on Broadway or in Hollywood and long years of subsequent emptiness, or about any group of Americans who pursue any occupation to their despair.

Most of life is a falling-away, a gradual surrender of the dream. The reason sports provide such dramatic material is that the climax comes so early in a man's life, the decline so swiftly. For a truly great athlete like Jimmy Foxx to enter the downward slide in his mid-thirties is tragic, because of both the magnitude of his fame and the totality of his collapse. But his story merely intensifies the story of us all. What a book I could write about the young authors of promise I have known whose descent to oblivion was as swift as Foxx's but less well publicized. Sports provide an added poignancy because we make such a fuss over the young athlete and are so quick to forget the has-been.

As I worked on these paragraphs, trying to clarify my attitudes toward sports in literature, I received vivid demonstration of the conflict that always exists between the normal and the dramatic. I attended the fiftieth reunion of my championship basketball team and was happy to see that the boys I had played with had all become solid citizens of our society. George Waddington had retired from a substantial job in Philadelphia. Ed Twining was treasurer of our principal bank and the father of three sons whose athletic prowess has brought him much gratification. Peg McNealy was the father of three sons, too; his had tended toward the artistic and had done well. Bill Polk had served a long career in the army, with honor. No tragic declines here, and as we gathered I could hear again the song which some inspired 1924 cheerleader had set to the tune of 'Just Give Me a June Night, the Moonlight and You':

> Just give us McNealy, and Twining and Polk,
> Michener too, and Waddington, and then watch our smoke.

It had never seemed strange to me, in those old days, to hear an entire student body, from first grade to twelfth, chanting that song of praise. We were, after all, athletes and we deserved the roaring plaudits. In my home-town newspaper I am described till this day as the high-school athlete . . . who happened to write books.

But then I thought of Harry Bigley, that golden lad who had played forward with me, the champion of champions, first in our area to shoot equally well with either hand, the kid without nerves who could net nineteen out of twenty-one foul tries when one player shot them all, the handsome, straight-A lad for whom everything was possible. At an early age he had been struck with a back infection that left him so sorely crippled that when an ice storm came he slipped and, lacking control, killed himself. If I ever watched a heroic character pursued by envious Greek furies, it was he, and I suppose that if I were to write now about our team, I would find myself focusing on him. He had stood at the apex, in college days a forward on little Ursinus, who defeated mighty Penn almost single-handedly in the era when Penn ruled. And he had seen the glory fade.

Coaches

The coach is a special kind of athlete, the quintessence of the breed. If you take the salient characteristics of the athlete, and cube them, forcing them all into the mold of one hypertensive man, you have the foundation for a coach.

To understand the complexity of the coach's job I recommend two books which have recently appeared on Woody Hayes, for until you have read them you cannot comprehend the pressure cooker in which the big-time coaches live. The books are radically different. The first, by Jerry Brondfield, is *Woody Hayes and the 100-Yard War* and is a frank hagiography written from the inside. It makes the volcanic Ohio State leader one of the most endearing, cantankerous and capable men in America. I especially recommend pages 100–198 as a day-by-day dissection of just what a coach does, and why he earns his salary, however great it is.

The other biography, *Buckeye,* by Robert Vare, was written from the outside and is certainly not a puff job. It depicts a brutal disciplinarian, an organizing genius and a wild man in his instantaneous responses to distressing situations. Here I recommend pages 77–101, which explain how a big-time university finds and recruits its players, and pages 102–126, which show how a football machine fits into a university structure.

From close study of these and half a dozen similar accounts, and from what I have observed at close hand of the work of outstanding football coaches like Ara Parseghian, Bo Schembechler and Bear Bryant, and Frank McGuire in basketball, I have reached certain conclusions.

No other member of any faculty is subjected to the close and constant scrutiny which the coach experiences. He is written about in the papers, criticized on radio and television, and reviewed constantly by the alumni who pay the bills. If he is of a sensitive or retiring type, he has no place in coaching.

Nor is any other faculty member subjected to the rigorous performance-evaluation which a coach must undergo. If he is deficient, a crowded stadium witnesses his failure, and he is not allowed to remain deficient very long. An ordinary faculty member can get away with murder for decades without detection.

Few other members of the faculty exert the degree of constructive leadership manifested by the coach. The testimony on this point is overwhelming; perhaps athletes are several degrees more simplistic than non-athletes and are thus predisposed to absorb the leadership their coaches exert, but too many athletes have testified to the moral importance of their coach to deny that it exists.

Most coaches more than earn their salaries. Since the curious system devised by America requires schools to provide public entertainment of a professional caliber, it is to the successful coach that we must look for the creation of a team that will enlist a maximum following. A basketball coach like Frank McGuire is worth a fortune to the University of South Carolina; a football coach like Don Shula is worth millions when he converts the Miami Dolphins first into contenders and then into champions. From the point of demonstrable worth, I would suppose that most successful coaches are severely underpaid insofar as salary is concerned, about correctly paid if television contracts and other perquisites are added in.

Coaches tend to be simplistic, conservative and dictatorial, and the outstanding ones have these characteristics to a marked degree. They operate in a pragmatic world in which raw success is measurable and determinative. John D. Massengale, himself a head coach at Eastern Washington State College, has compiled an excellent summary of what the coach should be: a member of a closely united occupational subculture operating somewhat against the grain of the rest of the faculty. His paper can be found in *The Phi Delta Kappan* for October 1974; in it he argues that coaches inherit a particular set of behavior patterns, values, language tricks and general life style. With machine-gun brevity Massengale lists some of those characteristics:

> Coaches as a group are aggressive and highly organized, seldom paying attention to what others say. They display unusually high psychological endurance, persistence and inflexibility. Coaches appear to dislike change and tend to be very conservative politically, socially and attitudinally. They are often formally educated in the field of physical education. Physical-education majors tend to have little in common with other students in the field of education. They have a more traditional philosophy of education and a slightly lower social class

background. They tend to be more dogmatic and appear to have different social values from other prospective teachers.

Massengale places heavy emphasis on the solidarity that coaches feel toward their profession and all members of it:

> Allegiance to the subculture's values is reinforced by professional coaching organizations and coaching journals. Most teacher-coaches, regardless of their teaching field, tend to ignore teaching journals and become devoted readers of coaching journals. They also tend to ignore educational conferences, but regularly attend coaching conventions, clinics and workshops. Open opposition from the academic community strengthens the isolation caused by the uniqueness of coaching. That hostility reinforces the subculture by creating alienation and polarization; the separation is maintained by the complete or partial exclusion of the coach from the academic in-crowd. The result of this extreme polarization between the coaching and the academic communities is the creation of an in-group/out-group relationship. The two groups identify each other as opponents, and each group regards itself as the guardian of its members' virtues, values and loyalties. The out-group becomes viewed as a threat to the cherished values of the in-group.

I commend this article enthusiastically for its conciseness and relevancy. A more detailed analysis can be found in the carefully researched article by George H. Sage, 'An Occupational Analysis of the College Coach,' in Ball and Loy's *Sport and the Social Order*.

Coaches unquestionably intrude upon the civil rights of the young men and women who serve under them. Rules about hair, bedtime, living arrangements, associates, what women to date, the taking of medicines and sometimes the deprivation of medical care would not be tolerated in any other kind of activity, yet coaches seem generally to believe that it is their prerogative to lay down such rules and to enforce them by such economic sanctions as terminating scholarships.

When Dee Andros, football coach at Oregon State, was accused by his players of depriving them of their civil rights, the president of the university appointed a Commission on Human Rights to investigate the complaints. This drew the ire of Max Rafferty, California's State Superintendent of Public Instruction, himself a former coach with a 51–5 record, and in a speech which has become famous he took off after the critics: 'Andros is of Greek descent, like Spiro Agnew, and he's just as good at football coaching as Agnew is at pointing out the faults of the news media, which is pretty darned good.' Then Rafferty suggested that Andros told his players: 'If you want to play for me, fellows, no girlish necklaces and cutesy medallions, no Iroquois scalplocks, no hair-mattress beards and no Fu Manchu mustaches. You can sport these execrable excrescences and still go to Oregon State, but you can't massage your egos thus publicly and still play football for Dee Andros. Period.'

Rafferty then proceeded to call anyone who questioned such coaching dictates 'Communist agitators, the hairy, loud-mouthed freaks of both sexes who infest our campuses today like so many unbathed boll-weevils, the pseudo-intellectuals, the beard-and-sandal set, crum-bums, kooks, and members of the Filthy Speech Movement.'

A few coaches bring disrepute upon their profession by adopting unethical practices. They brutalize their players. They play men who are obviously unfit medically. They connive to circumvent whatever rules are established for their own protection. And they provide their players with very poor models of behavior. They are found at all levels of coaching, from Little League through high school and college and in the pros, but fortunately they rarely predominate. The standard coach is more often like the Allen Gardy I knew in high school, a man of surpassing rectitude, or the Bud Wilkinson that Billy Vessels knew at Oklahoma.

Finally, I could not possibly play for some of the dictatorial coaches operating today. I would not be able to tolerate their nonsense for even one week, let alone four full seasons. (That would not worry them; they would see rather quickly that they had little to gain from a skeptical, self-directed oaf like me.) On the other hand, if I were a poor boy locked in some ghetto who saw athletics as my only avenue of escape, I might seek out one of the tyrranical coaches, trusting that he would make me mean enough to land a job with the pros.

Now for an elaboration of certain points made above. The average fan cannot comprehend the pressure that accumulates on a major coach as the football season progresses. Take a typical example. An independent football power—one not belonging to a conference—could balance its athletic budget only if it got on national television a couple of times a year and finished with a bowl game. But this year it had unexpectedly lost an early game when the right tackle allowed his opposing lineman to crash through and block a vital field-goal attempt.

Its record now stood 4–1 with a big game looming. If another loss were sustained, the record would be 4–2 with little chance of television appearances, but if the coach could rack up a win his record would be 5–1 with a chance for television and a bowl game too.

So in the week before this critical game the coach drilled his right tackle on how to chop down the lineman coming through to block a kick, and he spent so much energy heckling his tackle, hammering at him until the boy almost staggered, that an observer complained, 'He's brutalizing that poor boy.' But his efforts paid off.

The big game was a barn-burner, going right down to the final minutes with the coach's team trailing 23–21 but in possession of the ball. Through a series of well-drilled plays sent in by the coach, the quarterback maneuvered his team into field-goal position.

The whole season would now culminate in one play. Would that right tackle be able to protect the kicker? The ball was snapped. The line held. The field goal was good. The coach had a 24–23 victory and a 5–1 record. This one play meant that he would be invited on television twice before the season ended, earning about $200,000 each time, and he would gain a bowl game, which would mean another $500,000. One play, by one boy, meant $900,000 to that school. And this doesn't happen very often in chemistry class, or in the study of Chaucer, or in a course on ethics. That autumn no professor at the school could compete with the football coach in achieving public recognition; only his endless perfectionism enabled his school to pick up a quick nine hundred thousand.

Regarding the dictatorial coach, seeking vainly to sweep back the ocean of social change, everyone connected with sport has his own anthology of hilarious incidents, but the better coaches easily adjust to new situations. Not long ago the Associated Press circulated a feature page quoting ten major college coaches as to how they accommodated their one-time prejudices to the newer type of high school athlete. Hayes, Schembechler, Broyles, McKay and Parseghian confessed that they were bending with the times. Darrell Royal made an interesting comment:

> In the 1950s my team had two-hour workouts morning and afternoon with no breaks for water. Now we stop at least every twenty minutes and let them have all the water or saline solution they want. In my opinion we coaches are just as strict as we once were. We have been taught or have learned better training methods.

But there are others who have made no concessions; like guardians at the gate they fight to prevent any social change from gaining entrance to the stadium. The consequences can be ridiculous. For example, coaches have fought a long battle against hair. Close-cropped themselves and inheritors of a Marine Corps tradition, they have sought to impose their standards on athletes who would prefer to follow the styles of their own generation. The coaches have heaped ridicule upon such men and have tried to enforce arbitrary rules, which the courts have struck down.

I was on one campus when the famous edict of J. Edgar Hoover appeared: 'I cannot respect any man who wears long hair or a beard.' A football player who had stubbornly resisted attempts to make him cut his hair responded, 'Well, I guess that takes care of Jesus Christ and Ulysses S. Grant.' Several coaches of professional teams have gained national attention by insisting that their players be shorn, but in reading their justifications, I have always wondered how they interpreted the Bible account of the athlete Samson. While his hair remained long, like that of a proper warrior, he was more powerful than an NFL linebacker; when he allowed it to be cut, the way the coaches advocate, he lost his strength.

In recent years two college coaches have received much attention, one in football and one in basketball. Frank Kush, a graduate of the Pennsylvania coal fields and Michigan State, has been presiding over the football team at Arizona State, building a local powerhouse which has the distinction of sending an unusual quota of graduates to the professionals. As one such player has said, 'If you can play for Frank Kush, you can play for anybody.'

Hailed as 'the new Vince Lombardi,' Kush specializes in bone-crunching offense, savage defense and the strictest training regimen in the nation. Late in August each year he takes his charges to a private camp he owns at the edge of the desert and there puts them through incredibly rigorous drills, featured by obligatory charges up Mount Kush, a nearby rock pile four hundred and fifty feet high and guaranteed to knock the wind out of even a super-athlete. For even a minor infraction during training, Kush barks out, 'One mountain for you,' and after practice the guilty one—'he came off the line too slow'—chugs up that steep and dusty incline.

Kush has produced an unbroken series of winners against better than average southwestern opposition, but not the real big time, has taken his teams to one bowl after another (1974 was a mediocre season, 7–5 and no bowl game, but in 1975 he was again 12–0 and ranked second in the nation) and has been invited to coach at various other colleges and in professional leagues. He lacks the charm of Vince Lombardi, and the ability to adjust to new situations, but he has compiled an impressive reputation as the toughest coach in the country. Three major magazine articles have featured his unique system, with numerous case histories of the remorseless manner in which he drives his players.

Mike Tomco, a three-year veteran from Anchorage, Alaska, tried to get his coach in focus for David Wolf of *True* magazine:

> 'College football is an ugly business,' said Tomco. 'Kush just does what he thinks is necessary to win. I can take what he hands out—and it's helped me —but a lot of kids can't handle it. They go through the gate. We all hate him now, but later, most guys see he's really made them play their best. You know, I've seen him do some awful things—stamp on hands, humiliate and emasculate guys till they quit football and left school, call 'em "wops" and "dagos," and drive kids till they passed out. Still, aside from my father, there's nobody I respect more. See, Kush is honest and fair. You can count on him in the clutch. He knows life is hard, so he's teaching us to get up when we're knocked down. He's a different guy after the season. Like Jekyll and Hyde. Last winter

I was broke but I wanted to take out my girl friend. I called Kush to see if he knew somebody who'd loan me a car. He gave me his car and ten bucks for dinner.'

Kush is not hesitant in discussing his philosophy of sport. Graduate of a tough system himself, he makes no apologies for his hard-nosed approach:

> My job is to win football games. I've got to put people in the stadium, make money for the university, keep the alumni happy and give the school a winning reputation. If I don't win, I'm gone.
>
> Football is pain and agony, and our kids are prepared to pay the price. Our kids get mentally prepared for violence. In a pro camp it may depend on how much pain you can take.

The case of Jim Harding, who is reputed by even his enemies to understand the science of basketball better than anyone else, is illustrative. An Iowa boy who claims he won letters which records at the University of Iowa fail to confirm, he graduated with a degree in physical education and into a series of the routine small-time jobs that such would-be coaches land at the start of their careers. West Liberty High School in Iowa, Marquette High in Milwaukee and then college jobs, Loyola of New Orleans, Gannon College in Erie, Pennsylvania, and finally a big-time assignment, LaSalle in Philadelphia.

Through the years he made himself into a fierce disciplinarian, a tyrant and a man who used his coaching position as a base for psychological warfare. He abused his LaSalle players so flagrantly that he ran afoul of the sportswriters on the Philadelphia papers, and Frank Dolson of the *Inquirer* wrote a series of stories which made Harding's position untenable.

He then shifted to the professional Minnesota Pipers, a tough, knowledgeable bunch of playground graduates, including Connie Hawkins, one of the great players of his day, spending his days in exile from the NBA. Jim Harding, vainly endeavoring to enforce his silly rules on these old-timers, drove them to distraction and himself to a heart attack. One of the most haunting things I have heard in sports is Hawkins' confession that when Harding returned from his heart attack, partially recovered, his players purposely allowed the score to narrow in the final moments of each game, hoping that the excitement would knock him off for good.

It became impossible for Harding to continue with the Pipers, but after a respite he landed on his feet once more, this time with the University of Detroit, another Catholic school which was giving up football and seeking to go big time in basketball. They could have done it, too, for they had one of the best college ballplayers in the country, Spencer Haywood, and a solid supporting cast of good ball-handlers.

Then the blows began to fall. Haywood quit school to enter the pro-

'No Rose Bowl, no Sugar Bowl, no Cotton Bowl, no . . .'

fessional ranks in Denver, from where he would jump to the Seattle Supersonics, before moving to the New York Knicks. Then the Detroit players began to rebel against the drills Harding insisted upon, and several promising candidates quit. Harding was accused of threatening others with the loss of their scholarships, an illegal act under NCAA rules. The team lost cohesion, was riven by factionalism, and drifted to a 7–18 record, pitiful for a man who had often proclaimed: 'I know more than 99.9 percent of the basketball coaches in the country.' After another year he was through, a man from the sixteenth century trying to operate in the twentieth.

I am surprised that more big-time coaches don't go the way of Jim Harding. The pressures on them to win are cruel, and the penalty for failure inescapable. I know of no other occupation where the evaluation of a man's work is so incessant; they say, with some justice, that a writer is no better than his last book, but he doesn't produce a book every week, eleven weeks a year for instantaneous review. He can lick his wounds and recoup his energies, but the coach is on the firing line constantly.

He is trapped in an impossible bind. To keep his job he must win, but if he wins, it means that Coaches Y and Z at the bottom of the ladder must be losers, and sooner or later they will be fired.

Is it fair to penalize a man when the system itself is rigged against him? For some years I toyed with the idea that what we must do is educate our alumni to a realization that it was morally indecent to blame a coach for what it was mathematically impossible to avoid. (When my little college Swarthmore went 9–0 one miraculous year, I organized a group of alums to write letters of protest to our president, warning him that we had not intended to get our degrees from a football factory. He replied that he appreciated our letters, because after losing seasons he received so many complaints the other way, but he thought even the most rigorous school could absorb a winning season now and then.)

After long consideration of this problem, I have devised 'An Irreverent Plan for Protecting Coaches.' Its merit is that it ensures that every coach will have a winning season every year. Each alumnus can boast in his club, 'This year we tied for the championship,' and he can do so year after year. The plan is this. All colleges and universities are grouped together in conferences with twelve members. This is essential to the plan, and no deviation will be permitted. Since football teams play a schedule of eleven games, each member of the conference will play each other, and there will be an understanding that this year Team A wins its game against Team B, but that next year Team B will win.

At the conclusion of the tenth Saturday of each season, the conference standings will be as shown in the first column.

AN IRREVERENT PLAN FOR PROTECTING COACHES

Team	Standing at End of Tenth Saturday		Standing at End of Final Saturday	
	Won	Lost	Won	Lost
Avengers	5	5	6	5
Barracudas	6	4	6	5
Challengers	5	5	6	5
Destroyers	6	4	6	5
Executioners	5	5	6	5
Firestorms	6	4	6	5
Gladiators	5	5	6	5
Hooligans	6	4	6	5
Invincibles	5	5	6	5
Javelins	6	4	6	5
Killers	5	5	6	5
Limpets	0	10	0	11
Totals	60	60	66	66

On the last day of the season the Avengers play the Barracudas and win. The Challengers defeat the Destroyers. The Executioners wipe out the Firestorms, and so on down the line, with every 5–5 team clobbering every 6–4, and with the Killers annihilating the Limpets as usual, 55–3. The final standing is shown at the right, with eleven teams having winning seasons and all of them tied for the championship.

Obviously, the key to this system is the Limpets, who are required to lose every game every year in order for their fellow conference members to triumph. How are the Limpets to be persuaded to undergo this perpetual humiliation?

Simple. The university whose proud colors the Limpets wear will be granted, by the conference, enough money every year to build a new music auditorium or a theater or a cyclotron or a dormitory for women, plus a large grant for the purchase of books for the library. This money will come from donations which admiring alumni will contribute to the other eleven teams, each of which will have had not only a winning season but a share of the conference championship.

In addition, the coaches of the Limpets will have lifetime tenure at salaries equal to those paid by winning teams, and during the winter banquet season the Limpet coaches will speak on the moral values to be gained from football, and when they proclaim, 'At our university we stress character, not winning,' everyone will know they're telling the truth. To coach the Limpets will not be all bad, not by any means.

But what of the players? How can we persuade high school athletes to join the Limpets when their record over the past nine years has been 0–99?

Very simple. Limpet recruiters will tell their prospects what all recruiters say, 'We're interested primarily in your education, not your football ability.' But they will be able to prove it. 'Of the one hundred boys who played for us, ninety-nine graduated. Hoskins didn't. He got a girl in trouble and fled to Mexico. Our alumni found a job for every boy who wanted to go into business. Our placement bureau found a slot for every boy who planned to enter medical school. We have the best library in the Missouri Valley and the newest science buildings, thanks to the grants we get each year.' And if the student is perverse enough to ask what it would be like to spend four years playing football with the Limpets and going 0–44, the recruiter will say solemnly, 'As Grantland Rice himself pointed out,

> For when the One Great Scorer comes
> To write against your name
> He marks—not that you won or lost—
> But how you played the game.

You join us on the Limpets, and every week you'll recognize the truth of those noble lines.' I believe with the proper recruiters we could make playing for the Limpets actually attractive.

The conference, too, will profit. When cynics complain that athletes at Barracuda are not graduating, the officials there and at the other conference schools could point proudly to the Limpet record of graduating ninety-nine out of a hundred athletes and let that stand as surrogate for the whole, the way the Pacific Eight Conference now does with the Stanford record.

There is one tactical problem I haven't solved. If bowls contribute major funds to university programs—over $35,000,000 in television money over the last ten years, plus a like amount in gate receipts—our conference might find it obligatory to produce only one champion each year, so that it could move on to some bowl, sharing its income with the other eleven members. This could be solved relatively simply. Let the Barracudas, in the example given, *win* their last game against the Avengers; this would give the Barracudas a 7–4 record and the title. Of course, the Avengers would then become losers at 5–6, which might be disastrous, except that when we force the Avengers to lose this year, we would also promise them that next year in the final game they would win, have a record of 7–4, and pick up some bowl money, which should be enough, I believe, to save their coach's job.

The more I think about this reasonable plan, the more I like it. At least it's as sensible as the various plans being followed today. And not the least of its virtues is that after ten or fifteen years of concentrating academic excellence at the Limpets' university, we would have in each area of the United States one institution of real merit. Its growing departments, its enhanced library and its constantly improving faculty would be a positive boon to the nation.

The plan has three serious weaknesses, all financial. 1) If the outcome of a game can be known in advance, what will happen to the multitude of football pools and gambling lines across the country? That's something to worry about. 2) Would ABC or CBS show any interest in televising a midseason game from such a conference when the standings of the best team could be no better than 4–3? 3) And would any self-respecting bowl committee select a team, even if it did win the championship, if it had only a 7–4 record? Millions upon millions of dollars are at stake here and I shall have to work further on my plan.

I must make two final observations about athletes and their coaches, each of a seemingly irrelevant nature but each instructive. Of the sixty athletes I have known, fifty-nine have been Republicans, only Stan Musial having been a Democrat. I have never so far heard of a coach who was a Democrat, although some of the Southwestern Conference men may be so nominally. Joe Paterno, I believe, was the son of a Democratic father, but he quickly changed when a coaching career became feasible.

The athlete and his coach move in a world of conservative values and are surrounded by conservative types. Very few Democrats among the alumni have private jets, or good jobs to dispense, or the spare cash to endow athletic scholarships or build press boxes so that the university 'can go really big time.' Also, coaches know that conservative, hard-nose procedures pay off. For every hotshot newcomer who throws passes all over the place, there are ten tough old buzzards like Woody Hayes and Bear Bryant who work on the system of 'four yards, a cloud of dust and a bucket of blood.' They're the ones who remain in coaching till their mid-sixties.

If I were a coach I'd recruit all my boys from underprivileged Democratic families and convert them to Republican linemen and back-court strategists. I wouldn't have a single Democrat among my assistant coaches and I'd quickly identify the businessmen in my area who had private jets. I would not be a coach like Jim Harding or Frank Kush. Ara Parseghian and Joe Paterno are more my type.

The reasons why athletes and their coaches tend to be conservative Republicans have been well explained by Rick Sortun, who played varsity football at the University of Washington and later in the NFL:

> You are subtly channeled into an educational rut. Your advisors suggest fairly simple courses, like PE [physical education] or business. The practices leave you too tired to study more than what you need to get by. You're definitely too tired to think on your own. You're told to be suspicious of hippies and

radicals. You end up avoiding the kind of associations—the serious bull sessions, the intellectual give-and-take with people of various philosophies—that are really as much 'college education' as what you learn in the classroom.

Increasingly, you accept the philosophy of the locker room. Physical strength and the ability to withstand pain are the most positive virtues. Women are things. Bookish people and little people are suspect. Finally, with the scholarships, the alienation, and the practice hours, you come to view it all as a job.

In recent years the athletic profession has had three heroes, Spiro Agnew, Richard Nixon and General Patton, and it has had bad luck with two of them. It is understandable that coaches should have revered the first two: they talked football language, were no-nonsense men, and showed little sympathy for the radical life styles that were sweeping the campuses and threatening established routines. I have a score of quotes from sports figures regarding these heroes; a couple have crept into this manuscript, but the kindest and most typical, I think, appeared in the 1973 Nebraska guide, a lavish full-color 200-page job that sold for $2.00 and was worth it:

> Honor piled upon honor for Devaney, his staff and players for 1970 and 1971 —the AP and UPI trophies, Grantland Rice Trophy, the MacArthur Bowl, Big Eight and Orange Bowl Championships, all-America honors and many others —but the greatest honor came after the 1970 season when President Richard M. Nixon visited Lincoln to speak to a University of Nebraska convocation and presented Devaney and the Husker co-captains with a plaque proclaiming the Cornhuskers the 'No. 1 Team in the Nation.'

I have spoken to only a few coaches about Nixon. They felt that he was innocent of any real wrongdoing and that he had been persecuted by the same kind of long-haired radicals who give coaches so much trouble on college faculties. I have heard of no coach who thinks otherwise, and this is understandable, because President Nixon was always on their side; he did telephone lockerrooms; and he did uphold verbally the old-fashioned virtues that they uphold.

The athletes have had better luck with General Patton. His reputation has grown and his principles of battle have been shown to be correct in most respects. He was a superior athlete himself—at the 1912 Olympics he placed fifth in the Military Pentathlon; he carried a seven-goal handicap in polo with ten the highest, had won two hundred cups for horsemanship, and was topflight in shooting and handball. He might be said to be the beau ideal of American sportsmen.

In his famous address to his troops who were about to invade Sicily he spelled out his philosophy of both war and sports, and all subsequent men who have related the two in locker room exhortations are indebted to him:

Battle is the most magnificent competition in which a human being can indulge. It brings out all that is best; it removes all that is base. All men are afraid in battle. The coward is the one who lets his fear overcome his sense of duty. Duty is the essence of manhood. Americans pride themselves on being he-men and they *are* he-men.

We Americans are a competitive race. We bet on anything. We love to win. In this next fight, you are entering the greatest sporting competition of all times. You are competing with Americans and with Allies for the greatest prize of all—victory; and the one who wins the prize is the one who first attains victory —captures his objective. Never forget that. And remember also that the Deity, in whatever form you think of Him, is with us.

There was another side of Patton which is duplicated in many of the top athletes. He was an intensely emotional man, and his biography is replete with situations in which he wept. To his record I append some additional instances:

General Patton: When he spoke of the German enemy 'tears came into his eyes several times.' When the navy with whom he had been battling offered him a flag for his new army 'Patton was crying.' After he slapped the sick soldier 'he began to sob.' When a French general paid him respects 'the gesture moved him to tears.' When he delivered the routine fighting talk he called Form Number 7 'he wound up with tears.' And when in Los Angeles, at the end of the war, he looked at his medals and said that not he but gallant men had won them 'tears welled up in his eyes and he could not go on.'

Vince Lombardi: When he had to cut Joe Scarpati, a wonderful fighting ballplayer, 'he cried.' When admirers handed him a plaque which read 'Yea, though I walk through the valley of the shadow of death, I will fear no evil, for I am the meanest son of a bitch on the hill,' he wept.

Woody Hayes: When he beat Michigan in 1972 he cried like a baby and was photographed doing so.

Don Meredith: After making his hard final decision not to play football at Texas A & M 'he cried.'

Bear Bryant: When he went on television to deny charges that he and Wally Butts had rigged the Alabama-Georgia game 'he broke into tears.'

Mickey Mantle: When he left home to play professional ball 'sobs rose up and choked me.'

Dave Meggyesy: When his high school team lost the championship: 'I remember sitting in the corner of the locker room, crying my head off.'

Connie Hawkins: When his Pittsburgh Pipers won the 1968 ABA title: 'Washington, who had taken down twenty-seven rebounds, sobbed uncontrollably: "I tried, I tried. I did the best I could." "You were beautiful, Wash," Connie said softly. Then he was crying, too, the tears wetting his mustache and dripping off his chin. Then Arthur Heyman had his arms around both of them, burying his sweaty hair in Wash's chest. All three men were weeping.'

Joe Namath: When he announced to a press conference that he was succumbing to the dictate from Commissioner Rozelle and surrendering any financial interest in his gambler-frequented night spot, Bachelors III, 'he broke into tears.'

I have a score of other citations, but these seem the most macho. I cite them for a peculiar reason. Male America, and I suppose female America too, deems it rather manly when an athlete weeps in public; certainly one of the greatest sports photos of all time, endlessly reproduced, shows Lou Gehrig unable to fight back his tears. For such men it's all right, because we know they are manly.

But when Edmund Muskie allowed tears to come into *his* eyes for a far more justifiable cause, the honor of his wife, the American public rejected him brutally. For he was *not* an athlete who had already proved himself to be a man. He was a lanky Maine politician, and as such, he had to be suspect.

IX

The
Inescapable Problem

This brief chapter poses a special problem which no athlete escapes: 'After a long period of vigorous physical activity during school and college, how can I devise a program of moderate exercise that will keep me healthy till age seventy?' The question can best be explored through the case history of a young football player I shall call Lew Cobberly.

I first met him in prep school, a hefty, well-coordinated tackle weighing 222 at age eighteen. He was a good student, but his main delight was smashing into opposition backfields to haul down quarterbacks.

It was obvious that the football colleges would offer him a plethora of scholarships, but he surprised me by choosing not one of the powers but a lesser university with an outstanding course in business administration.

He played three years in college and gained one of those one-newspaper nominations as all-American. The designation was questionable, but enough to win him a round-nineteen draft into the pros, which he entered while eight credits short of a degree. He barely survived the cut the first year, played spasmodically the second, and was cast adrift at the end of training camp the third.

With unusual perception he told me, 'The fact that I shied away from testing my luck at Ohio State or Alabama betrayed the fact that I really lacked the killer instinct. I mean, in the pros you go up against men who know nothing but football. They're out to tear you apart, and if you don't devote every thinking minute of your life to crushing them before they crush you . . . Simple fact is, I never had that kind of dedication and the professional coaches saw it.'

So at age twenty-five Cobberly found himself unemployed, but by no means unemployable. He hurried back to his university, obtained his degree, landed a good job in Detroit, started a new life. He had never intended becoming a football casualty, and he didn't.

His tragedy lay elsewhere. Having played games from age nine, he was now fed up. With his gift for self-analysis he acknowledged that in college he had allowed football to cheat him of a real education, while the pros had considered him no more than a low-grade commodity. Sports held no further glamour for him and he said, 'To hell with it.'

He quit all exercise, put on forty pounds, lost his edge, became a sedentary slob. Through two decades I watched him deteriorate, twenty-five through forty-five, and visited him in the hospital after he suffered a relatively mild heart attack. He should have recovered easily, but he was so flabby, his heart so encased in fat, his lungs so deficient in elasticity that he died.

Any athlete should be able to make the transition from hyperactivity to relative inactivity with ease, but young men like Lew Cobberly fail the test. To understand why, three preliminary questions must be disposed of. 1) At what age are human beings at their apex, physically? 2) Is their retreat from that apex so rapid that they can no longer find pleasure in playing games at which they once excelled? 3) Is it safe, or even desirable, for men and women in middle and advanced years to engage in exercise?

At what age do the physical reactions of a human being start to slow down? During World War II, I handled the paper work on a study sponsored by the British and American military authorities who wanted to know at what age a young man was best qualified physically to pilot a jet fighter. He would be alone in the cockpit, depending only upon his own judgment and particularly upon the speed of his automatic reflexes. After applying a battery of tests to thousands of young men, the scientists decided the optimum age, if physical response alone was considered, to be sixteen years and eight months. After that, the young man was over the hill and really too old to pilot a jet fighter. But if other attributes like judgment and character were cranked into the equation, the optimum was something like twenty-two years and seven months. After that, regardless of what criteria you used, it was all downhill, and whereas a super-pilot might still do good work till he reached the advanced age of twenty-six, he was an exception, for the odds were heavily against him.

Tests have shown that a human being reaches his or her maximum aerobic capacity, one of the best overall measurements of athletic capacity, at an age somewhere between nineteen and twenty, and that this capacity diminishes thereafter, first slowly, then swiftly.

It is obvious that swimming champions are usually young, seventeen being a ripe age, after which skills decline rapidly. Harvey Lehman, of Ohio University, made an extensive study of when the athletes of the preceding decade had peaked (*Research Quarterly* [October 1938]), and while his figures cannot apply to today's professional football and basketball, for those sports were not well established then, his others deserve attention:

AGES AT WHICH ATHLETES REACH THEIR MAXIMUM PROFICIENCY

Football	24	Pistol shooting	27
Ice hockey	24	Baseball, non-pitchers	28
Boxing	26	Bowling, regular	32
Cornhusking	30	Golf	30
Baseball, pitchers	27	Billiards	32
Indianapolis 500 drivers	27	Bowling, duck pins	32
Tennis	27		

Since the Lehman study, more accurate figures have become available for the newer professional sports. An average football player now peaks at somewhere around twenty-eight, a basketball player at twenty-four, and a hockey player at twenty-seven. But Lehman's other figures still hold. The master athlete tends to be a has-been at thirty-five.

Stan Musial, who functioned longer than most, told me a bittersweet story. 'One of the saddest days of my life was when I found out about my eyes. Before age forty I hadn't felt the slightest loss in seeing. Then my eyes started to go bad. The ball looked so much smaller than it used to. First base seemed to be actually farther away. So the Cards sent me to the top eye doctors, and they examined me for a whole morning with the latest machines, and at the end they gave me the bad news. "There's absolutely nothing wrong with your eyes." I was just getting older, like everyone else.'

I played very rugged sports through age thirty-nine and would acknowledge no diminution of power, but at forty it was as if an iron gate had suddenly clanged shut. I could scarcely believe the finality of it. Lew Hoad told me at his tennis club on Spain's Costa del Sol, 'I can still go out and beat any of them . . . the first day. But in order to recover for five sets the next day, I have to go right to bed after the match and sleep twenty hours. After the second match I have to sleep twenty-four hours. After the third I need twenty-eight. My legs, my muscles, my lungs. Who wants to punish himself like that?'

From researching most available studies on the subject I conclude that a man's total physical-psychological equipment reaches its apex of efficiency somewhere before thirty-one. Thereafter he is in decline, whether he knows it or not. True, in sports like golf or trapshooting, which exact little physical demand, he can prolong his period of excellence. And obviously, in harness racing, which exacts practically no demand, he can last into his seventies.

'Boys, we all remember how Stretch Madden almost single-handedly
sank the Lakers in the last game of the playoffs with eight consecutive dunks.
Well, I'm delighted to announce that Stretch has agreed to apply
those same competitive skills to the marketing of our budget lingerie.'

But for most of us, in most of the active sports, we are clearly on the way out by thirty-five.

After the age of thirty-five do human beings retain the capability for active though diminished participation in sports? Lehman, in the study just cited, added a table which showed the most advanced ages at which individual athletes had accomplished outstanding performances, including world championships, in sports which did not require strenuous physical contact. His old-time big-league pitchers had twirled thirty-seven masterpieces between the ages of forty and forty-four, a feat not matched in recent years. Rifle and pistol marksmen at that age had won eighty-two major championships. And in the age group fifty-five to sixty-four, fourteen different men had turned in top performances in such diverse sports as bowling, target shooting, billiards and golf.

Similar reports are becoming commonplace. A few years ago the Tournament Players Division of the Professional Golfers Association issued a quick rundown of one season's play: halfway through the 1971 tour four of the top-ten money winners were over the age of forty; seven of the thirteen best scorers were over forty; and every low-scoring record had been racked up by a player over forty.

Ernst Jokl, analyzing the ages of all participants in the 1952 Olympics held at Helsinki, found men competing successfully at these ages: canoeing, thirty-six; track and field, forty-two; swimming, forty-five; gymnastics, forty-five; and fencing, forty-nine. The senior women contestants were somewhat younger, except in canoeing, where they were two years older.

James W. Whittaker, himself forty-six and the first American to climb Mount Everest, says, 'The ideal age for mountain climbers is between thirty-five and forty. One member of the Italian team who conquered K-2 in 1954 was forty. What counts is mature judgment and how tightly you are wound.' I like that last clause; it says so much about the athletic individual.

Clarence DeMar, the indefatigable marathon runner turned in his best times between the ages of thirty-four to thirty-eight and completed his last race at the age of sixty-six, covering the twenty-six-plus miles at an average rate of slightly over eight minutes per mile. And Percy Dawson, an early advocate of physical fitness, walked six or seven miles one day each week at age ninety-two.

In 1970 *Sports Illustrated* carried one of the funniest sports stories ever. In it John Cottrell recalled a famous bicycle race run in Sweden in 1954 from the northernmost tip of the country to the southernmost, a distance of one thousand miles. All the top professionals were competing, but the race soon degenerated into a classic farce because a bearded old duffer named Gustav Hakansson, seventy years old and grandfather of five, insisted upon entering without official sanction. He turned up at the starting line riding a woman's beat-up antique bicycle with a cowcatcher in front and wearing an improvised uniform consisting of overalls. At the end of the first blistering day he was a figure of ridicule trailing the field by ten miles; at the end of the first three hundred miles he led the pack by twenty!

> The old man's remarkable progress was explained by one vital difference in his racing strategy. He cheated. Unlike the other riders, he did not observe the rule by which competitors were required to stop each night at check points and restart in the morning. After an hour's rest the first night, Gustav was back in the saddle, plodding on alone through the darkness. Still, since he was not an official entrant, one could hardly complain that he was taking an unfair advantage.

Soon he was leading the field by more than a hundred and fifty miles; with only one hour's sleep in each twenty-four he plugged on, giving a remarkable demonstration of endurance. He covered the thousand miles in five days and five hours, then sought refuge in a jail cell to catch up on his sleep. And in 1958 Steel Grandpa (as he was called) at seventy-four, made a whole new set of headlines by traveling from his home in Gantofta, Sweden, to Jerusalem on a motor scooter.

Even more astonishing is the fact that lean, energetic Sanders Russell won the Hambletonian, premier event of harness racing, in 1962 when he was sixty-two and hampered by a dislocated right ankle encased in a heavy bandage. In 1975, at seventy-five, he won a major race at Wilmington, Delaware.

My own attitudes on this matter have been determined by fortunate personal experiences. I played rugged basketball till forty, then shifted to volleyball till forty-five, and now hope to play tennis for the rest of my life. Some of the most tenacious doubles I have experienced were played against former Vice-President Henry Wallace when he was seventy-six; I lost. I also lose to a remarkable man in his mid-sixties who has a plastic hip; he can beat any of us.

Obviously, then, men and women can perform capably in selected types of sport regardless of what decade of their lives they happen to be in, and I should like to offer a recommended list of sports appropriate for each of the decades:

A LOGICAL PROGRESSION BY DECADES
ILLUSTRATIVE ONLY, NOT TO BE CONSIDERED COMPREHENSIVE

Decade	Highly Recommended	Worth Investigating	Demanding But Possible
5–15	Walking Swimming Tennis	Baseball Basketball Soccer Skiing Boating Bicycling	Track and Field Football (not before age 11) Hockey (not before age 10) Golf (not before age 9)
15–25	Walking Swimming Tennis Golf Baseball Basketball	Soccer Skiing Boating Bicycling	Football (last decade) Track and Field Hockey Rodeo Handball Squash

25–35   This is the crucial decade, because what happens here may determine the quality of subsequent life. Unusual attention must be paid to making an orderly transition into lifetime sports, if this has not already been done.

Walking Swimming Tennis Golf Boating	Softball Volleyball Bowling Skiing Soccer Bicycling	Track and Field (last decade) Baseball (last decade) Basketball (last decade) Hockey (last decade) Handball Squash Rodeo

35–45	Walking	Bowling	Rodeo (last decade)
	Swimming	Volleyball	Soccer (last decade)
	Tennis	Fishing	Handball
	Golf	Skiing	Squash
	Boating	Horseshoes	Softball
		Bicycling	Volleyball
45–55	Walking	Bowling	Handball (last decade)
	Swimming	Bowling on green	Squash (last decade)
	Tennis	Fishing	Volleyball (last decade)
	Golf	Skiing	Softball (last decade)
	Boating	Shuffleboard	
		Horseshoes	
		Bicycling	
55–65	Walking	Shuffleboard	Skiing (last decade)
	Swimming	Bowling	
	Tennis	Horseshoes	
	Golf	Bicycling	
	Boating		
	Fishing		
	Bowling on green		
65–75	Walking	Shuffleboard	Tennis (last decade)
	Swimming	Horseshoes	Golf
	Boating		Bowling (last decade)
	Fishing		Bicycling (last decade)
	Bowling on green		
75–85	Walking	Shuffleboard	Golf
	Boating	Horseshoes	
	Fishing	Swimming	
	Bowling on green		

This table invites several important generalizations. Swimming is, as some have claimed, the ideal sport in that it is highly conducive to well-being, exercises all the big body muscles, expands heart and lung capacity and can be practiced over a total lifetime. Tennis and golf permit an extended participation, too, but it is walking, that ever-available, no-equipment exercise that tops the list. It could almost be called the criterion of the functioning human being.

On the other hand, the table makes clear why, for the average human being, football is such a restricted sport, combining as it does the heavy probability of body damage and a severely limited number of years during which it can be practiced. That schools should devote so much of the athletic dollar to a sport which offers such restricted benefits is remarkable;

financial and emotional advantages which accrue to football are the only explanation.

Enthusiasts may be surprised to notice that I have not included hunting or boxing. The first is a lively outdoor activity but one for which I can generate no empathy whatever. I cannot think of any legitimate grounds for recommending boxing to anyone.

But with such a variety of engaging sports available—and I have not covered attractive alternatives like lacrosse, badminton, archery and croquet—it is a bewilderment why everyone does not acquire, in his youth, a group of sports which he or she can enjoy through life. The rougher games can be phased out early; the more compatible ones can be played at varied levels of competition forever.

Should one continue to exercise in middle and advanced years? In Chapter III, I summarized my thinking on this subject; three points merit repetition.

If you haven't kept up your muscle tone, your heart resilience and your lung capacity, you could kill yourself by rushing precipitately onto a tennis court or into a squash enclosure for a sudden and vigorous game. No formerly energetic person who has allowed himself or herself to grow flabby should resume active sports without the supervision of a doctor.

If you are one of the many persons who can lead a satisfactory life without much or any physical exercise, and if such a regimen keeps you alert and happy, don't change, especially not past the age of forty.

Finally, there is no evidence that vigorous athletic participation will prolong your life; indeed, as we have seen, there are several disturbing studies which indicate that it may shorten it. But, as I argued earlier, I strongly suspect that these negative studies reflect not on sports but on the sloppy way in which athletes who were active in college discipline their lives after they leave.

I have discussed this problem with various groups of people who have remained active through their sixties, and one man, who has worked with extraordinary intensity in a demanding profession well into his seventies, summed up the general thinking in these apt words: 'In view of the studies, I mustn't claim that engaging in vigorous games has prolonged my life, but I'm sure of one thing. Those games have made what life I have had extra productive and extra enjoyable. I'm convinced that I was able to maintain my mental health only because I discharged my nervous aggressions on the tennis court, and that tranquillity alone has justified all the effort.'

My friend's opinion is supported by the testimony of experts. E.V. Cowdry, in his book *The Care of the Geriatric Patient*, says:

> Adults need regular exercise even into advanced years. Older muscular systems do respond. Exercise is needed for: maintenance of posture; correct joint align-

ment and mobility; to preserve strength; to keep good locomotor skills; to stimulate circulation; and to give emotional satisfaction from physical competition and independence.

The President's Council on Physical Fitness has issued an excellent statement entitled *Adult Physical Fitness* (Government Printing Office). Along with an illustrated program which intimidated me, since the man photographed seemed destined to rip telephone books apart with his bare hands, it summarizes current thinking:

> There is strong authoritative support for the concept that regular exercise can help prevent degenerative disease and slow down physical deterioration that accompanies aging. The evidence is conclusive: individuals who consistently engage in proper physical activity have better job performance records, fewer degenerative diseases, and probably a longer life expectancy than the population at large. By delaying the aging process, proper exercise also prolongs your active years.

If the evidence is so persuasive and so clear, why do so many Americans fail to make the easy transition from vigorous youthful sport to the more productive lifelong kind? Seven reasons, some spurious, have been advanced to explain our indolence.

The first is psychological. We have been brainwashed into believing that only those sports which entice spectators to sit in large stadiums to watch are manly or endowed with high acceptability value. Football, basketball ice hockey and baseball are the regal sports, and they are the ones that are to be encouraged in junior and senior high school and supported financially in college and university. Yet active participation in such sports is ended by the twenty-five–thirty-five decade, leaving the practitioner, in his crucial early-middle years, bereft of a sensible program for maintaining good health. The intensive propaganda deifying spectator sports has psyched the athlete out of those alternative patterns which might prolong his life.

The second reason is that athletic programs in schools and colleges are dominated by this spectator psychology, and decisions are made which support it rather than the welfare of the student body as a whole. I have already marveled at the fact that St. Jude's would spend $7,000,000 on a basketball facility to be used by only sixteen players out of a student body of eleven thousand, and that each of the sixteen would drop the sport before he was thirty-five and most of them before twenty-five.

The third reason is also psychological. Many former athletes have testified that they gave up all participation after their varsity years in college because their obvious drop in ability made competition at a lower level of performance distasteful. They would rather sit around in idleness than exhibit their growing deficiencies. Much as I deplore such reasoning, considering it extremely juvenile and narcissistic, I do understand it. To be an ex-athlete with fading powers is a demanding role from which most of us, fortunately, are excused.

In the second game of the 1973 World Series, when the New York Mets and Oakland were battling for the championship, with the Mets having lost the first game, they called upon a superannuated Willie Mays to help pull them through. It was a travesty. In the late innings they used him as a pinch runner, and that was all right. But they kept him in the game, and in the ninth inning, on a critical fly to left field by Deron Johnson, Mays ineptly lost the ball in the sun, misplayed it, and with his legs tangled converted an easy out into a run-producing double. However, the Mets tied the game, and on his next at bat Mays lined a hit into the outfield, stumbled at the plate, recovered partially, ran in a wavering line toward first and looked the fool.

Mays must have been embarrassed, for this was his farewell appearance in baseball and he simply was not capable of performing. He was damaging the chances of an entire team and should have known better. But I quickly rejected this special pleading. If Willie Mays, with his tremendous career behind him, wanted to play a few more games, he was entitled to make the effort, and if he damaged his team, his coaches ought to have forced him to quit. I had felt exactly that way back in the late 1920s when Tris Speaker and the incredible Ty Cobb ended their playing days going through the motions with the Philadelphia Athletics. They weren't what you'd call really good, but by God they were Speaker and Cobb, and I saw them.

I cannot accept possible embarrassment over waning powers as an excuse for quitting participation in sports. I still recall the shock that swept over me when Mark Spitz, having won an unparalleled seven gold medals at the Munich Olympics announced, 'I'll never swim again.' Of course, at his advanced age of twenty-two he should quit Olympic competition, and I hope that's what he meant. But to give up entirely a sport which had meant so much to him and which had done so much for him was incomprehensible.

Coaches have a responsibility here. If a man's life reaches its climax at age thirty-one, after which he will be of diminished value to his coach, the latter is obligated to see that an orderly transition is made, to protect the athlete's physical well-being if nothing more. And this should be the responsibility of coaches on all levels, from Little League, where, as we have seen, a boy can reach the apex of his life at age twelve, to the championship professional football or basketball team, where the shock of quitting at thirty-one may be even more damaging.

The fourth reason is that while our society prizes spectator sports, lavishing money and attention on them, it actually denigrates lifelong sports, or did until recently. During the most active years of my life the communities I lived in had too few tennis courts, swimming pools, golf links and general playgrounds. There were some communities with no facilities for lifelong sports for men or any sports at all for women. Budgets were pathetically out of line, and the prevailing mood of spending most of the budget on football was well expressed by Bear Bryant of Alabama in an interview with John E. Peterson of the *Detroit News:*

> Asked why his University of Alabama football players were housed in a luxury dorm, fed a diet twice as expensive as that provided other students, and given private tutors, the legendary coach Paul 'Bear' Bryant replied: 'Our first concern is to teach these kids to play hard-nosed football. If they do, we'll keep filling that stadium and we'll be able to keep on giving scholarships to athletes who might never have gone to college otherwise. Sure, Joe Willie (Namath) never graduated. We got eleven players in the pros (professional football) right now and only two of them graduated. But Joe Willie, he signed with the Jets for more than $400,000, and the rest of them, they average about $30,000 a year. You know your typical college graduate, even if he's magna cum laude . . . he's going to be damn lucky to start at $10,000 a year.'

Today even the most gung-ho athletic directors recognize the need for broader programs, and some which will incorporate women. Universities are providing excellent facilities for tennis, recreational skating and sometimes even golf. Frisbee, a delightful way to waste an afternoon and still work up a sweat, has had an amusing impact on the sports establishment. When *Sports Illustrated* dared to run an article on it as a semi-legitimate sport, various outraged macho types protested that whereas they beat themselves to death playing real sports like football—with bruises to show for it—now a pantywaist affair like frisbee was being accorded equal status.

Some of the most enjoyable nonsense of my life has been centered on this game, which I discovered late while working at Kent State University. Later on, Chip Cronkite, son of the television broadcaster, and I held the championships of Hong Kong, Bali and Tahiti. Our culminating performance came on the last-named island, where we completed 122 consecutive long throws *around a coconut palm.* I can still recall the disdain with which a famous jock asked, when told of this feat, 'Frisbee? A grown man playing frisbee?' I took the trouble to indoctrinate him into the mysteries of the flying saucer and he became an addict.

Park boards now build tennis courts and swimming pools, as well as golf links and fields for baseball, and some cities are providing facilities for soccer and lacrosse. But in my area at least, major funds still come from private enterprise. I know of no covered tennis courts available for year-round use which have been built at public expense. I know a score that have been put up with private funds, and perhaps that's the way it should be done, except that then the underprivileged child is excluded from developing his or her skills.

The fifth reason is pervasive. At home, at school, at college and in public life a person can spend his or her first twenty-five years without ever being told that plans ought to be made for a lifelong health program. I had a better education than most and I can recall not a single hour of instruction on this most vital of topics. In sixth grade I did have an enthusiastic teacher who lectured now and then on hygiene—horrible word—and one day she told us something which had a lasting effect. She said, 'Each morning when you get up you must drink a full glass of water. This washes out your insides, and this is important, because as you walk to school you might be hit by an automobile and they'd rush you to the hospital and cut you open and then the nurse would see that you hadn't washed your insides.'

The likelihood that this was going to happen to me so dominated my thoughts for the next few weeks that I could see nurses standing about the operating room looking at one another in horror, saying, 'He didn't wash out his insides today. I suppose he never does.' And I became so fearful that I started drinking a full glass of water immediately upon rising, a habit I continue till this day, to my considerable benefit.

That may have been a silly approach to teaching health, but it worked, and I judge that if similar instruction had been given on the necessity for acquiring lifelong exercise habits, I would have been just as receptive, but I received none, and most young Americans in the age group five through twenty-five receive none either. The teachers of my youth did not have the knowledge. Now they do, and they should share it.

An orderly program of health instruction should be provided at various levels in our educational system. In elementary school, the foundations of good health habits should be established. In high school, instruction should be given in the tenth grade so as to catch the maximum number of students, and I would wish the teaching to be emphatic, reminding the student that it is the well-being of fifty or sixty productive years of life that are at stake. In college, a concentrated review of basic health principles, including diet, should be offered in the sophomore year, possibly without credit but with emphasis on the truism that no man or woman can function at maximum effectiveness if health is allowed to deteriorate.

The sixth reason stems from American custom. As a nation we do not sponsor adult sports to the extent that many foreign countries do. We do not have the gymnastic competitions of Czechoslovakia, nor the addiction to cross-country skiing of the Scandinavians, nor the industrial soccer teams I found in Italy and England, nor the planned cultivation of an outdoor life that one finds in Germany. I would rate our public adult participation below

'When he played at Southern Cal they clocked him in 4.5 seconds for 40 yards.'

that practiced by any of those countries. Taking all the countries of the world, I would rate us in the low upper middle, better than the median but not much. This is deplorable, for we have the wealth to provide a satisfactory program and the intelligence to know that we need it.

The seventh reason and the last is one we shall hear more about in the future. As a nation we run the risk of forgetting the salutary effect of play. As adults we penalize ourselves unnecessarily by losing our capacity for it: the lazy flight of the frisbee with grown men and women chasing it ridiculously, running through the woods at a picnic, chasing with dogs over a freshly mown field, romping with kids on a lawn, playing stickball in the street, exhibiting lost prowess in a pick-up softball game, laughing with a beer can in the left hand while trying to toss a quoits ringer with the right.

I prize the sheer nonsense of play above almost anything else in sports, for it keeps one young in spirit; it should remind us of our animal inheritance; and it loosens us up. I subscribe without reservation to the sagacious judgment of one of our leading psychologists, Dr. William Menninger:

> Mentally healthy people participate in some form of volitional activity to supplement their required daily work. This is not merely because they wish something to do in their leisure time, for many persons with little leisure time make time for play. Their satisfaction from these activities meets deep-seated psychological demands beyond the superficial rationalization of enjoyment.
>
> Too many people do not know how to play. Others limit their recreation to being merely passive observers of the activity of others. There is considerable scientific evidence that the healthy personality is one who not only plays, but who takes his play seriously. Furthermore, there is also evidence that the inability and unwillingness to play reveals an insecure or disordered aspect of personality.
>
> Good mental health is directly related to the capacity and willingness of an individual to play. Regardless of his objections, resistances or past practice, any individual will make a wise investment for himself if he does plan time for his play and take it seriously.

While sitting passively in the great stadium or watching in grim-lipped silence some game on television, we surrender ourselves to the deadly seriousness of mere observing. This might be permissible as a diversion, but too often we allow watching the professional to serve as our total association with sports, thus missing the joy and benefit that come from playing the game oneself. There is another pitfall. The young man or woman of twenty-five who quits physical activity to concentrate exclusively on progressing at a job is overemphasizing economic competition, underemphasizing the benefits of play, and endangering his or her life.

So much for the negative aspects. What can we do to improve the situation?

Parents must assume responsibility for inculcating in their children a positive desire to build health habits that will produce well-being throughout life. During the past fifty years our society has learned much about caring for teeth, eyes and obesity. Now we should shift to more general goals, and a primary one must be the cultivation of lifetime participation in vigorous physical activity.

Elementary and high schools are particularly responsible, and boards of education should see to it that verbal instruction is given, even though facilities for swimming, tennis and golf may not be available. The child may not actually acquire the skills for these sports in his school program, but he will at least be aware that he ought to be acquiring them outside.

Colleges and universities have a special obligation, for they are educating many of the people who will be making community decisions later on. The man or woman who in college becomes addicted to watching football will be likely in later life to lead community drives to pay for public stadiums in which only that sport can be exhibited. But what college graduates should be voting for in their communities are more tennis courts and playing fields on which boys and girls can engage in the less heavily structured games.

The media should achieve a better balance in their coverage of lifelong sports, but newspapers are under heavy pressure to publicize only the spectacular professional contest, for that's what sells papers. I see some hope in television. Its generalized sports programming has begun to include a commendable scatter of types.

Governing authorities should give strong support to these lifelong sports and provide public facilities on which they may be pursued. To do less is to short-change the health of the general population.

However, the responsibility for devising a lifelong program of exercise that will enhance general well-being rests upon the individual. The serious athlete has a particular responsibility. Handball and squash are ideal first steps after varsity or professional competition. These can be supplanted later by less energetic tennis and golf, with walking, fishing and boating for the really advanced years. It could all be so simple.

Two athletes I met during the course of this study have been exemplars of how transitions should be made. The Sewell brothers, Joe and Luke, formed one of the preeminent brother acts in big-league baseball. They were born in the small Alabama town of Titus, Joe in 1898, Luke in 1901. Joe was picked up by the Cleveland Indians, with whom he played shortstop and third base for eleven years, ending his career with the New York Yankees three years later in 1933 at the age of thirty-four. He was a good batter—.353 one year, .312 lifetime—and still holds the record for being able to defend himself at the plate. In 1930 he struck out only three times during the entire season, and he repeated this feat in 1932. He told me, 'I still have the bat I used in batting practice. In the fat part there's a stain just a little bigger than a baseball. That means I hit the ball every time the same way—right on the button.'

Luke also started for Cleveland, in 1921, as their catcher, and ended his playing career an amazing twenty-two years later with the St. Louis Browns in 1942. He passed easily into a long tenure as manager, St. Louis Browns at first, then the Cincinnati Reds from 1949 through 1952, when he quit baseball.

I met the brothers at a celebration when they were aged seventy-six and seventy-four respectively. They were sharp-eyed, about the weight they had been in their heyday, alert, witty and delightful to be with. If you wanted to talk about the old days, they were willing to spin yarns about Babe Ruth and Ty Cobb. Catcher Luke could tell you the strengths and weaknesses of the major batters. 'Lou Gehrig didn't have any weaknesses,' he told me as we yarned.

But if you preferred talking politics or business or the coming election, they were just as informed. When Joe left baseball he had found a job at the University of Alabama which allowed him spare time to farm. Luke had become a banker in Akron, Ohio, specializing in business loans.

I asked these unusually bright septuagenarians what had helped them make the transition from professional ball to private life, and Luke explained: 'Two things. You get hungry. And you open your eyes.' Sport had revolutionized the lives of these two farm boys. But they had always known it to be a sometime thing, and when their playing days were over they intelligently hacked out a place for themselves in the larger world. They had maintained their active lives, found new occupations, and guarded their health. Talking with them about either the old days or the present was a privilege.

It is this kind of orderly transition that I wish for everyone. In the case of the professional athlete, his failure to make the shift is tragic; his success in making it heart warming. But it is the average man and woman in whom I am principally interested. We should not end our active lives at twenty-five, nor at forty-five, nor at sixty-five. Life should be a constant progression, filled with those testing and rejuvenating activities appropriate for each passing decade.

X

The Media

If the individual's participation in sports can best be understood as a form
of dance, professional performance must be studied as a form of entertainment. Newspapers, radio and television, aware of this fact, have prudently
presented sports as entertainment.

Consequently, one of the happiest relationships in American society is
that between sports and the media. This interface is delightfully symbiotic,
since each helps the other survive.

In the early years of this century baseball prospered mainly because it
received at no cost reams of publicity in daily and Sunday papers. Coverage
which any other business would have had to pay for as advertising was given
freely because of its entertainment value. The newspapers knew what they
were doing; by offering exciting news about the Cobbs and Speakers they
maintained their circulation and increased it. One of my first jobs as a boy
was picking up the Sports Extra of the *Philadelphia Bulletin* each summer
night at 6:05 and rushing copies through our village so that fans could learn
how their Athletics and Phillies had done that day. I remember how avidly
the men grabbed for my wares.

In recent years radio and television have given golf and football the same
kind of free advertising, enabling those two sports to mushroom into fantas-
tically profitable forms of entertainment. Of course, radio and television
grew along with the sports, and at times because of them. I have often
speculated as to which explosion, golf or football, represented the bigger
television marvel. One is tempted to say football, but this commanded an
audience as far back as the 1890s; all that television did was to increase

football's existing excitement some thousandfold. But in the case of golf, television took a game which had not previously enlisted much public support and converted it into a compelling event. For this reason golf may be a profitable takeoff point for a discussion of what changes overtake a sport when it is transformed from a private exercise into a public entertainment.

Golf had been a game for gentlemen, begun in Holland but now governed by royal and ancient rules developed at St. Andrews in Scotland. It was traditionally played in an atmosphere of austere silence before few or no spectators. The most interesting tournaments were conducted under the rules of match play, in which the total number of strokes required to complete a round of eighteen holes mattered little. Two men completed one against the other, and what did count was the number of individual holes each won. A match would be over if Player A was three holes in the lead with only two left to play. Obviously Player B could not catch up, so A won, 3 and 2. But if Player A had won the first ten holes in a row, Player B couldn't possibly catch up, either, and then the score would be 10 and 8.

This was exciting golf, and two of the four championships Bobby Jones won when making his grand slam in 1930 were match play. Its fatal weakness when television arrived was twofold: no one could predict how long a match would last, and it could be decided on a hole where no television cameras were stationed.

When I attended my first golf matches, the players would rebuke anyone on the course who dared make a sound during play, and newsreel cameras were absolutely forbidden.

With the advent of television all this had to be changed. Since cameras were essential, they had to be endured. In the early days one irate champion said, 'I'll never accept a grinding camera on the course when I'm playing,' and a television executive observed, perceptively, 'When we start to offer big money, he'll learn to.'

Match play, with its essentially difficult system of keeping up with the score, simply had to be abandoned in favor of the simpler medal play, in which a player's total score for 72 holes competed against the total scores for dozens of other players. But this raised a new problem. Was Player A, who was on the final green with 271 and about to take two putts, ahead of or behind Player B, who was on the sixteenth green with 263 and about to take one putt? I remember those first televised tournaments; no one could keep the comparative scores straight or know who was winning.

But then some genius came up with the solution: state at every point during the 72 holes how each player relates to par for the holes so far played. Thus, in the example just given, Player A, who is going to two-putt the eighteenth, will wind up with a score of 273, and since the par for one round is 71, he will be eleven strokes better than total par of 284, and the board will show a —11.

Player B, at the sixteenth, is going to one-putt, and he will be 264 at that point, with a par 4 seventeenth and a par 5 eighteenth awaiting him. He, too, should end his round at 273, which means as he finishes the sixteenth he is also — 11. The two players are tied, but if Player B can score even one birdie on his last two holes he will finish with a — 12 and will win outright.

If not, the two players will end the tournament in a dead heat, at 273 each. In the old days this would necessitate a next-day play-off of eighteen holes, a solid test of who was the better man. But with a huge Sunday-afternoon television audience already tuned in to the entertainment and eager to know who will win, the continuation of a tournament final till Monday, when people will be at work and unable to follow the tube, is unreasonable, so a sudden death has been devised. Take the two or three players who tied for first and have them start playing another round, with victory going to the first man who wins a hole outright.

This is a brilliant concept, somewhat opposed to the traditions of golf, to be sure, but a reasonable solution to a television problem and a satisfying compromise for the audience. However, the competing players cannot start their confrontation at the first hole, because no semi-permanent cameras have been installed there. There are cameras, however, at holes 15, 16, 17 and 18. So sudden-death eliminations start at hole 15, proceed to hole 18 if necessary, and if the players are still tied, return to hole 15 for another sequence.

Traditionalists deplore such changes. They argue that match play, one man against one, is the toughest test a golfer can face, because he must remain at top form every day and defend himself against the unknown who is on a hot streak and eager to knock him off. 'Look at the way Jack Nicklaus wins a tournament,' a classicist told me mournfully. 'He cards a 73 the first day, then pulls himself together, finishes with two 66's, and is hailed a winner. Hell, in match play he'da been out on his duff that first day.' The purist also objects to sudden death, claiming with some justice that it is unfair to require a player who has struggled doggedly to achieve a tie over 72 holes to hazard everything on one lucky shot on the sudden-death fifteenth.

Old-timers also resent discarding the former pattern of eighteen holes on Thursday, eighteen on Friday and a really demanding thirty-six on Saturday. 'That showed who the real men were,' the traditionalists argue. But television cannot easily absorb two rounds played on a single day, so it has dictated one round each on Thursday through Sunday.

I like every one of these changes, for they have made watching golf accessible to millions. Without them, the game could not have been utilized by television, and the entertainment feature of the sport would have been either lost or severely circumscribed. In an average year television pumps $4,000,000 into golf, allowing players to earn incomes like these for 1974: Johnny Miller, $353,021; Jack Nicklaus, $238,178; Hubert Green, $211,709. If a sport is to draw down its share of the fantastic amounts of entertainment money now circulating, it must accommodate itself within reason to the peculiar demands of television. I judge that golf has not been required to alter its basic characteristics or endanger its basic honesty. Its deal with television has been an honorable one, and it has sacrificed no fundamental. Certainly, it has not prostituted itself the way baseball did in the 1972 World Series.

Cincinnati was playing Oakland for the championship, and Commissioner Bowie Kuhn decided, wisely I believe, to schedule the weekday games for night viewing so as to attract the maximum audience. Gone would be the spectacle—on Monday through Friday of World Series week —of the American businessman casting one eye at the company ledger, the other at the television set secreted in the corner of his office.

But to provide night baseball was easier said than done, because Oakland is three hours behind the huge viewing audience of the east coast. If the game were really played at night in Oakland, say at eight o'clock, it wouldn't come on the tube in New York City until eleven, which would mean that it would end sometime around one-thirty the next morning.

An appalling solution was devised. Start the game in Oakland at 5:30 P.M., which would place it on eastern screens at the best possible hour, 8:30 P.M. The only trouble was that the actual playing of the game in California would take place in half-twilight, when the ball would be difficult to see and when nature's light would be intermixed with electric.

That was a dubious concession to make in the first place, but worse was to come. A sudden rainstorm on Tuesday night forced the cancellation of the third game of the series in Oakland. This was a stroke of bad luck which Commissioner Kuhn could not have foreseen, but it forced postponing his schedule a day. This required some gymnastics. By the time the fifth game came around, it had to be played in Oakland in half-light, after which the two teams had to scramble into airplanes, fly to Cincinnati, and with inadequate rest plunge right into an afternoon game there.

This was indefensible. Translating all times onto Cincinnati clocks, the fifth game ended at 10:56 P.M. Friday night in California; the sixth game started at 1 P.M. Saturday afternoon in Cincinnati, with the players having spent what night there was flying at thirty thousand feet. This is a pretty high price to pay for television income, but Commissioner Kuhn saw nothing wrong:

It would have been a terrible thing to postpone Saturday's game in Cincinnati. The thousands of fans who had bought tickets could not have used them on another day. Besides, the players had eight hours' rest, fully enough. I don't think we acted in an unprofessional way.

Two comments are essential. The decision to play the weekday games at night was not forced upon baseball by television; it was the baseball powers, eager for that big night audience, who made the decision, forcing it upon the network. (Television, whose big fall season coincides with the World Series, was not eager to disrupt regular scheduling lest viewers who did not watch baseball be attracted to the new fall shows on the other networks.) But Commissioner Kuhn was right in his prediction that the World Series at night would be a fantastic success; it even outdrew *All in the Family* and smothered its football competition. On Saturday afternoon it drew a 20.1 rating as against 9.1 for the Oklahoma-Colorado game; on Sunday it out-rated the Detroit Lions-San Diego Chargers game 25.7 to 11.8. But to many the violations done to the spirit of the game seemed far too high a price for favorable television ratings.

The guardians of each game will have to keep close watch on the concessions required by television. There is nothing unusual about this. Writers have to maintain the same kind of vigilance, and so do businessmen. Sports, however, are subject to special pressures because of the magnitude of the money involved, and their protectors will have to be trebly strong to resist improper inducements.

We must keep in mind the size of the television pot. In 1963 television paid football—college and professional—$13,900,000. By 1966 this had grown to $41,100,000, and in 1968 to $54,700,000. In 1970 it was $58,000,000, and in 1975, $60,000,000.

Pro football is a good litmus test. In 1963 television paid $926,000 for the NFL title game. From 1970 through 1975 Super Bowl tabs have hovered at $2,500,000. Colleges and universities participated in the outpouring of the cornucopia, gathering $5,100,000 in 1963, $10,200,000 in 1968, $12,000,000 in 1970 and $16,000,000 in 1975.

Golf has enjoyed a similar bonanza. In 1961 it gleaned a miserly $150,-000. Ten years later, in 1971, $3,000,000. In 1976 it should go to $5,000,000.

Baseball's profits from the tube have been equally spectacular, and when radio income is added, positively startling. In 1960 nationwide and World Series rights went for $3,250,000. In 1970, $16,600,000. And in 1974 nationwide rights alone were worth $43,000,000. Local rights for 1976 should be another $35,000,000.

The overall television expenditure for sports, counting the specials and the oddball events, is a staggering $200,000,000 per year. (In an Olympic year add another $19,900,000.) And this is money, by and large, that was not available to sports two decades ago. This bonanza produces three consequences: professional leagues must get their fair share of the television dollar or expire; universities must figure out some way of distributing the television dollar more equitably than now, or many schools with great names in football will have to quit the sport; since profits have been so vastly multiplied, the potential for corruption has also grown.

Sport by sport, let us observe what changes have been forced by television and judge which of them have been justified and which not.

We have already seen how consideration for television can determine how a World Series shall be played. I object to playing a twi-night game in California; I think it a perversion of the sport. But given the time differences between west coast and east, I see no way to avoid this, and I suppose the teams will have to learn to adjust to it. But forcing teams to fly cross-continent without adequate rest, to fit into a television timetable which could have been revised, is a violation of common sense and should not be tolerated. Nor would I permit, in order to retain the big Saturday-afternoon audience in Cincinnati, the cancellation of a Friday game in California, to be replayed later at some more convenient date. The upsetting of the home-away schedule with its subtle advantages would be contrary to the best interests of baseball.

Colorful uniforms, decorative ball parks like Three Rivers in Pittsburgh and Royals in Kansas City, and the use of the go-carts to haul pitchers in from the bull pen, innovations encouraged by television, are commendable, and I would like to see more of them. New rules to hurry up the game would also be in order: fewer warm-up pitches except in case of sudden injury to the starting pitcher (which would mean that the bull-pen pitchers might not be ready) and the granting immediately of intentional walks. I am not satisfied that the designated hitter (the innovation whereby an older slugger who can still hit but is not spry enough to field bats regularly in place of the weak-hitting pitcher, who never bats) adds much to the game; in the games I've attended he has batted about .214, which hardly compensates for the disruption of the orderly statistics of the sport.

I am shocked by the proposal that giant-screen television be installed so that the calls of umpires can be second-guessed by spectators, accompanied by the riots that would surely ensue. This should not be allowed, and my stricture here goes for football, hockey, basketball and tennis, too. The umpiring of any game is a chancy thing, as is the Norns' umpiring of human lives, and we are all better off if we learn to live with that fact. In the games I have played, the chance call of the umpire has been a constant factor: the tennis shot that may have nicked the line; the strike that could have been a ball; the cornerback who might have interfered with the pass receiver; and that most difficult of calls—did the basketball player dribbling the ball charge into the guard, or did the latter block him?

I think we ask too much of games if we demand a godlike finality in umpiring; we would take a giant step backward if we installed great screens where the fans could participate in the reaching of decisions, because a fundamental of play would have been violated: the uncertainty of judgment. I am not, however, opposed to the officials' having somewhere an unexposed screen to enable them to review their judgment on close plays, or on any play in which the official responsible for the call was not in position to see it.

I remember the 1973 Cotton Bowl in which Alabama was defeated 17–13 by a late-period Texas touchdown in which the Texas halfback clearly tiptoed down the white chalk mark on his way to the goal, placing himself out of bounds on three separate steps. The official watching the play missed the infraction, which any television replay should have shown. But in a startling number of cases the television camera does not resolve the problem. For example, after this same Cotton Bowl, not one Texas coach, viewing the game films, would acknowledge that his halfback had stepped out of bounds. The cameras had been at the wrong angle to catch the missteps.

I am gratified to learn that the Italian National Soccer Federation has seen fit to petition the TV people not to show instant replays of crucial decisions, lest fans in the area of the stadium see the facts and rush forth to slay the referees, as has often been attempted in the past, sometimes successfully. I wish American sports could agree on a policy of keeping instant replays out of the stadiums.

The changes in tennis have been all to the good and there should be more of them. The new colorful uniforms, allowing the spectator to differentiate between players, are excellent. I still wear pure white, and so do my opponents, but we are from an older school and the new is better. Of course, the introduction of sudden death has saved the game for television, and for the players too. This has been a most happy solution to the problem of those 21–19 sets that I used to play, and I find few players or spectators who object to the new system, providing that the winner must be ahead by two points before he can be declared the winner of the tie-breaking game.

But now a new problem threatens. Tennis as now played, even with sudden death, is not yet ideal for television, because probable duration of play cannot be predicted. When John Newcombe plays Jimmy Connors the best three out of five sets, the afternoon may require only three 6–1 sets and be over in a jiffy, or five 7–6 sets, in which case, close to three hours might be required.

There is some talk of doing with tennis what television did with golf, quit the indeterminate set system (comparable to match play in golf) and switch to a system whereby a competition consists of three sets, with the total number of games determining the winner (like medal play in golf). In fact, the professional World Team Tennis League has already come up with something close to this. Two teams of men and women compete in six different sets: first man versus first man, woman versus woman, second man versus second man, men's doubles, women's doubles, mixed doubles, each one set. Add up the total score in games, and the team that won the most games wins the match. This keeps the evening to a predictable length; it provides the spectator with a good mix of fast tennis; and I deem it reasonable, but only for play that is primarily entertainment.

I would object, and I think those responsible for tennis should too, to any system which would do away with sets in individual competition and substitute mere games won. There is a finesse to set play which is beautiful to watch and excruciating to participate in; an older player has won the first set from a younger opponent, lost the second, won the third. In the fourth set he loses two quick games, then makes a sober calculation. If he fights with all his energy to regain ground in this fourth set and fails, he will have worn himself out, and will have no reserve for the fifth, which he will lose too. So he allows his opponent to run off the fourth set 6–0. Then, in the fifth, he is ready for an all-out fight, which his superior tactics and conserved strength give him a very good chance of winning.

If the final result depended on total games won, the younger man would win, with that one 6–0 bulge in his favor. But the men are not playing single games; they are engaging in a subtle competition in which mere games do not mean a great deal. The trick is to win three sets, and sometimes it is justifiable to throw away four quick games in order to get on with the real contest.

One development in tennis requires close watching. When a gambling hall in Las Vegas in company with a television network can put up $450,000 for a Laver-Connors match, and then $1,000,000 for Newcombe-Connors, it is usurping the traditional rights of the tournament director, it is dictating unfair procedures, and it is destroying the orderly processes of the game. It is one thing for Las Vegas to announce that John Newcombe and Jimmy Connors are the two top stars of the game; it is quite another for Newcombe and Connors to enter a field of sixty-four or thirty-two and battle their way slowly through the rounds, with the possibility of being knocked off by Bjorn Borg or Vijay Amritraj or Roscoe Tanner, and surviving to the semi-finals as true champions, to meet in the finals for the purse. I do not want the judgment of television executives to be substituted for time-honored systems of play.

In the summer of 1974, if such executives had been allowed to determine *ex cathedra* the semi-finalists in World Cup soccer, they would surely have selected Brazil and West Germany and Argentina and one other, and they certainly wouldn't have selected Poland, who beat practically everybody while Brazil and Argentina were foundering. As honest sport, the two Connors matches were a bad show; as an afternoon's entertainment exhibition, a triumph. But the two should not be confused. A major fault with such matches is that they siphon away from a sport vast sums of money which should be more equitably distributed through a large field of competitors.

Ice hockey has been a disappointment on television, even in the major cities which sponsor NHL teams. The game, which is so very difficult to follow and which suffers from infrequent scoring, ought to be more acceptable than it is; in the rink itself it can excite wild passions, and its partisans often consider it the best game in sportsdom. When I started work on this book I knew none of the intricacies; attendance at some of the Flyer barnburners quickly rectified that deficiency, and I have since watched every game I could find on television. It's a game of marvelous movement, swift change and exciting pileups. To watch a Bernie Parent or a Ken Dryden in the goal is to see the instantaneous beauty of great ballet; to watch Bobby Orr and Phil Esposito, when they played for Boston, tearing the Philadelphia defense apart with minutely calculated moves was one of the most fluid moments in sport.

But whether it can be translated onto the television screen remains uncertain. There has been talk of a fluorescent puck, but I doubt if even it could be followed through the mysterious shifts and changes which are so commonplace in a good hockey game. I have sat with numerous unindoctrinated friends as we watched the moves on a little screen, and they all complained, 'I can't see them when they score.'

'Watch the replay,' I advised.

'I do, and I still can't see it.'

The problem of offsides, as in soccer, is a difficult one to explain, and I have heard serious proposals that this be discontinued. Let as many skaters as wish be where they want. An advocate says, 'You'd have more nine-seven games with all the added excitement that would mean.'

Having received much of my education in Scotland, where soccer was king, and having been a most loyal partisan of Dundee United, in those days the nothing team of the league, I have often pondered this problem of offsides and have concluded that it is a refinement that no American will ever really comprehend. It is generic in hockey and soccer, and to abolish it would probably destroy the lovely balance of these two games.

No one was surprised when, at the conclusion of the drab 1975 play-offs,

NBC announced that it was dropping hockey. No other network leaped at the chance of taking over, and it may be that hockey is fated to become the grand opera of sports: something not for the lay multitude, but for the perpetual joy of the connoisseur. I cannot foresee much change that it can undergo to make it more acceptable to the television audience, and maybe that's all to the good. It will remain the sports lover's sport.

Basketball faces serious limitation insofar as television is concerned. It is monotonous, and it had better make some changes or it will find itself far in the rear where the television dollar is concerned. I am, as I have previously confessed, a complete devotee of this marvelous sport, considering those who practice it well among our greatest athletes. But the domination of the game by hyper-pituitary seven-footers and the frequency with which the total focus of the game is compressed into the last three minutes make its appeal on television limited.

I have found the ABA rule, whereby a field goal made from beyond the twenty-five-foot circle is worth three points, a good one; it should be adopted by the NBA immediately. Other recent changes which have eliminated that incessant march to the foul line have been commendable, but the lane from foul line to basket should be widened and the basket perhaps raised in height so as to introduce more variation in play.

In other words, instead of basketball's having been harmed by television, it has been delinquent in making those reasonable changes to accommodate the camera that would have strengthened the game and made it more popular. But perhaps basketball is a special case; its rule changes have been so prolific during the past forty years that it almost looks like a sport trying to find itself; for my money, most of the rule changes have been to the good. When I started, one man shot all fouls; we had jump balls at every opportunity; play was not continuous; a player was expelled after four personals; the zone, which would later be outlawed, had not yet been developed; the one-hand shot was not approved; the jump shot was frowned upon; the running hook was a scandal; and a championship game could go 16–14. The modern game is much better; the problem now is to fit it more exactly into the age of television, and if this cannot be done, its popularity will fade.

Halfway through the 1974–75 season a situation arose which pinpointed the ethical niceties that arise when television dominates a sport. I stress the fact that no one was at fault here, other than the exigencies of the game. When it became apparent that the Los Angeles Lakers and the Milwaukee Bucks were not going to make the play-offs, and that the New York Knicks might also miss, CBS awoke to the fact that they were in the middle year of a three-year $27,000,000 contract with the NBA and that this season was falling flat on its face. With the three top draws in the league going nowhere, who cared, asked the television people, what Kansas City-Omaha was doing?

Milwaukee was a dead duck because Kareem Abdul-Jabbar had missed a good portion of the season as a result of having broken his right hand when he slammed a strut in disgust at his own play. The Knicks were in pitiful shape because their two big horses, Willis Reed and Dave DeBusschere, had retired, leaving the team without muscle. And the Lakers had simply withered on the vine, with Wilt Chamberlain, Jerry West and Elgin Baylor gone. In the first days of league play it was apparent to serious followers of the game that the Big Three had become the Three Blind Mice and that upstart teams lacking in charisma, like Washington, Buffalo and Golden State, were now going to dominate.

The ethical problem is complicated. It appears that basketball cannot survive on television if two major markets, Los Angeles and New York, field wretched teams. (Since those cities are the fountainhead for other media too, the flood of exciting publicity which followed the ascendancy of the Knicks vanishes if they vanish.) But if television does not continue to pour money into basketball, seventeen of the eighteen NBA teams will be in mortal danger, and any survivors in the ABA. So, would it not be both reasonable and profitable for the new leaders in the league—Kansas City-Omaha, Buffalo, Washington—to trade away or even give away a good helping of their best players in order to rejuvenate New York and Los Angeles?

I had figured this out for myself; I was surprised when Paul Silas, a player for the Boston Celtics, was willing to ventilate the problem publicly. No rivalry is greater than the Celtic-Knick, yet here was a star of the Boston team seriously proposing that his arch-enemy be strengthened, for the good of the league:

> Pro basketball needs a strong franchise in New York. The league is very dependent on how well the Knicks do. The NBA grew up with the Knicks' success in the last half a dozen years or so. Some people think it's about time to focus on other cities, other good young players, but it doesn't work that way. New York is where the media and the crowds are.

Silas, in addition to being a Celtic star, was also president of the NBA Players' Association, and it was his responsibility to see that the league remain strong and retain its television income so that large salaries could continue.

Not long after he made his statement, Abdul-Jabbar was traded away by Milwaukee, an inexplicable deal until you found where he was going . . . to Los Angeles. And George McGinnis, the superstar of the ABA, was filched by the Knicks and promised $2,400,000 despite the fact that NBA rights to him were owned by Philadelphia. This latter piracy was so blatant that the incoming president, Larry O'Brien, simply had to cancel it, but New York's attempted steal was economically justified by the fact that the city had to land a couple of superstars if the rest of the league was to remain solvent.

This is a ticklish point, one on which I cannot clarify my thinking. Certainly, the 1974–75 NBA season was a disaster, and the play-offs were worse, with a Washington–Golden State finale that could excite no one, but can this be corrected only by allowing television to reassign players in a pattern more interesting to viewers? A purist argues: 'To modify a game for such a reason would be immoral.' A realist counters: 'But if basketball can survive only if it keeps getting television money, then the league must make whatever changes are demanded.' An expert told me, 'There's a third choice. To hell with television money. Let the eleven weakest teams, financially, in the two leagues fold. Then place the fourteen survivors in a rational league paying rational salaries.' Of the three positions, my guess is that the middle one will prevail. Television will certainly call the shots.

The game which has profited most from television is football. Starting with a spectacle which already had the ingredients—power, speed, varied movements, choice of plays, enough pause between plays to allow the man at home to decide what the quarterback ought to do, plus an alluring violence —the rules makers and Commissioner Rozelle have been uncanny in their ability to make the right decision at just about the right moment.

The massive rule changes prior to the 1974 season are a case in point. When I started intensive work on this book in 1972 many football people asked me my opinion of their sport, and I spoke for a majority of fans when I said, 'Looks to me as if you're running into two serious problems. The offense has been shackled, and it's plain improper for an end to be knocked down four times while trying to get downfield to catch a pass. And the field goal is pretty soon going to bore the paying spectators. I side totally with Alex Karras, who said, "Twenty-two straining giants in perfect condition fight for fifty-nine minutes. Then some European runs onto the field, kicks a fifteen-yard field goal, wins the game, and shouts, 'Hooray! I keek a touchdown!' " If I were you fellows, I'd change the rules.'

Sports experts across the country had already begun issuing the same warning: I was merely parroting what the people I had been interviewing were saying. And even Don Meredith at the conclusion of one extremely dull game in which most of the scoring had been achieved by desultory field goals, actually said on the air, 'It was a good game . . . if you like field goals.'

In spite of these danger signals, I had concluded that the men running the game would listen politely to the criticism and refuse to make changes.

I was not remotely prepared for the flood of changes they did make: moving the goal posts back to where the collegians had had them for several decades, thus making field goals more difficult; moving the kickoff back so as to encourage more runbacks; replacing the ball, on a missed field goal, at the point where that play started so as to diminish the times when a team could take a wild shot at the crossbar, knowing that at worst the ball would be brought out to the twenty; protecting the receiving end so that he could get down field to catch the ball; eliminating the crack-back in which a man in motion was able to poleax a man from the blind side; and the institution of sudden death to diminish the number of tie games.

No other sport would have dared make such a congregation of radical changes at one time, and during the first season at least, each appeared to improve an already superior game. The important question is: Did these and other changes encouraged by television pose any threat to the inherent character of the sport? We have seen how television demands nearly wrecked a World Series game. Now let's look at four additional instances of interference.

The first involves the behavior of the new football officials required by television. It was to serve broadcasters that a linesman was added, holding a flag to indicate the spot from which a team takes over possession of the ball. And there he stands, holding his flagged pole at that sacred spot while the action of the game moves far from him to the other end of the field. His purpose is to enable the announcer to say, 'The Falcons' drive started at the eighteen-yard line.' To me this seems a silly waste of manpower, but it does no harm.

One other official has been added, this one not in uniform and not listed in the program. He is the television network man, often wearing an iridescent orange vest, who instructs the real officials when arbitrary time-outs are to be called for advertisements. It is his job to see that the game is halted often enough to enable the network to unreel its commercials. Normally, he creates no problem, for the orderly flow of a football game presents numerous normal opportunities: after a punt, after a recovered fumble, after a score, at the two-minute warning. Interruptions like these affect the progress of the game in no way.

But tradition requires fourteen such time-outs in a game, 3–4–3–4 by quarters, and if toward the end of a half they have not come normally, it is the job of the network man to impose them. He signals the referee that he is hurting, and it is up to the official to find an excuse for a break. That's when the announcer says, 'Well, a time-out on the field, and now a word from the sponsor.' No reason is given for the break; the rule is that it must not impede the normal momentum of the game.

But I saw a game at Veterans Stadium in Philadelphia in which the hometown Eagles were holding on by their fingernails to a 24–20 lead late in the game. The New York Jets kicked a field goal, making it 24–23, then kicked off to the Eagles, who got the ball deep in their own territory, with 3:35 to kill.

Prudently, they started running plays that used up a lot of clock, and the Jets could do nothing about this, because they had no time-outs left. But at this point the television man in the orange vest started signaling frantically that he had three more commercials to squeeze in. His arm-waving reminded the referee that the network was entitled to one more time-out, so in the midst of the Eagle defensive maneuvering, the referee called an arbitrary time-out, killing the clock, penalizing the Eagles in their attempt to use up time, and conferring a huge advantage on the Jets.

This was an indefensible interruption and it could have caused the Eagles to lose, except that their fired-up defense did manage to stifle the last Jet effort. This kind of intrusion ought not be permitted.

The second intrusion occurred during the summer of 1974. Notre Dame had a game scheduled with Georgia for Saturday afternoon, November 9. ABC found that if it could persuade the two schools to move the game up to Monday, September 9, and play it at night, the network would be able to broadcast the game to the nation at the opening gun of the fall season, to the delight of fans and the considerable enrichment of the two schools. The change was quickly agreed upon, and while such supine surrender to TV caused adverse comment, the more mature reaction was that of Bear Bryant, who growled, 'We think TV exposure is so important to our program and so important to this university that we will schedule ourselves to fit the medium. I'll play at midnight if that's what TV wants.'

I can't decide what I think about this case, the two sides of my nature being in conflict. As a sports purist, I don't like the idea of a university's allowing itself to be pushed around by television executives who are in the business of selling advertising; but as a citizen who has had to spend a good deal of his spare time trying to raise money for good causes, I shudder to think of any worthy institution's kicking away $200,000 in defense of a questionable virtue. Rescheduling a Notre Dame game far in advance is not the same as refusing to reschedule a World Series game when the sleep of the players is sacrificed to a commercial schedule.

The third interference came in April 1974. The New York Knicks and the Boston Celtics had faced grueling competition in the first round of the NBA play-offs, Boston requiring six tough games to eliminate Buffalo, New York seven to down Baltimore. Yet as soon as those games were over, CBS ordered New York and Boston to start immediately the next round, so as to catch the big Sunday audience. Bill Bradley, rarely one to complain, had to protest: 'You'd think the owners would be too tired from watching to start the next round only thirty-six hours from now. But I guess not.' Boston annihilated the weary Knicks, 113–88, and Phil Jackson of the losers pointed out: 'If television didn't run the league, it would have been a different game. Especially when you have two teams like these, both with players over thirty coming from tough series that ended Friday.'

The fourth case was a shocker. On December 19, 1975, the Blue-Gray College All-Star Game was played in Montgomery, Alabama. The Miz-Lou Television Network had contracted with numerous stations throughout the country to provide a closely timed three-hour package, and when confusion at the start gave warning that the game might run long, television officials unilaterally ordained that the first period consist of twelve minutes instead of fifteen. But the game moved faster than anticipated, and it looked as if there would be empty space at the end. So the television people ordered the third quarter to be stretched ·out. Still too fast! Additional minutes were slipped into the fourth quarter, and in the final thirty-one seconds of what was loosely called a game the Blues scored a touchdown to win 14–13. Actually, the game had long since ended, and Bill Moseley, of the Blue-Gray Committee, apologized publicly to the Confederates, tacitly admitting that they had been robbed by television. The broadcast ended as planned, whereupon the stations in my area screened a fourth or fifth rerun of an episode from *The Untouchables.* Flagrant abuse like this calls into question the integrity of sports.

Of the five instances of television interference one was justifiable (shifting the date of the Notre Dame-Georgia football game), one was debatable (jamming the Celtics-Knicks basketball game to Sunday so as to catch a large audience), two were reprehensible (making the World Series baseball teams fly all night to an afternoon game, and allowing the television official to interrupt a crucial situation in the Eagles-Jets football game) and one was scandalous (manipulation of the clock in the Blue-Gray football classic.) Now I should like to cite a case in which substantial interference produced beneficial results for everyone.

In the old days the various bowl games used to compete for attention during the afternoon of January 1, and there was no possibility for one viewer to catch all the action. The committees who ran the bowls could not be expected to relinquish voluntarily their traditional spots, and since no outside force was strong enough to make them do so, chaos prevailed. But with the advent of big television money, the networks were able to dictate rational scheduling. Thus the Rose Bowl was allowed to retain its traditional late-afternoon timing (east coast), after which the others fell naturally into line: Sugar Bowl at night on New Year's Eve; Cotton Bowl early on New Year's afternoon; Orange Bowl on New Year's night, after the Rose Bowl had finished; plus various other bowls strung along over a couple of weeks. It seems to me that everyone has profited from the new system.

One aspect of sports television leaves me perplexed. Why is it that broadcasts of the football Super Bowl have been so uniformly dull—fans call it the Stupor Bowl—while telecasts of the baseball World Series have been so superlative?

At first glance it would seem that as a television spectacle, football had everything in its favor, and its enormous popularity proves that this is so.

And yet football is to baseball as checkers is to chess. I would suppose that any thinking man or woman who loves finesse would, after a season of exposure to both games, realize that baseball was the game worthy of closest attention, the one with the most subtle variations, the one that has the capacity to make the viewer hold his breath with sheer joy.

As I was working on this chapter I found myself, because of airline scheduling, in Kansas City with an evening to waste, so I went out to the spanking new Royals Stadium in the Harry S Truman Sports Complex to watch a game between the Kansas City Royals and the California Angels. It was an appalling game, 11–10 in thirteen innings, highlighted by the fact that every time Harmon Killebrew came to bat, Kansas City had the bases loaded, and poor Harmon, the designated hitter, went 0 for 7 and left eleven stranded. The game produced eight recorded errors plus two others that the scorer mercifully called hits. There were nine pitchers; the game lasted four hours and twenty-two minutes; and it should have been a real yawner.

But as it unfolded I saw three of the most exquisite plays I have ever watched in any athletic contest, gems so lovely they gleamed in the arc lights, leaving the watchers first choking with amazement, then limp from cheering. In the tenth inning Kansas City had a man on first with one out. The batter lashed a clean single into the hole between first and second, and it should have moved the runner from first to third. Denny Doyle, the California second baseman—who would be traded to the Boston Red Sox in time to star in the 1975 World Series—had no possible chance for an out, but he sped into right field, pursued the ball on a converging line, threw himself prone, grabbed the ball in the webbing of his glove, pivoted on his hip, sprang erect, and rifled the ball to third base, holding the runner at second. The next Kansas City batter drove a long fly which would have scored the runner had Doyle not held him at second, and the next batter grounded out, if I recall the sequence properly.

The point is, Doyle postponed defeat by a superhuman effort that accomplished nothing. He didn't get his man out at first. He didn't throw the runner out at third. He delayed the outcome by three innings, but in the end his team lost. As we left the park, everyone was talking about Doyle's unbelievable play.

The other two plays that caught my attention were routine outs. A

California batter, two outs and a runner in scoring position, swung vigorously at the ball, topped it, drove it into the ground about six inches in front of the plate, and ran like mad for first as the ball took an enormous high bounce toward short. Fred Patek, the Kansas City shortstop and the smallest man in big-league play, leaped forward, dashed at breakneck speed toward where the ball would bounce on the turf, trapped it with his gloved hand without looking, then leaped high, whirled in the air and threw the ball with a snap-wrist action that nipped the runner by half a stride.

The third play was an outfield masterpiece. I can't say who made it, because each team used so many players in the final innings, thirty-six in all, that my scorecard became jumbled and I don't really know who was playing left field when a Kansas City batter slammed a clothesline drive into left center. Again there was a runner on base, and from where I sat the game was over, but the California fielder sped to his left, never hesitated, appeared to intersect the trajectory of the ball, failed, then threw himself prone, and with his right gloved hand reached across his body, grabbed for the ball, and caught it in the webbing.

To have seen any one of these plays would have been a privilege. To have seen three in so miserable a game was one of the unforgettable pleasures of sport. They demonstrated the intricacy of baseball, that curious game of strategy and skill in which some lucky man determined that the bases should be ninety feet apart, a distance which enables a runner with a perfect sense of timing to steal second, while another just as swift but lacking that precision gets thrown out, a distance which permits the kind of play I've just described in which a daring shortstop with a rifle arm can gun down a runner a fiftieth of a second before his foot touches the bag.

I doubt that television could have caught the full poetry of those plays; baseball is not quite as good on the screen as football, which brings us back to that tantalizing question: Why then is the World Series so much more exciting than the Super Bowl?

The reason, I think, is that the World Series is indeed a series, with the tension mounting from game to game, so that no matter how nervous and inept the players may show themselves to be in game one, by the time the sixth game is reached, if it is, they have settled into their grooves, and they perform their minor miracles. Thus the sixth game in the 1975 Cincinnati-Boston Series was one of the supreme sports exhibitions. The Super Bowl, on the other hand, is a one-shot deal, and both coaches and players have disciplined themselves to play cautiously. No wild and sudden pass, no careless punt allowing the receiver to run back for a touchdown, no razzle-dazzle. If the Super Bowl were the best two out of three, you'd see some wild games in the second try, with a chance that game three could turn out to be a classic.

Certainly the elimination games in recent years have provided thrills comparable to the World Series: in 1971 the double overtime between Kansas City and Miami which was decided when two European-style soccer kickers attempted field goals (the Norwegian Jan Stenerud missed his, the Cypriote Garo Yepremian made his); in 1972 when Franco Harris of the Pittsburgh Steelers caught that incredible pass in the final moment to defeat Oakland 13–7; and perhaps best of all, the Raiders-Dolphin play-off game in 1974 when Kenny Stabler of the Raiders threw his desperate last-minute pass to enable his team to eke out a 28–26 victory.

I have suspected there might be an element of divine justice in the way recent World Series and Super Bowls have gone. Football is incomparable, but we need to be reminded now and then that a quieter game like baseball, which so many extroverts keep announcing as dead, still has the capacity to excite and astound.

One aspect of football captivates me, because it demonstrates how intelligence can aid a game. I have often asked but never discovered who first dreamed up the idea of admitting a wild-card team to the final play-offs. Each conference is divided into three divisions, and the champion of each is assured a berth in the play-offs. But an elimination with only six teams competing would be cumbersome or, if one team drew a bye, unfair. So some genius devised the plan whereby the second-place finisher with the best record in any one of the three divisions is awarded fourth place in that conference. This has the advantage of keeping interest alive throughout each conference, even if the champions of the three divisions have long been known. One year, in the final weeks of the season, twelve teams were still eligible for the play-offs, and it is not uncommon for one or both of the wild cards to be decided on the last Sunday of the season.

This has accomplished so much for the sport, and is such a congenial way of providing a second life for a team, I would recommend that even if the leagues expand to thirty-two teams, which would permit an orderly four divisions of four teams each in both leagues, thus eliminating the need for the wild card, some way be devised whereby it could be retained. It is one of the best inventions sports has come up with recently, and the man responsible for it should be voted forthwith into the Hall of Fame.

It is equaled, I think, only by a system devised long ago for the soccer leagues in England and Scotland and adopted later by other nations around the world. Soccer is such an inexpensive game to play, with little equipment and none of it costly, almost any community can afford to field a team. So numerous are the cities that wish to enter topflight competition, in all countries, they are divided into divisions of descending competence, A, B, C, D, etc. In Scotland, where I became an avid fan, the A division consists of eighteen teams, and the lesser divisions have the same number.

The neat trick is that each year the two teams who finish last in the A division are automatically dropped back to B, their vacancies being filled by the two teams who finished first in the B division. The same is happening at the tail end of C, and so on down the line.

Thus there is a constant mobility among the teams, and as the season draws to a close it often happens that the champion of A is pretty well known, whereas a real dogfight is under way to see which two teams at the bottom of the ladder will be forced to accept the ignominy of relegation, as the phrase goes, to the next lower league. Some of the worst soccer riots in history have involved partisans whose beloved team was about to be either relegated or promoted.

> For example, on May 18, 1969, the citizens of Caserta, a town of 70,000 northeast of Naples, were overjoyed when their League C team beat Trapani, because this meant that next season Caserta would be promoted to League B. The celebration, which lasted for several days, was dampened by ugly rumors that Caserta had won only because it had bought off one of the key Trapani players.
>
> Belatedly, on Monday, September 8, Italian radio carried the chilling announcement: 'Players involved in the scandal are barred for life. Caserta forfeits the game and is refused promotion to League B.'
>
> When the news flashed through Caserta, all shops closed and people started massing in the street. By afternoon the news was officially confirmed, but no damage was done. That night the citizens of Caserta found that the game scheduled for Sunday, when they were to play their first game in League B, had been canceled. On Tuesday a sullen, embittered mob began ripping iron shutters off store windows and setting fire to municipal buildings.
>
> When water pipes supplying the town were torn up, fires could not be checked, and barricades were erected in the streets. Football fans in nearby Naples, hearing that a first-class riot was under way, came to Caserta by bus, just to be in on the fun. By the time peace was restored, eighty people were in the hospital, ninety-nine in jail, and damage estimated at two billion lire had been done. Caserta was still in League C.

A Michener Miscellany: 1950–1970.

I have always been a supporter of soccer and from time to time have entertained fatuous hopes that it might become established in the United States as a major sport. It has so much to commend it, specifically its world-wide acceptance. As a nation we compete in very few true world championships—tennis, yachting and track are ones that come to mind—and it would be salutary, I think, if we fielded a national soccer team for the World Cup and played Argentina, let us say, home-and-home for a chance to go to the finals in Moscow, with total goals in the two games deciding the winner.

Suppose the first game were played in La Plata, with Argentina winning, 2–1. The second is to be played in Omaha, and with only a few minutes left in the game we are ahead 3–1, which means that we're about to win on total goals, 4–3. But the Rumanian referee spots an American foul—maybe it was, maybe it wasn't, but the Tunisian linesman nods yes—and Argentina is awarded a free kick at our goal. Our victory has been rubbed out by the referee, and he a Rumanian. Friends, it demands restraint for a fan to keep in his seat at such a moment. In Peru on Sunday, May 24, 1964, such a decision evoked a riot which caused the death of almost three hundred spectators. This explains why many nations are now requiring deep trenches to separate the spectators from the playing field. Too many referees were getting killed.

Things got so bad in South America that they were advertising for Europeans to come over and officiate: 'Good pay, good lodging and a decent burial.' In one small town near Khartoum the referee made so many dubious calls that toward the end of the game the losing team kicked him to death, and their supporters asked, 'Why did you wait till the second half?'

I saw some of my best soccer in Israel, but the fans were becoming so violent, they had to sit behind a basketweave of barbed wire to prevent them from running onto the field. During the winter of 1975 an Israeli judge found the rioting so endemic and severe that he canceled all league play.

It is strange that a game with such a powerful hold on spectators, one so popular throughout the world, should not have caught on in the United States. The answer, I think, is that in the three countries in which American-style football became established first—United States, Canada with slightly different rules, Australia with the wildest game of all—the superiority of the American game, with its violence, its variation in action and its more frequent opportunities for scoring, became evident, and fans could show no interest in the slower, more repetitive and low-scoring soccer version.

This brings us back to television. In 1967 a serious attempt was made to force soccer down the American throat, and CBS invested considerable funds in broadcasting league games on a regular basis. Danny Blanchflower, a famous, glib-tongued expert from England, was imported to do the commentary, and the result was a threefold disaster: 1) there was even less scoring than in hockey; 2) Blanchflower was an uninhibited realist who, when the local defenseman loused up a play, said so, to the consternation of the television people, who were accustomed to the ultra-sweet blandness of the American broadcaster; and 3) worst of all, the ebb and flow of soccer provided no reasonable stopping places for commercials, and when the referee did halt play to take care of that chore, he seemed always to do so just as the home team was about to run the opposition into a state of exhaustion. The enforced time-out, so alien to soccer, where the continuity of play is everything, gave the worn-down team time to recuperate, and the balance of the game was destroyed. CBS quickly got the silly game off the air and returned to hard-hitting American football, where the blood could be clearly seen as the opposition players limped off or were dragged away on stretchers.

A new attempt is being made to introduce soccer, this time with six players indoors in a confined hockey-lacrosse area with play continuous and no offsides. I can hear Danny Blanchflower telling his cronies in the local pub back in England, 'Sounds logical, if that's what a bloke wants in his football. But they ought to call it something else, because it's not the game we play.'

Soccer's big chance will come not on television, for it seems deadly dull when compared with American-style football—a comment I will delete if this book ever moves overseas, because nine-tenths of the world considers a television broadcast of a European final or a World Cup the supreme sporting thrill—but in the universities when the cost of fielding a football team of sixty or seventy players, with their ultra-expensive equipment, becomes insupportable. Soccer is one of the world's great games, and I have rarely experienced the thrill I did in the summer of 1974 when I went to Germany to follow a group of teams from varied nations as they battled for the World Cup. Such competition offers a new dimension in sport, better in some ways than the comparable Olympics, for the overall level of performance is higher, and I will personally applaud the day when the sport becomes part of the American scene, with or without the sanction of television.

There is another way in which television dominates sports. It plays a major role in determining where franchises can profitably be placed. If City A and City B are competing for a football, basketball or baseball franchise, and if each has adequate funds to pay for it and a stadium or arena in which to play, and if City B ranks only 33rd as a potential television market while City A ranks 21st, it is to the benefit of the league and of television to place the available franchise in City A with its much greater potential rather than in City B, which might have a higher raw population but which doesn't amount to much as a television market.

At present two measurements are used to determine the television potential of a city. Area of Dominant Influence (ADI) allocates every county in the United States to that metropolitan area which dominates its viewing habits. For example, a county in mid-California might be awarded to San Francisco-Oakland if its viewers habitually relied on San Francisco for news and entertainment, or to Los Angeles if they customarily tuned southward.

Designated Market Area (DMA) assigns districts according to their viewing habits during prime time and is therefore a more sophisticated measure of the advertising potential than the cruder geographical allocations of ADI. Here is how your area ranks:

THIRTY-TWO METROPOLITAN AREAS

Rank 1970 Census	Area	1970 Population	Rank ADI	Rank DMA	Rank Per Capita Wealth
1	New York	11,529,000	1	1	1
2	Los Angeles	7,032,000	2	2	4
3	Chicago	6,979,000	3	3	13
4	Philadelphia	4,818,000	4	4	25
5	Detroit	4,200,000	7	7	18
6	San Francisco/Oakland	3,110,000	6	6	5
7	Washington	2,861,000	9	8	6
8	Boston	2,754,000	5	5	22
9	Pittsburgh	2,401,000	10	10	24
10	St. Louis	2,363,000	12	12	31
11	Dallas/Fort Worth	2,318,000	11	11	11
12	Baltimore	2,071,000	19	20	27
13	Cleveland	2,064,000	8	9	28
14	Houston	1,985,000	14	14	14
15	Minneapolis/St. Paul	1,814,000	13	13	12
16	Seattle	1,422,000	15	17	2
17	Milwaukee	1,404,000	26	23	19
18	Atlanta	1,390,000	16	15	20
19	Cincinnati	1,385,000	23	24	21
20	San Diego	1,358,000	34	32	9
21	Buffalo	1,349,000	24	25	26
22	Miami	1,268,000	18	16	28
23	Kansas City	1,254,000	22	26	15
24	Denver	1,228,000	28	28	7
25	Indianapolis	1,110,000	17	19	10
26	New Orleans	1,046,000	36	35	32
27	Tampa	1,013,000	20	18	30
28	Portland	1,009,000	25	22	8
29	Phoenix	968,000	37	36	16
30	Providence	914,000	29	29	23
31	Rochester	883,000	60	67	17
32	Honolulu	629,000	81	80	3

Spot Television Rates and Data. Skokie, Ill.: Standard Rate and Data Service, April, 15, 1973. DMA: Nielsen Station Index markings by households within Designated Market Areas, September 1975. Last column: U.S. Department of Commerce: *County and City Data Book,* 1972.

These figures illuminate certain points in professional sport. The endemic weakness of franchises in either Baltimore or Milwaukee has been difficult to explain. The former has a population of 2,071,000, almost twice that of New Orleans or Denver and much bigger than Atlanta, yet it has represented a dubious sports market. Milwaukee has a population of 1,404,000, again, much bigger than that of cities whose franchises were doing well, while Milwaukee has had trouble.

The reason is found in the ADI and the DMA ratings. Baltimore was a fine city, with a large population, but its television viewers were siphoned south to Washington and north to Philadelphia. Its population rank was a high 12, its television potential a low 19–20. It really wasn't a very enticing market. Milwaukee, delimited by both Chicago and Minneapolis, was worse, its population rank being a respectable 17, while its television potential was 26–23.

The opposite was the case with Tampa. I was astonished when in late 1974 the NFL announced that it was thinking of awarding the city a franchise costing some $16,000,000, so I was not surprised when Tom McCloskey, a Philadelphia builder, declined to accept when the franchise was offered. 'He's no dummy,' I told my friends. 'Tampa hasn't the potential to support such a franchise.'

I was wrong. I hadn't looked at the figures. Tampa may rate only twenty-seventh in population, but rates 20–18 in television potential, ahead of established markets like Cincinnati, Buffalo, Denver, New Orleans and San Diego. Having checked these data, I was not surprised when Hugh F. Culverhouse, an attorney in Jacksonville, quickly picked up the Tampa slot. It looks to be a sound risk.

I do not think it proper that television should dictate where franchises go, but even so, if I were putting up my own money, I would think twice about locating a major franchise in Rochester, which shows an enormous differential between its population and its potential, and I would love to take an NFL team into Montreal, which dominates not only its share of Canada but also a good part of northern New England and New York. I would be most reluctant to invest my dollars in San Diego; the discrepancy seems too great; however, local pride might offset this, especially if the management happened to come up with a good team.

San Francisco and Oakland represent an interesting case. With a large population, impressive potential and an extremely high per capita wealth, this area could support one team in each major sport handsomely. But crowding two football and two baseball teams into this confined area puts too great a strain on the resources, and I was not surprised when it was announced that the San Francisco baseball Giants were going broke. Some of the other teams in the area may find themselves in trouble too, but when the sorting out has occurred, the survivors should prove healthy, with television's help.

Television's overpowering financial leverage must not obscure what I believe to be its greatest importance: its capacity to accelerate change. Consider these three cases.

For more than a decade football fans knew it was insane to conduct championship games in January in northern cities like Green Bay. Football played in a blizzard might be heroic but it wasn't football. Yet the fans were powerless to enforce a change, because the men running the game felt they could ignore the protests.

But in 1967 television showed that dreadful Green Bay-Dallas play-off with the stadium thermometer at seventeen degrees below zero, and the general public could watch Dallas end Bob Hayes running pass patterns with his hands inside his pants lest they freeze solid and break off. Don Meredith can now laugh at that excursion into the Ice Bowl: 'What we didn't know and Green Bay did was that our receivers were running their patterns two ways. If, for example, Bob Hayes was just the decoy on a play, he kept his hands jammed in his pants. But if he knew I might throw him the ball, he ran with his hands out. Green Bay had us taped all the way.' To play a game under such conditions was preposterous, and television forced a move to some more southerly city, where the January play-offs should have been all the time.

In the early days television sponsored safaris in which well-known sportsmen traipsed to far regions of the world, gunning down large animals. But when people began to protest that they did not want such scenes in their living rooms, the networks quickly left the high-powered rifles home and conducted camera safaris that were just as interesting.

In 1974–75 sports fans were subjected to two lamentable rip-offs, Evel Knievel's closed-circuit 'motorcycle' jump across Snake River Canyon, and ABC's telecast of the George Foreman fiasco in which he fought five so-called boxers in one afternoon. The outcry against such nonsense was immediate and unanimous. Knievel's jump had been falsely sold from the beginning; the Foreman fights would not have been allowed in a well-run corner saloon, let alone on national television. Dick Young wrote of it: 'This gimmickry, this phony trash exposes the ends to which TV producers will go for an audience. Boxing never sank so low as at this moment.' Jim Murray turned in one of his strong columns: 'I don't think I've ever seen a more degrading "sports" spectacle. Everybody who had anything to do with it should be ashamed. It set boxing back to the barges. The game was exposed for its essential bankruptcy.' But next year something equally trashy will be offered us, and we must condemn it.

Worthy innovations, like the Superstar competition, are needed; they add spice to the year. But television by itself cannot exercise the judgment required to sponsor the meritorious and condemn the meretricious. Only an alert public can do that.

I cannot leave television without grappling with the enigma of Howard Cosell. Into the bland and almost sophomoric world of television sports coverage came this rasping, opinionated, logorrheic, knowledgeable gadfly of whom a jealous critic once said, 'Howard is the only man in the world who changed his name and put on a toupee in order to tell it like it is.'

Let me explain how I became a connoisseur of radio and television broadcasters. I was working in Colorado back in 1936, and on a blustery Saturday afternoon I was driving home with my car radio on. It was a football game between two western universities, late in the final quarter. It was obviously a game of heroic proportions, with players from the home team—I forget its name—performing miracles. They really must have been playing over their heads, because although I didn't catch the score, they were socking it to their opponents, and the announcer was breathless in his excitement over the performance of his heroes. Then the game ended and he revealed the score. His miracle players had lost, something like 42–0, and I realized for the first time that the announcer's job was to create suspense, sustain tension, and give the listener the feeling that he had participated in a game which had been decided only in the final seconds.

Following that introduction I became addicted to the historic broadcasts of Frank Murray, the best P-Oner in the business. On days when his hometown St.Louis ball club was rained out he took bleak Western Union P-One transmissions (one paragraph), and using only his imagination and inside knowledge of what would probably have happened in a ball game, converted them into highly colorful re-creations which convinced the listener that Murray was sitting in the park in Boston, watching a thrilling game between the Red Sox and the Yanks.

The Western Union P-One reported: 'Foxx flies center. Higgins singles. Chapman pops third. Cramer fans.'

Here's the way Frank Murray would have handled this: 'Jimmy Foxx, second only to Babe Ruth, hunches his mighty shoulders and swings with all his power. Gomez fools him with a low curve that misses the bat by a foot. Jimmy steps out of the batter's box, rubs resin on his immense hands, and comes back, glaring. He takes ball one. Lefty Gomez studies him and delivers another tantalizing twister and again Foxx misses by a foot. Quick delivery, ball two missing the outside corner. Now Foxx means business. He crowds the plate, daring Gomez to throw at him. The ball comes in high, nothing on it, Foxx swings. [Here he raps the desk with his knuckles to simulate the sound of a bat on ball.] What a clout. DiMaggio goes back,

back, back. He's on the track, right up against the wall. A leap! He spears it in his gloved hand. The crowd roars. [Sound of crowd roaring] What a catch, and Gomez smiles that enigmatic smile of his as Jimmy Foxx slings his bat toward the dugout.'

Some of the best ball games I ever attended were those imaginary ones coming at me from that smoke-filled room in the back of a radio station in St.Louis. From it I progressed to the broadcasting greats—Graham Mac-Namee, Red Barber and Mel Allen—and then to the retired ballplayers like Waite Hoyt and Dizzy Dean. They were a sterling lot, able to evoke cascading memories with a single apt phrase: Red Barber's 'Joe DiMaggio is sittin' in the catbird seat right now, with everything in his favor.' Or Dean's 'They woulda had him at second but he slud.'

I was instructed in the power of the sports broadcaster one Sunday afternoon in Miami when the Dolphins scored a touchdown and the better part of the audience of 68,901 took out their handkerchiefs and fluttered them. 'What gives?' I asked, and the man sitting next to me explained.

'Look around you. More than half the people bring transistor radios to the game. They've always done that here. Some of those seats over there are pretty bad, and the scoreboard is not only lousy but from many seats it's invisible. So we watch the game with our eyes and listen to it with our ears. Rick Weaver, of WIOD, is about the best sportscaster in the country, and he explains what's happening. He gives us the inside analysis so that we understand what we've been seeing.'

'Where do the handkerchiefs come in?'

'One day he wanted to know how many of us in the stadium were listening to him, and the Dolphins had the ball first and goal to go from the nine-yard line. That's one of the toughest situations in football, and Rick said, "If we score, everyone who's listening wave a white handkerchief." We did score, and the stadium looked like a snowstorm.' Later I asked Weaver about this, and he said, 'We calculate that these days about sixty to seventy percent of the couples who attend the game bring at least one transistor.'

It was into this juvenile electronic age that Howard Cosell exploded. Long before Monday Night Football he had been broadcasting in both radio and television for ABC, making a slowly growing impact on the New York audience as a sensible commentator who tried valiantly to explain sports events and the milieu surrounding them in terms the listener or viewer could understand. I heard him infrequently in those years, but even then he seemed to me 'to be telling it like it was.' Just as newspapers and magazines were reaching the stage where their patrons were beginning to demand better reporting and more in-depth explanation, so television was getting to the point where the extreme blandness of normal videocasting was an insult to the perceptive viewer.

Cosell was the precipitant. When he was tossed into the television hopper, with his grating nasal voice and incredible vocabulary, the public quickly responded, initially with hate mail, then with accolades. I saw him first at a memorable snow-swept Monday-night game between the Eagles and the Giants. Television was unkind to him that night: 'If anyone ever looked like an on-camera drunk,' he later said, 'I did.'

But he was good. He generated excitement, knew how to bounce his street smarts off country-boy Don Meredith, how to utilize celebrity guests for maximum effect. Like all night-club performers, which is what he essentially was, he had certain shticks—time-tested bits he could rely on for certain applause—such as rattling off the rosters of teams without notes, adding the number of each player as he went along.

It might be said that I recognized Cosell's importance to television, but I did not admit how important he was until one Monday night in Miami when the Dolphins were playing Pittsburgh. I was sitting in the western curve of the stadium in a seat which would have allowed me to look back over my right shoulder and catch a good view of the suite from which Cosell would be broadcasting. I didn't look back, because I had come to watch the football game, which turned out to be a wildly fluctuating affair. That was the game in which during the first few minutes Dick Anderson intercepted two Pittsburgh passes thrown by the black quarterback Joe Gilliam, running each in for a quick touchdown.

But as I looked at this exciting game, one of the best played that year, I became aware that in order to see the field, I had to look over a veritable sea of faces. Everyone in my area was looking not at the players but back over his shoulder at Howard Cosell.

'There he is!' they reported breathlessly to each other. 'He's talking with someone now. Look! Look! It's really Cosell. I can see him!'

One man had brought not an ordinary radio but one specially geared so that it could pick up the audio from the television broadcast, and in my quarter he became the center of attraction. 'What's he saying now?' people begged. 'What did he say about that pass?' What Howard Cosell said about a play was much more important than the play itself. Many of the spectators in my row did not even see the play, for they kept watching Cosell, but even those who did watch the field wanted confirmation of what they had seen. It was as if only the presence of Cosell lent verity.

At intermission I was introduced into the world of the Monday-night banner, that strange development whereby otherwise sensible fans lug into the stadium cumbersome banners painstakingly lettered with innocuous and sometimes funny messages which the owners hope will be caught by the panning cameras, thus ensuring a brief immortality: 'Cosell, the Mouth that Roars' was one; 'Jacksonville Loves Howard Cosell' was another.

As I went for a drink I was accosted in the passageway by two young women who carried a large banner rolled on sticks, which the police would not allow them to take into the stadium. Apparently a quota had been set, and scores of huge productions had been interdicted. 'Would you please sneak this in for us?' they pleaded, although how they expected me to conceal so huge a mass, I did not understand.

'What's it say?' I asked.

Proudly they unrolled a portion. 'Parkersburg West Virginia loves you Howard.' That was the message.

'What's it mean?' I asked.

'It's well lettered, and if the cameras pick it up, there we'd be, on national television!' They were almost tearful in their pleading, two young women in their early twenties, so I agreed to smuggle their world-shaking banner into the stadium.

I got it past the guards by saying, 'I had it in before,' and as soon as I reached my seat the young women ran up, took the banner, and secreted themselves in a position from which they could spring forth when the roaming camera crew came their way to pick up that night's free publicity for ABC. And sure enough, late in the game the girls unfurled their banner right in the face of the camera crew, and I suppose their deathless message of devotion to Cosell flashed on the screen for six or seven seconds.

In the closing minutes of the game, when Pittsburgh roared back and threatened to win, the Dolphins decided on an unusual strategy, one slightly infra dig for a champion. They would direct their quarterback to down the ball intentionally in the end zone, surrendering two points to the enemy in the hope that the ensuing free punt from the twenty-yard line would place the ball so deep in enemy territory that no score would be possible in the remaining seconds.

In my area there was heated discussion of this cowardly strategy, with certain fans proclaiming, 'Givin' away a safety's a disgrace,' but the man with the specially wired radio assured us, 'Howard Cosell says it's a smart move.'

'He did?' the protesters asked, and a multitude of faces stared out of the arena to the glassed-in compartment where the oracle sat. If he had said it was all right, it was all right. Miami gave away the safety, got off a soaring punt, ran out the clock, and preserved their lead. 'Cosell said it was all right,' the fans around me repeated, and they were standing there when I left, staring toward the spot where the great man still sat before the post-game cameras.

Despite the spectacular growth which television made possible for football and golf, the success of a professional team still depends primarily on the coverage it gets free in the newspaper. The best thing that can happen to

'I'm afraid we're kind of tied up. Eddie and Paul are watching
Game of the Week, then the Tulsa Open, Aussie Tennis and the Big Fight reruns.
Karen's signed in for Wide World of Sports, Celebrity Bowling,
Gymnastics from Poland and the Roller Derby. I'm watching
the Innsbruck slalom trials, African Safari, free falls and gliding.'

a team, or to a player, is to have the local papers write enthusiastically, for then financial success is assured. Constant favorable mention, especially in columns, is better than paid advertising, better than radio, better than television. With it a mediocre team can prosper; without it even a good team can fade.

Of course fans enjoy seeing their team on the tube, but the opinion they form of that team stems principally from what is written about it. On television there is little opinion; when it does appear, it is apt to be pusillanimous, and when it is strong, it is apt to be uninformed. For a recapitulation of what he saw, and a judgment of its significance, the fan must turn to his newspaper; there his loyalty is engendered and his prejudices enforced. I have found that those papers whose opinions are most firmly voiced tend to be the most successful.

It is therefore not surprising that owners will go to extreme lengths to ensure favorable coverage, and some of the most scandalous newspaper behavior in the past fifty years was found in the sports department, where writers often accepted pay from both the paper and the team upon which they were reporting. If the sanctity of the press has been the holy grail of the editorial page, it has been a cup difficult to find in the sports section.

For the first hundred years of its existence, baseball had the press of this nation in its pocket. The true story of baseball was never told. The game received an unconscionable amount of free publicity, often written by men who were little more than paid lackeys of the owners, and the federal government was dragooned by popular opinion into granting the sport concessions and exemptions that continue to amaze.

And the public loved it. I remember so clearly those weeks, more than forty years ago, when Bing Miller of the A's went on a hitting streak that ran through some eighteen games. Toward the end a sportswriter for the *Philadelphia Bulletin* wrote a column in which he explained that whenever Bing went on such a spree, he had the custom of not changing his socks until the skein had ended, a kind of superstition not uncommon among athletes.

But then the writer went on to explain to his sports-hungry public that when Bing said *socks* he didn't mean the kind that you and I wear, nor the colorful hose that the spectator sees and which gave two teams their monickers, Red Sox and Pale Hose. No, he meant the flimsy white stockings which the player puts on first, and which are necessary because the visible socks have no feet. The writer went on and on, explaining where the stockings were made, how much they cost, how long they lasted, and the normal frequency with which they were laundered. Real inside scoop, the stuff that fans eat up. I can still see it on the page, high in the left-hand corner, framed in a separate box. 'Great writing,' I said.

Most of the stories of that period were like that, little glimpses into a make-believe world with almost never an honest insight into the ignorance, the bullying, the exploitation, the cupidity, the brief careers, the long years in the shadows. The social indifference of the sports pages was offset by the brilliance of the writing, and it was not by accident that so many of America's most cogent writers had sports pages in their backgrounds.

It was in the 1920s that the owners of *The New York Times* commissioned Professor William Lyon Phelps, the charismatic pundit of the Yale English department, to review the literary quality of their newspaper. He surprised them by reporting that whereas much of the paper was passably written, one department excelled. That was the work being done by John Kieran in the sports department. This represented the first public recognition that someone writing about sports could be a true artist.

Others shared Kieran's excellence: James C. Isaminger in Philadelphia, Westbrook Pegler for the Hearst papers, Ring Lardner of the *Chicago Tribune* and Paul Gallico of the *New York Daily News.* Reporters started to move from the sports page to the editorial; some shifted completely to the writing of short stories or books. Ernest Hemingway, John O'Hara, Bob Considine, Walter Cronkite and James Reston began as sportswriters.

The sports page was an exciting place to work for several reasons. Tonto Coleman, former czar of the Southeastern Conference, has summed it up best: 'I turn to the front pages of my newspaper to read about men's failures. I turn to the sports pages to read about their triumphs.'

There is a sweet finality to the sports page. Team A met in deadly struggle with Team B and there was a specific outcome, which can be recorded. Even the appearance of the old morning sports page, with those eight baseball games with their line-ups in neat boxes, and the line scores underneath, was reassuring. Especially appealing to the eye were the box scores of games in which nine players on one team played the whole nine innings against nine on the other side, with perhaps a couple of doubles, one triple and three double plays listed in the smaller type below. 'The beauty of agate' a newspaperman once called this as I stood with him looking at proofs of that day's paper. He was referring to the small clean type in which box scores were printed. Many writers have testified that they derive real pleasure from a box score properly presented. (I have never watched any baseball game, so far as I can recall, in which I did not keep a full play-by-play score.)

The second advantage of the sports page in those days was that every significant act could be codified, recorded and compared with similar acts being performed by other players and other teams. The statistical data of baseball were narcotic. As a boy I could recite the batting order and batting averages of every team in the two leagues, and I have watched with interest in recent years when grown men, who have retained this mathematical interest, have patiently gone back to recalculate batting averages and slugging percentages and record every time that Babe Ruth came to bat, finding five instances, when, under previous rules, he had come to bat in the ninth inning with his team one run behind and two men on base and hit some tremendous blast right out of the park, only to have it recorded as a double because that would have sufficed to drive in the winning run, making the home run superfluous.

I have often wished that I could associate myself with a good sports historian and a topflight computer expert with an interest in sports. We would take every World Series game ever played—because this is a neatly closed system of definable characteristics—and compute the coefficients of correlation between all known variables. In a World Series, who performs closest to the averages of the preceding season—the pitcher or the batter? A left-hander or a right-hander? Which is the crucial game to win? In an extra-inning game, what is the best strategy for using pinch hitters? And of course, the most debatable question of all, in a short series does the pitcher predominate?

I have a score of other questions we could attack, but I will not bore the non-statistician; besides, the figger-filberts, as they have been contemptuously labeled by the sports press, will already have anticipated the questions.*

One of the permanent delights of baseball is the minute accuracy of the mathematical data. I am appalled at the sloppy records of basketball, the hit-or-miss way hockey assists are awarded, and the general chaos of football statistics in which the heroic work of the linemen down in the pits must go unrecorded and unremembered. Again, the comparison of baseball with chess comes to mind: every move of the most intricate chess game can be recorded in a logical notation, imprisoning it for future reconstruction. When I state that Joe Sewell, a splendid fielding shortstop, batted .353 one season and .312 lifetime, I am offering a startling bit of information for the baseball addict, for these figures mean that this little man excelled most recorded competing shortstops, who are expected to field well but who can play the position today if they can bat no more than .238, an acceptable average for that spot.

The sportswriter has this known body of information about which to write, and his task is made easier because he can assume that most of his readers will be keyed in to these basic data.

*When this manuscript was completed, Skip Myslenski, of the *Philadelphia Inquirer,* advised me that such a book had already been printed: Earnshaw Cook's remarkable *Percentage Baseball.*

The third advantage of the sports page is that it deals not only with current scores but also with past heroics. Nostalgic recollection is the basic commodity of the sportswriter, and I have noticed that even in the best journals, three signed columns out of five are apt to deal with remembrance of past glories.

If a player is traded, or performs some outstanding feat, or visits a town in his retirement, or dies, the event becomes an excuse for recalling the interesting trivia of his life. I shall not soon forget that during an evening I shared with columnist Red Smith, I introduced a variety of topics on which he could not possibly have been prepared, and listened as he spun one relevant tale after another, conjuring up names long forgotten and providing details of what this player had said or done, always with a delightful twist of whimsy or outrageousness. At one point we were speaking of sports and government, and without time to reflect he said, 'Best example of that I ever witnessed was when the city council of Snohomish, Washington, passed an ordinance prohibiting the high school football coach from using one of the school's all-around athletes, Earl Torgeson, on the football team. The city fathers had guessed that Torgeson might have it in him to play major-league baseball, and they didn't want him to break any bones as halfback. They were right. The Earl of Snohomish, as we called him, went on to play first base for the Boston Braves, gaining considerable fame for his hometown.' And it occurred to me, as I listened to this skilled narrative, that Smith must have had several thousand such recollections, all codified, all relevant and all stimulating.

One of the major rewards of my own writing life was that I worked for about a year on the old *Information Please* show with John Kieran, who, as he so often proved, possessed an extraordinary memory for everything from light verse to bird habits. Before and after going on radio, Kieran and I would talk for a while about varied topics, but I liked best those periods in which he would recollect some preposterous sports story, telling it with acerbic Irish wit. His treasury, like Smith's, was inexhaustible.

The best contemporary sportswriters have this valuable felicity, though less developed than the masters Smith and Kieran. Dave Anderson, of *The New York Times,* is approaching them in the grace with which he can summon past performances and make them relate to current topics.

No other writer on the daily paper would dare to indulge in nostalgia the way the sportswriter does. His readers would command him 'to get on with it.' If President Ford is in trouble, I am not breathlessly interested in knowing that President Buchanan once faced the same problem and solved it by delaying decision. But the sportswriter is actually cherished for his ability to link past with present, for his witty charm in keeping faded figures alive. It must be fun to be reminded so constantly of afternoons enjoyed, of nights filled with exciting victories.

But the greatest advantage the sportswriter has is freedom. It is not by accident that so many of our good writers once wrote sports, and not politics or business or city government. It was on the sports page alone that they were free to write evocatively or sardonically or brashly or alliteratively or pompously. Numerous former sportswriters have testified to the fact that the top editors left them alone; the sports pages were an arcane region which the big brains of the paper never really comprehended.

The sportswriter was encouraged to develop a personal style, or even to become as irascible as Westbrook Pegler. It was one of the best jobs in the world, for it dealt with finite things in an infinite way. The unfolding of the season established the calendar, and the championship game brought everything to a known conclusion; but within that finite universe the sportswriter was free to indulge himself almost as he wished. I started my writing career as a fourteen-year-old sportswriter for our local newspaper, and one of the saddest days of my life came when I failed to land a job with the *Detroit Free Press*. It was clear to me that they needed some young writers with spark and affection for games, but I was unable to convince the editors and my sports career ended.

With the advent of television, the old patterns had to change. Fans now had the scores before they went to sleep, and there was no need for 'the beauty of agate' to inform them in the morning. What they now needed was inside information revealing why the score ended as it had. As soon as I perceived the revolution, I started watching the big newspapers to determine which was responding most intelligently to the new challenge.

The best single performance in the new dimension that I have so far seen appeared in the *Dallas News* after a 1973 football game in which Los Angeles defeated Dallas unexpectedly, 37–31, with Harold Jackson catching four touchdown passes from John Hadl. The *News* gave the score and a brief rundown of the game, but then had three full pages of captivating analysis of why the debacle had occurred, with sensible quotes from both coaches, many of the players, Jackson the Los Angeles hero, plus a full page of photographs of the crucial plays.

This was sports coverage at its best, but whether a newspaper in Dallas was entitled to award so many pages of newsprint to a football game, when the city had so many other problems of pressing nature, is a question I will beg for a moment.

Three newspapers seem to me to have made the shift from mere press agentry to solid reporting with some distinction: The *Philadelphia Inquirer,* which I read daily and for which I may have a small predilection; the *Washington Post,* whose Shirley Povich I have been following since 1943 when I was stationed in that city with the navy; and the *Miami Herald,* which I have been seeing fairly often in recent years. In most editions of these papers the connoisseur will find some article worth his attention, an article which probes a little deeper than the ordinary sports story used to.

But the two papers which have been preeminent in forging new policies are *The New York Times* and the *Los Angeles Times*. I have oscillated between the two when trying to determine which was the better; I see the former more regularly than the latter and am inclined toward it. I particularly enjoy its spectacularly wide coverage; no other paper in the country can match its reportage on such sports as hunting, boating, tennis and squash and such games as chess and bridge.

A sophisticated friend, who prefers either the *New York Post* or the *Daily News*, suggests that perhaps I am still a 'prisoner of agate,' and that what I prize is mere coverage and not interpretation. His position was strengthened when the *Times'* sports department was hit by two scandals in a row: the first dealt with its solicitation and overuse of free passes to sporting events; the second was a savage article by Martin Ralbovsky, the sportswriter who did the book on the Schenectady Little League champions, who revealed the department's improper reliance on publicity handouts, which young reporters like Ralbovsky were directed to rewrite as legitimate news.

The appointment of James Tuite as head of the department had two salutary effects: the malfeasance just cited was stopped, and the paper began encouraging its reporters to dig rather deeply into the sports scene and start depicting the realities rather than the myths. The *Times* series on recruiting in colleges was a commendable performance, as were its occasional articles on the financial chicanery in the sports empire and its harsh condemnation of the growing violence in sport.

In addition, Tuite instituted an opinion page in the Sunday editions where some of the gripping topics of contemporary sport were discussed. This was a real contribution, with the letters to the editor proving the intellectual depth at which many of the readers were prepared to grapple with these problems.

But upon reflection, I had to decide that the best sports pages in the nation right now appeared in the *Los Angeles Times*. (If I were able to read the paper every day, I might think differently; I may have been lucky in seeing a relatively few exceptional issues.) In these pages I have found a surprising variety of topics treated, and almost never casually. I have found articles which probed high school sports, and the experiences of former athletes, and the negotiations of contracts, and the financial wizardry of franchise movements, and the role of women. The writing, too, has been above average, and there has been a knowing sophistication.

In the late spring of 1973 I happened to be storm-bound in a remote town in New Mexico, and the only paper I could see was a local sixteen-sheeter. But the weekend I was there chanced to be the one in which the state-wide basketball championships of New Mexico were to be decided, and I started reading about the contending teams—towns I had never heard of—and the writing was so professional, the sports lore so topflight, that I found myself obsessed with wanting to know how the Class C and D semi-finals came out.

For the writers on this little paper were using all the best techniques employed by either the *New York* or the *Los Angeles Times.* There were the interviews with players, the anguished statements by coaches, the careful predictions by experts, the editorials praising fair play, the accusations of unfairness on the part of the referees, and even a betting line.

I became so involved with this small-time tournament—I was worried whether the Class C former champion, a town with 3,000 population, could repeat—that I stayed by my radio to catch the breathless announcer intoning the sad news that my team had lost.

My point is that sportswriters around the world are able to generate this enthusiasm. They are uniformly good, some of the very best being the English and Australian fanatics who rely excessively on the pronoun *I,* making the sports event seem something that was engineered primarily for the benefit of the writer, who is now able to confide what earthquaking thing it was that the coach said to the malingering center.

I have written elsewhere about one of the most dramatic instances of influence I have witnessed. While working in Córdoba, Spain, in the spring of 1968 the local newspaper advised the Córdobans that in last Saturday's soccer game at Palma de Mallorca the Palma rooters had so terrified the officials that they made every critical decision in favor of the home team. 'The audience is the twelfth player on the field, and if Córdobans do not come out en masse this coming Saturday and terrorize the officials, we are not going to defeat Madrid Atletico.'

I went to the game, and during the first half the Córdobans may not have terrified the officials but they did me. Even so the score was tied 1–1. But as the half ended, a young Córdoban rushed onto the field, swinging a heavy camera in an arc over his head. Bringing it with full force down onto the cranium of the referee, he knocked that poor man silly, and when the second half resumed the officials began calling the shots more fairly, in the judgment of the Córdobans, and the home team won, 2–1. Next day the local sports pages reported that the behavior of the Córdoban fans had been exemplary, just what was needed if the promise previously shown by Córdoba was ever to be realized.

But the experience which best illustrates the relationship between the sports page and the sports enthusiast is exemplified by what happened when Joseph Avenick, the young man from New Jersey who helped me track down details for this book, worked as a beginning sportswriter for the *Philadelphia Bulletin*. He recalls:

> Like most tragedies, it started innocently. As a beginner in the department I was on the lobster shift, responsible for compiling those six-line trivia squibs used to fill out the tag end of a column. You've seen them:
>
> > Detroit, June 23. Fans here remembered Bob Fats Fothergill, pudgy right fielder for the Tigers, who led the American League in 1929 in pinch hits, with a total of 19.
>
> That's the whole story. A big newspaper will use up several dozen a day, and it was my job to find them, keep them short, and provide usable headlines. 'Cager Nets 29.' 'Trapshoot to Jackson.' 'Lefthander Runs Skein to 16.'
>
> I got my ideas from two sources. The barflies who'd call at two in the morning to ask, 'Who hit nineteen homers for the L.A. Dodgers in 1959, their second year on the coast?' (Answer: Wally Moon.) And what we called 'squib beggars,' who'd call at all hours to see if they could persuade the paper to print the score of their favorite team, whether anybody had ever heard of it or not.
>
> So one night it occurred to me to use the results of my father's bowling team, Belmont Garage, which competed against such famous outfits as Filter House, 260 Club and the DeBuggers. I still have the first squib I ran: 'Belmont Rolls Past 260 Club Behind Peitsch.' I gave the three top scores of Pop's team and the three best of the opponents, and the item created a sensation among the bowlers. Their names were in the paper!
>
> It also caused complications. Word got out that if a team played Belmont Garage, it would get its name in the *Bulletin,* and they did week after week. 'Joe Reeser (209), Howard Sheetz (195) John Warfield (186).' So every team that faced Belmont Garage was at peak form, with freshly laundered uniforms and new bowling shoes. Result was that Pop's team lost every game.
>
> Its record fell to 2–13, but every week the squib reported the latest defeat as a major upset. 'Mighty Belmont Bowled Over,' 'Belmont Bullies Bounced,' 'Belmont Leaders Edged by Upstarts.' Playing Belmont was taken as seriously as a game against the New York Yankees.
>
> Well, late in the season Pop asked me if I could please not mention his team any more, it was humiliating, week after week. Even semi-pro teams who played in obscurity wanted to schedule Belmont, just so they could get their names in the paper. Pop said, 'We're trapped. It was the biggest mistake I ever made. The publicity destroyed us.'

This hunger for publicity characterizes almost everyone associated with organized sports, and extraordinary measures are taken to ensure that a team receives its fair share. Whole departments within the corporation which owns a team sweat to see that the locals get their names in the paper with sufficient frequency, and big-time universities often have large staffs to circulate stories and pictures. Everyone writing about the scandal of recruitment has been aware of the role that publicity plays in persuading a high school boy to sign with this university instead of that: 'I pointed out to his parents that if he came with us, their son's friends could see him on national television.' Ray Barrs, a blue-chip high school senior from Albuquerque, in explaining why he finally decided to enroll at Colorado rather than some smaller college, said frankly, 'The conviction that at Colorado I would get more national exposure.' Al Stump, writing in *TV Guide*, has summarized my experience when he quotes an unnamed West Coast scout:

> Lots of kids being recruited don't ask for much extra if you can promise them six to eight appearances in three years before a U.S. television audience. The publicity, what it means to their ambitions to turn pro, is enough to sell them.

We are raising a generation of athletes who will do anything to get on television, but what it will contribute to them in the end they do not seem to ask. Like the girls with their Cosell banner, just to get on that tube is enough.

With the burgeoning interest in sports, the time was ripe, on August 16, 1954, for the appearance of a new magazine focusing on the inside stories of the sporting world. There were satisfactory magazines already in existence, notably *Sport*, an adjunct of the MacFadden publishing empire, but it was cast in an old-fashioned mold. Time, Incorporated produced an attractive, well-illustrated, brightly written journal which they very much wanted to call *Sport* but which, being unable to acquire that title, they called *Sports Illustrated*, or *SI* in the trade.

Dan Jenkins, the author of *Semi-Tough*, that hilarious yarn about professional football players at the near-literate level is, of course, a writer whose work appears regularly in *SI*, so he must not be accepted as an impartial witness, but even so, he is accurate in his novel when he has his hero Billy Clyde Puckett refer constantly to *SI*: 'The Jets are still hot at the magazine because none of them made a cover during the regular season.'

SI has become the bible of the industry, and it has done so because it appreciated from the start the facts that faced printed journalism in the age of television: don't give the scores, give the inside stories behind the scores. And deal openly with those topics which men in saloons talk about in whispers.

Slowly *SI* began issuing those excellent four- and five-part series on what might be termed the sociology of contemporary American sport: Jack Olsen on the black athlete; Bil Gilbert and Nancy Williamson on women's rights in athletics; and Eddie Arcaro and Whitney Tower on the art of riding thoroughbreds. William Johnson, in the issues starting on December 22, 1969, had a somewhat complicated five-part series on the electronic revolution in sports, and there have been others which combined high reporting merit and social insight.

In other words, *SI* is doing many of the things it ought to be doing, and its success, after an agonizingly slow start, attests to the high regard in which sportsmen hold it. I have been especially interested in its style, for I judge that much of its acceptance has derived from this. Only *The New Yorker,* among contemporary magazines, has been as effective in sponsoring good writing with a certain wry touch, and if the style of *The New Yorker* has been correctly described by one critic as 'Yale-Vassar smart-ass,' then the decreed style of *SI* has got to be 'Texas-Oklahoma refined jock.' Here are some of the stylistic devices preferred by the magazine.

The unexpected juxtaposition: 'They are Pancho Gonzales and Pancho Segura, two men who have been around so long they have to mix Geritol with their Gatorade.'

The unexpected metaphor: 'So the losers in this [chess fiasco] are Fischer and Karpov. And don't forget the wood-pushers of the world.'

The backwoods simile: 'Down among the moss and live oaks of a South Carolina retreat the Masters juices were starting to flow like the channel bass in Calibogue Sound.'

The deft alliteration: 'Clowns, that crazy congregation of mirthful minutemen.'

The great one-liner: 'Roone Arledge, as anyone at ABC will tell you, was born in a manger.'

Refurbished oldie: 'As ill as the phainting phantoms Jimmy Connors and Ilie Nastase.' This is an apt reworking of the superb phrase in which some acid-tongued newsman described Phil Scott, the British heavyweight challenger who had a propensity for early collapse: 'Phainting Phil, the Swooning Swan of Soho.'

And the ploy I envy, the cliché apologized for: 'There is a timeworn wheeze among pro golfers that you drive for show and putt for dough.' The beauty of this device is that you get the benefit of the apt cliché, yet imply that anyone else who borrows it is a dunderhead. I've always wanted to use this shtick, but have never had the guts.

On the other hand, *SI* can become too cute. Toward the end of the 1975 college basketball season USC and UCLA made their annual weekend foray out of Southern California and into the perilous wilds of Oregon. Each of the California invaders would play a crucial Friday-night game against either Oregon or Oregon State, and then on Saturday night switch partners. A good deal hung on this pair of doubleheaders, and there could be many interesting consequences, depending on how the four games came out.

SI ran a delightful essay on the confrontation, replete with clever phrases, choice Americana—Oregon version—and allusive data. But it was too clever by half. One yearned for a good old Associated Press opening paragraph which stated in precise terms what was at stake in the two doubleheaders, plus a crisp summary of who won on Friday, who won on Saturday, and what the effect had been on the standings. But in spite of such lapses the magazine is a tonic. The sports explosion needed a journal just like *SI*, and we are fortunate that the one which came along had editors with insight into the kinds of explanatory stories that were needed.

In recent years books on sport have matured. During most of my life the average sports book was a disgrace, a puff job about some team or local hero written by an overworked press agent who batted it out during free periods. At its best it was hagiography; at its worst, servile press agentry. Year after year I sampled the flood and found it little better than that ancient story about Bing Miller's white socks. A portrait of sports was being painted which had so little relation to reality that it was preposterous. A whole decade would go by without one decent book on an activity that preoccupied millions. I pondered this anomaly and concluded that sports books were like sports movies: doomed to mediocrity because they were forced to deal with events which were colorful on the field but jejune on the printed page. It seemed impossible to write a sports book that was anything more than a compilation of records.

And then the long years of drought ended. Jim Brosnan's fine book on baseball, *The Long Season,* related the events of one season in mature terms. Jim Bouton's iconoclastic *Ball Four* looked at the same material from a more irreverent perspective, and it became apparent that professional sports could be presented intelligently.

Then came Roger Angell's *The Summer Game,* the first American book with the high literary quality of the best European books on sports. But the work which caught the imagination of all who loved sports in a grown-up way was Roger Kahn's *The Boys of Summer,* clearly a work of art and a joy to read.

It was not by accident that these ground-breaking books concerned baseball, for it is the most cerebral of our games and the one most worthy of reflective attention. But Jerry Kramer's remarkable *Instant Replay,* written with the substantial help of Dick Schaap, was both commanding and the essence of football. However, the best book on football I've read is Robert Daley's novel *Only a Game.* When I first read his chilling passage about what it means to a professional athlete when his knee gets conked, I said, 'This must be one of the best passages on sport ever written,' and in succeeding years I have met half a dozen students of the game who have told me, 'If you want to catch the essence of what sports are all about, read that bit Bob Daley did on knee injuries.'

The best book on basketball, perhaps the best on any sport insofar as the jungle of competition is concerned, is David Wolf's *Foul,* the study of what happened to Connie Hawkins. If I could read only one sports book, I would choose this. Wolf makes Hawkins a little bigger, a little more skilled than he actually was, but he can be forgiven for having become attached to his six-foot-eight subject. This is a book noble in intent, strong in execution. Blacks in particular should read it.

The best book on golf I've read so far is Dick Schaap's remarkable minute-by-minute re-creation of the Masters tournament of 1970, in which he follows the field through the anguishes and triumphs of that culminating test. Hubie Green assured me that what Schaap said about him was faithful to the way he was feeling and performing.

For the inside story of sports technique, I have preferred Leonard Koppett's two fine books *A Thinking Man's Guide to Baseball* and *The Essence of the Game Is Deception,* an analysis of basketball. Koppett's approach is so encyclopedic that he lulls you to sleep with a recitation of simple facts you already know, then snaps you awake with some fascinating original idea that you have never considered. In the baseball book he claims that the single most difficult feat in sports is for a batter to take a narrow piece of wood and with it endeavor to hit a small baseball thrown at one hundred miles an hour by a pitcher like Bob Feller or Sandy Koufax. The more I visualize myself standing at the plate with my Louisville slugger facing a pitcher only a few feet away, the more inclined I am to agree.

In his basketball book he captivated me with an analysis of what the supposed home-court advantage consists of. First he proves that it exists: In twenty-six NBA seasons through 1972, the home teams won 63.1 percent of over 10,000 games played! But then he asks how this advantage operates, and his mental gymnastics are exciting. In the end he concludes that maybe it's because the traveling team is worn out from one-night stands, while the home team has the advantage of rest, home cooking and the support of friends. I had figured that out for myself, but then Koppett surprises by saying, 'Not so,' and he proves his point by an ingenious bit of research. He looks at what happens on the first night when the travel-weary New York Knickerbockers return home to play a team which has been well rested over the preceding ten days. The result should either be a stand-off, or the rested opponents should have a substantial advantage. But they don't. The Knicks, back home, win that opening game 58.8 percent of the time, a preponderance that is statistically significant; that is, it couldn't have happened by chance. Then Koppett tells you what he thinks the home-court advantage really is:

The crowd noise affects the referees. When a home crowd keeps roaring, all through a game, all in one direction, very few referees can resist the subliminal effect so vehemently rejected by their conscious minds. Every little bounce in favor of the home team brings cheers; everything against it brings boos. It takes exceptional psychic strength to be the man who abruptly turns off the cheers and turns them to boos. This situation will exist until someone invents robot referees.

This is so similar to the conclusion of the Córdoban sports editor—that the home-town crowd is the sixth man on the basketball team, because it terrorizes the referee—that I judge Koppett to be right. His two books contain many such insights.

The best book on tennis is a short, deft account of how Arthur Ashe confronted Clark Graebner in a Forest Hills semi-final for the United States Open Championship. It is *Levels of the Game* by John McPhee, and it explains what goes through a player's mind in the tensest moments of a grueling match. It also describes how these two very different young men reached the apex of their sport, and one finishes the book knowing more about the workings of tennis than he could otherwise have learned.

Tom Meschery's *Caught in the Pivot* is about basketball, and not only is it written by a poet of recognized merit, it's also the best book on managing a team I've so far encountered. It deals with the heartbreak 1971–72 season in which as a rookie coach he tried vainly to drill some sense into the team billed as 'Tomorrow's Champions Today,' the Carolina Cougars—thirty-five wins, forty-nine losses—who were pioneering a new concept in big-time professional sports, a team without a hometown. The Cougars would have three rotating hometowns—Greensboro, Charlotte, Raleigh—none of which was prepared to accept wholeheartedly a team whose major stars were black.

And those stars! Meschery classifies Joe Caldwell as 'a superstar in the ABA. In the NBA a great sixth man.' Joe had a no-cut salary and had to be played. Jim McDaniels was the hero of the season and of the book. Another no-cut, must-play star, he had quit Western Kentucky in the middle of a college season to join the Cougars, who offered him a million dollars to do so. Of him Meschery said, 'Potential unlimited but weak on fundamentals. Obsessed with money. Heralded as the super rookie around which a Cougar championship would be built. Has received more than a million dollars strictly on potential.'

I found Meschery's book unusually interesting because I had been following Jim McDaniels' career for some time. I had already come into possession of the brochure his college had issued on him: 'All-American—On the Floor or Off.' But his coaches had said that before their all-American quit them to become a pro. His year with Carolina did not work out well.

Meschery, who had been one of the real gut players in the NBA, knew what a seven-foot hotshot was supposed to do, and he kept warning McDaniels that he wasn't ready for the big time, that he didn't know how to play defense, that the truly great centers of the NBA would eat him up.

He was unable to penetrate McDaniels' vanity, and at the apex of the season the seven-footer's agent let it be known that McDaniels was about to jump to the NBA. In a series of meetings almost too painful to report, McDaniels' agent, Al Ross, spelled out the demands which would have to be met if the unproved superstar deigned to remain with the Cougars:

> Mac wanted his $1,500,000 contract paid over fifteen years instead of twenty-five years. He wanted incentives—$25,000 for making the play-offs, $25,000 for Most Valuable Player. He wanted a life insurance policy for $100,000 and his yearly salary changed to a once-a-year lump sum. He also wanted Mr. Munchak's personal guarantee on his contract. Finally, Mac wanted, according to Al Ross, $50,000 cash immediately as an aggravation fee for all the crap he claimed that he had had to put up with while playing for the Cougars and living in North Carolina. Crap? Hell! We've all had to put up with crap. Who hasn't felt some aggravation during this season?
>
> When the sixteen points had been stated, Carl [Scheer, president and general manager of the Cougars] asked if there was anything else. There was. Mac was upset that his name was not nationally known, that he had not been given enough publicity. Ross referred to Mac as 'This man so blessed with talent, etc., etc.' Carl told me that at that moment Ross could have told Mac that he was Jesus Christ and he would have believed it.

About this time Meschery was obligated to make a speech on the virtues of sports and how great our athletes are:

> I felt like going to the banquet and crying in a loud voice, 'This whole business stinks of whores and pimps. You fans who look upon these fine athletes as though they represent models for your own children are looking in the wrong direction. Many of you look in disgust at the young who search after new life styles, who lament over the senseless bombing of other people, who scream that something is dreadfully wrong with the system. But these are the real models, these are the men of tomorrow, not our pro athletes. The pro athlete is a product of the commercial state. He should be looked upon as an anachronism.'
>
> I returned home sick of myself. Instead of truth I had given platitudes and funny stories. I had joked and laughed. I had put on a hilarious mask. I had promoted the sport like a robot performing his master's commands. At the banquet I had sold eight tickets for a future Cougars game. I had made fans for a sport that was fast becoming something else.

McDaniels made the jump, to the Seattle SuperSonics of the NBA, and I followed his new career with added interest. As Meschery had predicted, the superbly trained centers of the NBA crucified the newcomer, who didn't know how to position himself or how to put up even a mediocre defense. In his first game against Bob Lanier of Detroit, the latter scored fourteen points in two minutes and McDaniels scored none. Later, against Nate Thurmond of San Francisco, McDaniels was again unable to score, and when the San Francisco coach pulled Thurmond, because he was no longer needed, Thurmond went over to McDaniels and said, 'Okay, kid. You can score now.'

The next year Bill Russell, perhaps the most knowledgeable of all ball handlers, took over as coach at Seattle, and one brief look at McDaniels satisfied him that there was no way this untrained, undisciplined young man could play for him. 'But, Bill, we paid a million dollars for him,' Russell was told, and he is supposed to have said, 'You wasted your money.'

When I was in Europe a few months back an American television man told me, 'My next big story is supposed to be a report on the American college stars who couldn't make it in the NBA, so come over here to play for the German and Italian basketball teams. They get a pretty good salary for a couple of years, then go back home. Maybe you can tell me about the man I'm supposed to track down. Fellow named Jim McDaniels. Used to play for the Seattle SuperSonics.' So far as I know, the television show never materialized. But Meschery's book did, and it's a first-class look at the inside of basketball.

The writer about sports whom I most admire, as opposed to the sportswriter on a daily newspaper, is Herbert Warren Wind, one of today's most graceful masters of the English language. He writes mainly on golf, and has never been excelled, but an occasional article like one on jai alai or on John Wooden of UCLA is also perceptive and gracile. He is as good on golf as the great English writer John Arlott is on cricket, a man who epitomizes the game. Wind's one drawback is that he writes everything as if he were an English country gentleman reporting on a country scene sometime around 1923, and I often wonder how his gentility would handle a maverick like Lee Trevino. I imagine he's written about him, and rather well, but I haven't seen it. I do find that anything he puts his pen to, and it usually appears at good length in *The New Yorker,* is worth reading, for he is an adornment to his profession, and his reputation must grow with the years.

Recently Wind has been challenged by the appearance of a gifted writer with a real flair for the intellectual and artistic implications of sports. George Plimpton's first book, *Paper Lion,* was an ingenious working-out of the Walter Mitty fantasy. An enthusiastic amateur, with no pretensions to athletic professionalism, he talked his way into the training camp of the Detroit Lions, where he participated in scrimmages and took notes on how NFL players actually conducted themselves. His book enjoyed such wide success that he followed it with similar works on baseball and golf, plus a revisit to the Lions. How did the professional athletes respond? They spoke admiringly of his courage and conviviality. The reaction I liked best was voiced by a Lion: 'You could tell George was a rich guy by the way he kept inviting us to have beer with him and leaving us to pick up the tab.'

Plimpton will probably write even better books about sports, because he has an appreciation for the 1970s and a sense of what the 1980s are going to bring. He is unfettered by the antique allegiances which hamper us older men, but we were somewhat confounded when he flew to Zaire and wrote rhapsodically about the boxing match there as if it were a legitimate sporting event rather than an amusing entertainment. I for one was pleased to see black enterpreneurs ripping off the white establishment; blacks have not been treated well by white promoters, and if there is great nonsense afoot, they should be cut in on the boodle. But I doubt that the frolics thus presented should be reviewed with the gravity that writers once accorded a fight between Joe Louis and Max Schmeling.

I read all the sports columnists I come across and find myself liking Dave Anderson of *The New York Times* increasingly, although I deplore his addiction to that evasive phrase made so popular by *Time* magazine: 'This just might be the best this-or-that of the season.' That's a weasel phrase which should be avoided, but the other day I caught myself telling a friend, 'Dave Anderson just might be the best sports columnist in the business.'

My affection for John Kieran and Red Smith is considerable; they have added luster to the sports page. Many of my friends believe Jim Murray of the *Los Angeles Times* to be their inheritor, and he has been named sportswriter of the year numerous times by a restricted group of experts who always choose Chris Schenkel as the television pundit.

Murray is one of the funniest men alive, and a short, quick collection of his best lines would rate high: 'This club has a chance to go all the way. So did the *Titanic.*'

But Murray has a bad habit which his young imitators work into the ground. He takes one subject, usually something worthy of comment, then beats it to death, with crack after crack, belaboring the idea long after the dullest reader must have tired. Of Luis Rodriguez, the Cuban welterweight, he says: 'The face is old, yet young. The eyes are merry, yet sad. It is not a fighter's face, it is a clown's face. Fernandel in burnt cork. Grimaldi without bells. Durante in boxing shorts.' This habit of excessive citation can be seen at its most flamboyant in his introduction to his book about football.

And yet, he can frequently come up with a series of preposterous comments which are as funny as anything I've read. The last sentence in this series is one of his best:

Palm Springs. It is a place where every palm tree has its own spotlight, swimming pools come marked His and Hers, and anyone caught riding two to a Cadillac gets a ticket . . . It has so many golf courses that when an architect starts a new house he finds out first where the owner wants the first tee . . . Some people come down here for the 100-degree heat, but most come down for the 100-proof whiskey . . . Some of the hotels are so incredibly lavish that if the Queen of England ever came here, she would go home and set fire to Windsor Castle . . . They have so many swimming pools here, you could go home at night by canoe.

Among the day-by-day professional writers who do both columns and hard reporting, Frank Dolson of the *Philadelphia Inquirer* maintains a consistently high standard of pertinence without flashy overwriting. It was he who led the campaign against Jim Harding when that immortal coached at LaSalle, on his way to catastrophes in the west. Dolson figured in an interesting exhibition of how important a sportswriter can become to a city. After a long tenure at the *Inquirer* he suddenly jumped to the *Bulletin,* which is like the Pope's becoming head of the Lutheran Church. There was great fanfare and the *Bulletin* trumpeted its coup as a major cultural event, but within a few weeks for obscure reasons Dolson jumped back to the *Inquirer,* which promptly plastered the city with boastful signs: 'Frank Dolson is back where he belongs.'

For adventurous reporting solidly based on scoops, it is difficult to surpass the hard-working legmen who write for the *New York Post.* As Larry Merchant proved in his compelling book on big-time betting, *The National Football Lottery,* they know how to write with force and sometimes fury. Allan Malamud, sports editor of the *Los Angeles Herald-Examiner,* says admiringly, 'The *Post* has probably the best sports section in the country, and they do it with beat reporting and columns. They do it with good writers.'

The smaller cities in the hinterland produce first-rate sportswriters, as I learned when I came to know Alf Van Hoose of the *Birmingham News.* In that sports-crazy town Van Hoose could get away with murder, writing as loosely as he cared; instead he produces some of the most compact and chiseled prose I have ever read on a sports page. His paragraphs are so tightly wound that they could have been written by a professor of English, one who was especially attentive to style.

Some time ago I began noticing the refreshing copy filed by a young man writing for the *Philadelphia Bulletin.* D D Eisenberg always displayed a novel touch, a kind of offbeat, sardonic approach, and I was pleased when the paper called to ask if he could interview me about sports. I invited him to our hill but was taken aback when a beautiful, lively young woman appeared. 'I use only my initials to forestall the die-hards,' she explained. Later I discovered that she was the granddaughter and heiress of Abe Plough, the multi-multi-Memphis-millionaire of Schering-Plough. A good example of her approach came when Bobby Riggs sashayed into Philadelphia on one of his promotions to find that he had been challenged by D D. She won. But of course she enjoyed a minor advantage: Riggs had to play in a wheelchair, pushed about the court by a young friend of D D's who was eight months pregnant.

I am respectful of sportswriters, but find that even the best are subject to certain occupational hazards of which they seem unaware. Glenn Seaborg, the University of California's Nobel Prize winner in chemistry, was also a sports fanatic and served as his school's faculty representative in athletics prior to becoming chancellor. He told me, 'The most difficult aspect of dealing with sportswriters is their assumption of moral superiority. They insist on advising everyone.' At the same time, they ridicule anyone else's serious attempts to clean up unsavory messes in sports, like their contempt for the NCAA's efforts to police eligibility or the AAU's desire to preserve amateurism. They seem addicted to bigness and show disdain for the respectable little effort. Partisans of big-time collegiate sport, they go out of their way to demean small-college games, as if there were something shameful in not being the University of Arkansas or Oklahoma.

Frank Dolson makes fun of the fact that Delaware and Central Michigan are going to be on television for their small-college championship game in Sacramento. 'Delaware is such a household name they spelled it Deleware on the official stats.'

Jim Murray, in castigating golf czar Deane Beman for defending the Quad Cities Open in Bettendorf, Iowa, as 'part of the heart of the U.S. tour': 'Oh, sure, and Ursinus vs. Muhlenberg is the heart of football and would be wrecked by the Rose Bowl if it conflicted.' I know Ursinus well. The fact that it produced J. D. Salinger was just as significant in American life as if it had produced a 275-pound tackle who played three undistinguished years for the San Diego Chargers. Sports columnists got off some great cracks when my little college, Swarthmore, lost thirty-six football games in a row, overlooking the fact that young graduates in science were picking up three Nobel Prizes.

It is this arrogant assumption that only the big are worth watching which accounts for the scandal in the NCAA-ABC arrangement whereby the television network is allowed to decide which college games shall be shown on television, because 'only the biggies draw.' In the period 1966–73 ABC broadcast eighty-seven football games nationally, paying in the latter years $244,000 to each team appearing in a game. In order to spread this windfall among the maximum number of schools, a rule was promulgated whereby no school could appear more than three times in a two-year period. In spite of this, a few teams dominated the screen and hauled down the loot. In the decade 1966–75 Notre Dame and Texas each appeared twenty-one times; Alabama, Southern California and UCLA, nineteen times; Ohio State, seventeen; Nebraska and Penn State, sixteen. Following close behind were Arkansas, Auburn, Louisiana State, Michigan, Michigan State, Oklahoma, Tennessee. Obviously, the rich were getting richer and the poor, poorer. In spite of this imbalance, at the close of the 1975 season the NCAA and ABC negotiated an astonishing new contract: the network would shell out $36,000,000 for a two-year exclusive; financial returns per team would escalate to more than $250,000 a game; and since television wanted only the real biggies, the dominant teams would be allowed to appear four times in two years instead of the earlier three.

This severe imbalance, if long continued, can have only two consequences: it can force the formation of the super-conference of which Frank Broyles has spoken and it can drive the lesser schools away from football. It seems to me the media have a responsibility to see that good schools are not squeezed out, but I see no evidence that television and newspapers are prepared to fight for a more rational system of distributing the athletic wealth in talent and dollars, or of even being aware that they ought to be doing something.

It was well explained one Sunday morning when I asked the sports editor of a paper catering to one of the big-time powers whose coach appeared ready to shift to another job, 'Will your paper be concerned about the selection of his successor?'

'You better believe it! On a Sunday morning after a Saturday loss at the stadium, we sell nine thousand fewer papers, and at fifty cents a shot, that's a lot of money.' The symbiotic relationship between sports and media exists more strongly today than when I first became aware of it.

In recent years members of the sports media have had to absorb one bit of criticism which seems either overemphasized or naïvely uninformed. Even the Federal Communications Commission got into the act with a policy directive which would henceforth govern public broadcasting, whether radio or television:

> Licensees and networks are hereby notified that, effective October 16, 1974, they will be required to disclose clearly, publicly and prominently during each broadcast of an athletic event, the existence of any arrangement whereby announcers broadcasting that event may be directly or indirectly, chosen, paid, approved and/or removed by parties other than the licensee and/or network upon which the event is broadcast.

This is an attempt to counteract the effect of those sports broadcasters who are paid their salaries not by the stations but by the home teams, and who are suspected of disseminating not news but propaganda.

Vince Scully, for example, is one of the best baseball broadcasters in the business, but he happens to be an employee of the Los Angeles Dodgers, and the new directive requires that he announce this fact to his listeners lest they get the idea that from Scully they are receiving unadulterated news. I am not sure what good will be achieved by such a confession.

I have listened to radio and television broadcasts for many decades, and I have enjoyed the blatant 'homers,' those men whose loyalties were all with the home team. I recall especially the media people in Denver whose hearts bled with the Broncos. As a matter of fact, I never knew who paid them; if they were on the Broncos' payroll, they delivered the goods, and if they were not, the Broncos were getting a lot of free advertising. In either event, their broadcasts were informative, personal and fun.

The same was true of the Philadelphia broadcasters who covered the NHL Flyers, and I would have been disappointed if these men had not shown a partiality for a gutsy team which performed miracles in dragging down two Stanley Cup championships in a row. I've also heard some highly partisan broadcasting coming out of New York in favor of the football Jets and the basketball Knicks, especially the latter.

When I pointed out to a friend in Alabama that Alf Van Hoose seemed to be rather partisan where Bear Bryant and his Big Crimson Machine were concerned, my friend replied, 'He damn well better be, or we'd shoot him.'

I am in favor of local partisanship. That's what sports are all about, and to enforce a bland neutrality seems wrong. If I were a sportswriter or broadcaster I would certainly be for my home teams, and I would not try vainly to mask the fact. I would also hope to be a just critic of their failures and would endeavor to give my audience a clear report of the various shenanigans the locals were up to. Whether that would make me a 'homer' I can't say, because that term has pejorative overtones implying corruption, and I'd want to avoid that. But if it came down to a World Series between the Phillies, whom I have always supported, versus the Yankees, whom I have always deplored, I feel sure that even a moron would be able to detect where my enthusiasm lay.

There remains the question of whether the media have subjected sports to overexposure. On a recent weekend in my home, television offered seventy-five and a half hours of sports programming. It was May, so the plethora could not be blamed on football, but we did have basketball play-offs, hockey Stanley Cup games, baseball night and day, boxing, tennis spectaculars and tournaments, golf, track and field, various anthologies and four hours of wrestling and roller derbies for laughs. This was rather much, even for an aficionado like myself.

Last autumn we had high school football on Friday, collegiate on Saturday, three professional games on Sunday, one on Monday and one on Thursday. This was ridiculous. On Monday mornings, after the NFL game, certain metropolitan dailies ran seven pages of sports, with whole pages being given to close-up shots of the preceding day's action.

My concern here is not with the finances of such overexposure—I shall deal with that later—but rather with the general common sense of the matter. In a reasonable society should the basketball season extend from September almost to June? Should a competition with as honorable a tradition as ice hockey have its play-offs in Buffalo when the summerlike temperature is so high that the arena is filled with fog so dense that the players cannot find one another and the goalkeeper has difficulty seeing the shots coming at him?

In a column which attracted wide attention in April 1972, James Reston reflected on this question:

> There isn't a single professional sports season now that doesn't go on at least a month too long. Baseball starts in football weather, and football in baseball weather, and basketball overlaps them both.
>
> Even an old geezer and sports buff has to wonder whether the sports promoters are not going on too long and getting into trouble. And one day, if they all go on too long and demand too much, they will lose the magic. The game has gone on too long.

Jim Barniak, sports columnist for the *Philadelphia Bulletin* and a true believer, shocked his readers toward the conclusion of the 1975 ice-hockey season when he wrote:

> I would like at this time to announce my farewell to ice hockey for the 1974–75 season. As for the remaining two, or possibly three, games of the current Stanley Cup championships, I will be there in body, but that's all. My mind is completely blown. The game is no fun any more and, so, I'm getting out.
>
> The irony of all this is that I was on the verge of becoming a real hockey fan there for a while. I actually bought tickets to games during the past season, which may be the greatest tribute a sportswriter can pay to a sport. But now, quite frankly, I'm sick of it.
>
> Whatever bursts of peak form the players had left from an overly extended regular season looks to have been all but drained from them by these senseless intrusions into late May. The thing I will remember most about the series is forty dog-tired players skating through a dense fog.

I phrased my reaction more harshly. When I watched the worn-out skaters, the blankets of fog, the synthetic hoop-la, I switched my television off and said, 'That's a disgrace. I'll be no part of it.'

One of the surest ways to kill a sport is to overexpose it, make it mechanical, dilute the quality of its players, and extend its season arbitrarily. Even football could be killed if half a dozen wrong moves were made, and David Halberstam uttered the first serious warning to this sport in the December 16, 1974, issue of *New York* magazine. Now I grant that Halberstam is not your ordinary office worker who forms the mainstay of sports support. Even worse, he's an intellectual. But it was men like him who started the publicity ball rolling for football, and if men like him now start to abandon the game, there's bound to be trouble. They are the style-setters, and God help any sport in America when the style-setters make it unfashionable:

> In those days football seemed the most perfect sport and it seemed unlikely that we would ever get enough . . . We rooted for the Jets against the Colts. We did in a perverse way root *against* certain teams—Dallas in particular because of its sudden infamy, and because to me at least Tom Landry was the least sympathetic of the coaches, looking more like a regional director of the FBI than anything else.
>
> What also made the game so good in those days was the quality of the teams and the sense of identity they projected. There were only twelve teams and they were, by and large, good ones. They had character and identity and continuity.
>
> Part of the problem is the fan. We must confess our own guilt. We have, for some fifteen years or so, simply seen too much. If there was a network greed which was matched by an owner's greed, then it was also matched by a fan greed. Football was there every Sunday, it was free, or almost free, and so we watched it. One game was not enough, so we watched two.

Anyone who believes that football is home free, permanently, should read Halberstam. His could be the handwriting on the wall. Even more important than satiety and length of season is a more basic problem. Do we not make ourselves look like a nation of boobs if we enshrine schoolboy pastimes as a commanding function of our society?

It would be inappropriate to conclude a discussion of sports media—a characteristically light-hearted segment of our society—on so gloomy a note. After all, the sports report in television is known as the Happy Hour, and properly so, for it deals, as Tonto Coleman said, with man's successes. Sports columns are best when they report humorous or outrageous situations, and no big-time coach could survive long if he lacked a good supply of stories for the winter banquets.

Over the years I've collected the best yarns from such sources, and none surpasses the one told by Doug Layton of WERC in Birmingham:

It was Pete Maravich's senior year at LSU. Most charismatic college player in the country, flopping hair, dangling red socks, dynamic personality. Eighteen thousand people out to watch him every time he played. It was against Mississippi, and they knew they had to cut Pistol Pete down to size if they wanted to win, so they bumped him, hacked him, tugged at his shorts and stood on his toes. Well, this caused great anguish in the heart of Press Maravich, the boy's father who coached LSU and who had devised a system whereby his son could shake himself free for twenty or thirty easy buckets a game. The Mississippi ruffians were making it impossible for Pistol Pete to get free for his easy layups, and Press Maravich began heckling the officials. 'Look what they're doin' to my boy! Are you gonna allow them to do that to my boy? You've got to give some protection to my boy.' Finally the referee could take no more and he slapped Press Maravich with a technical, but the barrage kept up, 'They're killin' my boy.'

So the referee stopped the game, went to the LSU bench and asked in a voice of sweet reasonableness, 'Now, Coach Maravich, I don't want to hit you with another technical. What seems to be the problem?' This conciliatory attitude disarmed Maravich Senior, who replied quietly, 'Mr. Referee, you're letting them kill my boy.'

'Mr. Maravich,' the referee asked, 'which one is your boy?'

XI

Financing

This chapter deals with troublesome questions. Who should pay for stadiums? Who should own the teams that play in the stadiums? How much should the players earn who play on the teams? These questions, and others of a related nature, are discussed extensively in Roger G. Noll's *Government and the Sports Business.* My analyses were completed before the appearance of this classic work, but I had used earlier studies by three of the contributors: Roger Noll and Benjamin Okner on basketball finances, James Quirk on the reasons why professional teams shift from one city to another. No one should discuss the financial realities of sport without careful attention to the writings of these men.

I shall tackle the problem of stadiums first, because their costs involve readers directly, especially when the stadium is to be paid for through public taxation, as 70 percent of them are. On this question I confess to a firm predilection, stemming from a lunch I had one day in 1958 at Toots Shor's. The Brooklyn Dodgers had just left Brooklyn for Los Angeles and the New York Giants were leaving Manhattan for San Francisco, and some of us were discussing the consequences when a gentleman whose name I didn't catch made this observation: 'A city is a place where a large collection of people do the things that a city ought to do.'

When we asked what this meant, he explained, 'To qualify as a city, any collection of people must have an orchestra, a large library, a system of parks, a transportation system, a university and, yes, a public stadium in which to gather and a professional team to play there. If a town doesn't have these things, it's got no right to call itself a city.'

He had a point. You can defend building a city stadium on the questionable grounds that it will bring more business into the city. (It does, to taxicabs and saloons like Toots Shor's.) Or that it will help bind the city together. (It might have the opposite effect if a team excites partisan riots.) Or that it is essential for the city's image. (What image does a losing team create?) Or for a variety of other dubious reasons.

The real reason is that a city needs a big public stadium because that's one of the things that distinguish a city. I would not elect to live in a city that did not have a spacious public building in which to play games, and as a taxpayer I would be willing to have the city use my dollars to help build such a stadium, if that were necessary. I am therefore unequivocally in support of public stadiums.

My reasons are not all pragmatic. I believe that each era of civilization generates its peculiar architectural symbol, and that this acquires a spiritual significance far beyond its mere utilitarian purpose. First we had the Age of Pyramids, in which I would include such edifices as the ziggurat in Babylon, Borobudur in Java and Angkor Wat in Cambodia. They came along at much different periods chronologically, but at comparable stages in the development of their local civilizations. Those societies which built well in this age of massive structures are well remembered.

Then came the Age of Temples, symbolized by the Parthenon, followed by the Age of Stadia, symbolized by the Colosseum. One of the most revealing explorations I made was through Turkey-in-Asia, where in one small forgotten town after another I found huge stadiums which imperial Rome had erected for the entertainment of its remote citizens. One finds more Greek and Roman ruins in Turkey than in Greece and Rome combined.

Then came the glorious Age of Cathedrals, and much later the Age of Bridges, when flying arches were thrown across all the rivers of the world. One of the best periods, architecturally, was the Age of the Railroad Stations, when a functional need was met by heavy but inspired buildings that lent dignity to small towns and big cities alike. In Europe some of the railroad stations—Munich, Helsinki—were masterpieces, and in the rural area in which I live they were low, solid and sometimes majestic forts.

Quickly came the Age of the Skyscraper, then the Age of the intricate Traffic Circle, the sprawling Airport and the splendiferous Shopping Center, which created merely blight and disruption without contributing to architectural beauty.

But now we are once more in an Age of the Stadium, and I shall not anticipate the favorable things I have to say later by designating those American stadiums I find creative. In Madrid the great Estadio Bernabeu, sunk in a hole in the middle of the city, is a masterpiece. In Rome the hideous oval marked by the statues of athletes is a surprise, and in Mexico City the huge bullring, set deep in a saucer, is adventurous.

We live in an age when cities are compressing much of their creative instinct into stadiums, and some very good things are being done. A major city ought to have a major stadium, but before it starts building, it ought to appoint a commission not solely of businessmen or architects to decide what kind of stadium would best serve and where it ought to be located. To rush either of these basic decisions is to court disaster.

Let us suppose that NEW, a younger person with contemporary imagination, and OLD, an older hand who has kicked around a lot of stadiums, are members of that commission. Their preliminary discussion might run like this:

NEW: We might as well get one thing straight right now. Throughout all these discussions, no matter how long they run, I'm going to be insisting that we build only where there is adequate parking. Sports and the automobile are inseparable partners, and it's plain folly to build a stadium where no one can get to it, or away from it after the game's over.

OLD: I'll say amen if you make that transportation in general, instead of just the automobile.

NEW: What other kind of transportation is there? Really available, I mean?

OLD: Now, not much. In the future, maybe a lot.

NEW: I accept your correction. But my prime consideration leads me to think that we must build not in the city but in the suburbs, where the kind of people who can afford twelve dollars for a ticket live. I do not want my stadium tucked away in some corner of the city where there's no parking and where people are afraid to visit because of hooliganism and worse. I opt for the suburbs without question.

OLD: The traditional site for a stadium is in the city. One of the best in the world is that bullring in Sevilla. Right in the heart of the city. Even in America today the really fine stadiums are those which have kept to the city. The Vet in Philadelphia. Three Rivers in Pittsburgh. Riverfront in Cincinnati. And one of the best, old Yankee Stadium in New York. And the current marvel, one of the most ambitious stadiums ever built anywhere at any time, the Superdome in New Orleans. You can walk to it from the downtown hotels.

NEW: And not one of them has adequate parking. They're all antiquated before their bonds are paid off. The stadiums in this country that I like are the ones out in the countryside, with enough parking for the suburban customer who foots the bills. Shea in New York, an admirably placed stadium with plenty of space for autos plus subway availability. Foxboro some twenty miles south of Boston. Pontiac twenty-five miles north of

Detroit. And the only sensible stadium construction in recent years, that marvelous twin pair of stadiums in Kansas City well east of the city.

OLD: I'm disturbed by your insistence that it's the suburbanite who foots the sports bill. I think we have to differentiate here. You may be right that the suburbanite supports football, which offers at the most nine or ten home games a year. Maybe the well-to-do suburbanite can handle that. But in baseball it's the city man who supports the team, and not at twelve dollars a throw, and not a mere nine or ten times a year. Baseball has eighty-one home games a year, and its stadium had better not be any twenty-five miles to the north of the city. Same with basketball. Hockey? I don't know. Maybe it's a suburban game, too, but I noticed that my team played a hundred and seven games this year, and if half of them were at home, that means fifty-three home dates, and their playing area had better be close to the city.

NEW: It sounds to me as if you're making the survival of sports depend upon the survival of the city.

OLD: I am. Anything which arbitrarily weakens the city, weakens the base on which sports have always existed. The metropolitan newspapers, the radio and television stations, the subway alumni, the tax base on which to build and supervise the stadiums. Without that interlocking web, you haven't the infrastructure necessary for sports to exist.

NEW: You're fifty years in the past. We live in a new age, with the automobile instead of the subway. Our market is the people living in the surrounding areas, and unless we can pull them in comfortably, we're going to go out of business. As between the old-fashioned help the city can give, and the new-fashioned strength to be found in the suburbs, I'll take the latter every time.

OLD: You overlook one thing. I suspect that the age of the automobile, as we've known it, may be past. Families aren't going to have three cars in the future. The gas-guzzlers won't be here ten years from now. Shopping centers on the far edge of town are going to find themselves in trouble. Stadiums twenty-five miles out in the country are going to be unreachable. Some form of public transportation will be essential, and it will bring people back into the city, not out of it. I'll feel a lot safer, economically, if we have our new stadium as close to downtown as possible, because that's where the action is going to be.

NEW: Dead wrong. America will never give up its automobile. Our ingenuity will devise some alternative way of fueling, and ten years from now we'll be more mobile than we are today. I want my stadium out in the country, with space so that we can macadam about sixty acres and park all the cars that will ever want to patronize us. I want to see Kansas City complexes all across the nation, because that's the wave of the future. New Orleans Superdome? Seats eighty-four thousand. Has parking for twenty-five hundred cars. It was obsolete three years before it was finished. Your Yankee Stadium. The bill for refurbishing it was supposed to be twenty-three million dollars. I read the other day it'll cost a cool hundred million. And when it's completed you have an old-fashioned dump in an old-fashioned area with no parking. The city stadium is doomed.

OLD: Looking at the splendid jobs Philadelphia, Pittsburgh and Cincinnati have managed, I'd say the age of the new city stadium is just beginning.

NEW: You keep avoiding the basic problem. The city as you knew it is doomed. New patterns of living are evolving, and the city will be relegated to a ghetto subsidized by the suburbs. But the action will be in the suburbs, and so will the stadiums.

OLD: The city has survived for five thousand years as the center of civilization. The automobile has damned near killed it, but its resilience will be amazing. Keep the stadiums in the city, and give it help in surviving.

NEW: The game's the thing. Sports aren't a sociological agency. Having a good team and winning and attracting loads of paying spectators is the name of the game. And you can't do any of those things in a city any longer.

OLD: Will you grant me one thing? Maybe football can flourish in the suburbs, but baseball can't. And even with football I see the day when the fickle suburban fan abandons the game the way he abandoned boxing and wrestling. Then real sports will return to the stadiums in the city.

NEW: Football is good for another quarter-century. Nothing could damage it. So it ought to go where the big buck is, and that's in the suburbs. We break ground next Monday, twenty-three miles north of the city.

Competition between communities struggling for the sports dollar can become ridiculous. The New York football Giants, unable to find adequate quarters in their home city, decided to move their franchise to a garish new sports facility which the State of New Jersey promised to build for $291,000,000 just across the Hudson in what the brochures called the Hackensack Meadowlands, more popularly known as the Jersey swamps. A feature of the new installation would be a massive race track, which could be counted on to siphon customers away from the New York tracks at Yonkers and Aqueduct. This would mean a substantial loss in taxes for New York, which garnered at least 17 percent of the pari-mutuel handle.

So New York retaliated in various conniving ways. First it threw the New York Giants out of the field they were using, on the logical principle 'If you're going to desert us eventually, get out now.' Then state officials announced that they were planning to build a $275,000,000 sports complex —flat racing, harness, football—at an imaginative site on a platform over an old railroad center. (This had the collateral effect of making it impossible for New Jersey to peddle her bonds for her projected sports center, because if New York's plan succeeded, it would divert customers from New Jersey, which would mean that the New Jersey complex might go broke, making the bonds worthless.) New York had another salvo in its guns. It threatened to cut its share of the race-track handle on win-place-show from 17 percent to 14 percent, which meant that if New Jersey wanted to attract bettors, it would have to cut its take too, and this in turn would diminish its profits. This internecine war has not yet been resolved, but as one New Yorker said, 'That'll learn 'em not to meddle around with the Rockefellers,' it having been widely rumored that the New York retaliation had been spurred by the Rockefeller brothers in an attempt to protect their New York financial interests.

In the meantime, poor New Jersey, preoccupied with battling her enemy to the north, was being attacked on her southern flank by Philadelphia. A group of hotshot race-track operators from my home county erected a spanking new track called Keystone, and entered into competition with the long-established New Jersey tracks at Atlantic City and especially nearby Garden State. While New York was siphoning money away in the north, our boys would be draining it off in the south, verifying the famous description Ben Franklin once gave of New Jersey: 'A keg tapped at both ends.'

New Jersey might be powerless to contest the depredations of the Rockefeller brothers, but it was no paper tiger where Philadelphia was concerned. It waited till Keystone had announced its racing dates, then scheduled precisely those dates for Garden State, and since the New Jersey track was much better established, it blanketed the newer one in Pennsylvania. But even so, New Jersey was sorely damaged by the competition—its average attendance slumped from 10,944 to 7,942 and its daily handle from $1,624,492 to $885,750. By clever statesmanship, New Jersey may be able to fend off its two enemies and arrange some kind of reasonable truce. In the meantime, chaos reigns.

A more amusing competition has been taking place at the opposite end of the nation. San Francisco, long established as a sports center, has had to watch upstart Oakland, a few miles across the bay, surge to prominence, winning championships regularly in both football and baseball while San Francisco teams foundered in wind-swept Candlestick Park, which seated only 43,400.

Oakland entered the big time with a bang, erecting a stadium which seated 54,500, whereupon San Francisco renovated Candlestick, providing 61,100 seats. This was interpreted by Oakland as a dare, so they issued contracts to raise their capacity to 63,000, after which the San Francisco baseball team announced that it was going broke.

Baltimore, always in competition with Washington, clung to its outmoded Memorial Stadium, hardly a fit place for man or beast, and watched

Washington build its fine new Robert F. Kennedy stadium, seating 45,016. Thereupon Baltimore increased its seating to 60,238, which encouraged Washington to raise its total to 53,041. At this point Washington lost its baseball team altogether—leaving the stadium in perilous financial condition, and Baltimore lost its basketball team, with the possibility that it might lose football and baseball too. To forestall this, there was talk of building a big domed stadium to house both teams.

Once a decision has been reached on whether a new stadium is needed, and where it should be placed, the problem arises: How shall it be financed? Four possibilities are available:

Public taxation. After prolonged public discussion of need, location and cost, a proposition to build is placed on the ballot and a public referendum is held. If a majority of the voters approve, public tax funds are used to build the stadium, but only after a score of lawsuits test the authority of the government, delay the schedule, and double the costs. This was the route taken by New Orleans in building its Superdome, by Philadelphia in building its Veterans Stadium, by Denver in adding to the capacity of the stadium it already had, and by a suburb of Kansas City in building its superb pair of stadiums.

Existing institution. Some institution, usually a university, allocates its own funds to the building of a massive structure. Thus the University of Pennsylvania built one of the most congenial stadiums in the country, Franklin Field; Yale built its famous Yale Bowl, still serviceable even for professional football; Michigan built its mammoth stadium, which can seat 105,500 spectators, and the University of South Carolina built its Coliseum, perhaps the finest basketball court in the world.

Group cooperation. Certain districts, having struggled for years to build a stadium through public taxation, become irritated by delaying tactics and lawsuits, and decide to quit the major city and its infamous politics and build the stadium with their own money. This was done in Foxboro, Massachusetts, and Pontiac, Michigan, and it is a strategy that many other communities should consider, even though it forces the builders to elect a suburban solution on practical rather than philosophical grounds.

Individual initiative. A few communities, faced by the same frustrating indecisions mentioned in the preceding instance, are lucky enough to contain citizens of great wealth who, in impatience, cut the Gordian knot. They acquire a large piece of land, hire architects to design the best possible structure, finance and build the stadium themselves, and arrange some complicated procedure whereby the construction will ultimately pass to public ownership. Clint Murchison did just this when Dallas could not agree to supplant its rickety old Fair Grounds with a new football stadium; he went northwest to the suburb of Irving and did the job himself. Abe

Pollin, in the Washington-Baltimore complex, waited vainly for years, hoping that his region would come up with a sensible plan for a sports complex. When decision became impossible, he went to Landover, Maryland, and built a fine installation, using his own money.

In each of these four options there is bound to be chicanery, for the building of a massive sports complex is never uncomplicated. The hucksters at New Orleans went before the public with a solemn promise that a Superdome, 'much better than Houston's,' could be built for a mere $35,000,000, and in 1961 and 1962 they received voter approval for that amount, with an implied promise that the limit agreed upon would not be exceeded. Deplorable acts by labor, by subcontractors, by politicians and by operators never identified, escalated the cost to $68,000,000, then to $110,000,000, and finally to something around $163,000,000, not counting operating expenses. Furthermore, a little-known clause in the authorizing legislation provided that in the case of emergency, and God knows this became an emergency, the whole financial burden could be shifted to a public authority which could spend and tax until the job was paid for. Starting to build a stadium is taking the first step in an open-ended commitment of which the final cost may double or treble. And once started, the operation cannot be called off, so that a community runs the danger of undertaking a massive future tax burden mainly to gratify the building mania of men and women long since dead.

The so-called free gift of a public benefactor like Clint Murchison and his Dallas Cowboys' stadium isn't always so free either. The stadium was paid for by sports fans who bought bonds, that's true, but the roads leading to it, the added facilities that were needed, the tax rebatements that were offered, and the lost taxation in future years were paid for by the public. Though after forty years Texas Stadium passes into the ownership of the suburb in which it is built, by that time it will have become outmoded and, as in the case of Yankee Stadium, it will probably cost the taxpayers some $100,000,000 for refurbishing.

A basic question has arisen recently. Should public money, either as hard-cash contributions or tax rebatement, be used to build pleasure domes for the use primarily of the wealthy few? This was first questioned in the case of Lincoln Center in New York, where the city taxpayer was required to pick up huge incidental costs while forgoing normal taxation on what had become tax-exempt real estate. At the same time, since the seats in the opera house and concert hall were both overpriced and oversubscribed, he could never buy a reasonably priced ticket, or even any ticket, to a house which his money had helped build. The problem was compounded when it was disclosed that most of the ticket holders lived outside the city, so that city taxpayers were subsi-

'Keep shooting! Wilt the Stilt has signed for a million eight!'

dizing the suburbs at the same time that city tax rolls were being diminished.

Did the city of Philadelphia, for example, have a reasonable right to obligate itself not only for the original cost of its Veterans Stadium, which would be used by private football and baseball owners for their personal enrichment, but also to contribute $1,500,000 each year for operations? Did the State of Louisiana have the right to spend $163,000,000 on a building whose primary purpose would be to aid private owners of teams? And perhaps more pressing, did voters in the Kansas City area show reasonable judgment when they built two massive stadiums, side by side, one for football, one for baseball, at a total cost of some $75,000,000 when the State of Missouri had social problems of a pressing nature which could have profited from the use of those funds?

I have wrestled with these moral problems for many years and have concluded: 1) a city had better have a good stadium if it wants to maintain its morale and its public acceptance; 2) city politics have become so totally corrupt, it is almost impossible to avoid paying about 100 percent graft on any major operation, but if pressure can reduce this graft, it should be applied; 3) legitimate overrun costs are to be expected; 4) it would always be preferable to finance a stadium by private rather than public funds; 5) but this is usually impractical, so a city is justified if it builds with tax funds.

But I would hope that city fathers would explain honestly what the stadium was going to cost, rather than hiding behind the subterfuges common today.

On one philosophical point I am adamant. Ninety-nine out of the hundred greatest buildings in world history—pyramids, Parthenon, Chartres Cathedral, Rockefeller Center—would never have been built if approval from the general public had been required. You cannot construct a beautiful city by plebescite; someone with vision must force the issue, override trivial objections, and ensure that the job is finished artistically. Therefore, I would not want the building of great stadiums to be subjected to picayune supervision by the general public. Let the project be explained, justified and funded honestly; then let the men and women of vision proceed with the actual work.

In most of the new stadiums a tradition has evolved whereby one tier is enclosed in glass and divided into sumptuous private suites, which are then peddled to large corporations or wealthy individuals in the community. The cost is high and is borne by the lessor and not immediately by the taxpayer, but it is obvious that a large part of the basic construction of the suite was carried by the taxpayer, and that the yearly rental is written off as a public relations cost, so that in the end it is the taxpayer who picks up most of the tab.

I would like to invite you into one of the more luxurious suites in one of the recently built stadiums. It is on the forty-yard line, about halfway up the side of the stadium. It consists of two large rooms plus bar and bathroom on one level, three bedrooms and two baths on the next level above. The entire floor area is covered with expensive carpeting from Belgium, on which have been placed massive pieces of Renaissance furniture providing seats on the main floor for some sixty guests. The wall decorations are paintings from Europe, mirrors with heavily carved frames imported from Europe and tastefully arranged scenes from former football seasons.

The bar was imported from London, a stupendous affair along which forty or fifty of the guests can stand comfortably. At convenient spots are pull-out tables on which the guests can place their trays while dining from the lavish smorgasbord. The upstairs bedrooms are done in French provincial style with ornate furnishings of considerable value. The bathrooms are marble and gold.

Because I am a nosy man with unpolished manners, I asked the owner if he would review with me the costs of such an establishment, and he laughingly agreed, with the understanding that I not use his name.

> If you wanted one of the more modest suites, you could get it for $18,000 a year, with a five-year obligation, and you pay years one and five in advance. My suite, which is a little more pretentious, is $31,000 a year, obligation for five years.

For that I get four bare walls and an uncarpeted floor. I paid about $75,000 for furnishings and decorations, but my tastes are lavish in some things, and I don't like to stint. You could furnish yours for much, much less. Say $15,000 and everything you put in remains your property, which you can sell to the next owner if you ever decide to give up your suite. Incidentally, in this stadium all the suites were sold six months before opening, and there have been no turn-overs.

Now, you can't just walk into your suite. First you have to buy a ticket to the game. Not only for you, but for your guests too. I buy seventy seats for every game. You understand, we get those seats right in front of the suite, so the guests move in and out of the suite as the game progresses. I pay $12 a seat, or $840 a game, seven games during the season, which is I don't know exactly how much.

The suite owner cannot bring his own liquor into the stadium, so he has the day catered by the stadium restaurant. I spend about $1,000 a game for drinks, $1,500 for food, which makes it $2,500 a game times seven games.

I studied these figures for some time while my host attended to other visitors. Adding up the details, I figured that this suite cost him, counting in a prorated cost of the furnishings and tips, not less than $79,000 a year. When I showed him this calculation, he said, 'Something like that, but it's worth it to my business. When I fly customers in from other cities and tell them, "I'm putting you up at the stadium . . ." '

I had missed a point. 'You mean your guests sleep here on game nights?' I asked.

'No. The suites are open 365 days a year, if you want to use them. I do. Most of my entertaining is done here. You ought to see this place on a snowy night, with only four lights illuminating the stadium . . .'

'Then your costs are a lot higher than I indicated.'

'Much,' he chuckled. 'But I wasn't going to correct your figures.'

I was afraid it might be insulting to ask him if this was all tax deductible, but obviously it was. It's the way America does business these days, this cross-fertilization of sports and industry, and it accounts in part for the tremendous boom in sports sponsorship.

Frequently the suburban county that declared a jubilee when it lured the stadium out of the city learns to its dismay that large stadiums almost never become self-sufficient, especially those far removed from cities. Even Houston's legendary Astrodome cannot break even of itself; the income that saves it comes from ancillary operations, including rental on a building put up nearby to accommodate those very cultural and business events that were supposed to keep the dome lighted. I have studied the prospectuses for a dozen projected stadiums, and every one was filled with phony promises. The 'other activities like conventions, business gatherings, Billy Graham revivals and Frank Sinatra concerts' which are depicted so glowingly could not possibly materialize. One cynic has said accurately, 'A huge stadium built principally for football is often peddled as a multi-purpose center. Well, such a stadium is good for football, and marching-band competitions . . . and nothing else.' (I once calculated that if Billy Graham were to rescue all the stadiums into which he had been thrust by publicity brochures, he would have to hold evangelist services 431 nights a year.)

Arlington, Texas, learned the cruel facts when it built Arlington Stadium, a baseball field halfway between Dallas and Fort Worth. Its dream of riches started to come true when it seduced the Washington Senators to Texas and lined up lucrative radio and television contracts. But the ball team proved a bust, one of the worst profit-and-loss operations in history, and the media income did not eventuate. Arlington faced the inevitable: assume financial responsibility for the operation and force the local citizenry to pick up the tab through real estate taxes.

It would be preferable to build stadiums from the beginning with tax money, openly acknowledged. But this honest way of doing things is difficult, so devious routes must be resorted to. It is probable that stadiums which have been recently built with the promise 'that no penny of taxpayer's money will ever be spent' will ultimately have to be shifted onto the public at a total cost of about one billion dollars.

The problems an architect faces when planning a new stadium intended for both baseball and football are exemplified in New York's Shea Stadium, built originally for baseball but converted belatedly to football too. A playing field adequate for baseball requires an area of 150,000 square feet, but football needs only 90,000. So to build a bi-purpose stadium you must first make it large enough for baseball, and then, by some device or other—retractable seats is a good one—scale it down for football. But then a problem arises. The average baseball city needs no more than 48,000 seats; football can use 86,000. Also, as architect Ron Labinski points out:

> Each game has its own pace—baseball fairly slow, football with constant action. That makes spectator facilities different for each sport. In baseball you have about eighteen opportunities to get up, walk around, go to the bathroom, buy a beer; in football, all of that is concentrated at half time. For football you need fast food service, high turnover and a limited menu; baseball allows time for slower service and more choices. Sales are greater at football games, and more vending facilities are needed. Ticket sales differ too; season tickets are the thing in football, but baseball seems to draw a walk-in, one-game-at-a-time crowd.

The most ineffective design for any stadium, other than one for bullfighting, is a circle, for then most of the seats have got to be poorly situated. The best design for baseball is a modified V, with the arms reaching out along the base paths to first and third and no distant seats in center field. The best design for football would be two gently curving arcs focused on the fifty-yard line and with no seats in the end zones.

Shea Stadium, an open-ended horseshoe, with lots of seats along the base paths and none behind the center fielder, is almost ideally adapted to baseball, but when a football team has to use it, the deficiencies become appalling. It provides 55,300 seats regularly—which baseball in New York can occasionally fill—and this can be upped to 60,000 for football, which is far too low. Its design means that it can never be suitable for football, but if the open end of the horseshoe, out beyond center field, were closed in, which could be done at no great cost, football attendance could grow to 83,000, enough to make the game profitable. But baseball refuses to allow those extra seats, for they would stand glaringly empty most of the year. An impasse has been reached, one that is experienced whenever these two popular sports try to occupy the same stadium. Since baseball cannot use a restricted field, it is football that suffers.

The inescapable problems at Shea have been multiplied in recent years. The baseball Mets were supposed to have the stadium to themselves, but then the football Jets were moved in. Then the baseball Yankees lost their home while it was being refurbished, so they were crammed in too. And the football Giants, having announced that they were moving to the Jersey swamps, discovered that that promised nirvana might never be built. They tried playing their home games in Yale Bowl, not happily, and finally they, too, were thrown into Shea.

So a rather modest stadium intended for one baseball team now had two, plus two football teams, and it required a computer to arrange schedules, with both football teams forced to play the first half of their schedules as away games, since the home field was still being used by baseball. To defer playing before hometown fans until the club has absorbed four or five drubbings on the road is grotesquely unfair. New York is undersupplied with stadiums, because even when Yankee Stadium is redone, the city will still have no field adequate for football.

A compromise was attempted in building Philadelphia's Veterans Stadium; the architect devised an octorad, a squarish-looking circle consisting of eight arcs which smooth away the deficiencies of either the square or the circle. This unique design provides major seating for football, satisfactory space for baseball, with 6,000 seats moved out of sight and 9,000 more screened off behind center field. It is not ideal, by any means, and the shifting of seats is never as easy as it sounds, but it is an ingenious solution. A better, of course, would be to build two separate but adjoining stadiums, one for baseball and one for football.

One of the more captivating ball parks I have seen is that little jewel in Montreal—Jarry Park. It seats only 28,000, and may be uneconomical to operate but ballplayers love it. Howie Reed, an American who had a good experience as an Expo pitcher, told me, 'I've pitched in those big, sterile stadiums in the States, and believe me, it's much better to play a ball game in Jarry. Intimacy is an asset.' Other ballplayers who felt the same way explained why Jarry was so much fun; the spectators were down in the game, part of it. Reed concluded, 'I'd not hesitate in calling it the best place in the world right now to play baseball. It actually adds to the enjoyment of the game.' I used to feel the same way about Fenway Park; that left-field wall was part of every game, but Jarry seemed even better.

But in spite of its quiet excellence, it may be doomed. The 1976 Montreal Olympics require a large domed stadium, and the proposed design is most interesting, with a giant cantilevered hook hanging down above the roof of the stadium, issuing cables that will lift the roof in summer and lower it in winter. Clearly, Canadian politicians will apply pressure on the baseball team to quit Jarry and move into the great vacant arena, about as unsuitable a locale for baseball as could be imagined and with none of Jarry's intimacy. Politics and finances may make the move inescapable; the baseball people will probably be unhappy, but because they are associated with American interests, they may find themselves in a position where they do not dare to protest.

Some of the newer centers combine cultural activities and sports. The best I've seen is the one about to be finished in Alabama. The Birmingham-Jefferson Civic Center comprises a massive exhibition arena, a symphony hall, of splendid dimension and sound, seating 3,000, a theater seating 1,000, a large central esplanade, and a basketball-hockey arena seating up to 20,000, all smack in the center of town, and well related by ramps and tunnels to the art museum and other cultural activities. It is beautifully designed and imaginatively interlocked. It was so symbolic of the future that I went back three times, to attend a business exhibition, to listen to a Rachmaninoff piano concerto, and to watch a ballet rehearsal. I wish I could have seen a basketball game, but that part wasn't finished. Except for the inevitable lack of parking, this handsomely arranged center establishes a standard which any medium-sized city ought to be able to meet, but only if architectural imagination is applied from the start.

The Superdome in downtown New Orleans is the sort of flamboyant elegance every nation ought to sponsor . . . once. Even in its unfinished state it delighted me, a stupendous building that enlarges the mind of the unprejudiced visitor, an enormous ring supporting a roof so towering, it looks as if it must collapse from its own weight. A jaundiced critic sought to disenchant me, reciting those grotesque cost overruns of which I have spoken, but I told him, 'I'll bet it works. I'll bet it more than earns its upkeep. In the years ahead the city will derive enough profit from it to justify the cost of construction.'

'If it wasn't already built, would you authorize going ahead now?'

'Unquestionably. If it didn't exist, it ought to.'

'But do you know about the scandals?'

'Deplorable. Those responsible should go to jail. But even so, when I look at it my heart skips a beat, just for the sheer hell of it. When I become more sober I see four things. First, the cost was excessive. Second, the chicanery connected with its financing and building was disgraceful. Third, it's a stunning building and I wish we had it in Philadelphia. Fourth, it will be a focus of nationwide attention for the next forty years, after which it may have to be torn down to be replaced by something better. But you have a bargain, pal, and in time you'll appreciate it.'

I spent long hours, repeatedly, inspecting the Superdome, and it excited me as no other building of its magnitude has ever done. It's a major effort, handsomely designed and well built. It looms above the city like some gigantic growth in a jungle, its dome glowing in the sky, so huge that it can be comprehended only from afar. It dwarfs any other stadium; the Houston Astrodome could be slipped inside with space to spare.

An effort has been made to make it adaptable: for rock-and-roll it can seat 97,363; for a Super Bowl football game when Chicago is swept by blizzards, 75,795; for baseball, 60,543; for basketball, with all seats close to the playing area, 19,678.

I doubt that the cost can ever be amortized, but the dome should earn operating expenses. A tax on hotel rooms will help; so will parking fees and rentals. While I was expressing this confidence, my critic kept intoning his miseries: 'It has eighteen hundred seats which can't see the scoreboard. They forgot to provide dugouts for baseball. I hear they put men's urinals in the women's washrooms.' And I said to myself, 'Here they build one of the prime architectural inventions of this century, and it has three little errors which can be corrected over the weekend. Who really gives a damn?'

When I spoke to the man who had been in charge of putting the whole majestic concept together, he said:

> We built an open doughnut first, just those flared upright walls. See how the upper lip of the wall forms a concave receptacle. When the walls were completed, with no roof at all, we came inside and built sixteen tall towers. On them we constructed the large domed roof, with its lower edge convex, so that it would slip into place when the towers were lowered, convex edge of the roof fitting into the concave lip of the wall.
>
> So the day came when we started to lower the towers, hydraulically, a quarter of an inch at a time, all sixteen towers together, with the dome slowly descending. Finally only a quarter of an inch separated the roof from the wall.
>
> We decided to slip the thing into place early one morning. Everyone was in position. We all had walkie-talkies and each tower would report to me. It was

now or never, so slowly we lowered the towers for the last time. That roof weighs tons, many tons. And without a sound it slipped into position, found its balance, not an inch out of line. When the last tower called in, 'No pressure here,' and it was home safe, I burst into tears.

New Orleans is not yet home safe with its Superdome, and I suppose it will never be. But after the years of travail the city will have a masterpiece. You have to have faith in men who have the nerve to call their artificial turf Mardi Grass.

The best solution to the stadium problem for a major city that I have so far seen is the Harry S Truman Sports Complex in suburban Kansas City. Had it been erected within the city proper, it would be ideal; as it is, it is well-nigh perfect as a suburban solution.

Its merit lies in the fact that it consists of two complete stadiums about one hundred yards apart, one designed especially for football, the other for baseball, and with adequate common parking for both. The interiors are artistically handled and the movement of people has been rationalized.

The original public authorization, voted by a single county east of Kansas City but within the metropolitan area, was $42,000,000, but as should have been expected, final costs were something like $75,000,000, which seems within reason for a dual structure of such excellence. However, many of the things I liked existed only because two very wealthy men owned the teams that were to play there. Lamar Hunt is the subject of one of the best recent sports stories; when he lost a bundle in the first year of his operation of an AFL football team in Dallas, a family friend complained to crusty H.L. Hunt, his billionaire father, that 'Lamar has dropped a million dollars in one year,' and H.L. replied, 'Well, at that rate he can't last longer than a hundred and fifty years.' Lamar Hunt now owned the Kansas City Chiefs, who would play in Arrowhead Stadium, seating 78,000.

The Kansas City baseball team, which would play in Royals Stadium, seating 40,762, was owned by Ewing Kauffman, who controlled a fair share of Marion Laboratories. Hunt is reputed to have plowed in $14,000,000 of his own money to make Arrowhead just a little closer to what he wanted. I was told that Kauffman 'had kicked in $6,000,000 to make Royals Stadium a little nicer.' And the things these two millionaires added helped make the difference.

The most daring solution to the football-baseball conflict has been devised in Honolulu. Aloha Stadium is built in six sections: two, seating 22,000, are fixed; four, seating 28,000, are able to pivot and move into interesting new patterns. (They ride on compressed air, operated hydraulically.) For football the sections are arranged in an extended oval, with most of the seats in good position along the sidelines. For baseball the sections waltz into a compact double horseshoe, with most of the seats along the base paths. Will it work when finished? They say so.

I am encouraged by a small operation which was undertaken by the unlikely town of Pocatello, Idaho, population 40,000. Idaho State University is located there, registration 6,000, and its football teams faced a problem—extinction. An official explains:

> We played our games in the Spud Bowl Stadium, a worn-out affair with wooden stands built in 1936 as a WPA project. Seated 5,000. Weather in Pocatello is a menace especially in early winter, and sometimes we had to play in heavy snow. That meant we couldn't play our games Saturday night. But we oughtn't to play them Saturday afternoon, either, because in Idaho half the population goes hunting then. We were withering, with no attendance, no money, no scholarships and damned little interest. We were spending $100,000 a year and taking in $20,000. It had to stop.

Into this dismal picture stepped a group of local men with soaring imaginations. Dubby Holt, head of athletics at the university, said, 'Problem's simple. We've got to have an all-weather stadium so we can play at night, regardless of blizzards.'

Bill Bartz, the university's business manager, said, 'That means a domed stadium, and they cost upwards of sixty million dollars. Impossible, but if we could build one for about five million, I'd be willing to sell bonds, backed by student fees to get the money.'

John Korbis, the university's engineer, produced the startling news: 'I've been fooling around with plans for a totally different kind of domed stadium. I'm positive I could build it for—hold your breath—two million, three hundred thousand.'

Bud Davis, the energetic president who had once coached football, said, 'Sounds feasible. I'll back you all the way. Go ahead and build it.' And for this sanguine judgment he was promptly dubbed by the local press 'Idiot of the year for southeast Idaho.' They called the venture 'Idaho's Half-Astrodome.' Officially it became the Mini-Dome.

What this innovative team did was dig an immense hole in the earth, so that the cost of building side walls would be minimized. Then, across the opening they slung their version of a Quonset steel roof, well arched. This gave them a covered area in which a standard-sized football field could be laid out, plus commodious seats for 14,000 for football, 18,000 for cultural events.

The interesting thing is that the football field is laid out, not along the long axis of the domed building, but *across* it. Tests had been made, and no football kicker in existence could strike the top of the arch, 108 feet high, with a punt; field goals are kicked into the sloping sides of the roof, just as they are kicked into the end stands in an outdoor stadium.

At this point Cedric Allen, an architect with an artistic eye, was called in, and he painted the inside of the building in six different bright colors, so that all seats are color-coded with corresponding entrances and exits. The result is one of the sauciest buildings in America, sprightly, well suited to its purposes and practical. It's air conditioned, too, by means of large fans that suck in the cool outside air. Holt says:

> Over a heavy gravel bottom we laid a two-inch base of asphalt, topping it with one-half inch of a special rubber plus a three-sixteenths-inch composition pad to absorb the shock of landing. Then we installed a synthetic turf which is ideal for football but also good for track. We have a movable basketball court, and that's it.
>
> To our surprise, we have been able to schedule major events for about three hundred nights a year. Football, of course, and basketball and track. But also high school sports from miles around. Art shows, roller derby, plays, operettas, jazz concerts, religious meetings. This one building has revolutionized social life in this section of Idaho.

I had startling proof of its versatility. Onto the turf had been pasted, with inexpensive adhesive tape, the lines for a tennis court. Two questions perplexed me: 'Will that tape stay down through a real set? And will the ball bounce on the turf?' The problem was solved by finding me a racket and an opponent, and I played part of a set, scuffing into the lines and finding them stable, running for well-hit balls and finding them bouncing up much as they would from a good grass court. The tennis was not only possible, it was enjoyable, for the surface was much softer on the legs and feet than the courts I was accustomed to.

I commend the Pocatello experiment most enthusiastically to northern communities. Already a variety of colleges and universities have been to Idaho to see how this innovation might be adapted to their needs. Holt says:

> The danger is that each community wants to alter the design a little here and there, and in doing so they lose our simplicity and our very low cost of $2,300,000 for basic construction, $2,800,000 for everything. Last case I heard of was coming in at $7,000,000. Costs have gone up, of course, but you should be able to do it for less than $5,000,000, and have a domed stadium which avoids whatever errors we allowed to slip in. And with imaginative management, it can be utilized more than three hundred nights a year. Whether it could be self-sufficient if you had to pay for the land—we got ours free, of course, because we're a state enterprise on state land—I can't say. But you can certainly pay the overhead and repairs.

The worst example of stadium building I have ever seen, or heard of, occurred in Denver. The Broncos, a privately owned professional football team, used Mile High Stadium, which seated only 50,656. Football became so popular that more seats were obligatory, especially if the team were to operate at a profit.

The stadium was owned by the city, which received a decent rental from the Broncos. If an additional 23,360 seats, which could be easily constructed, were added, who would pay the cost of $24,726,000? It was decreed that the public ought to pay, through taxation, but this was objected to on the rational argument that real estate taxes were already high and it would be immoral to tax all citizens to pay for a facility that would be used only by a few and to the profit of a private company.

So an ingenious plan was devised whereby football, baseball, basketball and ice hockey were lumped together as entertainment, and a tax of forty cents was assessed on every ticket sold for any seat at any entertainment held within public buildings or facilities owned by the city. Thus, those who attended games would be paying for the increased facilities used by the teams playing those games.

Reasonable enough, ostensibly. Such a rule avoids taxing the property of all for the use of a few. But the real impact of the proposal was to levy a forty-cent tax on everyone who attended an opera, or a play, or a symphony orchestra concert, or the performance of a string quartet, or a lecture on modern French art, so that the local football team could add 23,360 more spectators to each of their seven scheduled games.

This incredible proposition was put before the voters of Denver, and incredibly, they accepted it, on the obvious grounds that football was more important to the community than a symphony concert. The vote, held on September 10, 1974, was 50,972 in favor and 48,448 against.

This action is so abominable that I find no words sharp enough to condemn it. I am for sports. I am for stadiums. I am for the use of public money to build stadiums when no other way is feasible. And I patronize all kinds of sports with my own income, so I must not be condemned as being anti-sports. But to tax symphony-goers in order to make the operation of a privately owned football team more profitable is such a confusion of priorities that I cannot believe a city which I admire, and of which I have written with such affection, could approve. It did, and the whole city should be ashamed of itself—the sportsmen for having allowed such a thing, the politicians for having dared to put it to a plebiscite, and the voters for having approved it. In ancient Rome, stadiums were financed by imposing a tax on brothels, proving that the citizens of Rome had a clearer sense of values than those of Denver.

The good stadiums are substantially better than the bad ones, and the difference isn't always in the amount spent. The cost of an average seat in the New Orleans Superdome is $2,000; in the refurbished Yankee Stadium, $1,480; in the Denver addition, $1,060; at Pittsburgh's Three Rivers Stadium, $700; in the Houston Astrodome, $640; in Atlanta in Atlanta Stadium, $315; and in Pocatello's Mini-Dome, $128. The real difference is often in the imagination of the architects who add those finishing touches.

The job in Pocatello would be much less congenial if those bright colors were missing. The new stadiums at Kansas City would be much less effective if the ramps for quick entrance and exit were absent. The Superdome in New Orleans would be much less imposing if its circular design were merely ordinary.

One of the most interesting events connected with recent stadiums occurred in Philadelphia, when after agonizing delays and the waste of much money, a design-of-desperation was finally rushed forward and about to be accepted because no way of avoiding it could be found. Woody Bond, civic leader and former basketball mate of mine in college, had the guts to put his foot down. 'This looks like an old-fashioned garage. It would add nothing to the posture of this city.' he said. And he forced the architects to go back and draft something more in tune with the modern world. And getting it right didn't cost a great deal more. The result was a stadium adjusted more or less to both football and baseball, one with many accouterments and a façade that is at least acceptable. It could have been better. It is infinitely better than it was going to be.

Any commission charged with building a new stadium for its community should visit the good ones to learn how class can be obtained by the exercise of good taste. Unpretentious installations like Foxboro should be inspected, and modestly priced ones like Seattle. Specifically, preposterous scoreboards which dance and explode cannons and lead singing can be avoided, especially when they cost $2,000,000 to install. If this is to be an Age of Stadiums, let us erect some of timeless quality, like those noble affairs the Romans built in Turkey two thousand years ago.

The commission should also face squarely the possibility that financial disaster may overtake any stadium, no matter how carefully planned. The cost overrun at the new Yankee Stadium in New York, the heavy tax burden placed upon the citizens of Philadelphia, the impending financial crisis of the baseball stadium in Arlington, Texas, represent the normal expectancy. The New Orleans Superdome, which excited me so much, was open less than six months when it ran into financial catastrophe. A deficit of $5,500,000 loomed, and Louisiana State Attorney General William Guste issued the statement that many citizens had anticipated when the stadium was announced: 'If the Dome Commission is going to get the money, Governor Edwin Edwards is going to have to call a special session of the legislature.' Purpose of the session? Additional taxes.

Unforeseen disaster can also strike. Honolulu had barely finished its revolutionary stadium with the pirouetting segments when the World Football League ran into mortal trouble. I was in Hawaii one Wednesday when the local team had no quarterback for the forthcoming Sunday game. They telephoned a fellow in some city like Seattle and asked him if he'd like to call signals, and he flew out to take over. Shortly thereafter the league folded, leaving the splendid new stadium with no major occupant. A community plays a sophisticated brand of Russian roulette when its enthusiasts proclaim, 'We'll show the world we're really big time! We'll build a stadium! And while we're at it, let's put a dome on top!'

In the early years of every professional sport, the owners were men of great dedication and expertise: in football, George Halas of Chicago; in baseball, Clark Griffith of Washington; in basketball, Eddie Gottlieb of Philadelphia. They added affection, folk humor and business mismanagement to the game, and stories about them are legion. Connie Mack and John McGraw became the epitome of the manager-owner.

Their type was soon superseded, however, by the business tycoon who made his fortune in trade, then dabbled in sports ownership both as a means of advertising his product and finding community approval. The beer barons—Jacob Ruppert with his New York Yankees, and Augie Busch with his St. Louis Cardinals—were prototypes; they became famous across America and the sales of their beer did not suffer in the process. It is interesting that when William Wrigley, the Chicago tycoon, wanted to buy into the National League, he was strongly opposed by Colonel Ruppert, who feared that such ownership might be used to commercialize chewing gum.

Then came the third echelon of owner, the corporate manager who bought a club not only to publicize his business enterprises but also to take advantage of a curious development in federal tax laws. This new owner could afford to pay $20,000,000 for a franchise, ostensibly lose $1,000,000 a year in its operation, meld his sports activity in with his other businesses, apply his sports losses against his his business profits and actually earn a profit on his sports team, a wonderland of juggling not open to the non-millionaire who might want to run a sports franchise and nothing else.

There is nothing wrong with the basic law that made this fairy tale possible. It is called the law of depreciation, and it governs all business activity in the United States. Over the years our business and taxation experts have determined the normal life of all the tools, equipment and resources used in business ventures. A heavy truck, for example, costing $20,000 can be expected to be serviceable for four years; therefore, its original cost can be depreciated over a period of that time. This means that during each of the four years, the owner can charge one-fourth of the cost of the truck, or $5,000 a year, to depreciation, counting it as a deductible cost of doing business.

Even in my profession the law of depreciation operates. The office in which I work, being a solid structure whose counterparts in other parts of the country remain usable for thirty-five years, can be depreciated over that period of years. If I pay $20,000 to build my office, I can charge a yearly depreciation of one-thirty-fifth of the original cost, or $572 a year. I am presupposing straight-line depreciation. In some fields it is lawful to use accelerated depreciation—a lot the first year, little the last. My electric typewriter can be depreciated in four years. The car I use in doing research depreciates to nothing in three years. My general office furniture in eight. (If at the end of the normal period of depreciation, when the value has been reduced to nothing, I can still use the item, fine. I get a bargain. But I can no longer charge depreciation against it, for in the phrase that covers this, 'the depreciation has been used up.')

When applied to general business, this is a good law. It brings order and justice into a difficult field. And it allows business to operate in a reasonable way. I have sometimes heard complaints against the particular rate of depreciation allowed for an item; businessmen would usually prefer the quickest possible depreciation, for this allows them to charge off the item promptly, which enables them to pocket an immediate tax saving rather than a deferred one. But I have never heard a reasonable man complain against the general concept of depreciation.

In sports, the law has been applied in an interesting way. When an owner purchases a franchise, he is buying two things: an intangible license to participate in organized league play and profit from the experience of the other twenty-three or twenty-seven teams in the league; a tangible batch of proved professional players whose life expectancy in the league is limited. It is not possible to depreciate the license to participate, for it does not wear out, nor does its value diminish. But the new owner can certainly depreciate the value of his athletes, for they do wear out, just like an electric typewriter or the reserves in an oil well. Suppose that the owner buys a new player from one of the other clubs for $1,000,000. His ability to play cannot last longer than ten years, so the owner has the legal right to depreciate this cost at the rate of $100,000 a year over a ten-year period. If the player lasts twelve years, that's a bonus, but his depreciation has been used up.

If this were the only problem, depreciation in professional sports would be no different from depreciation in any other enterprise, but in sports, there is one whale of a difference, and it is this which has accounted in large part for the recent revolution in sports, and particularly in the ownership of teams. Follow this hypothetical case.

Seller S has owned an NBA basketball team for a long time. Every knowledgeable person agrees that it is worth at least $5,000,000, and when word escapes that S is willing to sell, at least six groups of buyers are eager to take the team off his hands. There is no argument over the sales price.

Buyer B bids $5,500,000 and gets the team, and the sale is approved by the NBA.

Now an interesting complication occurs, and prior to the winter of 1975 this was the situation. Seller S wants to allocate as much of the $5,500,000 sales price as possible to the intangible license, good will and name of the club, for then he will be allowed to treat the money as capital gains and get a favorable tax break on it. But it is in the interest of Buyer B to allocate as much as possible of the $5,500,000 not to the intangible license but to the tangible ballplayers, for then he can begin depreciating them. Thus the interests of seller and buyer are diametrically opposed. The government, believe it or not, used to allow each man to allocate the $5,500,000 in whichever way was most profitable to him, within reason. Therefore the sale of the basketball team was organized in this way:

BUSINESS DETAILS IN THE SALE OF A TEAM
BY SELLER S TO BUYER B FOR $5,500,000

Seller S, seeking maximum present capital gains, allocates 82% intangibles; 18% tangibles.
Buyer B, seeking maximum future depreciation, allocates 17% intangibles; 83% tangibles.
Therefore, each determined his value of the twelve players as follows:

Player	College	Bonus Paid	Seller S Allocation	Buyer B Allocation	Yearly Salary	Years to Play
Adams	UCLA	$ 10,000	$ 80,000	$ 350,000	$ 62,500	6
Baker	Michigan	None	40,000	275,000	25,000	6
Czykonski	Pittsburgh	15,000	60,000	450,000	100,000	3
Dalhart	Texas	50,000	70,000	450,000	30,000	7
Evers	Memphis State	None	90,000	175,000	25,000	5
Flood	Grambling	25,000	80,000	560,000	100,000	4
Gabbage	North Carolina	30,000	165,000	690,000	125,000	3
Holcomb	Baylor	10,000	60,000	210,000	23,000	6
Isaac	Columbia	20,000	50,000	225,000	27,000	7
Jenkins	UTEP	75,000	185,000	800,000	250,000	2
Koop	Indiana	5,000	60,000	330,000	40,000	6
Larson	Oregon State	None	50,000	50,000	25,000	1
	TOTALS	$240,000	$990,000	$4,565,000	$832,500	
	PERCENT		18%	83%	$ 69,000 (average)	

It seems ridiculous that the value of Jenkins, the powerful center from the University of Texas at El Paso, could be valued by Seller S at $185,000 when his known salary was $250,000, and by Buyer B at $800,000 when his known life expectancy in the league could be no more than two years, but that's how the deal was arranged, and the government approved.

The beauty of this purchase was that as soon as Buyer B got title to the team, he could start depreciating the twelve players from scratch, disregarding the fact that Seller S had already depreciated them almost totally under his ownership. By the time Jenkins quits basketball, he will have been depreciated twice, once by S and once by B, for many times his true value. There is nothing illegal about this; a man builds a building, uses up all its depreciation, then sells it to another, who starts his depreciation anew. Finally he sells it to a third man, who then starts *his* depreciation.

The deal was further complicated by the fact that the law allowed depreciation of a basketball player over a period of three to five years, a reasonable adjudication. But this had a crucial bearing on the conduct of sports, because it was no longer profitable to retain ownership of a team after the five-year depreciation period had elapsed. It was infinitely more profitable for Buyer B to obtain possession of the basketball team, with that $4,565,000 depreciation dangling before him like a rich lollipop, than for Seller S to hang on to it, after his depreciation had diminished to nearly zero.

Thus it became much more profitable for B to buy a team than for S to keep one. And after the new buyer had held on to it for five years, and used up his major depreciation, it was advisable for him to get rid of it, take his capital gains, and look for another team for sale in another sport.

This explains the wild shifting about of franchises over the past fifteen years. I have been privy to the proposed sales of four top franchises; always I have urged men of wealth who had any interest in sports to get into the turmoil, believing that they could have fun doing so and perhaps even make a contribution to their communities. But the accountants always asked:

> Have you a collateral business making enough money so that you could use it to offset paper losses of four or five hundred thousand dollars a year? Would the ownership of a local team, with the publicity that ensues, be of specific advantage to you in the conduct of your business? Would you get fun out of ownership, and the upgrading of the team, and a possible chance for a divisional title? If the answer to those three questions is yes, go right out there and bid $20,000,000 for the team, because you can probably arrange the whole thing through banks for an outlay of no more than $2,000,000 in cash, and apply depreciation against your normal profits.

Unfortunately, the critical question was never 'Do you love sports?' because that had become irrelevant. How could one of the owners back in 1910, who loved baseball, possibly afford to buy a team today if he did not have a collateral business to absorb the losses that might accrue or, of greater importance, profit from the depreciation legally allowed?

Because this is the strange thing about depreciation. If you have no profits to charge it against, you derive no benefit from it. Let's go back to the illustrative case. If Buyer B establishes $4,565,000 as the cost of his players, he can charge off close to $900,000 a year depreciation. But if his ball club doesn't make that much, the depreciation is of no value to him. (He can carry it forward, of course, but if his club merely breaks even in the years ahead, he never uses it up.) However, if Buyer B has a large nationwide trucking firm which makes a lot of money, he can then apply the $900,000 depreciation allowed to his losing baseball club against the $1,800,000 profits made by the trucking firm, and he's in great shape.

But at the end of five to seven years he'd better get rid of his team because then it will not be generating enough depreciation to keep it attractive. Of course, it might actually be making money, or it might have won a championship, and B might want to hold on to it for sentimental reasons, but it will probably be wiser for him to sell to New Buyer Z, because then B can pick up a capital gains advantage, while Z can start the depreciation all over again. The justification for this strange system is that depreciation encourages industry to be innovative, to reinvest earnings, to gamble on the future.

That they operate destructively in the ownership of sports teams is an accident that could easily be corrected. All that is required is that the tax people in the government become involved after the sale of a team has been negotiated. Then let a rule of reason apply in allocating the sale price as between the intangibles and the tangibles; let a common schedule be drawn up as to what center Jenkins is worth, to Seller S and Buyer B alike, and let the deal go forward from that agreement. In effect, this rule of reason has always operated: buyer and seller could not establish ridiculous allocations; they had to be approved by the government. But the rule was never stringently applied, and some sales went through with allocations not much different from the imaginary example I cited. Noll and Okner in 1972 summarized the situation in these terms:

> The fast write-off of nearly all of the purchase price of a sports franchise through amortization of player contracts appears to be highly questionable. It is not that the profits this practice creates are inherently evil, but that they create socially undesirable incentives for team owners. Except for a very few teams, the maximum profit a team could hope to earn is a few hundred thousand dollars. This is dwarfed by the tax avoidance made possible by depreciation. The gains to a rich individual or a corporation from owning a team depend very little on the quality of the team or its operations. In fact, among the most profitable teams are the lowly NBA expansion franchises. They field poor teams and do poorly at the gate, but the fast write-off of the expansion fee saves the owners half a million to a million dollars a year in income tax. According to our conception of the public interest, society would be better served if the profitability of a team depended upon its ability to please the fans, not the tax accountant.

Five or six years ago it became apparent to everyone that this preposterous way of doing things could not continue for long. And in 1974 the federal government finally decided to take a close look at the way these transfers were being conducted.

The case was ideally suited for adjudication, because the confrontation between the owners and the government was clear-cut, the difference between their two positions radically different. In 1966 a group in Atlanta acquired from the established clubs of the NFL a franchise to launch a new club to be called the Falcons. For this privilege they paid $8,500,000, of which $727,086 was for debt service. This was subtracted from the sum in contention, and we will not hear of it again. The effective sales price was $7,772,914, and the new owners, as in the example cited above, wanted to allocate most of this to player cost, which would permit depreciation in the future, whereas the government wanted to apply most of it to the cost of the franchise, which would diminish depreciation and lead to immediate taxation as soon as the new club started to collect money.

This discrepancy, as we shall see in the next table, was so great that a lawsuit became inevitable. Known as *Laird*, Federal District Court Georgia, it was followed with more than usual interest because it epitomized the whole problem of sports ownership. As the case progressed, I consulted with various interested parties and concluded that the government would win, that depreciation allowances would be revised downward radically, and that the five-year switch of owners would be halted because it would no longer be profitable. When pressed, I pessimistically predicted that owners who had been allocating as much as 90 percent of their purchase price to player cost would be cut back to something like 20 percent. The financial holiday that professional sports had been enjoying was over.

I was surprised and pleased when Judge Frank Hooper handed down a most judicious award. The allocations involved were as follows:

LAIRD, FEDERAL DISTRICT COURT, GEORGIA
COUNTERCLAIMS AND DISPOSITION

Component	Buyers' Allocation	Percent	IRS Allocation	Percent	Judge's Award	Percent
Franchise value	$ 50,000	00.65	$6,722,914.	86.42	$460,871.*	5.96
Television rights					4,277,043.	55.04
Player cost	7,722,914.	99.35	1,050,000.	13.58	3,035,000.	39.00
Total	$7,772,914.	100.00	$7,772,914.	100.00	$7,772,914.	100.00

*Actual award, $410,871, to which must be added the $50,000 agreed upon by the buyers and not in contention.

The fact that the buyers were trying to allocate 99.35 percent of their purchase price to player cost probably alerted the IRS to the fact that in such cases a decision now had to be made. The fact that IRS wanted to allocate 86.42 percent to non-depreciable costs meant that the owners had to contest the decision, in defense not only of themselves but of all professional sports. The judge's award of roughly 60–40 in favor of the government was much more favorable to sports than I had anticipated; in retrospect it qualifies as Solomonic. If the case is appealed, some rough division like this could possibly be approved by higher courts, and if so, the owners of professional teams will be able to handle their franchises in a reasonable way.

One practical outcome of this decision will be that owners will no longer have a built-in compulsion to sell at the end of five or six years, because the depreciation awaiting the new owners won't be large enough to make the purchase enticing. Buyer B will no longer be able to determine arbitrarily what percentage of his purchase price will go to depreciable player costs, to be offset by profits he makes in his non-sport businesses.

One aspect of recent ownership has been disturbing. In far too many cases teams have been owned not by local people interested in the welfare of both the team and the community, but by outsiders, sometimes from the opposite end of the nation, who happened to be in a financial position in which ownership was a practical rather than an athletic consideration. I once had dinner with four major owners, not one of whom lived in the community in which he owned his club. They were interesting men, intelligent, street-smart and responsible. In their regular businesses, they were not fly-by-night operators, but it seemed to me that their ownership of sports teams had been dictated more by curious national law than by allegiance to sports. I preferred the old system, in which a local family dedicated itself to the sponsorship of a team, and rose or fell with its fortunes. I am afraid Congress has served us poorly by allowing laws which were reasonable when applied to business to dictate how games should be run.

Of course, the ideal sports operation is not one that builds up a loss which can be charged against profits elsewhere. The intention of every owner is to have a winner, and if he does, he usually makes a considerable profit. But even if he comes up with a loser, he can still make a profit over a span of years. In 1953 the Cleveland Browns were bought for $600,000. Eight years later they were sold for $4,000,000. In 1969 they were valued at $14,000,000 and now they are worth about $20,000,000. The New York Jets showed a comparable growth, and the Chicago Cougars of the upstart World Hockey League were established in 1972 for an outlay of $25,000 and two years later were worth $6,000,000. Similar stories could be recited about scores of teams whose value has multiplied spectacularly.

In fact, such success stories aroused the cupidity of hundreds of otherwise sane businessmen and they began laying out huge sums of cash to acquire franchises being peddled by an imaginative pair of young men from California who organized three nationwide leagues in three different sports. Gary L. Davidson, forty years old at the time, and Donald J. Regan, one year younger, sensed that America was ripe for a picking, and in quick succession they sold eleven franchises for a new basketball league (ABA in 1967), fourteen for a lively hockey league (WHA in 1972), and twelve for an improvised football league (WFL in 1974).

At the same time a radical new idea was being promulgated in professional tennis: a league composed of sixteen teams of men and women affiliated with large cities, playing a regular schedule throughout most of the year. A soccer league was beginning to flourish. Box lacrosse, a vigorous game much like ice hockey but more lethal, had its own league and was catching on in various eastern and Canadian cities. And groups of highly skilled volleyball players—four men, two women to a team—were organizing themselves into a league in the southwest, with a fair chance for success.

It was a sports explosion of bewildering proportion, and many critics began wondering if there were enough fans to support the proliferating teams. In New York, for example, there were the Mets, the Jets, the Nets, the Yankees, the Giants, the Stars, the Knicks, the Rangers, the Islanders, the Cosmos, the Tomahawks and the Sets, and few could identify what sport each represented.

It was obvious that some of these new teams were going to be in trouble, when I saw that the newspapers were not giving them traditional coverage. There were no interesting stories about the players, or the theories of the coaches, or the trades that were under consideration, and as I have stressed before, I do not believe professional sports can survive without constant and favorable newspaper attention. I think the papers wanted to cover the new teams but there was neither the space nor the interest, and the innovators found themselves in peril.

When an economic depression slowed ticket sales, gloomy statistics began to emerge. This was the situation as described in the August 12, 1974, issue of *U.S. News and World Report:* of twenty-four baseball clubs, one-half were losing money; of twenty-seven basketball teams, twenty-two were losing; of the twenty-six super-prosperous NFL teams, two were not breaking even; of the twenty-eight hockey teams, ten were losing. Also, all teams in the new tennis league were in distress, as were most of the teams in lacrosse. But it was the World Football League that was in the direst predicament; all fifteen of its teams faced potential trouble in the 1975 season. Davidson, who had created the WFL, confessed, 'Some clubs are put together with string, baling wire, stickum and gum. I spend half my time on the phone shoring up financial deals.' Peddling doomed clubs to hopeful new owners seemed the way out, and many proposals were floated. At the end of seven years' existence, the ABA had only one team which was still owned by the men who had launched it originally; all other teams had been sold and resold, some of them three times. The great sports boom had peaked.

Consider what was happening in Philadelphia. The tennis Freedoms dropped a bundle, called it quits, and moved to New York. The lacrosse Wings came close to financial collapse but were picked up by a new owner prepared to give the fledgling team one more whirl.* The hockey Firebirds lost $450,000 in cold cash but resolutely decided to field a team in 1975. The basketball 76ers had a dismal season, and the Bell of the WFL admitted losses of $1,500,000 but kept hoping that things would turn for the better next year. (On the other hand, the baseball Phillies had a good year at the box office, while the hockey Flyers played the entire season without an unsold seat; when they nabbed the Stanley Cup for the second year in a row, one and a half million people tore the town apart in a victory celebration. The city had to spend $186,000 to clean up the mess and another $46,000 to repair the joyous vandalism done to the transportation system.)

But in 1975 the ax fell. The ABA, caught in the vise of indefensible salaries and diminishing attendance, saw its roster of teams drop to seven, with Baltimore, Utah and San Diego abandoning the game and dissolving their teams. The cash loss must have been substantial. But the WFL collapsed altogether despite heroic efforts by the Honolulu businessman Chris Hemmeter to keep it afloat. Reports said that the owners who had so eagerly grabbed for the original franchises dropped at least $34,000,000.

One final word must be said about owners. Many are difficult for a sports lover to tolerate; they seem obsessed with financial manipulation rather than the welfare of the game or the players. They are obtuse in clinging to archaic rights which the courts will soon be striking down, and they show contempt for the public. They are warts on the body of sports, and that they should be in positions of power and control is indefensible. James Quirk has shown, in a remarkable article in *Law and Contemporary Problems* (1973), that most recent franchise shifts were dictated by commercial considerations: the departing team was doing as well as could be expected in its present home; in its new home it did pick up extra customers, but usually only for a few years; the change was typically made in order to garner television income, was rarely permanent, and accomplished little in stabilizing the league. In other words, rapacious carpetbag owners were allowed to perform unsocial acts for personal profit.

However, the majority of owners that I have met are like Joe Robbie of

*The league folded in 1976, but may be resuscitated later.

Miami, real devotees, men and women to whom the building of a respectable team becomes a passion, and they add luster to the sporting scene. Some of them may originally have bought their teams for financial advantage, but they soon found themselves bewitched by sports. In the end they are willing to make extraordinary sacrifices in order to build a winner, and their loyalty to their team often excells that of their players. Once when a group of us were discussing the transfer of a franchise, the owner of a club made this revealing statement:

> If you've never owned a big-time club, you can't appreciate what it means. I was a pretty good businessman in this town, and nobody gave me the time of day. But when I bought the team I became somebody. The newspapers asked my opinion on things. The television guys wanted to interview me. People would stop me on the street and say, 'Hey! I saw you on TV!' When I came into a restaurant people stopped and I could hear them whispering, 'He owns the ball club.' And the more good things like that happened to me, the more I determined to do for this town what Art Rooney did for Pittsburgh. Give them a champion. It may take me ten years, but this town is going to have a winner. Me sell? Even if the depreciation is used up? Are you crazy? Owning a team's the biggest thing's ever happened to me.

Clint Murchison, who masterminded the building of the stadium for his Dallas Cowboys, spoke for the legitimate owners when he said, 'You could make more money investing in government bonds. But football is more fun.'

In discussing player salaries, one basic fact must be kept in mind, and unless it is, much nonsense will ensue. Superstars like Kareem Abdul-Jabbar, Bobby Orr, O.J. Simpson, Joe Namath, Nolan Ryan and Billie Jean King earn for their teams something more than twice as much as they are paid. This means that if economics is to be the sole criterion, our twenty or thirty top athletes are grossly underpaid.

The reasoning is this. Roger Noll, using sophisticated correlation techniques, identified nine measurable factors that relate, perhaps causally, to the success of a professional basketball franchise:

Number of competing teams in area	Stadium capacity
Team won-and-lost record	Per capita income
Price of average ticket	Years located in city
Population of area played in	Number of superstars on team
Number of home dates played	

Two of the factors were found to exert a negative influence: the longer a team stayed in one location, the more likely it was to run into box-office trouble; and the more competing professional teams in the area, the smaller the cut for each. (Later Noll cranked in a tenth variable and found that the higher the percentage of blacks living in the area, the lower the attendance:

'The connection is simply that ball parks located in undesirable neighborhoods tend to be old stadiums in very large cities in the north and midwest, and these cities also tend to have atypically large black populations.')

The major factor determining success was the size of the population in the hometown area. (We have seen earlier that television viability was also a major factor, but it, too, was a measure of available audience.) The owners could do nothing about this population factor except move to a larger city. There was one variable, however, that they could control: the number of superstars on their team. This really mattered, because the team with the superstar drew at the gate, whereas another team with five journeyman players might have an equally good won-lost record but be unable to generate enthusiasm. That club lost money. Noll and Okner have summarized the situation in this way:

> Having a superstar on the team is worth 25,000 attendance during the season. This figure, of course, is an average for all teams and for all seventeen players in the two leagues classified as superstars by our criteria. Still using the $4.50 average ticket price, this means that about seventeen professional basketball players produce about $100,000 a year in gross revenues for their teams beyond whatever contribution these talented athletes make to the won-lost record of the team. Including the contribution the superstar makes to his team's winning percentage, the results suggest that basketball superstars are worth salaries exceeding $100,000, as measured by the contribution they make to team revenues.
>
> Furthermore, a player such as Lew Alcindor [Abdul Jabbar] is probably worth much more. If he is the difference between winning and losing in twenty percent of the Bucks' games and if he is twice the fan attraction of the average of our seventeen superstars, then, by himself, he accounts for nearly $500,000 a year in gate receipts for the Bucks. Despite the acknowledged statistical error in such regression estimates, the evidence is strong that Alcindor is grossly underpaid in relation to his value to his team—even if he earns $250,000 annually.

The problem is, therefore, not with the superstar. If Nolan Ryan or Catfish Hunter pitches thirty-five times a season, and if their pitching rotation is well publicized, each may attract an additional 15,000 paying customers every time he goes to the mound. At an average admission of $3.50, this means a windfall of $52,500 per game, or $1,837,500 for the season. Now, the salary paid to Ryan or Hunter has already taken much of this augmented income into consideration, but it is obvious that baseball could pay these gifted pitchers at least twice as much as it does.

The problem comes with the next flight of players. What is the guard worth who helps Jabbar on defense and feeds him on offense? The superstar does not play in a vacuum; without the help of extremely able assistants, he cannot accomplish much. Even Jabbar was unable to get his team very far until his supporting cast of players was sharply strengthened; Oscar Robertson was needed to augment the unusual talents of the great center.

But even this formidable pair did not click until other positions were filled with truly able players. I learned this truth about the superstars when I followed the history of Lombardi's superlative fullback Jim Taylor. When paired with Paul Hornung behind that formidable line led by Jerry Kramer, Taylor was well-nigh unstoppable, and many people, including me, considered him one of the best fullbacks, all things considered, ever to have played in the NFL.

But then he was traded to New Orleans, and I remember telling my friends, 'He'll turn that franchise around.' He did nothing of the sort. Behind a weak line, without the one-two punch of Paul Hornung to divert opponents, he accomplished little. He didn't tear the opposition apart, as he had at Green Bay, and he didn't score. He may once have been a superstar, but without topnotch support he quickly subsided into just another journeyman ballplayer.

I would estimate that at least 40 percent of the superstar's performance derives from his supporting players. He always has the capacity to break loose in some breath-taking exhibition—for a brief, dazzling spell—but he cannot win games consistently without first-class support. Consequently, if Jabbar is paid $400,000 a year, the steady pros who enable him to play his game, and especially to win, must be worth 40 percent of that, or $160,000.

So I conclude that the star-slightly-under-the-superstar is also worth a high salary. But that brings us to the fifth and sixth men on the basketball team, or the last three men in the baseball line-up, or the journeymen linemen in football. Games have become so highly technical, and coaching so perceptive, that the presence on the opposing team of even one weak player is enough to send the troops crashing into him and scoring almost at will.

How often have you watched a quarterback, advised by phone from coaches perched high in the stands, isolate an inadequate opposing cornerback and throw so many passes in his zone that the poor man becomes dizzy? A really inept defensive back might throw away three touchdowns in one half, and there goes the game.

One Sunday afternoon I watched Earl-the-Pearl Monroe, the best one-on-one player in the heat of the game I have so far seen, isolate a New York Knicks guard—Earl was then playing for Baltimore—and pump in some thirty points at critical junctures of the game. His shots were beyond believing, but they were made possible by a guard who couldn't quite keep up with him. In the next game New York slapped Dave DeBusschere on him, and that was the end of Earl-the-Pearl.

The question is, if the inadequate player in a minor position can lose a game for you, what should you be willing to pay to get an adequate one who will help you win? Sixty to seventy thousand would not be out of line, because if you string along with the inadequate man you can get cheap, you neutralize the abilities of the superstar whom you pay $400,000.

Rationalization like this explains the salary schedule for a run-of-the-mill team like the Philadelphia 76ers. (Says Mark Heisler, a staff writer of the *Philadelphia Bulletin*, who compiled this list, 'When in doubt, I guessed low.')

Billy Cunningham	$300,000	Allan Bristow	$70,000
Doug Collins	200,000	Fred Boyd	70,000
LeRoy Ellis	100,000	Don Smith	30,000
Fred Carter	90,000	John Tschogl	25,000
Clyde Lee	75,000	Harvey Catchings	20,000
Steve Mix	70,000	Coniel Norman	20,000

Total: $1,070,000

These figures highlight the fact that it is basketball, with its five-man teams, which pays the highest salaries. The following table, abstracted from various sources, shows the rough relationship among the four major sports:

AVERAGE SALARIES IN FOUR MAJOR SPORTS

Sport	1971	1974	Number of Players per Squad
National Basketball Association	$50,000	$90,000	12
National Hockey League	32,000	75,314	19
Major League Baseball	31,000	37,000	25
National Football League	27,800	28,000	43

The low salaries in football are a result of the relatively short season, the few games played and the large number of players per squad. The high average salary for hockey is startling, and reflects the recent rapid expansion of this sport. Clarence Campbell, in an interview, bemoaned the inflated salaries:

In 1965, when we had six teams in the old NHL, the average player's salary was $16,333. The average ticket price was $2.50, arenas were filled to 96 percent capacity and it cost an average of $850,000 to operate a team.

Now we have eighteen NHL teams, an average charge of $6.61 a ticket, and it costs $3,500,000 to operate a team. Attendance has dropped to just above 90 percent capacity, and the average player's salary is $75,314.

Before we enter a discussion of the moral justification for high salaries, it will be instructive to compare a few outstanding ones, insofar as rumored estimates allow:

PROBABLE INCOME, EXCLUDING ENDORSEMENTS AND PERSONAL
APPEARANCES, FOR SELECTED ATHLETES IN VARIOUS SPORTS

Pelé	$800,000	Herve Filion	$250,000
Wilt Chamberlain	600,000	Jack Nicklaus	238,179
Nate Archibald	455,000	Dick Allen	233,000
Joe Namath	450,000	Chuck Fairbanks	200,000
Walt Frazier	450,000	Catfish Hunter	200,000
Kareem Abdul-Jabbar	400,000	Bobby Orr	200,000
Johnny Miller	353,021	Hank Aaron	200,000
Laffit Pincay	322,000	Tom Seaver	140,000
Angel Cordero	306,000	Billie Jean King	119,000
Billy Cunningham	300,000	Bob Griese	80,000
Ron Turcotte	278,000	Derek Sanderson	80,000
Bill Shoemaker	251,000	Larry Csonka	65,000
Pete Maravich	250,000	U.S. Congressman	44,625

Educated guesses from various reports, not all for the same year. Pincay, Cordero, Turcotte and Shoemaker are jockeys. Filion rides a sulky. Chuck Fairbanks is the former football coach at the University of Oklahoma who moved to the New England Patriots. A rough calculation of athletes who are earning over $100,000 yearly showed fifty basketball players, forty-five in hockey, thirty in baseball, sixteen in golf and only ten in football.

Up to this point my reasoning on sports salaries has been relative. No moral absolute or social imperative has been considered. If superstar Jabbar produces additional earnings of $1,000,000, the owners can certainly afford to pay him $400,000. And if he gets that much, his supporting stars are entitled to $160,000, and if they earn that much, it is not illogical to pay the journeymen who make the game possible $60,000 or $70,000. But now it is obligatory to raise the social issue: Is it desirable that *any* of these players receive salaries of that size?

Before we grapple with that treacherous problem, let's take a look at what really happens in our paying of athletes, and those associated with them. Not long ago (in *Sports Illustrated,* February 15, 1971) Melvin Durslag unearthed details of the deal arranged by coach George Allen when he shifted from the Los Angeles Rams to the Washington Redskins. Durslag is a witty writer, always on the lookout for a laugh; therefore, I cannot verify what follows, but he swears this was it: a base salary of $125,000; a bonus for signing of $25,000; use of a $150,000 home; incentive bonuses each year of $5,000 for getting to divisionals; $10,000 for a conference championship; $15,000 for getting to the Super Bowl; a car and driver; a $250,000 life insurance policy; a generous expense account; traveling expenses; hotel

'*$100,000 . . . $200,000 . . . $300,000 . . .*'

expenses; moving expenses from Los Angeles to Washington; six weeks' paid vacation; total possession of any revenue from radio, TV and endorsements; and an option to buy 5 percent of the club stock for $500,000. (The stock would probably be worth $1,000,000 on the open market.)

In a deal like that, there is a degree of insanity, but the same can be said for many American salaries. Mike Douglas earns $2,200,000 for talking on TV. Charles Bronson gets $1,500,000 for making a sadistic motion picture. Mick Jagger earns $3,000,000 for singing songs that few over the age of twenty-two can understand. Erika Jong makes more than a million dollars for composing the sexual memoirs of an addlepated young woman. Sally Struthers picks up $156,000 for acting in *All in the Family.* And a Harvard philosophy graduate with a Yale M.A. in theology is lucky if he can earn $10,000 a year. Dr. Harvey R. Rutstein, in a letter to *The New York Times,* analyzed this phenomenon:

> Many women and men study, at significant financial investment, ten to twenty years to attain a doctoral degree. Recent developments and economic setbacks have decreased demand for these intellectually trained people. They now drive cabs, tend bars, sell insurance. Athletes, many of whom were high school dropouts, are building $200,000 homes.
>
> The answer is depressing but inordinately simple. There are few 'gray' zones in sports. A puck goes in the net or misses, the ball through the basket or out,

and clearly there is always a winner and a loser. Soul-searching is not required, a weighing of dismal alternatives obviated. We have escaped to the black and white of sports from the frustrations and confusions of such gray zones as the Vietnam war, police corruption, morality of abortion, bounding inflation, dismal political leadership alternatives, safety on the streets.

In ancient Rome, citizens befuddled by the complexities of the waning empire found in the battles waged by the gladiators precisely this simplistic relief from the governmental problems of their day. Cynics are always citing the downfall of Rome as a gloomy precedent; the relevant fact is that after the introduction of those gigantic athletic festivals in the Colosseum, Rome survived rather successfully for another four centuries, and I suppose we can survive our excessive sports salaries.

But then the moral problem arises. Should a well-run society divert so high a percentage of its gross national product into sports, when there are so many other aspects of our national life which cry for attention? A recent study has shown that we spend about one hundred billion dollars a year on sports and recreation, considerably more than we spend for national defense. If this vast sum went for the improvement of the national health, fine. If it encouraged our citizens to become active participants and to avoid physical and mental deterioration, fine. And if it encouraged young people to build patterns of living that would serve them throughout life, fine.

But if a great deal of this investment is merely subtracted from the creative processes of the nation, and siphoned into the hands of a few essentially brash young men and women, the consequences can only be destructive. Our nation may be generating deep resentments in establishing and promulgating such unbalanced priorities.

An interesting case developed with Bill Walton of UCLA. In the final game of the 1973 NCAA finals against Memphis State, Walton gave an overwhelming exhibition of how basketball should be played, on television, watched by more than 30,000,000. He shot twenty-two times from the field and sank twenty-one, an unheard-of percentage. He was also devastating on defense, and with that one game, showed that he would be worth whatever the pros might decide to pay him. Therefore, when the Portland Trail Blazers signed him for $2,500,000, it was confidently expected that he would be 'the white hope' in competition against the great black centers of the NBA.

He was a bust. In his early games he was downright inept when going against older, experienced hands like Jabbar or Thurmond. Then he developed bone spurs. Then he began to sulk, complaining that the coldness of the Portland floor aggravated his feet. Then he fell into some kind of unspecified trouble with the FBI over his supposed knowledge of the whereabouts of Patty Hearst. Then he gave a jolting interview in which he excoriated both the FBI and the United States. And finally he drew down his enormous salary after having played few games and making little contribution when he did play.

I talked with seven notable athletes about this extraordinary performance, sometimes at length, and those over the age of thirty were disgusted with Walton's behavior, saying that it brought discredit to sports, but those under thirty unanimously defended him, arguing that Walton represented the sports star of the future, the player who would not allow himself to be pushed around by owners, or press, or public opinion, or the FBI. One superstar told me, 'If his feet hurt, no obligation to play. If he has a bone spur, he owes the management nothing. The day is past when outsiders are going to tell us when to perform and how and for what purposes.'

Bob Briner, long associated with sports, wrote a scathing article on incidents like this, well before Walton surfaced, in which he said:

> Americans who fear that there has been too much emphasis placed on victory should be relieved to know that winning or losing has become nearly irrelevant with large numbers of our major league players . . . The salary drive used to be restricted to the last few weeks of a season. Now the season is the salary drive. The pros play the statistics game for eighty games, then play basketball if they make the play-offs.

Salary schedules for black players raise unique problems. It is not widely known that the typical black athlete consistently earns more than the typical white. The statistics on this are overwhelming, but what they mean is that in order to stay on a big-league team, the black has to be so much better than his white competitor that he is forced to be almost a superstar. If a team has seven blacks and seventeen whites, a good few of the latter might be marginal players, which would mean that their modest salaries would bring the white average down. But none of the seven blacks could be marginal; to land a place on a team, the black must be a star, so he earns a star's salary.

But when it comes to matching a particular black star against a comparable white, the latter almost always earns the higher salary. As *Ebony* pointed out, in 1971 Carl Yastrzemski earned $35,000 more than either Hank Aaron or Willie Mays, although both of them excelled him in reputation, performance and years in the league.

If one is able to accept the gross imbalance existing in all American salaries, there should be no complaint against those paid to athletes. The Pelé case summarizes the problem. Originally it was announced that he would earn a yearly salary of $7,200,000, which was incomprehensible. But then it was revealed that this was for three years, not one, which was still perplexing. Next it was announced that it would be $4,500,000 for three years, which was approaching reason. And finally we discovered that the figure included all sorts of business deals, advertising income and collateral perquisites. As in similar cases, the final figure made sense: about $800,000 a year for athletic skills, the rest for serving as ambassador for soccer. It was a sound business deal, and the results started coming in right away. Each of the first games in which he appeared drew 20,000 more customers than usual; he was photographed with the President; and he appeared on television constantly, selling soccer.

But I must reiterate that sports salaries are earned while the athletes are young, which means that most of the money will have vanished before the player reaches forty. Also, in every publicized deal there is a substantial amount of hot air; most of the vaunted millionaires never materialize; and on prudent reflection I still think the young man who trains himself to be a certified public accountant does better for himself, over a lifetime, than the hotshot nineteen-year-old athlete who picks up a contract which evaporates after three years, leaving him with no profession and no pension.

The lack of noblesse oblige among the newer crop of athletes disturbs me. The appalling frequency with which players break contracts, use blackmail to force renegotiation of old ones, and express contempt for the public makes me think that American sports may soon be in danger. Once-ardent fans will back away from supporting such ingratitude, and one franchise after another will find itself in deepening trouble.

As teams move from place to place, athletes shift from city to city, never staying long. They become wandering mercenaries, much like the German knights of the late Middle Ages, generating few local loyalties. They pick up their high pay for a few years, but it will be difficult to hold on to, and in the end they will have found more disappointment than satisfaction.

There must be a better way, for the profession of athletics goes back at least four thousand years, and many men and women have found honor and satisfaction in it.

XII

Government Control

To compare America's appetite for sports with that of the rest of the world's is impossible unless one carefully stipulates what period he is discussing. Looking at the world sports scene as it existed in 1970, I can state categorically that compared with many other nations, the United States did not then over-emphasize sports. Had I never lived abroad, I might have believed otherwise, but to accept the charge that our nation was then sports-mad would be to misread our situation and ignore conditions in the rest of the world.

I believe that in 1970 our emphasis was just about what it should have been, as the following tabular summary of my judgment proves. I constructed this table in that year and trust that it represents conditions as they existed then. Observe that in each of the four categories numerous additional nations could have been listed; the four chosen are merely indicative. Also, the rank order within each category is meaningful, the nation at the top of a category being considerably more sports-minded than the one at the bottom.

COMPARISON OF SIXTEEN SELECTED NATIONS
AS TO THEIR EMPHASIS ON SPORTS IN 1970

Excessive Emphasis	Well Above Average Emphasis	About Right Emphasis	Well Below Average Emphasis
East Germany	Japan	Great Britain	Mexico
Russia	Australia	United States	Ireland
South Africa	Italy	Belgium	Sweden
Brazil	Hungary	Spain	India

Concerning the relative ratings of the first four, I have no compunctions. Those nations are sports-crazy to a degree barely understood in the United States. In the second group I vacillate in my ranking of Japan and Australia; I used to think the latter a scene of sports frenzy, but I am told by responsible observers that in recent years the sports addiction in Japan has multiplied. I place Great Britain ahead of the United States for two reasons: the excessive betting there, and the disgraceful and riotous behavior of the British soccer fans, their excesses being far worse than anything we see in the United States—so far. It is possible that Belgium ought to be ahead of us, too, considering its maniacal behavior when Eddy Merckx and Jackie Ickx were competing in international races. I also have mild doubts about the proper placement of Ireland; it lacks major teams, but its devotion to horse racing, under ideal conditions, might warrant a higher rating.

The significant point is that prior to 1970 America rated just about where it ought to have been: a wealthy nation capable of supporting professional teams, but doing so within a rule of reason. Problems arise with the post-1970 period, when new leagues in old sports began to proliferate and when new sports which had never before fielded professional teams organized leagues in such sports as lacrosse, tennis, volleyball and box soccer. Whether this explosion has escalated America into the category of Excessive Emphasis is for each critic to decide for himself.

My own judgment is that it has not. We are still well within the bounds of reason and are protected, since non-viable leagues will perish financially if they do represent an unhealthy overemphasis. But for an American critic to imagine that even with our post-1970 expansion we equal East Germany in our devotion to sports is to misunderstand available data. For example, Austria, with a population of only 8,060,000, has just passed legislation which will permit government to spend $60,000,000 a year on sports. To equal an expenditure like that, the United States, with a population of 210,000,000, would have to budget $1,564,000,000, which is many times what our federal government provides.

There is, however, a psychological danger in the recent explosion which does merit attention. The emphasis on sports is not of itself regrettable—our nation has the energy and the money to support the expansion—but when sports are encouraged to preempt financial and psychological support that might be spent on more worthy projects, society could be drifting into trouble. Apprehension about this tyranny of sports was voiced in *Education of the Gifted and Talented,* a report to the Subcommittee on Education of the United States Senate, March 1972:

> Gifted adolescents as a group have reduced the extent of their reading from junior high to high school, perhaps because of fears that they will be

viewed as 'grinds' or have suffered group pressures unless they exhibit athletic prowess . . .

The waste of talent has been emphasized by Pressey in several writings. In one article he compared the eighteenth-century European society, which valued the arts and nurtured many outstanding composers who produced works of lasting benefit, to the twentieth-century American society, which values athletics and provides outstanding opportunities and rich rewards to those who reached stardom. Consequently, Europe of one and two centuries ago experienced the remarkable achievements of Handel, Haydn, Mozart, Chopin, Liszt, Verdi, Schubert, Rossini, Mendelssohn, Debussy, Dvorak, Berlioz and Wagner, all of whom played, composed and/or conducted their own compositions between the ages of six and seventeen. In the United States, with similarly high valuation on athletics, Pressey noted the remarkable accomplishments of Bobby Jones and Marlene Bauer in golf, Sonja Henie and Barbara Ann Scott in skating, Vincent Richards and Maureen Connolly in tennis, and Mel Ott and Bobby Feller in baseball, all before the age of eighteen.

All of the individuals listed, whether musician or athlete, had the benefit of strong familial and social encouragement, early opportunity to develop their abilities, superior early and continuous guidance and instruction, individualized programs, close association with others in their fields, and many strong successes.

Eighteenth-century Europe produced musicians because society of that time prized creative talent; twentieth-century America produces athletes because our society obviously treasures sports more highly than creativity. John Leonard of *The New York Times* has summarized this predilection as follows: 'This is a culture of little boys who would rather grow up to be Pete Rose than Gustave Flaubert; whose cathedrals are paved with Astroturf; a nation womanless, artless, Indian-killing and as point-scoring as the factitious West.'

I have already quoted the housewife who told me that any self-respecting American mother would want her daughter to be a cheerleader so that she might have a chance to marry a football player. I have heard fathers say, 'If a son of mine could be either an honest, God-fearing football player or a long-haired musician, I'd despise him if he didn't choose football.'

This unhealthy psychological overemphasis manifests itself in the recent attempts throughout the United States to forge an alliance between sports and nationalism. Our political leaders have been goading sports into performing three improper functions, and if this trend continues, sports will be hopelessly contaminated. 1) Sports are being asked to serve as propaganda in support of specific political parties. 2) They are being used to buttress military goals. 3) They are being grossly misused to create a fuzzy, shallow patriotism.

I do not warn against such abuse as an outsider. I am a politician who has run for various elective offices. I could be classified as a militarist, for I volunteered to serve in war. And I would hope that I was a patriot. But I am beginning to feel most uneasy when I watch sports being asked to serve as handmaiden to politics, militarism and flamboyant patriotism. A halt should be called. Sports are games played by children and vivacious grown-ups; they serve us best when they are restricted to their proper sphere.

In the years 1969–74 I searched in vain for published material focusing directly on this problem and found nothing substantial, although some authors did make casual reference to the unholy holy alliance. In 1975 I discovered two excellent treatments, Brian M. Petrie's 'Sports and Politics' in Ball and Loy, and Robert Lipsyte's amusing and irreverent 'Please Rise for Our National Pastime' in his *SportsWorld*. The following incidents chosen from scores which have occurred recently, illustrate what Petrie and Lipsyte are worried about:

• In the fall of 1974 my wife and I attended a major college football game, and the mayor of the city, knowing that I enjoyed sports, arranged to have a motorcycle escort take us to the game. Through the crowded streets our one-car motorcade sped, attended by four state troopers, their sirens wailing. At the game, some two hundred police officials guarded the stadium, and one told me, 'Our best duty comes in the fall, when we go out to the airport to meet the big sportswriters and escort them to their hotels.'

• It has been calculated that in the 1972 football season, 40 percent of all seats sold to games played by the Chicago Bears were deducted from income as business expense, and 54 percent of all tickets sold to Houston Oiler games, highlighting the interrelationship between sports and government.

• In 1972 I attended one important game at which a squad of marines, assisted by an army band, raised the flag at the start, then assembled at midfield during half time, assisted by three troops of National Guardsmen and two of Boy Scouts to honor America's participation in the Vietnam war, while a Catholic priest, a Jewish rabbi and a Protestant clergyman offered prayers for our boys in Asia, and a member of the home team's squad for the previous year marched on crutches to a receiving stand where the president of the university awarded him a medal and the verbal assurance that he, and not the unruly protesters in the streets, was the true American.

• In various eastern states I watched attentively as politicians arranged for local athletes to enroll in National Guard units rather than be drafted for Vietnam. These men, scores of them, never went overseas. Others were offered athletic scholarships to college, and this kept them from the draft. As Jeff Kinney, halfback at Nebraska, confessed, 'Football has been my whole life. Without it, who knows where I might be now. Vietnam? Jail?

Or what?' To use football as an escape from civic duty is indecent.

• In 1972 the Kansas City Royals came up with a rational plan to play *The Star-Spangled Banner* only on special occasions, hoping that this would remind the patrons of the true significance of the anthem. Howls of protest prevented them from doing this. 'Every game in every sport should begin with the National Anthem' was a common response.

• October 6, 1972, was proclaimed by President Nixon as National Coaches Day, in tribute to those men who best exemplified the true spirit of our nation.

• In 1975, when New York city teetered on the abyss of bankruptcy, Governor Hugh Carey realized that he ought to issue a clarion call for courage. He did not refer to moral absolutes, or to economic irrefutables, or to the history of our republic. Instead he summoned up images to which most of the population would respond: 'New York is a comeback city. It's the place where Roy Campanella made a comeback, where Jack Dempsey made a comeback, where the "Boys of Summer"—the Brooklyn Dodgers —made a comeback. We'll be here.'

• When Bill Walton spoke out against certain aspects of life in America, and especially against the FBI, the owners of the Portland Trail Blazers felt it incumbent to apologize to the public, on the presumed grounds that sports and patriotism are so interlinked that professional athletes were obligated to represent traditional values.

• On Monday night, September 17, 1973, during half-time ceremonics at the game between the Green Bay Packers and the New York Jets, Melvin Laird, then Secretary of Defense, appeared on the field to conduct ceremonies during which ninety young men volunteered to join the navy and were sworn in for active duty. This was loudly approved by the spectators as sports' answer to the peaceniks.

• When the big-league baseball headquarters put out a handsome four-color thirty-two-page brochure extolling baseball as the heart of American sports, they said this about one player:

> To George Scott, who once picked cotton for $1.75 per 100 pounds, baseball means a gold-plated Cadillac, $250 suits, a $175,000 home, a World Series ring . . . and *more*. 'I achieved my life's ambition. When I was a kid I wanted to be like Willie Mays or Mickey Mantle. Both were $100,000 players, and now so am I. That's why I've got a lot to be thankful for. When the National Anthem is played, I have my hand over my heart and thank the good Lord, who blessed me with a healthy body and a talent for working hard.

• At one point in 1975 the Senate was considering seven different bills on sports; the House, thirty-four bills; and the Senate found time to consider Resolution 144, which called upon the International Olympic Committee to restore posthumously the gold medals it had taken from Jim Thorpe and to declare him winner of various events back in 1912.

• Many big-time schools designate one coach or faculty member to protect the young athlete from the law. This ombudsman fixes traffic tickets, keeps his charges out of police courts, silences girls who have 'gotten into trouble,' and manipulates social agencies lest they annoy the athletes on the eve of a big game. Not surprisingly, several of our most famous universities have found themselves involved in ugly scandals when whole segments of a team have engaged in gang-rape, a jovial collegiate version of *jus primae noctis* in which the football hero expects to be accorded seignorial rights while the local sheriff stands guard.

There was a calculated move in the Nixon administration to align sports and politics in such a way that nationalism became the end product. The telephone calls to victorious teams, the granting of plaques symbolizing national championships arbitrarily decided, the prominence of coaches and ex-coaches in the entourage, the excessive entertainment of sports figures and the dabbling in quarterback decisions prior to big games made many observers uneasy, and I for one was not surprised when Watergate revelations uncovered the sports philosophy that underlay much of the thinking in that White House.

When James McCord gave signs of following his own inclinations rather than participating in a cover-up, he was told: 'The President's ability to govern is at stake. The government may fail. Everybody else is on the track but you. You are not following the game plan.'

When Herbert L. Porter was asked why, when he had interior doubts about hiring unsavory characters to perform dirty tricks, he still went ahead and hired them, he explained: 'Because of the fear of group pressure that would ensue, of not being a team player.'

When anyone let it be known that he was going to stonewall it, and refuse to cooperate with the grand jury, he was said to 'tough it out,' a football phrase. The code name for mining the North Vietnamese harbors was 'Operation Linebacker.' Nixon's own code name during the attack on Cambodia was 'The Quarterback.' And when John Mitchell, formerly the chief legal officer of the nation, was consulted on a matter involving a real test of conscience, he answered with a phrase right out of coaching: 'When the going gets tough, the tough get going.'

As someone said at the time, 'What the White House needs is less Vince Lombardi and more Abraham Lincoln.' Dave Meggyesy had written, long before Watergate:

> A militaristic aura surrounds football. Not only in obvious things like football stars visiting troops in Vietnam, but in the language of the game—'throwing

a bomb,' 'being a field general,' etc., and the players' obligation to duty. The game has been wrapped in red, white and blue. It is no accident that some of the most maudlin and dangerous pre-game patriotism we see in this country appears in football stadiums. Nor is it an accident that the most repressive political regime in the history of this country is ruled by a football freak, R. M. Nixon.

I am disturbed by any effort to identify sports with patriotism: Olympics, World Cup, Davis Cup, European rugby. This is an improper alliance, two good things melded together to form one of doubtful merit. If we continue down this dubious path, sensible people are going to turn away from the presumptuous alliance and our national sense of patriotism will suffer. A young man with glasses who prefers medical research can be just as representative of his nation as one who plays football, and we had better remember that.

I first became suspicious of the popular alliance between sports and patriotism during World War II. Before enlisting, I had heard a good deal of hoop-la about our sports heroes who had joined Commander Tom Hamilton's physical-fitness program in the navy. Throbbing stories were written about these heroic young men and I expected to find them storming the beaches. Where I found them was at land stations here at home, conducting one-two-three gymnastic exercises, and never in the destroyers or on the beaches. They were at Dartmouth and at Patuxent River and Great Lakes, and later at the posh headquarters in Honolulu and Guam. If I retain an admiration for Ted Williams it's because he was out there . . . twice. If I have betrayed a fondness for Bear Bryant, it is in part because he served in the navy, spotting patrol planes.

In the 1936 Olympics, Adolf Hitler became the first to exploit sports as an arm of nationalism. In the 1968 Olympics, East Germany was caught heating the blades of its bobsleds with blowtorches, 'for the greater glory of the state.' In the 1972 games, Arab nationalists gunned down Israeli athletes in order to prove a political point. The world was outraged. Sober critics began to warn that if this unbridled nationalism were to continue, the Olympics would have to be halted.

In all Olympics the scoring of events like figure skating and high diving became so ridden with national animosities as to make honest competition impossible. I remember being in Finland on that Sunday in 1972 when two Finnish long-distance runners scored outstanding victories, and I know with what wild delight the little nation cheered its successors to Paavo Nurmi and Ville Ritola. That was legitimate national pride. That afternoon some Finnish sportsmen and I sat together watching the telecasts from Munich, witnessing the appalling manner in which partisan officials stole the basketball championship from the United States. For some years I had been telling my friends, 'It'll be a healthy day when some other country knocks us off in basketball. And I expect to see it happen soon.' Normally I would have applauded a Russian victory, just as I thought it salutary when the Russian ice-hockey team gave the smug Canadians such a drubbing in the first games of their match.

But to have a game stolen, and so blatantly, and against the judgment of the responsible officials on the floor, was outrageous, and I said so. 'Sure it was a steal,' the Finns chided, 'but what can you do about it?' At the time, nothing. But later that year when the people of Colorado had to vote on whether to host the 1976 winter Olympics, I happened to be working in that state, and numerous voters, knowing my interest in sports, asked my opinion, I always reminded them of the abominable nationalism of the Munich games, and I asked the rhetorical question, 'Do you want to sponsor such nonsense here in Colorado?' The plebiscite was 358,906 for the Olympics, 537,440 against, and the games were thrown out of the United States, as they should have been. The Olympic Committee can countenance misbehavior like the basketball game if it wishes, but it cannot then come to the persons outraged and seek their approval.

I would be in error if I did not point out the constructive aspects of sports nationalism. The rejuvenation of East German spirit, after the bleakest kind of communist oppression, started with a renaissance in sports and peaked in the 1972 Olympics, when the little nation won some twenty or thirty times the places to which it would be entitled on a per capita basis. Sports in Hungary have had the same beneficent effect.

A perceptive article by Janet Lever, 'Soccer as a Brazilian Way of Life,' in Gregory Stone's excellent *Games, Sport and Power,* explains that when the São Paolo soccer team wins over the weekend, production in the city's factories rises by 12.3 percent in the following week. But when the home team loses, industrial accidents rise by 15.5 percent. It is a matter of historic record that in 1966, when Great Britain won the World Cup in London in the most exciting competition so far conducted, with at least a dozen games in the masterpiece category, emigration from Britain to Australia and New Zealand dropped conspicuously, but when Britain lost, rather ignominiously in Mexico City in 1970, it rose. It was quite clear, in 1970, that a disastrous British soccer performance accounted in substantial measure for the loss of an election.

John Lindsay used the euphoria created by the Mets' surging World Series victory in 1969 as a major spur in his campaign for reelection, and Frank Rizzo did the same with the Flyers' hockey victories in 1975. I came upon a fascinating instance of sports nationalism when I visited Canada, whose major cities are stretched out along an east-west line just north of the American border. In the winter television viewers see Canadian hockey, played mainly in the United States, and basketball, played only there. In the summer Canadian viewers love the baseball games that appear on television, with the added excitement of having a major-league team of their own in Montreal. The problem came with football. Canada has its own version, with a bigger playing field, an extra man on each team and a more open style of play. The cities are divided into two rabidly competing leagues, an eastern with four teams, a western with five, and the struggle for the Grey Cup can be heroic.

But certain cities wanted to drop or diminish Canadian football and institute American, with Montreal joining the NFL, Toronto the WFL, and one of the western cities joining whichever league would have it. The money was available. The stadiums were ready. And certainly the population, nurtured on NFL games on television, was prepared to support the venture.

But the Canadian government, quite properly I believe, vetoed the proposal. As one official explained it to me:

> We have a hard time sustaining a sense of Canadian unity. Our cities are so far apart, strung like pearls on a chain, reaching east to west. Sports are one of our most powerful unifying forces, particularly Canadian football. It binds us together in a way that not even hockey can do, because the better teams are now in the United States, even though the players are all Canadians.
>
> But in football the pull is east and west. You ought to see a Grey Cup game! It even suppresses the animosity over the French and English languages. That's why we can't allow American-style football in Montreal and Toronto and Vancouver. Then the emotional pull would be north and south, out of Canada. And the Grey Cup would be nothing compared to the Super Bowl. American football would be destructive of Canadian unity.

It was during a Monday-night NFL half-time show that I first became aware that football games had become a heady mix of patriotism, sex, violence and religion. A bloody first half had barely ended when hordes of personnel flooded the field, carrying flags, and trumpets, and small cannon, and rifles, and Bibles. They were joined by eighty-six scantily clad girls in age groups ranging from fourteen years old to twenty-five. This was a combination of American values hard to beat, with marines and rabbis and priests adding sanction to the affair. It was difficult, at times, to tell whether I was in a strip-tease show, an armory, a cathedral or a ball park.

Anyone seeking the ultimate in such foolishness, plus a frank lampoon of our pretentiousness, ought to read the description of the half-time extravaganza produced at the imaginary Super Bowl game in Dan Jenkins' *Semi-Tough*. It requires four irreverent pages, 191–94, for the procession of fighter planes, marching units, long-stemmed American beauties and praying clergymen to pass.

Or perhaps you watched the half-time show at the Orange Bowl on January 1, 1975, when the pageantry set a new world's record for display and participants. Everything led up to this stirring climax:

> NARRATOR: America, the dream of a faithful few, who desired to bring into reality a nation of which they could be justly proud . . . where government by, for and of the people would be the ultimate goal. Steadfast these honorable forefathers stood . . . even laying down their lives for a cause they believed to be just . . . now the mantle has been passed to another generation . . . to those who believe that 'from sea to shining sea' America is the greatest country on earth.
>
> (On band crescendo *America, America, God shed His grace on thee,* giant flag begins to be unfurled. Flash bulbs ignited on cue.)
>
> And now to honor America, let's all join in the singing of our National Anthem.
>
> (Band strikes up. Audience participation. Dancers dance. Streamers open. Star umbrellas light on cue. All exit triumphantly.)

The dubious union of sports and religion ran into some heavy weather on Monday night, December 2, 1974, when the Miami Dolphins played host to the rampaging Cincinnati Bengals. Just prior to the game, a crucial one for both teams, Reverend Richard J. Bailar, of the local United Church of Christ, asked benediction on the night's proceedings. It could be called the prayer heard round the nation; trouble began with the fifth word:

> Creator God: Father and Mother of us all: We give you thanks for the joy and excitement occasioned by this game. We pray for the physical well-being of all the gladiators who run the gamut of gridiron battle tonight . . . but, knowing that the tigers are voracious beasts of prey, we ask You to be especially watchful over our gentle dolphins. Limit, if You will, the obfuscations of Cosell's acidulous tongue, so that he may describe this night truly and grammatically as it is . . . A great game, in a great city, played before Your grateful children, on whom we ask peace and shalom. Amen.

The last word of the invocation had barely echoed through the appreciative stadium when hell broke loose. The objections, so far as I was able to codify them later, were these: 1) The God of football could never be a Mother. He is a God of wrath and He strikes irreverent people like Reverend Bailar dead. 2) The fine American young men who play football, even those from Cincinnati, are not gladiators. 3) It was blasphemous to refer that way to the Bengals and Dolphins. 4) God has nothing to do with Howard Cosell, and to make fun of his, that is, Cosell's, grammar was ungenerous. 5) All the players and most of the spectators are Christians, and to use the word *shalom* was an insult to them. 6) But primarily, football is a sacrosanct matter, and so is religion, and to treat either in a jocular manner is impudent; to joke about both is sacrilegious and warrants the judgment: 'That son of a bitch ought to be shot.'

From reading the Miami newspapers—and remember that sportswriters are a major cog in this seamless welding of patriotism, sex, religion and violence—I got the impression that our total society had rejected Reverend Bailar's prayer. Certainly Reverend Archie Davis, of the local Presbyterian Church, had. Next day he fired off a letter to the *Miami Herald* which launched public discussion of the affair: 'I was on my way into the Orange Bowl on Monday night with headphone radio tuned in when the Invocation was made. I could not believe what I was hearing.' After severe criticism of the event, he concluded: 'I don't think he offended God, because I don't feel that God heard him.' In a private letter to me, Reverend Davis expanded his thesis:

> Theologically, let me say that I think he came to God in prayer in a flippant manner and not in a reverent manner, and I think that any time we approach God, that we ought to do it whether it is at a ball game, or in private, in a sense of aweness and reverence. The language of the prayer and the contents drew laughter from the crowd, after each sentence. To me, this is a mockery of prayer. Being a Christian minister, prayer should be based on Christology. We come through Christ who is our Advocate, and He pleads our cause before God the Father. He ended with A-men and not in Jesus' name, and in my opinion, the prayer did not make a dent in the mind of God.

I found it difficult to believe that Americans in general had failed to see in Reverend Bailar's prayer the exact balance between levity and faith that an invocation at a football game warranted, so I communicated with Bailar, and he sent me a detailed letter with these relevant sentences:

> When I say *deluge of requests* I have literal reference to the flood of written and phoned requests for copies. The news services had picked it up and evidently it was printed in every major paper in the country. The overwhelming response, about seventy-five to one, was of acceptance, praise, gratitude and 'right on.' Nothing in my twenty years of ministry has elicited the reaction of that forty-three-second invocation (extended another thirty-two seconds by applause, to the dismay of ABC's national timing), which is both humiliating and humbling, frustrating and gratifying. My picture and prayer reportedly are displayed in bars catering to sports folk; I am stopped in stores for my autograph. In short, I have momentarily become a minor celebrity. All of which says something about the sterility of religion and the idolatry of sports in America. Iconoclastically yours.

In the fall of 1973, of the twenty-six NFL teams, twenty-one held religious services prior to their games. I was permitted to attend four of these and they were moving experiences. Some athletes have protested the intrusion by the Fellowship of Christian Athletes as being divisive, since the members tend to look down on their infidel brethren, but if I were a cornerback on Sunday morning, going up against Joe Namath that afternoon, I am quite sure I would attend prayer, if only to stabilize my nerves. Televising such prayers, however, is using sports improperly to proselytize.

Numerous NFL teams carry their own chaplain with them, and so far as I know, always a Catholic, because, as one owner told me, 'they take sports more seriously,' and I see nothing wrong with this. Prior to the Super Bowl in 1975 the Pittsburgh Steelers gained a lot of amiable publicity when their good-luck priest, flown over from Ireland, announced that this might be his last big game. He had brought the Steelers victory in many crucial games over the years, but now, he said, 'I've prayed out my option.'

I think we have gone about as far as proper in interlocking sports and religion. (Why is it that only football teams carry chaplains? Is someone up there indifferent to basketball? Or has football become so violent that players might need last rites at any moment?) I can foresee people cynically turning away from religion if it is abused. Football is a game; it need not be so grim an occupation that one needs shriving before the whistle blows.

If sports must be kept clear of flamboyant patriotism and exhibitionistic religion, what legitimate relationship might they have with government in general? I propose to look briefly at seven situations which appear to require government action of some kind, and then to give an opinion as to whether intervention would be warranted: 1) the extra-legal existence of sport; 2) laws which have already been proposed; 3) the brawl over the Olympics; 4) gambling; 5) the television blackout; 6) excessive use of drugs by athletes; 7) a curious, little-known problem relating to our three military academies.

For an extended period in our national history, baseball was the major professional sport, and to many the only one, so an inspection of how it built a position of special privilege within ordinary public law will lay the groundwork for understanding how all professional sports rely on government intervention and protection.

On July 2, 1890, under pressure from President Grover Cleveland, and in response to the formation of the Standard Oil Trust back in 1879 and its monolithic impact on society, Congress passed the Sherman Antitrust Law, which declared in the clearest words possible that it outlawed henceforth:

> Every contract, combination in the form of trust or otherwise, or conspiracy in restraint of trade or commerce among the several states or with foreign nations.

If there ever was a law directed specifically at baseball, this was it, for the big leagues were a combination; they were in a conspiracy to keep players' salaries low; they were in restraint of trade, for the team in Cincinnati could not hire away a player on the team in New York; and since the three major leagues then operating comprised twenty-four teams located in eight different states, they were obviously engaged in interstate commerce.

But in the United States system of government, no one knows what a law means, no matter how clearly written, until the courts confirm. So as soon as the Sherman Antitrust Law was passed, the courts began to adjudicate what it meant. In 1895 the Supreme Court determined that the word *every* included labor unions, and in 1897 it decreed that railways were included too. Many felt that within a few years it would have to decree that the baseball owners were clearly in restraint of trade for these reasons: 1) they operated as a cartel; 2) they determined which cities could join the cartel; 3) they operated illegally in depressing player salaries; 4) they prevented a player from moving from one team to another in search of maximum salary.

But in 1922 the Supreme Court handed down a landmark decision, *Federal Baseball Club of Baltimore* v. *National League,* in which for sentimental, historical and business reasons it decided to exempt baseball from regulation under the Sherman Antitrust Law. The unanimous decision was written by that unassailable champion of logic and decency Oliver Wendell Holmes, and dealt with only one small point: Did baseball engage in interstate commerce?

> The clubs comprising the Leagues are in different cities, and, for the most part, in different states. Of course, the scheme requires constantly repeated traveling on the part of the clubs, which is provided for, controlled and disciplined by the organizations, and this, it is said, means commerce among the states. [Holmes then denied that it was interstate commerce.] The business is giving exhibitions of baseball, which are purely state affairs. It is true that competitions must be arranged between clubs from different cities and states. But the fact that, in order to give exhibitions the Leagues must induce free persons to cross state lines is not enough to change the character of the business. The transport is a mere incident, not the essence of the thing. Personal effort, not related to production, is not commerce . . . A firm of lawyers sending out a member to argue a case does not engage in such commerce because the lawyer goes to another state. [And then Holmes added one of the most callous judgments in constitutional law; because baseball was not engaged in interstate commerce, the owners were permitted to continue doing just about anything they pleased. The inherent injustice of the conditions under which the players worked was no concern of the court.] The restrictions by contract, and other conduct charged against the defendants, were not an interference with commerce between the states.

It was obvious then, and it would remain obvious for half a century, that Holmes had written a bad decision, one reflecting no credit on him or the Court. His apologists say, 'That day the great jurist was nodding,' but the fact is that the nation's supreme tribunal had given sanction to a kind of peonage in which young ballplayers, once signed by a team, became that team's property for the duration of their playing lives, unless their owners decided arbitrarily to trade them away. What was worse, the player in this servitude was obligated by law to play for whatever salary the owner elected to give him. A famous cartoon of the time showed Justice Holmes raising a commodious umbrella over a group of smug and gangsterish owners, giving them legal protection to engage in 'interstate business, slavery, blacklisting, restraint of trade, denying freedom of contracts and conspiracy.' I have never thought the cartoon an exaggeration.

In 1953 *Toolson* v. *New York Yankees* gave a different Supreme Court an opportunity to overthrow Holmes' error in *Federal Baseball,* but the new Court handed down a bewildering decision with seven major points: 1) professional baseball is a business engaged in interstate commerce; 2) it is exempt from normal federal law, but this is an anomaly; 3) the precedent case, *Federal Baseball,* is in error and should be corrected; 4) but it is best if this court stand by earlier decisions; 5) because baseball is unique and has unique privileges; 6) and it would be confusing if we reversed the earlier decision, even though it is wrong; 7) 'If evils exist as a result of *Federal Baseball,* they must be corrected by Congress and not the courts.'

But Congress refused to act. Owners, sentimental sportswriters on the big newspapers, an adoring public, plus the pleasant baseball memories of congressmen made the passage of any law disciplining baseball impossible. The sport went its way immune from ordinary legal supervision, but all other sports were specifically subjected to the law.

That was how things stood in 1972 when Curt Flood's case came on the docket, challenging baseball's extra-legal status. Many Americans found it difficult to agree with Flood's contention that he was being treated as a chattel when he was offered a salary of $100,000 by the Phillies and $110,000 by Washington, and Flood as well as other players lost much public support. But I kept thinking of the time I served on Guadalcanal under an army colonel who was a caricature of all deep-south plantation owners of the 1840s. He treated us white officers like dirt, and there wasn't a damned thing we could do about it, but at the same time he treated his black orderly to all sorts of perquisites—use of the colonel's jeep, extra booze, days off—if only the black would play the Stepin Fetchit role. Although he was well educated, he shuffled and mumbled and delighted visitors by calling his boss 'Mistah Colonel, suh.' Embittered by the treatment I was getting, I remonstrated with the orderly one day and said something like, 'You sure worked things out well for yourself,' and he replied, 'Having to do it this way, it's still slavery.'

When Justice Harry Blackmun began to read his decision in *Flood* v. *Kuhn* on June 19, 1972, the listener got ample warning in the first few moments that ballplayers were going to get it in the neck once more. Blackmun began by reciting the names of eighty-seven notable figures from baseball history, including even umpire Bill Klem, and a good percentage of these men had fought owners over unfair contracts. Then Blackmun said:

> And one recalls the appropriate reference to the 'World Serious,' attributed to Ring Lardner, Sr.; Ernest L. Thayer's 'Casey at the Bat'; the ring of 'Tinker to Evers to Chance'; and all the other happenings, habits and superstitions about and around baseball that made it the 'national pastime,' or, depending upon the point of view, 'the great American tragedy.'

That had to be one of the strangest paragraphs in legal history. What followed was equally so. He acknowledged that both *Federal Baseball* and *Toolson* presented difficulties, that baseball's special status was an aberration and an anomaly which ought to be corrected, and that something ought to be done, but he reverted to *Toolson* and concluded that if Congress had allowed Justice Holmes' original error to persist for fifty years, it was up to Congress to do something about it. 'If there is any inconsistency or illogic in all this, it is an inconsistency and illogic of long standing that is to be remedied by Congress and not by this Court.' Justices Burger, White, Stewart and Rehnquist concurred.

In dissent, Justice Douglas confessed that back in 1953 he had supported the *Toolson* finding but that he had 'lived to regret it and would now correct what I believe to be its fundamental error.' Chief Justice Burger, in a special concurrence, said simply, 'It is time the Congress acted to solve this problem.'

In the meantime football and basketball leagues had come into being, and each hoped that the cozy exemption from normal law which baseball enjoyed would be extended to them, but because they were newer forms of sports without the legendary aura of baseball the courts did not accord them the same privileges, and Congress refused to pass specific laws stating that they should be treated the same as baseball. This left a curious and frustrating inconsistency in the sports picture, which still exists.

Football was the first to grapple with it. As long as only one league existed, the NFL, its owners could *act* like baseball owners, even if they did not have the *legal* right to do so. They could determine which cities could have teams, and by means of a draft of players they could also decide what team a college star should be assigned to, in perpetuity, and for decades things worked well, for the owners.

But with the advent in 1960 of a second league, the AFL, backed by aggressive multimillionaires like Lamar Hunt, things began to fall apart. AFL owners were not bound by the gentlemen's rules of the NFL, and they could go into any college and bargain for the star players, escalating salaries overnight to astronomical dimensions. The most famous case was that of Joe Willie Namath, star quarterback for Bear Bryant at Alabama, who was signed by Sonny Werblin of the New York Jets for the announced salary of $450,000. Werblin is important in the story, because he had formerly been a theatrical agent and understood the publicity value of a huge salary, whether the actual details supported the newspaper stories or not.

At any rate, a salary war developed, and NFL owners complained that it was about to destroy the sport. So they went to Congress, and in 1966 gravel-voiced, silver-maned Everett Dirksen steamrollered special legislation which gave them roughly the same exemption from the law that baseball enjoyed. The NFL was free to absorb the AFL; a cartel could be established; college players would be assigned to the various teams in an orderly draft, and those fantastic salaries would be cut down to size. Once more the bargaining power of the athlete was destroyed by federal law, passed by Congress and approved by the courts.

Basketball provided the most interesting case. In 1971 a bill was proposed in Congress that would have given basketball the same exemption. However, it ran into two difficulties. It had no Everett Dirksen to run interference for it, and it faced vigorous and highly sophisticated opposition from some astute basketball players, who justly pointed out that it would favor a few owners while depriving many players of their right to bargain for a high salary between the two leagues.

I do not subscribe to what I am about to quote, but this view shows how far sports have come in a short time. A basketball player told me:

> To understand our case you must realize that basketball players are more intelligent than football players. We are fewer in number. We have a tighter player organization. And we had outstanding brains like Oscar Robertson and Kareem and especially Bill Bradley and Jerry Lucas. So when our basketball owners decided to merge their two leagues and lower salaries, we decided to cut them off at the pass. We went right down to Congress and testified against the bill and killed it. And that's why we earn those big salaries and the football players don't. They weren't minding the store. We were.

Hockey, being an international sport with its roots and its players in Canada, has not yet faced up to the problems just recited, and when it does, it is doubtful if the American Congress or the American courts will make the final decisions. On the other hand, one would expect comparable problems to arise and perhaps comparable stalemates.

Up to this point I have phrased my sentences as if I sided exclusively with the players. In law and logic I do; baseball and football players have received a rotten deal, with the connivance of Congress and the courts, and I do not see how any fair-minded man or woman could conclude otherwise. However, the management of so complex a social organism as a professional sports league involves much more than the mere satisfaction of the players. Balance, the maintenance of equal competition, the preservation of tradition and the adjustment to new opportunities like those presented by television, cable and pay TV all impose special responsibilities, and anyone with a sense of fair play will be hesitant to prescribe how the professional leagues ought to conduct their business.

Consider this case carefully. Starting around 1927 the American League began to dominate baseball, and with the cementing together of those remarkable Yankee teams, it became overpowering. In those years the league kowtowed to the Yankees shamefully, allowing them to steal players and dictate operating procedures. As a consequence, the Yankees won numerous pennants and a disgraceful number of 4–0 World Series.

But at a serious cost. The American League became stodgy, routine, unimaginative. It was the National League which brought in the great black superstars, the new stadiums, the night baseball, Astroturf, drum-tight pennant races, maximum attendance. By building the Yankees into a super-team, so that each home team could make a lot of money when the Yankees came to town, the owners condemned the American League to second-rate status, and they damn near destroyed it in the process. In other words, by being false to the very principles on which baseball had been given its exemptions—the maintenance of equal competition—they dissipated their advantages.

Roughly the same thing happened in football. In the days of Lombardi's ascendancy, his league, the NFL, was so far superior to the AFL that comparison was painful. After the 1967 Green Bay walk-away over Kansas City 35–10 in the first Super Bowl, Lombardi judiciously refused to compare the two leagues, but after his 1968 humiliation of Oakland, 33–14, he allowed himself to be goaded by sportswriters into admitting that he judged AFL football to be below par.

But at this moment of NFL ascendancy, the seeds of its decline were sprouting. It became complacent while the AFL, stung by Lombardi's honest evaluation, began initiating imaginative changes. It built better stadiums, attracted superior crowds, and within a few years its brand of football was visibly superior to that played in the NFL. It was then that teams like the New York Giants and the Philadelphia Eagles started their stumble into serious trouble.

The maintenance of honest competition is the essence of professional sports, and basketball is going to be in even worse trouble than it already is if it allows television to force the super-players into Los Angeles and New York in order to provide grist for the media mills. This is the Yankee syndrome revisited, and if basketball repeats the error that baseball committed, it will reap similar ugly consequences.

Justices Holmes and Blackmun were not talking idly when they spoke of the peculiar requirements of professional sports. Talented players must not be allowed to congregate on only the clubs of our biggest cities, those with the ability to pay the highest salaries. I would think that the Catfish Hunter case—in which the inept behavior of Charles Finley invited an arbitrator to declare Hunter a free agent, whereupon he threw himself into the marketplace, soliciting high bids—would terrify organized baseball. Presumed details of the Hunter settlement with the Yankees surfaced: 'One million bonus before signing anything, $200,000 in cash to pay his attorneys, $200,000 salary a year for five years, a ten-year retirement plan requiring $50,000 a year, $1,000,000 of life insurance on himself, and $50,000 insurance on his children.' This could be termed a fairly generous settlement, but I was assured by the owners of another American League team—in a smaller city—that they had offered Hunter $50,000 above whatever the Yankees might bid, but that some higher-up had deemed it in the interest of baseball that he go to New York, where media coverage would be greater. Frankly, that's a hell of a way to run a sport.

The problem was aggravated in late 1975 when labor arbitrator Peter Seitz handed down a decision declaring pitchers Andy Messersmith of the Los Angeles Dodgers and Dave McNally of the Montreal Expos free agents, in the Catfish Hunter pattern. This adjudication, which might or might not be upheld by the courts, would mean that henceforth any baseball player could refuse to sign the contract his club offered him, play out his option for one year, declare himself a free agent, and then sell his services to the highest bidder. The financial chaos that many feared and which Congress should have prevented by sensible legislation seemed at hand.

Like most fans I have become disgusted with the legal shenanigans in basketball: the Billy Cunningham contract-jumping case involving Philadelphia and Carolina; the Spencer Haywood contract-jumping case involving Denver and Seattle; the Jim McDaniels league-jumping case involving Carolina and Seattle; the George McGinnis case involving team-switching practically everybody. Each community has its own horror story of a basketball player who proved an ingrate and scurried to court to find legal justification for his cupidity. Basketball, and its players, should wake up to the fact that it is repelling fans by such misbehavior; much of the financial trouble that has overtaken the sport in recent years has occurred because fans have become sickened by the unconscionable battle for the buck and the constant recourse to the courts to justify the breaking of contracts. The mess proves that Justice Holmes and Senator Dirksen were correct when they sponsored special interpretations of the law to cover the requirements of professional sports, and a similar law had better be passed quickly to salvage basketball.

The solution is twofold. Obviously, all professional sports should be under one legal umbrella, with no advantage to baseball and no disadvantage to ice hockey. This umbrella should be structured by Congress with the affirmation of the Supreme Court. It should prevent the accumulation of all the best players by one or two teams, and I believe this can be accomplished best by relying not on the common sense of the owners, for they are deficient in this commodity, but on some kind of reasonable reserve clause protecting the owners, some kind of draft, with the lowest-standing team choosing first, and some kind of mechanism for adjudicating salary disputes.

It is the last item that is difficult. I have high regard for the new system devised by baseball. If Owner O and Player P reach an impasse in a salary dispute, binding arbitration becomes obligatory. By February 1 Owner O writes down on a piece of paper the highest salary he is prepared to pay. Player P writes down on his piece of paper the salary he thinks he is entitled to. The arbitrator, chosen from a panel of fifteen experts from outside of baseball, studies the conflicting demands, holds brief hearings between February 10 and February 20, and within three days thereafter must choose one figure or the other. He does not average the two figures, trying to find a compromise representing an approximation of justice, because to do so would be to invite the owner to submit a very low figure and the player a very high one. He must choose one figure or the other. This is a real rule of reason, because if the owner submits a ridiculously low figure, and the player a reasonable one, the arbitrator will surely back the player, and vice versa. So far the rule has worked well and has been widely accepted.

But many believe that the tested American, and Western European, way to settle salary questions is by strike, as the football players tried unsuccessfully to do in the fall of 1974 and the baseball players successfully did in the spring of 1972. Strikes are messy, they are frustrating, and they rarely lead to hard-and-fast solutions, but they are an ultimate recourse when the laborer feels that he has been aggrieved, and no better substitute has been found.

While the baseball strike was under way some ridiculous charges were made that this would ruin baseball. Ruly Carpenter of the Phillies predicted, 'This has taken all the fun out of the game. It'll never be the same again.' I deplored the decision to play a truncated season in which not all the teams would play the same number of games: San Diego, 153; San

Francisco, 155; Milwaukee, 156. 'It'll throw all the statistics haywire,' I complained, nodding soberly when one sportswriter warned that the National League West could end with a team standing of this order:

Team	Won	Lost	Percent
Houston	89	64	.582
Los Angeles	90	65	.581
Cincinnati	89	65	.578

How would you like to defend that one? Well, the 1972 season produced several excellent pennant races, in which mathematical monstrosities did not decide the outcome, and a cliff-hanging World Series in which the Oakland A's defeated Johnny Bench and the Cincinnati Reds in seven games. In retrospect, the great baseball strike did almost no damage except to owners who had lost the ticket sales from a few games.

The football strike of 1974 was uglier and had a curious psychological fallout. I spent the climax of the strike at an NFL training camp from which the established veterans were absent, and it became painfully obvious that the coaches, with no veterans to handle, were forced to spend so much time with the rookies that they were beginning to discover talents in the new men which would have gone undiscovered in a normal camp, when any coach could spend only a few desultory minutes a day with the rookies.

It was quite clear that the prolonged strike was having no negative effect on the stars, who would easily reclaim their old positions, but it was having a devastating effect on the older marginal player who was apt to be superseded by some recruit whom the coaches had accidentally discovered but who would normally have gone unnoticed. I was reminded once more of how brief and cruel the life of the journeyman professional can be.

Sports exist in an extra-legal shadowland, and I believe our government should take steps to clarify the ambiguities. But does this mean that the government should establish an administrative agency which would engineer a comprehensive set of laws through Congress and then apply them evenly to all sports?

This is a knotty question, and there is no better way to comprehend what it involves than to study bit by bit the extraordinary bill relating to professional sports which was introduced in the Senate on March 30, 1972, by Marlow Cook, of Kentucky, who entitled it *The Federal Sports Act of 1972.* In the moving speech with which he presented his bill to the Senate, Cook said:

> Until recently the world of sports was always different, always sacred. However, with the recent snowball of controversy in the sports world, the time has

obviously arrived for a new perspective. The sports world has been beset by a series of easily identifiable problems, all of which have resulted from the mass commericalization of sports. Until recently we have been reluctant to admit that sports are a business, as well as a national recreational form.

Few Americans have escaped the attraction of the sports world. Its drama, heroics and excitement involve over one-half of the American people every year. Indeed, it has been said that a sports event is a microcosm of life. Each participant begins his quest on an equal basis, each meets many obstacles along the way, and each finally experiences success or failure. The only difference is that the world of sports provides another chance of success, another hope of victory.

With that preamble, Cook unrolled his proposed law, which would provide these measures:

1. A Federal Sports Commission consisting of three salaried members, appointed by the President, with advice and consent of the Senate, serving staggered terms of five years, no more than two to be from the same political party.

2. A Sports Advisory Council of eight members—two owners, two athletes, two league representatives and two recognized leaders in the world of sports, including writers and broadcasters—to be paid $100 a day while working, plus travel and per diem.

3. The Commission, as advised by the Council, would have summary powers to promulgate rules, without specific adoption by Congress or prior approval of the court, relating to the granting of franchises to cities, the supervision of franchise sales, television coverage of sports, the legal form for all player contracts, and the orderly movement of school and college players into professional ranks.

4. Considerable powers for the enforcement of the rules promulgated under the preceding section, with civil penalties not to exceed $50,000 for those who do not comply and the right to invoke injunctions against them.

5. The right to collect relevant data plus the power of subpoena to get it.

This is a powerful proposal. That it did not become law does not mean that something like it will not be proposed in the near future, this time with a likely chance of adoption.

Does the sporting world need such governmental regulation? I think not. I have worked in Washington a good deal in recent years and am not overly impressed with the functioning of several of the commissions already established for the governance of industry, or aviation, or broadcasting. I concur wholly with James Quirk's conclusion at the end of his investigation of certain abuses in professional sports. Much of what he saw called for correction, and perhaps governmental intervention at the legislative or judicial level, but not to the extent that a federal czar was needed:

Certainly, the history of regulatory commissions is not one which instills overwhelming confidence in such a device as a protector of the interests of the general public. Businessmen involved in the day-to-day decisions of running their firms are in a much better position to make judgments than the bureaucrat. Furthermore, regulatory commissions have the unhappy history of often developing into more effective cartel organizations than could have been created by the businesses themselves. Hence, the suggestion to correct some of the worst abuses of professional sports by appointing a federal sports czar is not appealing.

There is one area in amateur sports in which governmental intrusion may be inescapable and even desirable. That is the feud which prevents the United States from sending to the Olympics, or other international competitions, our best teams. To comprehend the majestic silliness which thwarts us, the reader must be able to decipher four sets of initials: IOC, AAU, USOC and NCAA. And to do this, some appreciation of history is required.

In 1889 the government of France became aware that Frenchmen were lagging behind Germans and Czechs, then a part of Austria, in physical well-being. It appointed an amateur, Baron Pierre de Coubertin, to study the matter, and belatedly in 1893 he proposed a plan guaranteed to catch the imagination of young people. The Olympic Games, which had flourished in Greece from 776 B.C. until A.D. 394, when Roman corruption made them noisome, would be revived.

Baron de Coubertin and his counselors from various nations instituted what would become the International Olympic Committee (IOC), and early in its existence it stipulated that in each nation which wanted to participate in the Olympics, the selection of the participants and the organization of the supporting effort must rest in the hands of one committee independent of government. This prudent rule, so easy to state and so difficult to enforce, had as its objective the prevention of nationalism. A group of French athletes would be invited to participate as individuals, not as a team representing France.

Who in the United States should be accredited to the IOC as our legal, non-governmental committee? In 1888 a group of amateur sportsmen, increasingly concerned about the intrusions of an unbridled professionalism, had organized themselves into the Amateur Athletic Union (AAU) and had gradually assumed control over the conduct of some sixteen or seventeen individual sports as different as basketball and bobsledding. Almost inevitably it became the American authority for the first Olympic Games held in Greece in 1896 and has never relinquished that authority. It is the only committee recognized by the IOC, and without its approval there could be no American participation in the Olympics.

This requirement of 'freedom from governmental control' can produce Alice-in-Wonderland consequences. I recently met with the Olympic committee in a communist dictatorship in which the ruling cadre controls everything, even the weight of a loaf of bread. But the committee assured me that 'we are completely free of any governmental domination,' and they showed me a paper to prove it. The dictator had proclaimed, 'You are free of governmental domination,' and IOC must accept this affirmation. On the other hand, if the United States Congress seeks to bring order into our Olympic mess, it has to be careful, because we operate our government openly, and the communist members of IOC could well decide that our congressional action constituted governmental interference and kick us out of Olympic competition.

The IOC concerns itself only with the Olympics, and thus operates only once every four years. But each individual sport has its own international federation, and these have acquired considerable power in determining how sports shall be conducted. For example, in track and field, control rests with the International Amateur Athletic Federation, and any American organization seeking to participate internationally in track and field had better keep in its good graces. I shall not be discussing these individual federations further, but they are powerful.

If the chain of command between the IOC and the AAU had remained uncomplicated, American participation in the Olympics would probably have remained fairly stable. But two intrusions of a major nature occurred, and the Olympic picture was to become hopelessly muddled. In 1950, with the best intentions in the world, Congress entered the picture, creating by law the United States Olympic Committee (USOC), which proceeded to identify those American organizations entitled to accredit athletes. Ten of the organizations were already within the AAU, and the few remaining others were scattered among minor organizations. So day-to-day Olympic decisions still rested with the AAU, and USOC was nothing but a kind of athletic holding company.

To pause for a moment, if the arrangement I have outlined so far had obtained, the problem of the young man or woman who wanted to participate in the next Olympics would be simple, whether he was in college, or had graduated, or had never attended any school. He or she merely had to affiliate with some club like the Des Moines YWCA or the New York Athletic Club, which had membership in the AAU, and win meets sponsored by such groups, have his papers forwarded to the USOC, which would routinely forward them to IOC in Lausanne, and in due course the athlete would receive certification of his eligibility. USOC was no bar to orderly Olympic procedures.

But now the second intrusion appears, and it will become totally bewildering and sometimes quite frustrating. Who produces and trains most of our Olympic-quality athletes? Our colleges and universities. Who provides the scholarships, the skilled coaches, the competitive meets and the stadiums in which they are held? The colleges and universities. Who has the prime interest in a junior who would like to compete in the Olympics but who also has another year of eligibility on his scholarship? You know who.

In 1905, a long seventeen years after the organization of the AAU, President Theodore Roosevelt ordered representatives from thirteen schools to the White House to face up to the mounting tragedy of college football which, as we saw earlier, was killing batches of our best young men each fall. The university people not only solved that ugly problem—by outlawing the flying wedge and legalizing the forward pass—but under the leadership of Chancellor MacCracken of New York University, went on to form a permanent intercollegiate organization for the governance of all their games, the National Collegiate Athletic Association (NCAA). Quickly it became the governing body for intercollegiate sports, laying down rules, supervising eligibility, stating who can offer scholarships to whom, and supervising the collection and distribution of receipts.

And quickly the difference between the AAU and the NCAA became clear. The former was composed of well-intentioned and often bumbling gentlemen amateurs who preferred running amateur sport like an old-fashioned club, with the added privilege of going abroad to the Olympics every four years and wearing blazers. The NCAA, on the other hand, was composed of tough-minded and socially reactionary directors of athletics at universities, coaches and well-disciplined faculty representatives, all on salary, whose primary business was to see that collegiate athletics showed a profit. Conflict between the two groups was inescapable.

Briefly, the problem is this. NCAA members spend great amounts of time and money discovering, nurturing and coaching track and field talent, but when the Olympic year rolls around, they must relinquish control over their athletes and watch a group of amateurs bungle the job of administering the United States team at the games. In 1972 at Munich, those in authority couldn't even get the American sprinters into the starting blocks on time, couldn't even fill in reports that one of their swimmers was taking doctor-prescribed medication for asthma.

Patriotism demanded that some kind of modus vivendi be worked out, and various truce proposals succeeded, but only temporarily. If the Los Angeles YMCA wanted to hold a meet with the YWCA, that would be a closed meet, since it fell under only one jurisdiction, the AAU. And if in the same city, on the same day, UCLA wanted to hold a meet with USC, that also would be closed, but it would be conducted by the NCAA. But what if the YMCA wanted to hold a meet with the UCLA? That would be an open meet, and a jurisdictional dispute would arise.

Also, suppose that various athletes in California are invited to visit Russia to compete with athletes living in the Kiev district. California men and women from both the YMCA and UCLA would be chosen for the team, but now real trouble ensues. The former are under the jurisdiction of the AAU, and it is affiliated with the international federation governing track and field, but the UCLA athletes owe their allegiance to the NCAA, and it is not directly affiliated with the international federation. Therefore, it must turn its athletes over to the AAU. Rather than submit to this humiliation, the NCAA will quite often refuse to release its athletes to the AAU. The American team is inferior. The Russians win a big victory, by default.

In this struggle I am one of the few outside observers who have always sided with the NCAA. They produce the athletes, pay for them, and coach them. Also, they are professionals who work at their jobs the year round. And on the playing field they usually make the right decisions. I much prefer them to either the AAU or the USOC. But when one watches the NCAA in its routine decisions and sees the colossal stupidity of some of them, continued loyalty becomes difficult.

• The NCAA in an effort to apply at least a minimum standard, adopts an eligibility rule of some ingenuity. A would-be athlete coming out of high school must prove by tests and records that he has reached an educational level which will enable him to score in his college classes 1.60 on a 4.0 scale. 'Means he can handle the hard letters of the alphabet up to M.' Ivy League schools, with stellar academic records like Harvard and Brown, feel that they should enforce a more demanding standard. 'In those factories you gotta know the whole damned alphabet.' But the NCAA threatens to discipline these colleges if they operate under the more stringent rule.

• A Jewish athlete at Yale wants to visit Israel to participate in the Maccabiah Games, but the NCAA has decided not to cooperate with the AAU in authorizing those specific games, so all Yale teams are threatened with reprisals.

• Walter Byers, the permanent secretary of the NCAA, considers the official *Newsletter* a proper place to extol Vice-President Spiro Agnew's attack on freedom of the press, and to espouse other right-wing manifestations.

• An impartial study of NCAA disciplinary penalties shows that it is primarily black athletes who feel the ax, rarely whites.

• The NCAA passes high-sounding rules, then fails to enforce them. In one hilarious case involving a University of Richmond athlete who had already graduated, the NCAA granted one extra year of eligibility, after tearful pressure from the university.

• The NCAA has been especially arrogant in refusing to allow its players to participate in international competitions.

• The NCAA customarily sides with the big schools, because that's where the money is, and pays inadequate or no attention to health benefits from sports, intramurals or women's rights in the sports world. It is not by accident that many women coaches are fighting the belated attempts of the NCAA to take over jurisdiction of women's sports.

On the plus side, the NCAA does make an attempt to try to bring order into the chaos of intercollegiate sport. It has the power to discipline Long Beach and to declare mighty Oklahoma ineligible for two years—thereby depriving it of fat television contracts—for having altered grades of a high school hotshot. And it does stand for many of the best aspects of American sports. It is by no means a deficit organization.

I have consulted most of the available material on the AAU-NCAA conflict, and three serious studies seem preeminent. Ron Barak, in the *Southern California Law Review* (1968), compiled an extensive summary of the matter under the title 'The Government of Amateur Athletics; The NCAA-AAU Dispute.' Its 113 detailed footnotes indicate the available research. Unusually readable is the 56-page mimeographed *History and Current Status of Amateur Sports Problems* issued by an unidentified source on September 19, 1974. But the most challenging is a paper by James V. Koch, professor of Economics at Illinois State University, entitled 'A Troubled Cartel: The NCAA,' *Law and Contemporary Problems* (1973).

In his article Professor Koch investigates the NCAA in the coldly analytical way he would use in studying any other cartel:

> Despite the claims of the NCAA that it is a champion of amateur athletics and physical fitness in colleges and universities, it is in fact a business cartel composed of university-firms which have varying desires to restrict competition and maximize profits in the area of intercollegiate athletics. Economic theory in the area of cartelization has proven to be a remarkably accurate predictor of the stresses and strains which have beset the NCAA.

Koch quotes approvingly Senator Cook's acerbic statement: 'The NCAA is a body primarily designed to protect and defend its member institutions from the professional sports world and to make sure that collegiate sports gets its share of the sports business pie.' In his discussion, Koch always refers to 'university-firms' in order to remind the reader of the essential business interests of the cartel: 'NCAA rules limit the number of student-athletes that a given university-firm can purchase, how long these student-athletes may be used, and the prices that may be paid for them.'

Applying abstract rules governing all cartels, Koch says that the NCAA shift from the 1.60 proof of ability to the 2.00 was a normal concession to the big-time university-firms. Declaring freshmen eligible to play varsity ball was the cartel's gesture to cutting production costs. Breaking the membership into three levels was an effort to keep all groups happy. And the limitation of the number of scholarships to be granted will probably have to be revoked, because it poses a hardship on the larger university-firms.

The cartel is troubled, says Koch, because most of the member firms are losing money, and he says that proper cartel management would dictate the following changes: 1) severe cutting of costs; 2) shortening the time expended in recruiting; 3) establishment of a draft system, whereby the top high school prospects were distributed equitably; 4) increasing revenue by renting stadiums to professional teams; 5) sponsoring championship play-offs; 6) and above all, reaching some kind of agreement with the AAU to forestall government intervention.

It has been evident for some time that there is no possibility of self-discipline in the brawl between the AAU and the NCAA. After the 1972 Olympics had ended in recrimination, the NCAA withdrew from USOC, and Samuel Barnes of the NCAA said, 'The troubles in Munich are only the latest example of the continuous, countless bunglings of the USOC. We have had enough.' Walter Byers added, 'The situation is worse now than in the sixties. The only external force that has clout to bring about reorganization is the agency that gave USOC its original charter, Congress.' Arthur Lentz, executive director of USOC, retaliated, 'Logically, they have a point, though it's a great disappointment that they would make their point this way. It pours more fuel on the fire.' Jack Kelly, president of the AAU, defended his organization by saying, 'Walter Byers would like to be czar of all amateur sports in this country and has been frustrated in his attempt.' Chuck Neinas, commissioner of the Big Eight and supporter of the NCAA, made the serious charge that whereas USOC had a surplus of $1,300,000 in the bank, it 'could not feed or house the athletes at the Olympic trials in Eugene, Oregon.' And a USOC official charged Byers with sabotaging the 1976 Olympics by taking his organization out of the committee and asking his 664 member schools not to solicit funds for the 1976 teams.

Obviously, something had to be done, but the results of previous attempts to unravel this snarl had given no cause for hope. In 1962 President Kennedy had asked General Douglas MacArthur to mediate, in hopes of putting together a respectable American team for the 1964 Olympics, and a sort of truce was patched up, only to dissolve quickly thereafter. In 1963 Kennedy handed the job to Bud Wilkinson, with results even less permanent. Later that year Kennedy invited the professional management firm of Arthur D. Little to try to bring some order out of the chaos, and it accomplished little except laying the philosophical groundwork for Senator John

Tunney's Omnibus Sports Bill of 1973. This in turn became the proposed Amateur Athletic Act of 1974, which we shall be inspecting in just a moment. A Senate committee chaired by Senator Warren Magnuson looked into the troubles after the 1964 Olympics, and in 1967 Vice-President Hubert Humphrey appointed a blue-ribbon panel of five distinguished citizens—Solicitor Archibald Cox, Congressman Ralph Metcalfe, Cleveland publisher Thomas Vail and Marine Commandant David Shoup, headed by labor negotiator Theodore Kheel—to knock heads. It failed.

It should not be surprising, therefore, to find that members of Congress, irritated by such intransigeance on the part of the sports community, began bringing in bills which would discipline all parties. The bills about to be cited are quite different from the omnibus bill proposed by Senator Marlow Cook, which dealt with all professional sports; these restrict themselves to the confusion in amateur ranks.

Three distinguished former athletes who were also members of Congress brought in bills: Congressman Bob Mathias of California; Congressman Jack Kemp of New York; Senator John Tunney of California. Congressman James O'Hara of Michigan also proposed a measure which would untangle America's Olympic problems.

But after preliminary skirmishing, major attention focused on Tunney's Amateur Athletic Act of 1973, S.2365, which incorporated ideas earlier proposed by Senators James Pearson, Marlow Cook, Mike Gravel and Warren Magnuson. (In 1974 it would become S.3500.) It merits the closest study by anyone concerned about American amateur sports.

If passed, it would create two major bodies, both funded by the same authorization of $1,100,000 a year. Originally the government would also create a permanent fund of up to $50,000,000, provided private sources contributed a like amount, the resulting $100,000,000 to be invested so that yearly interest would be available for constructive sports purposes.

An Amateur Sports Board of five members appointed by the President, with advice and consent of the Senate, unsalaried but entitled to $150 a day while working, plus a per diem. This board would revoke all existing charters and issue new ones, seeing to it that possession of the new charters did not congregate in any one group, as present charters do in the hands of the AAU, which controls eight and possibly nine. The board would also resolve differences that might arise regarding closed and open competitions. Of great importance, the board would wipe the USOC slate clean by appointing nine fresh members to control American participation in the Olympics.

A National Sports Development Foundation governed by sixteen trustees, serving without yearly salary but entitled to $100 a day when working, plus per diem, to be appointed by the board, the trustees to appoint a president, who will make the seventeenth member. The duties of the foundation would be to collect and supervise funds, and to spend 'not more than $1,000,000 each year' in the furtherance of physical fitness, health, safety and general sports activity.

It would not be illogical for one to be against the Cook Bill because it established a bureaucracy to control all sports, but to be in favor of the Tunney Bill because it merely sought to unravel complexities in amateur sports. Adverse critics have charged that once the board had cleaned up the Olympics mess it would, like all previous commissions, seek new fields to control, with the inevitable consequence that we would find ourselves with a sports czar, whether we wanted one or not. The Tunney bill passed in the Senate 62–29 but could not reach a vote in the House.

I am impressed by the fact that twice before, Congress has intervened in American sports, each time with dubious results. In 1950 it granted a charter to USOC, which seems to have encouraged that group in its obstinacy. In 1964 it granted a charter to Little League Baseball, which encouraged that organization to make some rather foolish decisions.

Furthermore, certain critics of the Tunney bill have pointed out that all the administrative benefits that might accrue from that bill could just as easily be attained by merely having Congress revise the USOC charter.

One aspect of the Tunney bill merits the closest investigation. Would dictation by the United States government as to how USOC must conduct its affairs make all our teams ineligible for Olympic competition, since it would run counter to the basic Olympic law that national organizing committees must remain free of governmental domination? Many ridicule this apprehension, but Lord Michael Killanin of Ireland, who has succeeded Avery Brundage as president of the IOC, has issued a sharply worded warning. Arthur Gander, president of the international federation governing gymnastics, has said, 'The AAU is the only body in the United States who can arrange international competition with affiliated federations. Further, the AAU is the only body who selects an Olympic or World Champion team. The AAU has the right to do it. How it does it, it doesn't bother us, you know.' And the Marquess of Exeter has replied in answer to a specific question on this matter, 'The AAU is the affiliated member . . . and it alone is recognized. Whereas governments naturally have power in their own countries to set up any body that they like, any body set up in opposition to our recognized member (the AAU) would not be acceptable, and any athletes not affiliated to our official body would be ineligible for international competition, including the Olympic Games.'

In view of the way Iron Curtain countries circumvent this rule, I find it intolerable to think that either Arthur Gander or the Marquess of Exeter should presume to dictate to us how we should conduct our Olympic procedures. In the Colorado case we have given one example of our readiness to resist the Jovian decisions of Olympic committees; we dismissed the winter games from our slopes. In trying to find the right solution to our internal Olympic structure, we should pass whatever legislation seems just, and if this falls foul of some technicality laid down by the IOC, we should be prepared to skip a round of Olympic competition and allow other nations to see for themselves what the games would be without our competitors, our support and our infusion of television income.

If that sounds ultra-nationalistic, it is also ultra-sensible and reflects the reality of the situation. I doubt that the IOC would endanger its operations merely to support the rather attractive gentlemen of our AAU. And if the communist countries want to use this device to kick us out of the Olympics, we should know about it now. On the other hand, Congress should do nothing that would needlessly abuse the AAU and its friends abroad; certainly it should not establish a government dictatorship over sports, not because the communist countries would object but because it would be wrong to do so.

My sympathies still remain with the NCAA, but I fear it has become so imbued with big-time professionalism, so concerned with television contracts, and right-wing politics, and nit-picking to protect the interests of its bigger members that it had better be restricted to that wholly reasonable and even necessary aspect of cartel management. It is not the body to represent us as our USOC. I therefore find myself supporting the desired end of the Tunney bill but do have apprehensions lest it become the first step in federal domination of yet another field. I fail to find one commission in Washington that truly represents the interests of the general public; they all become trade organizations dominated by the powerful companies they are supposed to regulate, and a sports commission would surrender the same way.

Two things remain to be said about government control of sports. Few of us realize that high school sports are ruled not by schools, nor by school boards, nor by state boards of education, but by self-appointed lay organizations called state athletic associations. They have been dictatorial, conservative and indifferent to girls' rights, but generally efficient. I have been amused by the attempts of certain state organizations to hold back the tides of change—fighting women's rights, for example—but I have also been impressed by the wisdom of others in adjusting to new demands and in avoiding court battles over inconsequential matters. They serve 'a useful purpose and I see no reason why they should be supplanted by governmental bodies. It is, however, likely that their more dictatorial decrees will be increasingly challenged in the courts, and from the four or five cases I have studied, it looks as if the courts are going to favor appellant students rather than the boards.

The other development is this willingness of the lesser federal courts to intervene in matters that used to be the sole province of the sportsman, and to hand down adjudications in areas where Congress has refused to act. Such decisions are summarized in the comprehensive article by Michael Jay Kaplan, 'Application of Federal Antitrust Laws to Professional Sports,' in *American Law Reports* (1974).

Typical of the cases is *Denver Rockets* v. *All-Pro Management,* which Federal Judge Warren J. Ferguson used as an excuse for unloading a bombshell on the pros and the NCAA. The case was unusually complicated in that it involved Spencer Haywood, whom we last saw as he jumped from Detroit University to the Denver Rockets for a reputed million plus. When this, like so many offers of its kind, turned out to be more than fifty percent hot air, Haywood jumped to the Seattle SuperSonics of the NBA, for some real money. But now a rule designed to protect the colleges intruded. No athlete could be signed to a professional contract until four years after his high school class had graduated. (This was enforced in order to protect schools that might have invested large sums in recruiting and training the young man.) In compliance with this rule, Haywood's contract with Seattle was declared illegal. But Judge Ferguson struck this down on the logical grounds that it constituted a restraint against the right of Haywood to earn a living.

Of equal importance were two other legal decisions. In 1974 Federal Judge William Sweigert tackled the Rozelle Rule. Quarterback Joe Kapp had played a full season without signing a contract, which made him a free agent. But the Rozelle Rule said that if another team signed Kapp, it would have to pay the original owner of his contract an indemnity, which meant that Kapp was not truly free. Judge Sweigert not only struck down the Rozelle Rule but also declared the draft system itself unconstitutional in that it assigns bargaining rights to a graduating college football player to one team alone.

In 1975 Federal Judge Earl R. Larson, in a separate case involving fifteen professional football players, found the Rozelle Rule unconstitutional on different grounds: that it prevented open-market bidding for players. Both cases have been appealed, and it may be some years before the Supreme Court hands down a final decision, but imagine the confusion in professional sports if the findings of the lower courts are sustained.

Normally I would not want courts to solve such delicate questions. Everyone would be much better off if Congress recognized that sports are a major American industry, faced up to its responsibilities, and passed sensible laws regulating them. But since there is ample evidence that Congress will refuse to do this, we should be grateful when the courts do intercede.

I even find myself supporting the decisions reached in *Toolson* and *Flood*. The ancient legal principle of *stare decisis* (let the earlier decision stand unless it is in grotesque error) is a prudent one for courts to follow. It encourages an orderly continuity in national life, and had I been serving as a Supreme Court Justice when these cases were being adjudicated, I would have held my nose and voted with the majority in both cases. But I believe I would have written an obiter dictum even stronger than Chief Justice Burger's. It is disgraceful for Congress to remain inactive when injustice and confusion are so prevalent in American sports, and something should be done promptly. And it can be done, well short of establishing yet another czar.

Whether government wishes it or not, it is deeply involved in betting on sports. The total amount bet in the United States is impossible to ascertain, because only a small proportion is done legally and with proper records, but experts have suggested that it may run as high as $150,000,000,000 a year, including illegal football and baseball pools.

We know that legal pari-mutuel betting on horses totaled $6,386,613,302 in one recent year, and that of this, half a billion dollars was turned back

'*Free Agent!*'

to the states in profits and an undisclosed amount in racing-related state and federal taxes. If all forms of betting were legalized, the take of the states could run as high as $12,000,000,000.

I was raised in a community which taught that betting was a sin, and I am still shocked when I pass a church and see that semi-legalized gambling is taking place inside. However, as an adult I have come into contact with a lot of gambling, and participate myself, gingerly. Four experiences explain my changed attitudes.

By accident I once spent a holiday with the professional gamblers of Hot Springs, Arkansas, and learned from them the mysteries of the crap table. They taught me how to place my bets behind the line, so that I was betting with the house rather than with the thrower. At one point on my big night I was betting against Joe E. Lewis as he threw a spectacular sequence of numbers without any sevens. I had every point covered with fifty dollars or more and pocketed nearly two thousand dollars before Joe's streak ended. When Joe finally threw a seven, I lost over $500, but heavy covering was part of the system, and I didn't care.

But what impressed me in the Arkansas visit was betting on football games. It was the Christmas-New Year's period and a red-hot gambler and I pooled our resources and bet on eleven different college and professional games. He was quite knowledgeable and I moderately so, but the point-spread system had been devised to neutralize just such information as we had, and we lost eleven straight bets. In the meantime a much-less-informed gambler sat with us, watching the games on television, and won nine out of eleven. In disgust we asked him what inside information he had, and he replied, 'You'll notice I never bet until kickoff. Then I always back the team that starts on the right-hand side of the television screen.'

My second indoctrination also involved football, and the point spread. Late in the season I had gone to a critical NFL football game in which both teams were vying for a divisional championship. I backed Team A with a ten-dollar bet, giving six points. As the game drew to a close Team A was winning, just as I had hoped, but by only three points, which meant that I was losing my bet. Team B had the ball and in desperation threw a bomb. My left cornerback intercepted and in my opinion had a pretty clear run for a touchdown, which would put Team A ahead by at least nine points and win my bet for me.

'Go! Go!' I screamed, and he was on his way. But as he crossed the fifty-yard line two opposing players vectored in on him. I'm pretty sure he could have jigged or stiff-armed them and made his touchdown, but with a three-point lead and less than a minute to play, he prudently fell to the ground and curled himself around the football rather than risk a fumble which might allow Team B to win. I could have shot him. He had thought more about winning a divisional title than about my point spread, and I still remember both him and that game with distaste. My team had won, but I hadn't and I was sore about it. There was something sadly awry about my reaction.

My third experience came in Spain, where the population went mad betting win-lose-draw on Spanish football. One weekend an all-star Spanish team, representing the nation, was scheduled to play in Germany, which meant that regular league play had to be suspended. In my ignorance I supposed the weekly betting would be suspended too, but my favorite waiter disabused me of that foolish idea.

'Interrupt betting? Are you crazy? This week the Spanish teams don't play, but the pool goes on as usual. What do we do? We bet on games in the Italian leagues.'

He showed me his ticket, fourteen games between teams I had never heard of. 'How do you study up on the games? If they're played over in Italy?'

'Study? Who studies? We just bet for the hell of it.'

But the betting experience to end all others occurred on a hurricane Saturday in London. The storms were so bad that nine or ten important games had to be canceled and, as bad luck would have it, some eight of them figured in the weekly pools, on which millions of pounds had already been bet. Again I supposed that the wagers for that week would be canceled, but not on your life. This time it was an editor who set me straight.

'They're meeting right now. In a closed room with no telephones and carefully guarded by police. It's what they say that matters.'

'Who are they?' I asked.

'Five men of impeccable reputation. All of them well founded in sporting lore.'

'What are they doing in a locked room?'

'They are predicting how the canceled games might have come out if they had been played.'

'You mean, they're making up scores?'

'Precisely. They can be trusted to give an honest judgment. Win-lose-draw. We do this so that betting will not be interrupted. If you listen to the radio tonight, you'll hear their scores broadcast with those of the games that were played.'

Faced with this kind of mania in the world, I felt it necessary to study the problem of betting more seriously than I had originally intended. From research at various tracks, bookie parlors and offices where informal pools flourish, I have reached several tentative conclusions.

Gambling is a normal human instinct and is probably irrepressible. Sportsmen insist that it produces no deleterious side effects; social workers claim that it does, in unpaid grocery bills, failure to visit dentists, family arguments of a violent nature, and the incursions of organized crime. It appears to be growing in volume in the United States and probably requires some kind of legal attention.

I have never worked in any large organization in which pool cards on football and baseball did not circulate. Insofar as the individual worker was concerned, they represented only a trivial investment, productive of much good conversation, but in the aggregate in a large building they involved considerable sums, and the energetic men who ran them apparently made a modest bundle. This kind of betting poses few problems.

Nor have I ever lived in a community where it was impossible to place a football or basketball bet by telephone. Our local papers carry the week's betting line. The bookie charges eleven dollars for a ten-dollar bet, and you choose your team, giving or taking the points agreed upon. If you bet ten dollars on each of six games, win three and lose three, you do not break even. You owe the bookie six dollars for the convenience of having been allowed to place your six bets. The amount of money so wagered must be tremendous, and it is all handled outside the law, except that the bookie is obligated to pay an income tax on his profits. This is one of the major aspects of gambling which warrant governmental attention.

Numbers gambling and the lotteries which attempt to replace it in some states do not involve sports, and I know little about them, except that I live in Pennsylvania, which has for some years operated a fumbling kind of lottery, and next to New Jersey, which comes up with a new gimmick every month, and just north of Delaware, which had a disastrous experience when it launched its lottery prematurely and without adequate professional counsel. If such adventures are required to save America fiscally, we are doomed.

I have done more than my share of betting on horses, with undramatic results. But I have attended meets with various devoted gamblers and have done my best to understand their systems. The only one to have compiled substantial winnings for me was that devised by an inveterate horse player who always bets on the first three horses listed and boxes them for the Daily Double and Trifecta. He keeps a history of his bets, and told me, 'You'd be surprised at how often they come in, betting the first three.' And I have been.

The most interesting wagering I have come upon is that conducted by the sports departments in large newspapers. A group of twenty office people will combine, list the names of two hundred prominent living men and women in all parts of the world—Lindbergh, De Gaulle, Adenauer, the King of Saudi Arabia, to name four winners—and then draw lots so that each player receives ten names. The players then contribute ten dollars each, to make a pool of two hundred dollars. Whenever one of the two hundred immortals dies, his owner collects the money. This is called the Ghoul Pool.

The government's problem is twofold: how to bring order into this informal exchange of money, and how to ensure that the government receives its proper share in taxes? At present some $100,000,000,000 probably circulates outside normal tax structures.

In pari-mutuel betting, taxation is simple. Using the figures cited earlier, state and local governments siphon off about 8.4 percent. Take the two-dollar bet to win at a New Jersey racetrack. From the total pool bet on all horses to win the computer takes out the prescribed 17 percent. The remaining total is divided among all the win tickets and shows $6.99 as the value of the winning two-dollar ticket. But the winner does not receive $6.99, for the breakage is at the twenty-cent interval, so that the holder receives only $6.80, meaning that the total taxation was something like 20 percent. And if a heavy favorite comes in and can pay only $2.19, the payoff is cut to $2.10, which represents a 4 percent deduction.

On gimmick bets the government's bite can be even heavier. At Bowie, Maryland, recently the Trifecta produced only one winner. He had bet three dollars and got back $68,881, which sounds adequate. But the total pool had been $82,202. And when the lucky winner appeared to collect his allowed $68,881 the IRS was there to subtract more than $30,000 of it. So of the $82,002 gambled on that race, government had siphoned off close to $50,000, or almost 60 percent.

State-run lotteries are worse. The standard takeout for the state is about 50 percent, which means that if citizens buy $500,000 worth of tickets, the state pays back as prizes only $250,000. But on the gimmick lotteries, the state's takeout can run as high as 100 percent, which means that if $1,000,000 worth of tickets is sold, the state awards a prize, but at the same time keeps all the money. How is that possible? By reason of a delightful device called the Millionaire's Lottery, in which the prize is a million, as promised. The catch is that the prize money is not handed out in one lump sum; it is doled out at the rate of $50,000 a year for a period of twenty years. Since the state can earn at least 7 percent on its money, and probably more, this means that on the million which it continues to own, it collects at least $70,000 a year in interest, and pays out only $50,000 to the 'millionaire.'

There are many financial reasons why the government might want to legalize gambling, and a federal commission is investigating the problem now, with intentions of submitting a report in the near future. If gambling is legalized, what would be the effect on professional sports?

To appreciate the basic dangers, one must go back to the bad old days of the Calcutta pool. I participated in one in Reno, Nevada, and saw its menace. On the eve of a golf tournament the big gamblers of the area would each contribute substantial amounts of money to a pool. The names of the sixty-odd golfers competing the next day would be drawn by lot, and then you became intensely interested in your player. (In one version of the Calcutta, gamblers bid for the player they wanted.) If he won the opening round, you won so much. If he survived the cut, so much more. If he led at the end of any day, another return. And if he won the tournament, you got the remaining bundle.

A Calcutta could lead to some very unpleasant situations. In the one I joined, after the draw had been made, heavy gamblers wanted to buy the likely winners, and pressure was exerted to make the men holding those names sell. If a golfer who ought to have won went into a sudden slump, as golfers will, there were charges of his having thrown the Calcutta for a secret payoff. And through the three days of play there was an ugly tension. I believe it was the golfers themselves who, fearing they might get machine-gunned, shortly thereafter outlawed the Calcutta. To reinstate it, or anything like it, would be regression.

The fault of the Calcutta was that it placed the gambler and the golfer in a one-on-one situation; in a very real sense the gambler 'owned' the golfer, and I can remember snarling under my breath as my man faded, 'You stinking bum! You're quitting on purpose.' For a measly ten dollars I was reviling a man I had never met.

The ability of a sport to resist corruption by gamblers is a matter not of tradition, but of numbers. Football has not so far suffered a major scandal, primarily because one team consists of twenty-six or more players, and to corrupt all of those who might be able to influence a score would be so complex a task that it could not be kept secret.

Boxing was the most susceptible, because only one man had to be suborned, and he could engineer his own defeat with such skill that even experts could scarcely detect it. Baseball had nine players on a team plus the noblest traditions in American sports, but as the Chicago Black Sox proved, the outcome of a series, if not a single game, could be manipulated by corrupting the pitcher, the major sluggers and a few key fielders. The Spanish soccer pool was easiest of all to police, because the bettor was backing fourteen teams of eleven players each, and it would be ridiculous to try to buy off the 154 opposing players.

Basketball, on the other hand, with its five players, each able to determine the drift of the game, was peculiarly vulnerable to the Calcutta evil. It was not by accident that the major scandals in collegiate sport focused on basketball,* and it is a tribute to the men running the NBA and the ABA that they have been able to keep their leagues free of visible corruption.

*I find it Kafkaesque that our courts should be so eager to protect the purity of illegal gambling on sports events, and to punish college players for having done nothing more than control point spreads, and at the same time to ignore the truly criminal acts that are directed against the youthful players.

There were rumors some years ago that games were being thrown, and after some study of the matter, I concluded that at least one had been, but officials took swift action, rebutted all charges and escaped a scandal.

The classic example of how numbers affect morality came when New York, eager to glean a few more dollars from harness racing, introduced the Superfecta, a gimmick race in which eight horses competed, with the bettor required to place the first four in their exact finishing order. When I first heard of this preposterous arrangement I doubted that anyone would be silly enough to be tempted by it, but so many did that the papers began to circulate stories of people who had made sensational killings—$50,000 for a three-dollar bet.

I had suspicions about the Superfecta from its beginning, and the huge payoffs agitated my doubts, but I failed to spot where the danger lay. I reasoned: 'With the exact positions of four horses required to win, I don't see how any gambler would be industrious enough, and careful enough, to fix them all.' What I had overlooked was something the gamblers had spotted almost immediately. An old hand at Vernon Downs explained it to me: 'Don't worry about the four winners. Just make sure who the four losers will be. Because if you can guarantee that four horses will be removed from the race, you can then box the other four. That is, you bet every possible combination of A,B,C,D, which can be accomplished with twenty-four tickets, for a total cost of only $72. In return you get an iron-clad assurance that you have the winners of that day's Superfecta. If no one else knows which four horses have been bought off, your lone ticket could be worth up to $128,000.'

So what the gamblers did was fix the race, not the four winners, but the four losers. Secure in their knowledge that E,F,G,H were fixed to lose—the four winners had to be A,B,C and D—they wheeled those four for $72 and started dragging down enormous profits. But human life is self-corrective. These clever gamblers who had thought of everything were so stupid that they always sent the same person to collect their huge winnings, and for this crucial job they chose an eye-stopping blonde that no man at the payoff window could forget. After she had appeared to collect six or seven times, it was an easy job for the detectives to nab her and her gang. (The legal resolution of this case was interesting. Everyone agreed that the fix had been engineered by the gamblers, and the court so found, but it was also decided that no drivers had been involved.)

It is for fear of such shenanigans that the administrators of professional sports advise against legalizing gambling. When they do so, they are ridiculed in the press, which points out that vast sums are already being bet without the evil consequences that men like Rozelle predict:

Suspicions would be created whenever something happened that determined the outcome of a game or even threatened the outcome. Instead of rooting for his home team to win, the fan's basic interest would be in winning his bet by a certain number of points sufficient to beat the spread. You could have a stadium with 80,000 fans vocally supporting the visiting team's rally and applauding the home team's misfortune.*

And then Rozelle cites evidence from European sports to bolster his argument that heavy legalized betting would be more dangerous to the integrity of games than the informal system we now have. He refers to Great Britain's decision in 1960 to legalize practically all types of sports betting:

Prior to 1960 there had been two major soccer scandals. Since 1960 there have been at least eight major teams and fifteen players involved. Ten of the players either confessed or were found guilty of bribery in court. Several have been fined and sentenced to jail terms by criminal courts.

He then recalls the dismal experiences of Italy (four players suspended), Germany (thirteen players suspended for life), Czechoslovakia (eighty convicted in court). In a letter he spells out the rules: 'Our football players are allowed to gamble legally at race tracks or Las Vegas casinos, but not on professional football. However, the extent to which they gamble, the type of persons they may gamble with and the places in which they gamble may be cause for this office to warn them to stop doing so under threat of suspension. No professional football player would be permitted to own a gambling casino.'

When Congress, in the late summer of 1973, galloped through the legislative process in order to terminate arbitrarily football's traditional blackout on television within fifty miles of a game in progress, it did so for a group of persuasive reasons.

Politically, the legislators had been receiving flack from their constituents in large cities who complained, with logic, 'The stadium is filled. We can't buy tickets. And they have the gall to say we can't look at it on television, either.'

Economically, the complainers had usually contributed tax dollars for the building of the stadium from which they were excluded. And since no more tickets could be sold, the owner of the team couldn't be losing money if he allowed the game to be televised.

Legally, the congressmen had a presumed right to dictate how television

*What Rozelle feared occurred at the conclusion of the 1976 Super Bowl. Pittsburgh defeated Dallas, 21–17, to win the championship, but when the final whistle blew, the winning Pittsburgh fans were desolate while the losing Dallas backers were joyous. Why? A last-gasp Dallas touchdown had prevented Pittsburgh from winning by the seven-point spread the gamblers required. So everyone who had bet on Pittsburgh lost money, even though their team had won.

should behave, because, unlike a newspaper, a television station was free to operate only because the government had granted it one of the relatively few channels. And for TV to deny local taxpayers access to a game which people fifty miles away could enjoy seemed indefensible.

Personally, many congressmen were irritated and offended when they could neither purchase tickets in the nation's capital nor see the game on TV, especially since the revitalized Redskins, under George Allen's leadership, were tearing up the league. I knew several congressmen in this period, and they were bitter about it.

Tactically, it was dangerous for professional sports, which had just yanked the baseball Senators out of Washington and placed them in Texas —disastrous decision—to do anything which might infuriate the legislators further, because sports enjoyed unusual legal exemptions, which Congress could rescind if it became embittered.

So, in a rush rarely seen on Capitol Hill, the Senate voted 76–6 to force the NFL to drop its blackout, and shortly thereafter the House voted 336–37 to do the same. There have been few governmental acts in the field of sports that were so wrong. Commissioner Rozelle was correct when he warned that televising a game free in the city where it is being played must in the long run prove destructive. People will not pay high prices to sit in weather-tormented stadiums to watch what they can see for nothing in the comfort of their homes. In time, football under this system must become a television spectacular, played before what might be termed a small studio audience, for the delectation of the video public.

I am not going to argue this point economically, even though the NFL is correct when it points out that selling all the tickets to the game is not the whole story. The fan who has bought the ticket, and paid for it, still depresses the economy if he stays home. He does not pay for parking his car, or for the scorecard, or for the booklet, and certainly not four or five dollars for food and beverages. If the average person spends six or seven dollars at the game, and if 10,000 stay away—a low figure for some games —the loss to the club and to the city, which would have collected taxes on the sales, can be substantial.

Before I state my serious objection to this congressional action, let's look briefly at its effect. At the conclusion of the 1973 fall season, during which the new law was first enforced, the Federal Communications Commission issued a triumphant press release intended to prove that Congress has been justified in passing the law:

> The anti-blackout law appears to have had minimal impact on twenty-six member teams of the NFL in its first season of operation. It is unlikely that

season ticket sales will be adversely affected by the law because there seems to be an excess demand for tickets. In fact, 1973 was the best season ever for the NFL, and early reports on ticket sales for the 1974 season indicate a strong demand for available tickets.

Impartial analysis of those early data supported this claim. But with the 1974 season things began to take the track some of us had foreseen. In fact, the grim truth had begun to unroll at the end of 1973. On Sunday, December 16, I sat in Shea Stadium in New York to watch the Jets play the Buffalo Bills, with Joe Namath in top form and with O.J. Simpson poised to become the first two-thousand-yard gainer in football history. It promised to be a good game, but because it was being telecast throughout New York, 12,260 ticket holders failed to show, and O.J. went over the two-thousand mark to a vast collection of empty seats.

A year later, on Sunday, December 15, 1974, when the Atlanta Falcons hosted the Green Bay Packers, a shocking total of 48,830 ticket-holding fans stayed home. A week earlier, on December 8, I attended the Baltimore Colts-Miami Dolphins game, an important affair, and I was told there were 25,820 vacant seats. A few weeks before, on November 5, a total of 81,000 subscribers stayed away from NFL games, and in perfect weather. At the conclusion of the 1974 season, a total of 492,611 ticket holders had stayed home. And at the beginning of the 1975 season, the teams had nine million dollars' worth of unsold tickets.

So Rozelle was right when he predicted that Congress could not foresee the consequences of its action when it unilaterally killed the blackout. Football had taken its first giant step toward becoming a studio game, like boxing and wrestling.

But my apprehension is of a much different kind. I believe it to be socially desirable for people to congregate in groups and to share common experiences. I believe it to be psychologically and politically dangerous for people to experience great and moving events by themselves, with no one else to react with. I believe it to be destructive of our community way of life for people not to meet together at public spectacles, games or theaters.

The decline and destruction of our inner city—and of our small towns —began when citizens no longer went out at night to the movies and afterwards to the ice cream parlor or restaurant. The vital movement that keeps a community alive after dark was lost, and the core of the city was abandoned, to hoodlums. Now if our great stadiums are going to be deserted, too, we shall have surrendered one more part of the city, and in the long run we shall all be immeasurably poorer. To keep a community alive requires the interaction of many forces, and to kill off any one of them is to invite the collapse of others. A city cannot be kept alive by having one million people, each in his own cubicle, watching a game.

But the overriding danger, much greater than that threatening the city, is the psychological. If we become a nation of inactive observers, each huddling in his own darkened room and never going out to mingle with other human beings, we run the serious risk of becoming neurotic and even self-destructive. Human beings are animals who require constant interaction with others of their kind. Kids need to play with other kids, to get their highly personal corners knocked off. Young girls need to associate with other young girls and boys to find out what adolescence is all about. Young scholars must argue with other young brains to discover their capacities and what ought to be believed. And adults must not hide themselves away from other adults, living narrow cooped-up lives. The great danger of television is not only that it diminishes intellect, but that its invitation to isolation threatens psychological stability.

On the other hand, there is something positively therapeutic in being part of a crowd sharing a common emotional experience. It is probably better for a couple to attend a theater and share the reactions of a large group of people assembled for a common purpose than for one withdrawn woman or man to watch a late movie on television. The first experience is civilizing; the second can be quite anti-social.

We need more mass experience, not less. We need more civilizing contact with our neighbors, not less. To convert any of our major sports into television specials lacking human reality would be a major step backward. For those reasons, the anti-blackout bill should be repealed. It was a political success, a psychological disaster.

There is one area in which the federal government should intervene: the use of drugs in sports. The evidence is overwhelming that teams on all levels have been either encouraging their players to hype themselves with drugs, or refusing to acknowledge that it is being done surreptitiously. Some years ago popping pills became an accepted way of life for the athlete: amphetamines for super-effort; pain depressants to nullify damage; sedatives to induce sleep; and what seemed most dangerous of all, the taking of large amounts of anabolic steroids to induce rapid weight gain.

The rumors which surrounded the NFL, for example, finally surfaced in 1970 when Houston Ridge, a former player for the San Diego Chargers, brought suit against his team for having encouraged him to take dangerous drugs in order to heighten his physical capacity. Professional sports have been stubbornly tardy in facing up to these aberrations, insisting in the face of damaging evidence that nothing was wrong. In 1975 one Roxie Ann Rice, aged nineteen, was caught while serving as scheduled courier delivering quotas of marijuana to NFL players throughout the nation. 'She was quite large, with an African-type turban on her head. She said she represented Shirley Temple Black's office in Washington and wanted photo passes for representatives of the Ghana government.' When arrested, Miss Rice said she also serviced the basketball teams of Pan American University and the St. Louis Spirits, and had plans for branching out into baseball, 'because it would be more fun because it was warm then.'

As one tough-minded horse player said when butazolidin was legalized for race horses, 'The problem with administering drugs to horses or athletes is not what the drugs will do if given, but what they will not do if not given. To be perfectly just, the bettor will have to be handed a list at the start of each football game, "Halversam has taken four pep pills this week, but Atkinson has taken none. However, Gregory, who plays next to Atkinson, has taken a snootful." '

My apprehension about the anabolic steroids is that while they certainly pile on the weight, changing a puny 209-pound guard into a 263-pound terror in one year, they probably do so at the risk of physiological and sexual alterations which cannot be reversed. That's too high a price for a contract which will probably run no more than three and a half years.

A special problem our government faces in sports is the sad decline of athletics in our military academies. In the old days Army and Navy were powers, always in contention for national honors and often the champions. Those were the exciting days when Ed Garbisch of Army drop-kicked four field goals to defeat Navy, 12–0, going on to marry the Chrysler heiress in what seemed the ultimate American romance. They were also the days of Doc Blanchard going inside for Army while Glenn Davis roared outside. That was when Army would go undefeated and even beat Notre Dame 59–9. In those days an Army-Navy game at the big stadium in Philadelphia would draw more than 100,000 spectators and millions more on radio.

Well, it's not like that any more. What with Vietnam conditioning the minds of young people against all military activities, and the general poor-mouthing of the military establishment, the academies have fallen on bad times in football: Army 0–10, Navy 4–7, Air Force 2–9. The last few Army-Navy games have been television disasters, and there has been serious talk that TV would drop them except for fear of congressional reprisal.

In fact, things have become so depressing that well-intentioned citizens are gravely discussing the practicality of passing federal laws to alter the picture. This is the problem: When a blue-chip high school football player is faced with the choice of where to go to college, he is naturally approached by people connected with the military academies—but what have they to offer him, compared with what the big-time powers can offer?

If he goes to Army he must attend real classes. He will not be handed a convertible or money under the table. He must live up to a rigorous code of deportment. Other students cannot take his exams for him. And at the end of his eligibility he cannot traipse off to the pros; he must proceed immediately to fulfill his five-year commitment to active duty in the armed services, while his friends who went to a standard university can draw down large salaries in the pros. Also, if he is a real tall basketball player, the kind coaches need, he can't get in the academies because of height limitations.

So the last decade has watched the steady decline of academy sport, and not only in football. Though Army regularly used to win nearly 80 percent of all its athletic contests, in recent years it has won only 56 percent, and in football over a three-year period, only 29 percent. Part of the problem is that Army schedules, like those of most universities, are made twelve and fourteen years in advance. That explains why a really inept Army team, coming off an 0–10 season faced a line-up of these powerhouses, most of which had played in bowl games the previous season: Penn State, Notre Dame, Tulane and Vanderbilt. The combined scores of those games: Other teams 138, Army 42. A deeply patriotic man, reviewing this situation, told me:

> It cannot be in the interest of our nation for us to allow our military academies to be held up to ridicule. It is bad for national morale and worse for the morale of our armed forces. Pitiful exhibitions like recent Army-Navy games proclaim to the world that our military establishment is sub-par. I think Congress should pass laws right away encouraging real athletes to enroll in the academies. If we have to lower standards a little for the athlete, do it. Above all, change that stupid rule which says an academy man must, immediately after graduation, go on active duty for five years. If the boy is good enough to land a job with the pros, encourage him to take it, then let him come back later to serve his five-year obligation, after his stint with the pros is over. That would help to entice the high school athlete back to West Point.

It seems strange that athletics, which has long been idolized for having produced military leaders, should now boycott the military because easy money is available elsewhere. And the agents through which this boycott is applied are those very high school and college coaches who have boasted, 'We are training the nation's leaders.' This is more serious than it might seem. If we enthrone sports as a national virtue, it is dangerous to force one of our major national symbols, our academies, to live under rules which make sports accomplishment impossible.

In view of what I have said earlier about disliking the union of sports and the military, the reader might expect me to be indifferent if West Point and Annapolis were no longer able to compete with Nebraska and Arkansas, for the goals of the schools are different; philosophically it might even be in the national interest if West Point retreated in athletics to a position somewhat like Yale's: a great university so preoccupied with education that advanced club football is about the best it can produce. I would find it repugnant to lower academy standards just to attract football players. But I cannot be indifferent to the fate of the academies; their very nature stresses athletic competence and rugged competition, and I have found that anything which runs counter to inherent nature must always be suspect. The academies are in trouble, and for athletes to be encouraged to boycott them is disgraceful.

One final word on government and sports. I have never been favorably impressed with czars for sports, or for anything else. In a crisis, perhaps, but for regular fare, no. I think Judge Kenesaw Mountain Landis highly overrated; he was a posturing gentleman who sided with management against the rights of players, a dictator who impeded the development of the game at least as much as he enhanced it. He may have been necessary as an antidote following the poison of the Black Sox scandal, but the incorruptibility for which he was praised he acquired as a judge and not as a sports dictator.

Most of the other czars were inefficient, little more than tools of owners, but I do have high regard for Pete Rozelle. Essentially a public relations man, and without much obvious success when he later became general manager of the Los Angeles Rams, he seemed an unlikely candidate for sage and guide through the years of football's major development. He has been right on most things he has done: opposition to Congress on the TV blackout law; disciplining Joe Namath; and particularly the masterminding of television contracts which have brought so much income to the game.

He has made only two bad mistakes. In 1963 after the Friday assassination of President Kennedy he saw no reason to postpone the Sunday football games, and in 1971 he did not comprehend when many women protested against flooding their homes on Christmas with two NFL play-off television broadcasts. If, in 1977, when Christmas falls on a football Sunday, the NFL insists upon business as usual, I shall volunteer to ring bells for whatever committee is organized to prevent it. There are some things in this world more sacred than sports, and family unity in observation of our major spiritual holiday is one of them.

XIII

Competition and Violence

In recent decades there has been a noticeable attack on the evils of competition. In kindergarten, children are taught to control aggressiveness and learn cooperation. In high school, students are encouraged to work for self-development and not for grades, which merely show their relative standing in competition with their classmates. In college, many undergraduates have turned away from competitive sports, preferring those experiences which enlarge friendships rather than engage enemies. In business life, managers are warned to avoid the constant tension of competition, and workers are directed by their unions not to compete against fellow workers but rather to perform up to an agreed-upon standard and no further. And medical men are beginning to emphasize that it is stress and self-induced tension that kill prematurely.

In sports, this revulsion against overcompetitiveness has manifested itself in a vigorous debate over the tactics of Vince Lombardi, who became the high priest of competition while coaching the Green Bay Packers. He achieved immortality with his summation of the competitor's creed: 'Winning isn't everything, it's the only thing.' But he said some other things too, and they are worth exploring.

• 'Football isn't a contact sport, it's a collision sport. Dancing is a contact sport.'

• 'To play this game you must have fire in you, and there is nothing that stokes fire like hate.'

• 'I will demand a commitment to excellence and to victory, and that is what life is all about.'

- 'This is a violent sport. That's why crowds love it.'
- 'Don't talk about injuries to anyone. Don't even tell your wife. Keep your mouth shut. There are three things that are important to every man in this room. His religion, his family and the Green Bay Packers, in that order.'

After Lombardi died fans cast about for his successor, and by general consent his mantle fell upon George Allen, the super-tense coach of the Washington Redskins. He, too, has uttered a series of apothegms which illustrate his competitive stance:

- 'Every time you win, you're reborn; when you lose, you die a little.'
- 'The winner is the only individual who is truly alive.'
- 'One hundred percent is not enough. The world belongs to those who aim for a hundred and ten.'
- 'We took a city that was known for last place and united it. Blacks and whites, Marylanders, Virginians and Washingtonians, Democrats and Republicans, they all were pulling together for the same thing.'
- And, in words of great perception, 'Careers don't last forever, and the season is short.' He was exhorting players to maximum performance during the brief period they were on the scene. Coaches, of course, go on year after year, prospering from the plaudits their players have won for them; players enter and depart quickly, like fodder through a chopping machine.

A few other memorable quotes from coaches will complete the testament of winning. Darrell Royal of Texas said, 'Luck is what happens when preparation meets opportunity.' Frank McGuire of South Carolina said, 'In this country, when you finish second, no one knows your name.' Bill Musselman of Minnesota said, 'Defeat is worse than death because you have to live with defeat.' And Leo Durocher summed it all up when he said, 'Nice guys finish last.'

Ed McCluskey, coach of a ragamuffin little basketball team representing Farrell High School in the coal regions of western Pennsylvania, elevated the Lombardi ethic to a new high: 'Through the years I've developed my own philosophy about high school basketball. Winning isn't all that matters. I don't care how many games you win, it's how many championships you win that counts.' He had won seven.

The first doubt to be cast on the deification of Lombardi came when George Sauer, an all-American from Texas and one of the heroes of the Jets' victory over Baltimore in the Super Bowl upset in 1969, asked publicly whether a coach, to win, had to imitate Lombardi. He thought not, and cited Weeb Ewbank, the low-key coach of the New York Jets as proof. Sauer pointed out that Weeb had copped two national championships without feeling obliged to impose any psychological tyranny in order to make his players perform. Other professional footballers pointed to various abuses in the Lombardi program and pinpointed the many contradictions in that system. They voiced strong opposition to the manner in which he kept mature athletes in a state of juvenile dependence, making grown men tremble when he frowned, or rejoice when he deigned to smile upon them. Some players said specifically that they hoped the strategies used by Lombardi would end with him and not become the standard procedures for all sports; they felt that his harsh impositions were unnecessary in the conduct of what should be games played by mature men. There seemed to be a general rejection of the reign of terror he had imposed. There was also hope that his tactics would no longer dominate the thinking of coaches working with nine- and ten-year-old boys or of coaches in high school. The rejection of his methods was by no means universal, and it was shamefully late in coming, but it was substantial.

Once the professionals challenged the myth, critics felt free to question the necessity of the Lombardi approach. *Sports Illustrated* ran a horror story about a practice which had become common in the high schools at Louisville, Kentucky: If a boy quit football, his name tape was removed from his locker and pasted on a conspicuous 'Hall of Shame,' with the result that boys and girls in the school shunned him. The coach who instituted this psychological punishment explained that it was merely 'negative motivation'; it accounted for the fact that his high school had left the ranks of habitual loser and entered the group of winners. Parents, however, protested.

Douglas Looney, in a widely reprinted article in the *National Observer,* tore the football ethic apart as it applied to business and general living. Under such topics as *Competition is basically destructive* and *Winning doesn't prove you're a better human being,* he rebutted Lombardi, but not in a stupid manner. He admitted that competition appeared to be a natural component of human life, but argued that it was best when one competed against oneself rather than against another human being whom one wished to destroy.

Physiologists warned that an overdeveloped sense of competition induced tensions which damaged the nervous system and led to various forms of physical degeneration. Cardiologists added that such tensions explained why so many American men died prematurely. Business moralists pointed out that excessive competition often led to a business immorality that could wreck our capitalist system, and as proof they pointed to the use of industrial spies, fake packaging, illegal advertising claims and massive bribes to foreign agents.

In the years when this questioning was becoming popular, I was working with radical youth groups, and in every extended discussion young people told me that they had been turned off by the excesses of organized sports, the adults who controlled it and the jocks who participated. This did not surprise me, for disaffected youth have usually been contemptuous of sports; but what did startle me was the discovery that hordes of traditional, non-radicalized college students were beginning to feel the same way. 'To hell with all competition,' they said repeatedly.

I have often felt that President Nixon could attribute his loss of office in 1974 to his football attitude about winning during the election of 1972. His Committee to Reelect the President (CREEP) had collected some $64,000,000, which it refused to share with the various Republican senators then running for reelection, on the grounds that 'the President has to win big.' If large chunks of that money, some of it illegally obtained, had been pumped into close senatorial campaigns, like Gordon Allott's in Colorado, the tremendous groundswell of the 1972 race would probably have returned a Republican Senate, which would never have authorized a Watergate investigation. In this case, winning was not the only thing; winning a balanced government in accordance with rules was.

A statement about winning which has given me much difficulty was made by Jack Nicklaus. He was speaking with considerable contempt of his fellow golfers who lacked his fierce desire to win: 'What gets to me are the self-admitted non-competitors—the guys who pick up $100,000 plus a year without ever winning a tournament, and go around telling the world how happy they are to finish ninth every week.' He then extolled the ethic of always trying to be number one, and I thought at the time that to be number nine in United States golf, to be immeasurably better than twelve million other golfers, and to earn $100,000 yearly was not disgraceful. Had I, years ago, started playing golf, I seriously doubt that it would have been incumbent upon me to beat the world. I would have wanted to achieve the highest level to which my ability entitled me, but if I had landed at ninth best, I would have deemed my career as golfer a success.

I cannot support Lombardi and Nicklaus and the coaches. Losing a game is not equivalent to death. Failing to be *numero uno* does not make me a lesser human being. Over the past twenty years I have repeatedly played one fine tennis player who used to have a national ranking, and I have never once defeated him. This does not mean that he is a better man than I. (You should see what I did to him in bottle pool!) It merely means that he is the better tennis player. I would be delighted to play him again tomorrow, for losing 6–3, 6–2 to a fine player is more rewarding than beating some beginner 6–0, 6–0.

Of course I have found winning to be more satisfying than losing; if I had never experienced victory, I might have acquired some psychological dislocation, but I feel that the average man or woman ought to be able to absorb a fair ration of defeat, and if some superjock growls, 'That merely proves you're a born loser, and there's nothing in the world lower than a loser,'

I no longer argue with him. I can only look at him with bewildered compassion.

And yet I must confess that I am on the side of healthy competition. I love it. I seek it out. I prosper under its lash. I have always lived in a fiercely competitive world and have never shied away. I live in such a world now and I would find life quite dull without the challenge.

I find competition to be the rule of nature, tension to be the structure of the universe. I believe that normal competition is good for a human being and I am sure that flight from it hastens death. I am prepared to acknowledge every charge against fanatical competition, or senselessly prolonged tension, and I would not foist either upon young people. But I would not wish to avoid reasonable competition, for I like a world in which men and women test themselves against others or against abstract ideals. I applaud the schools which drop pass-fail marks and go back to A-B-C competitive grades. I do not want to see my nation fall into desuetude because its citizens are unwilling to meet the challenges of our time.

In nature I find no avoidance of competition. A cardinal has built his nest in the bushes outside my bedroom window, and at nesting time he is careful to delimit his territory and then to defend it against intruders. He certainly does not shy away from competition. Indeed, when he sees his reflection in my window and recognizes it as an invading male cardinal, he springs into action, attacks his reflection in the window, then looks at me with a sense of triumph.

Not long ago I was on the Serengeti Plains of Central Africa with John Owen, the Englishman who then supervised that vast preserve, and after he had shown me the lions and the wildebeest and the zebras he said, 'Now I'll show the most interesting thing we have.' And he helped me spot a small bird with a sac on its chest, and we watched as this bird flew from corner to corner of a fairly large area, halting at boundary intersections and rubbing itself against some conspicuous weed.

When the bird had completed its rounds, Owen and I went to one of the marked weeds, pulled it, and returned to our car, where we found that the weed had been stained with a highly aromatic substance which other birds of that species could recognize from a distance. This would warn them that this area had been appropriated.

'The fascinating thing about this,' Owen told me as we watched the bird come back and stain another marker to replace the one I had pulled, 'is that when an overly aggressive male invader comes along, he ignores the outer boundary, comes right across, showing no fear of the more puny male inhabiting that area. But as he flies closer to the heartland of the occupying bird, he begins to lose his aggressiveness, for now he knows that he is inside that little core of territory which the occupying bird must defend to the death. The bully may make a few half-hearted passes at the little defender, but when he sees the fury in the little bird's manner, he quickly retires. At the outer margin it's a game, at the inner core, death.'

The male deer that inhabit my woods do not shy away from competition; if they did they would be outcasts. I hear them clashing horns, not to the point of death but rather in the joy of competition. My dogs compete furiously for stones, but only so long as the game is fun. The minute boredom sets in, my little female, who seems more intelligent about these things than the male, calls it quits.

We live in a competitive world whose rules are harsher than we might prefer. But competition is inescapable, and much superior to a bland existence with no challenge and no defining rules. When a young athlete goes out for a basketball team, there are forty aspirants and only five slots. When he takes examinations, there are thousands to be graduated, but only one summa cum laude. When he applies for a Rhodes Scholarship, he has to go up against a host of young men, many of them better qualified than he.

Whenever I got a job, I did so in competition with others; one of the great disappointments of my life came when I applied for a professorship at a western university and was rejected on the grounds that my years of studying in Europe had not given me the precise bit of paper which I would have obtained had I stayed home and studied in the more conventional manner. I said, 'To hell with it,' and became a writer.

In politics I have competed against the best, and messy though the American system is, I see no superior alternative. Certainly, those nations which have eliminated political competition have failed to produce acceptable systems. It seems to me that after reverence has been paid to the lofty phrases of our great public documents, the finest axiom of American civic life is the old war cry, 'Throw the rascals out!' Whenever I have lived in an area long dominated by Republicans grown careless, I have been inclined to vote Democratic, and vice versa. I feel it my civic duty to do so, because the natural competition of the two parties is healthy for the nation. I would deplore the day when such competition died.

When I write a manuscript, it competes with a hundred others, each equally worthy of publication; when I work in television or theater, the competition is even more severe. In recent years I have done a good deal of consultation with young painters, and the job of each is to find a gallery which will exhibit his paintings; to do so he must compete with scores of others equally gifted who are likewise searching for space. In fact, I find no aspect of life which is free from competition, and I find it in no way degrading to enter that battle and to throw my talent upon its mercies.

Nations, too, respond to challenge. If they don't, they perish. I remember sharing a podium with Arnold Toynbee when he first uttered that simile which has become so widely quoted. He was ridiculing capitalist America's reluctance to face the competition of Soviet Russia. 'Nations are like trout who have a sluggish stream to themselves. They grow fat and perish. Therefore, it's a good thing now and then to throw a couple of fighting carp among the trout. They make the lazy trout bestir themselves so that the whole stream becomes more vital.'

Similarly, the human mechanism responds creatively to challenge. It is inherently good to expand the lungs, to put moderate strain upon the heart, to test the leg muscles and keep them in tone. One of the most compelling groups of statues left us from the days of antiquity are those which show exhausted athletes, such as the Charioteer of Polyzalos. When you look today at such a statue, you cannot tell whether the man has won or lost; all you know is that he has just completed a grueling test of some kind and that he is content. These statues represent the finest aspect of sports, the personal depletion at the end of the game, the exhaustion that leads to re-creation. It is this that the competitor seeks.

Finally, I believe that the human intellect also prospers from competition. It seeks challenges. It has got to test itself against tasks of magnitude. It wants to weigh itself against the great norm of its time. On the lowest level it is the small-town pool shark who dreams of the day when he can challenge Minnesota Fats. On the highest level it is the burgeoning scholar who wants to test himself against Spengler and Einstein. Flamboyantly, it is Ernest Hemingway boasting that he went into the ring against Flaubert and Pio Baroja and fought them to a draw. Less flamboyantly, it might be the businessman who says to himself, 'I think I've put together something that may stand for a while,' or Hank Aaron saying quietly, 'If I make it through till next April, I know I can break Babe Ruth's record.' Bruce Ogilvie, who has spent much of his professional life analyzing competition, has summarized his findings in these words.

> The *moment of truth* is axiomatic in the life of the great competitor. Therefore, it is to be expected that those who excel will have a higher than average potential for coming to grips with reality. Successful athletes are achievement-oriented people and derive personal satisfaction from their striving. All things considered, the successful athlete is at his very best when the odds are slightly against him. Ambitious people derive slight joy, if any, when their ability remains uncontested. The great athletes that I have interviewed do not dwell upon their losses, but concentrate upon that part of their performance that limited their excellence.

Those who are not great athletes can derive a comparable benefit from reasonable competition, and the best is when the individual assesses the capacities allocated to him by his genetic inheritance and determines to use them to the best of his ability. Such a person can ignore outside norms; if he plays baseball, he does not mourn because Hank Aaron can hit 750 home runs and he can't. He achieves his own sense of accomplishment by performing up to his standard. But for life to be meaningful, there must be competition, either external or internal; I therefore reject all recent philosophies based upon a theory of non-competition, because such theories run counter to the experience of nature, of the individual and of society. Destructive competition carried to neurotic levels, I cannot condone. Creative competition, which encourages the human being to be better than he or she might otherwise have been, I applaud.

Without apology I side with St. Paul, who at various times made cogent observations about athletics and competition: 'Know ye not that they which run in a race run all, but one receiveth the prize? So run that ye may obtain . . . Put on the whole armor of God, that ye may be able to stand against the wiles of the devil. For we wrestle not against flesh and blood, but against principalities, against powers, against the rulers of the darkness of this world, against spiritual wickedness in high places . . . I have fought a good fight, I have finished my course, I have kept the faith.'

I know of no comment on competition more felicitous than the famous editorial which appeared in an English newspaper on the eve of the 1966 World Cup final, when critics acknowledged that Germany stood a fair chance of winning the next day: 'If perchance on the morrow Germany should beat us at our national game, let us take consolation from the fact that twice we have beaten them at theirs.' The strangest comment came just prior to the 1952 Olympics when Japanese sportswriters began to realize that their swimming phenomenon, Hironoshin Furuhashi, was not going to sweep the races the way the general public had been led to believe: 'If tomorrow we hear that our beloved Furuhashi has lost, it would be improper for us to rush into the streets and commit suicide.' He did lose, they did rush into the streets, and some did commit suicide.

The problem, therefore, is not with competition per se but with the violence that excessive competition arouses. This should be the grave concern of everyone connected with sport. It is getting out of hand, in all nations, and a halt must be called. A philosophical analysis of the problem can be found in Michael D. Smith's 'Sport and Collective Violence,' in Ball and Loy. From some fifty savage incidents, I remind the reader of these, some of which he has probably seen on television:

• Of the many riots which have overtaken baseball in recent years—some extremely destructive and all disgraceful—the worst occurred in Cleveland on the night of June 4, 1974, when the hometown Indians and the Texas Rangers met for the first time after a bench-clearing brawl had marred an earlier game. They played, unfortunately, on a night when ten-cent beer attracted a boozy crowd of 23,134. In the seventh inning, the Texas manager had to close down his bull pen in right field; Cleveland fans were bombarding the relief pitchers with firecrackers and beer cans. But real trouble erupted in the ninth. Photographs taken of the fray show drunken fans invading the field, climbing atop the Texas dugout and threatening the lives of the visiting players. Only quick support from the Cleveland ballplayers averted a tragedy. Said one Texan, 'If it wasn't for the Cleveland players tonight, we would have got killed.'

• Basketball, with its fans practically sitting on the floor, is an invitation to rioting, and there has been plenty. Television viewers learned how ugly it could be when the nationally televised game between Marquette and South Carolina erupted into a free-swinging donnybrook, but a short time later they were horrified when a dreadful affair occurred during a Big Ten Minnesota-Ohio State game held in the former's gym. Minnesota had been expected to win, and prior to the game their hyped-up players had put on a Harlem Globetrotters routine of fast passing and wizard gimmicks calculated to excite the spectators. It did, but it didn't help Minnesota much, because Ohio State, by virtue of extra cautious play, went into the final thirty-six seconds with a 50–44 lead. I will not attempt to report what happened next, but it involved a knee in the groin of a player extending his hand for a conciliatory handshake, a player kicking a downed player in the face, and a general riot that could have resulted in loss of life. Some weeks before the game Minnesota's Coach Musselman had made his statement that defeat was worse than death; the governor of Ohio called the affair, 'A public mugging. Gang warfare in an athletic arena.'

• On May 14, 1974, I was lucky enough to have a ticket to the fourth game of the Stanley Cup play-offs between the Boston Bruins and the rugged, new-style, cut-them-to-shreds Philadelphia Flyers. The opening period, which should have been played in a little over thirty minutes, required sixty-seven because of the incessant fighting, stick waving and general mayhem. The game was a disgrace, with the Flyers winning 4–2 on their way to the championship. I was distressed at this exhibition, for I was not accustomed to games in which players were actually encouraged to engage in brutal fistfights with opposing players. However, a Flyer partisan told me, 'How do you think we defeated New York last week? Our knuckle boys beat the living shit out of them and they were afraid to skate.'

• I was not surprised, therefore, when two young men were killed playing hockey in Canada and when, on January 4, 1975, Boston's Dave Forbes smashed Minnesota's Henry Boucha in the face with the butt of his stick, damaging Boucha's eye so seriously that he needed hospital care for many days. Judging this to be a common assault, Minnesota police arrested

Forbes and charged him in court with a felony. The sports world exploded. Hockey players protested that the courts had no right to interfere in a game. Coach Fred Shero of the Flyers said, 'We have to police our own. We don't have to go to court. I don't think the law can dispense justice in sports.' Bobby Clarke, most valuable player for two years, said, 'If they cut down on violence too much, people won't come out to watch. It's a reflection of our society. People want to see violence.'

• Boxing has produced more than its share of riots, a typical one having occurred at the Felt Forum in New York on the night of December 9, 1974. Pedro Soto, a likable kid from Puerto Rico with ten straight wins against carefully selected pushovers, was finally going up against a real fighter, Mike Quarry, brother of Jerry, who had been grinding his way through the mill for some years. It was a massacre, with every judge awarding Quarry the victory. Soto's adherents, who had laid out good money to see their boy triumph, could not accept the fact that he had been outclassed. So they trashed the Forum, ripping out seats, tearing down ceiling panels, wrenching toilets from the wall, and setting fire to the joint.

• Horse racing, with its opportunity for outrage when the stewards disqualify a winner or hand down an unpopular decision, has produced more than its share of disgraceful performances. At Roosevelt Raceway on Long Island on November 8, 1963, an accident in the sixth race caused six of the eight horses to pull up. Fans thought the race should be declared 'no contest,' but the stewards allowed the abbreviated results to stand, whereupon a major riot ensued, with a good percentage of the 23,127 spectators smashing the tote board, setting fire to a sulky in the home stretch, attacking a patrol judge inside his booth, destroying concession stands and overturning cars in the parking lot. Firemen had to douse the rioters with water, and the chief of security at the track suffered a fatal heart attack.

• Football, the most violent of all games, has escaped such major riots, lending credence to the belief that seeing aggression acted out in a game diminishes the likelihood that the spectator will engage in it himself. (This is refuted by certain ingenious studies which tend to prove that watching aggression does inspire aggression.) At any rate, if the big teams have escaped, the little ones have not. In one American city after another, football games between local high schools have either had to be canceled because of threatened violence, or played on distant neutral fields, or played in secret before no spectators. Baltimore, Buffalo, Detroit, St. Louis have all experienced this phenomenon, but the Philadelphia case in the fall of 1968 was perhaps the most typical. Race riots and school rivalries were hot that year. Ugly incidents had proliferated, so when the big Frankford team (mostly white) was to play powerful Edison (mostly black), an ingenious bit of scheduling was devised. Ron Howley, assistant coach at Frankford, says that neither the players nor the coaches of either team were allowed to know where the game was to be played. All personnel were placed secretly on buses at each school, with only an official riding beside the driver knowing where the bus was to go. When the teams reached the playing field, reporters were sworn to secrecy, on the grounds that other games that year might have to be played there. Frankford won, 32–12, but I wonder if it should have gone into the records as a game.

• Box lacrosse, having been advertised as even more brutal than ice hockey, had to prove it. On June 3, 1975, the Philadelphia Wings met the Maryland Arrows in undeclared warfare, and the game grew so rough that ninety-six minutes' worth of penalties had to be imposed; both benches emptied for a prolonged fracas; and, as if this were not enough, the state's attorney charged three players with having broadened the fray by attacking fans with their lethal sticks.

• Because soccer is the most widely played sport in the world, it naturally provides the largest number of riots. We have seen that on May 24, 1964, in Lima, Peru, nearly three hundred spectators were killed in a brawl following a disputed referee's call. In Glasgow, Scotland, on June 2, 1971, the final minute of what had been a scoreless tie between the traditional rivals Celtic (Catholic) and Rangers (Protestant) produced a soccer marvel, followed by a great tragedy. With less than a minute to play, Celtic put together a fine drive and scored the winning goal. Disgruntled Protestants in the audience cursed and started to leave. But in the remaining seconds the Rangers retaliated with an unbelievable goal, and the wild cries from the stadium could be heard at the exits. So those who had already left rushed back, only to be met by a crush of exultant fans trying to leave. Sixty-six were crushed to death.

• The Glasgow tragedy should not, perhaps, be charged to sports. It was an accident that might have happened anywhere; competition between Celtic and Rangers had merely exacerbated emotions which made the tragedy unavoidable. But there had been other incidents when British teams traveled abroad that raised serious questions about the decline of British sportsmanship. Barcelona, Rotterdam and various towns in Belgium had felt the lash of British hooliganism, but the apex came on May 28, 1975, when Leeds United journeyed to Paris for the finish of the European Cup. The game against Bayern of Munich was being played on neutral ground to escape partisan excess; Germans would hardly want to make asses of themselves in France, and it was supposed that Leeds would seek to make amends for earlier British misbehavior. Sad miscalculation! After a 2–0 defeat Leeds fans set out methodically to ravage the stadium and anything else that got in their way. It was an appalling performance, so disgraceful that the British ambassador had to make a public apology to both the

French and German governments. Ian Woolridge, of the *London Daily Mail* described the typical Leeds fan as a 'foul-mouthed, crude, drunken, intolerable oaf, bereft of reason, poisoned by prejudice, grotesque with self-invested arrogance, bent on destruction of property and intent on abusing anyone who speaks a foreign tongue. We are not feared, we are despised. We are not seen as "characters" or "tough." We are seen as morons and degenerates.'

• No game escapes the violence. Recently on a golf course in Maryland two foursomes became embroiled over the slow play of one, and a general melee ensued, with golf clubs being used like machetes. The climax of the battle came when two golfers revved up their carts, made a cavalry charge, and knocked the enemy into a bunker.

• In his book *The Nightmare Season,* the psychiatrist Arnold J. Mandell tries to relate such violence to larger forces than sport. While relating a horrifying account of his experiences with the losing San Diego Chargers' football team, he tells in detail of one crucial game in which the fans turned against their team and came close to physical violence:

> I'm beginning to see that the real source of the madness is the unconsciousness of the crowd. I mean, I've been trying to blame the players, the coach, the owners, and the Commissioner for the ugliness, but really WIN OR BE KILLED is a thing in our culture. Those fans today were murderous. Wild-eyed. Angry. Excited. Ready to kill. It's a huge circle. No one is responsible. It's like a lot of other things in our culture—a lot of independent variables. It's everywhere, in all of us. It doesn't do any good to try to pin the blame on one scapegoat.

• As he so often does, Art Buchwald carried this mania to its logical conclusion. On November 16, 1975, the Washington Redskins faced the St. Louis Cardinals in a game that might decide the division championship and would determine the wild-card spot in the play-offs. Washington played well and led 17–10 going into the final minute, but St. Louis quarterback Jim Hart threw a desperation pass on which end Mel Gray made a sensational catch at the goal line, scoring the game-tying touchdown. Or did he? Incessant replays cast doubt on Gray's possession of the ball as he crossed into the end zone, but proved conclusively that the ball had been knocked from his hands before a touchdown would normally have been scored. The officials, after unprecedented confusion and consultation, decreed that Gray had held the ball just long enough. The score counted. The game was tied. And in sudden death, Jim Bakken kicked a field goal to win for St. Louis and destroy Washington hopes. The ensuing outcry in Washington was horrendous. Senator Warren Magnuson demanded a recount. George Patrick Morse, a local attorney, filed suit in federal court to reverse the wrongful decision, and there was talk of carrying the case to the Supreme Court. It was in the heat of this fury that Buchwald, a rabid Redskins fan, made the only sensible proposal: 'I'm asking for the death penalty to be restored.' He added, 'If St. Louis had any class, they would admit it was all a mistake and give us the game.' He said he felt sure that if Washington ever won a game on a bad call, George Allen would insist upon forfeiting it to the rightful winner.

Vince Lombardi, shortly before he died, looked back on his quote which had helped get such unbridled enthusiasm started. He told Jerry Izenberg, 'I wish to hell I'd never said the damned thing. I meant the effort . . . I meant having a goal . . . I sure as hell didn't mean for people to crush human values and morality.' I would like to think that that was his final word on the matter.

Others were not disturbed by violence. When the citizens of Pittsburgh rioted in the wake of a glorious World Series victory, with reports of crime, rape and multiple injuries, Police Chief Robert E. Colville had to rise in defense of his city. He said, 'I have called this news conference because of the many unfounded and, in some cases, completely fabricated stories which went out over national news media.' After assuring his listeners that there was nothing to such stories, the police admitted that there had been 128 reported injuries, 98 arrests, 25 store windows smashed, one taxicab overturned, one other car burned, and one woman yanked out of a passing car. 'But she wasn't raped,' the police insisted.

The most thoughtful attack on the growing violence was written by a linebacker for the Calgary Stampeders in the Canadian League. John McMurtry was an unusual type to begin with, a philosophy buff, and when he quit the big game he turned to the teaching of this subject in college. His essay appeared first in a Canadian magazine, *Maclean's,* and was reprinted in the January 1972 issue of the *Atlantic.* It is entitled 'Smash Thy Neighbor,' and is a provocative analysis of why football has to be so violent:

> Progressively and inexorably, as I moved through high school, college and pro leagues, my body was dismantled. Piece by piece. I started off with torn ligaments in my knee at thirteen. Then, as the organization and competition increased, the injuries came faster and harder. Broken nose (three times), broken jaw (fractured in the first half and dismissed as a 'bad wisdom tooth,' so I played with it for the rest of the game), ripped knee ligaments again. Torn ligaments in one ankle and a fracture in the other. Repeated rib fractures and cartilage tears. More dislocations of the left shoulder than I can remember. Occasional broken or dislocated fingers and toes. Chronically hurt lower back. Separated right shoulder, needled with morphine for the games.

I remember that when reading Jerry Kramer's *Instant Replay* and his account of the twelve major operations he had undergone in order to continue with football, the impact on me was quite the opposite of what was intended. I thought that for a man to undergo such destruction of his body in order to participate in a game was insanity, yet almost everyone I spoke to, especially young people, said something like, 'Wasn't it wonderful, the way Kramer stuck to it?' Constantly I have heard him held up as an American ideal, and whenever this has happened I have thought that the speaker must have acquired a most limited understanding of what the great ideals of history have been. They have not included self-destruction in a game. McMurtry speaks to this basic point repeatedly, and his suspicions are worthy of attention:

> It is arguable that body shattering is the very *point* of football, as killing and maiming are of war. To grasp some of the more conspicuous similarities between football and war, it is instructive to listen to the imperatives most frequently issued to players by their coaches, teammates and fans. 'Hurt 'em!' 'Level 'em!' 'Kill 'em!' 'Take 'em apart!' Or watch for the plays that are most enthusiastically applauded by the fans, where someone is 'smeared,' 'knocked silly,' 'creamed,' 'nailed,' 'broken in two,' or even 'crucified.' In football the mouth waters most of all for the really crippling block or tackle. For the kill. Thus the good teams are 'hungry,' the best players are 'mean,' and 'casualties' are as much a part of the game as they are of war.
>
> Competitive, organized injuring is integral to our way of life, and football is one of the more intelligible mirrors of the whole process: a sort of colorful morality play showing us how exciting and rewarding it is to Smash Thy Neighbor.

A classic case of what McMurtry was inveighing against was uncovered on June 10, 1973, when the *St. Petersburg Times* of Florida ran a story claiming that twenty-eight scholarship members of the football squad at Florida State had quit because they had been subjected to organized brutality, not during the game itself and not even during the season, but in the winter hardening drills. The class, presumably voluntary but actually obligatory if anyone wanted to keep his scholarship, met five times a week for six weeks, in a bare room in which a chicken-wire false ceiling had been suspended four feet from the floor. Under this, pairs of would-be football players were shoved to engage in what amounted to almost mortal combat, which was continued until one emerged clearly victor. Then the loser had to face a fresh combatant, and stay under the wire clutching and clawing and spitting blood until he finally defeated someone.

Eighteen of those who quit reported in a body to the newspaper, and one young man said, 'Puny players were forced to wrestle huge linemen under

'Okay, Old Buddy, get in there and play the game win or lose.
But remember, nice guys finish last, there's no such word as chicken,
and every time you lose you die a little.'

the chicken wire, and the losers had to keep wrestling until they won, always screaming and cursing and trying to draw blood like some kind of animals.' The final loser, who had been able to conquer no one, was forced to rise at dawn next morning and race up and down the steep stadium steps ten or twenty times.

Officials at the university stated that Florida State had done only what other universities were doing, and it was all sanctioned by the NCAA. This prompted *Sports Illustrated* to do a follow-up, which appeared in the July 23, 1973, issue. Wisely, it did not stress the Florida State case but focused on other schools, principally Kansas State, where the program seemed even tougher than at Florida. The report was sickening: sheer brutality, men told to vomit on their own time and not stop running, bloodied noses, sickening force applied for little reason. The most telling quote came from a man who had graduated from the pit and was now playing right end for the New England Patriots. Bob Windsor, who had experienced his hardening at Kentucky, said, 'It was jungle-warfare training. I've never experienced anything like it in pro ball. There they treat you like human beings. Not in college. I wouldn't go through that again.'

The moral problem of such attitudes first struck me when I read a passage in Robert Vare's book on Woody Hayes. It came toward the end and was of no apparent significance, but it left an indelible impact:

> An inordinate amount of folklore has sprung up already around the short happy-and-unhappy life of Harold Raymond Henson III. It begins with the story of how he got his nickname   how his father, then serving his country in Fort Eustis, Virginia, hitchhiked fifteen hours back to Ohio, eyed his newborn son and proclaimed, 'He's got to be a champ.' Six months later, according to another story they tell around Columbus, the older Henson, his own football career rudely ended by an appendicitis attack, carried his Champ out to the fifty-yard line of Ohio Stadium and set him down on the sod. *'Someday you will punish people on this field,'* said father to son. 'Someday you will be a Buckeye.'

The italics are mine. Why would the vital element in an athletic career be a boy's ability to punish someone else? Why would a father or a coach create an ideal for a boy in which destroying an opponent became the goal? Bill Walton was referring to this when he charged, after having left UCLA, 'There were many times in college when opposing players were out seriously to maim the players on our team.' I have heard linebackers boast, 'I love to destroy the runner.' And they mean just that. And it's just as bad in baseball, where throwing directly at the batter's head is standard. Doc Cramer once said:

> If you hit a home run, you'd expect to be knocked down the next time up. Or if you beat a guy in a ball game, you wanted to be ready next time the fellow

pitched against you. Johnny Allen was the worst I ever saw for that. I said to him one day, 'I believe you'd throw at your mother.' 'Oh, no,' he said, 'I wouldn't throw at her. But I might brush her back a bit.'

Such incidents raise the vital question: Are American sports especially violent because they are forced to reflect the inherent violence of our society? I think so. I have always believed that because of our frontier heritage, and our sentimental reliance on the gun, our society became somewhat more addicted to violence than others.

Within recent years the new frontier created by urban disruption has produced shocking levels of violence. I have just seen a report which states that in American schools last year there were 204,000 instances in which students beat up their teachers in the classroom, 9,000 cases of rape in washrooms, and about 100 murders during school hours. Such conduct is incredible, and there had better be a retreat from this dangerous addiction. One place to start would be sports, both in the way they are played and in the behavior of spectators. Ice hockey and football have become too violent, and they set a deplorable example for other sports. The other day I heard a radio advertisement for tennis which made this well-disciplined game sound like murder at high noon: '. . . the ball crashing at close to one hundred miles an hour . . . real men slashing at the net . . . superb athletes ready for anything.' The sales pitch for box lacrosse was even worse, for it was being peddled as more violent and dangerous than hockey, with bodies clashing and sticks smashing across heads. The people selling those games knew what a large segment of the American public wanted. It wanted violence.

But at the same time that sports adjust to satisfy this hunger, there is danger that the public may become surfeited and turn away from something that is no longer a game. Everyone connected with sports must keep in mind what happened to wrestling and roller-skating. Years ago they were legitimate sports, but they were tempted by the easy money that raw violence assured, and bit by bit they lost self-respect, becoming nothing but spurious exhibitions. Now they exist in grubby arenas and on late-night television, their vitality and authenticity destroyed.

But they are good burlesque. They say in effect, 'All right, if you want violence, we'll give you some. But it will be make-believe, and no one will get hurt, at least not on purpose.' Half the fun is the glib-tongued announcer who appears to take the wrestling nonsense seriously. He reports it dead-pan straight, appalled by brutality, exhilarated by the unexpected move so carefully rehearsed, outraged by unsportsmanlike behavior, and always sympathetic with the referee who goes through the motions of trying to keep order while the contestants are gouging, hitting one another with chairs, chasing opponents up and down the aisles, and committing various other forms of mayhem.

I also like the conclusion of the matches, when Chief Jay Strongbow, his Indian headdress in place, hurls his defy at Bruno Sammartino, or when the latest tag-team phenoms grab the microphone alternately to accuse the Visigoths of ducking them through craven cowardice. 'But we'll get you, Visigoths! And we'll tear your limbs off one by one. You better be afraid! Because you got the hearts of cowards, and everybody in Chicago knows it. Watch out, Visigoths! We're after you and there's no hole deep enough for you to hide in!'

I like my violence that way, in a make-believe world. But my real affection goes out to the roller derby, where vicious skulduggery that hurts no one is carried to the level of high dramatic art. While writing this book I had occasion to visit Hollywood and participate in awarding the Oscars. No actor in California does the job, week after week, that Bob Martin does in refereeing the roller game. He is a tall, slim, good-looking man, master of the leer, the sneer, the snarl, the snide put-down, a man who loves to smirk into the eye of the television camera and say, 'I'm in control because I'm smarter than the others. I use my brain and they have no brains.'

Martin's standard ploy is to fraternize with the bullies of the visiting team and to outrage the hometown fans by calling every infraction against them and none against the visitors. He is adept at large, irritating pantomime as he makes a call and in thrusting himself into all sorts of places where he is not wanted. Then, when the home team can bear him no more, they take after him with clubs and chairs and broken bottles, and he turns craven, running like a frightened deer to the protection of the out-of-town bullies. At this point total pandemonium erupts: furniture is broken; Little Richard, his leg in a cast, starts belting people over the head with his crutch; men and women alike engage in twenty or thirty fistfights, and someone clubs Martin over the head with a breakaway chair, while the announcer cries over the loudspeaker system, 'Bob Martin is the lowest snake ever to crawl from beneath a rock. I wish someone would crush his head like a grape.'

This is a burlesque of sports' machismo, and I find it therapeutic, a kind of divine nonsense. Imagine, sixty young people engaged in one massive brawl, with things being broken left and right and no one getting hurt! It's Mack Sennett transferred to the sporting arena, and the burlesque is not only fun but does not result in injuries. The audience gets all the thrills, cheap and fake to be sure, that come from a linebacker pulverizing a quarterback for real.

The highlight of the wrestling-roller-skating season came one Sunday afternoon when one of the hometown bullies, apparently able to stand no more of the terrorizing Referee Martin had been visiting on him, went berserk. In one unbroken sweep he punched a girl skater in the face, knocked her down, kicked her in the throat with his skate, jumped on her, kneed her between the eyes, and hit her over the head with a chair. He then turned upon the chief bully of the visitors, picked him up, threw him onto a breakaway table, then kicked him repeatedly in the face. He then grabbed Little Richard's crutch and belabored seven or eight of the visitors, knocked over all the remaining furniture, and lashed at three of the opposing girl skaters, knocking two of them down. He then went for Referee Martin and gave him an unmerciful beating, ending by throwing him bodily some feet across the arena, after which he clubbed him with chairs, a hunk of broken table and the crutch.

At the end of this volcanic eruption, in which not a single person was hurt, of course, pale and wounded Bob Martin hobbled to the television camera and said in a voice trembling with menace and frustration, 'He better watch out or he'll be disqualified.'

Why did I waste my time on such frivolity? Because I wanted to review the downward steps by which once-popular sports descended to ridicule. In 1946 boxing and wrestling and roller derbies were still taken seriously, but when they began to grab for the nearest dollar, the quickest laugh, the most grotesque parody of violence their credibility was destroyed. When enough people begin laughing at the exaggerations of any sport, it is doomed. The custodians of the game refuse to heed the first warnings, because the people who are ridiculing the sport don't appear to carry much weight: a few canny reporters from New York and Los Angeles, patrons in the know, people who write magazine articles, the younger editors of *Time* and *Sports Illustrated*. But once that fatal chorus derides a sport as phony, the death rattle has begun, for they are the opinion makers, and sports exist on good opinion.

I am worried about ice hockey. In the United States, I rarely hear a word against it, but in Canada, where they have known the game longer, there is fear that it may already have been so contaminated by violence that it is doomed. The fighting is largely fake and not required in the movement of the game. It is a cheap hype to attract American customers, and if it is continued, it will kill hockey, because opinion makers will start to ridicule it. The custodians of the game will have done to it what earlier custodians did to wrestling and roller-skating and boxing: made it a thing of scorn.

I first became aware of this danger during the 1974 season; it was even more apparent in 1975—not in the United States but in Canada. If the rate of deterioration increases, the game could be dead in another fifteen years. Crowds would still be going to see the games, especially in America, but it would have lost its television patronage except on the little stations, where

'My man don't wrestle till we hear it talk.'

it would be played primarily for violence and comedy. It can be saved only by preserving the basic nature of the game and avoiding ridiculous excesses. I abide by what Homer said of competition:

> O friends, be men, and let your hearts be strong,
> And let no warrior in the heat of fight
> Do what may bring him shame in others' eyes.

Housman, who knew his Homer, phrased the same idea in these words when sending his Shropshire lad off to the competition:

> Be clean then; rot before you do
> A thing they'd not believe of you.

I apologize for the use of *men* and *lad* in these citations, and for my repeated use of other masculine words in this chapter, but violence in sport is primarily a male aberration. There have, however, been warning signs that when women turn to professionalism, they embrace a rowdyism which often exceeds that of men. Four women wrestling in a pool of mud was one pretty example. The petite and beautiful roller-skater Judy Arnold slugging it out with 250-pound Erlene Brown is another. In other sports, like tennis, women professionals seem eager to go down that fatally wrong road of cheap sensationalism. If they succeed, it will be a pity, for they have an opportunity to give sports a fresh, clean start and to avoid the errors their brothers have made.

And now for one of the most perplexing questions in sports. If you are in favor of keen competition, yet opposed to violence, how do you react to the Lombardi ethic? Like all coaches of professional teams, including the big-time schools, he was required to win. In his remorseless world, only the won-lost percentage counted, and to protect it a player had to be ruthless and hate his opponent, because the penalty for relaxation was losing, and the penalty for that was extinction.

It would have been ugly enough if this machismo had been reserved for the professionals and the big-time schools, but violence-prone Americans applauded Lombardi so heartily that he became the norm for coaches in small colleges, high schools and even Little League. When I worked on Chapter IV, dealing with children, I met this complaint a score of times: 'Our Little League coach thinks he is obligated to behave like Vince Lombardi.' And always this was said resentfully; parents might enjoy watching violence on television, but they didn't want their children to be on the receiving end.

I like Lombardi's dedication to accomplishment. I like his doctrine that when you engage your opponent, you do so to win. But I deplore many of the methods he devised to ensure winning. And I especially dislike the psychological tyranny he imposed and gloried in. Perhaps he was the ideal coach for professionals who from grammar school had been so football-bound that they could not discipline themselves, but he is a poor model for amateurs.

One aspect of violence in American sports is accidental, but it requires special comment. From the most ancient times hunting animals and birds for the sheer joy of hunting has been an honorable recreation, and an imposing collection of art, poetry, and writing could be assembled from all cultures to demonstrate this. But in our country the gun which is used in sport is also used to take human life, and at a rate that is shocking. The city of Tokyo, with a population of 12,000,000, produces three firearm killings a year. New York, with a population of 10,000,000, produces five hundred. Per capita, Americans gun down thirty-five times as many victims as Englishmen do.

American 'tradition' defends the right of every red-blooded American man to tote his gun and bushwhack his neighbor, and of every American woman to flush out her husband and blast him with the family shotgun. In 1968 I served as statewide chairman for the reelection of Senator Joseph E. Clark, an excellent gentleman and a good public servant. But early in the game he had the effrontery to say that he thought it about time we stopped gunning down our political leaders like John Kennedy, Robert Kennedy and Martin Luther King, and from that moment on, he was a dead duck. When I went to Erie, the hunting capital of our state, I was told by the committee of loyal Democrats that welcomed me at the airport, 'We're delighted to have you with us, Michener, and you can speak all night about Hubert Humphrey for President, but if you say one word in favor of Senator Clark and his bill to take our guns away from us, we'll run you out of town.' (There was no such bill.) And in the November election good Joe Clark and his moderate stand against guns went down to a crushing defeat.

In my home district, I would not dare to speak out against guns. Some hunters killed a little boy waiting for his school bus a couple of years ago. 'He moved,' they said in explanation. It was a wooded area and he could have been a deer. Other hunters shot at a deer in our back yard last year, and the bullet came ripping through my study and into my shelf of books. Had I been sitting at my typewriter, I would have been shot through the head. A Pan Am pilot who lives not far from me remonstrated with hunters who had invaded his property. They shot out one of his eyes and fled the scene, leaving him on the ground.

To protest such actions gets nowhere. If the President of the United States, coming from a gunners' region, inveighs against gun control, how can I advocate it? But I do wish everyone would read a report by four Cleveland doctors which appeared in the February 19, 1973, issue of *The Journal of the American Medical Association.* It is entitled 'Homicide and Suicide in a Metropolitan Area,' and in dispassionate terms it simply records the shocking rise of gun-related deaths in the period 1938–71:

> The controversy over firearms control, especially as it relates to handguns, has many passionate advocates on both sides. Public debate is sure to continue. From 1938 to 1962 there was an average of 87 homicides per year, with firearms involved in 50% to 60%. We now have more than 300 homicides annually, and guns claim 80% of the victims! Since approximately 90% of firearms homicides are handgun fatalities, we interpret this as an unmistakable and tragic consequence of the availability and abuse of handguns.

The report occasioned so much discussion and controversy that the four doctors went back to their figures, verified them, and came up with a finding even more startling than the one they had previously disclosed: They reported this in 'Accidental Firearm Fatalities in a Metropolitan County,' *American Journal of Epidemiology,* Vol. 100, No. 6:

> One hundred and twenty-three of the 148 accidental firearm fatalities (83%) resulted from mishaps with handguns. Over three-quarters of these fatalities occurred in the home (78%), and the majority of them (67%) occurred when someone was handling or 'playing' with a gun . . .

Our data also suggest that guns in the home are more dangerous than useful to the homeowner and his family who keep them to protect their persons and property. During the period surveyed in this study, only twenty-three burglars, robbers or intruders who were not relatives or acquaintances were killed by guns in the hands of persons who were protecting their homes. During this same interval, six times as many fatal firearm accidents occurred in the home. We conclude that a loaded firearm in the home is more likely to cause an accidental death than to be used as a lethal weapon against an intruder.

As I work on this passage, a lovely sixteen-year-old girl living down the road has been killed by a friend who did not believe that a gun largely dismantled could contain a bullet that would go off. It did.

I cannot foresee any substantial decrease in guns in family lockers during the rest of this century. Gunning people down is an American trait which will not easily be altered. In parts of the west that I know well, even to suggest that guns be controlled is tantamount to treason, and I no longer argue the matter. But people should realize that when they buy guns, it is they and their families who are in gravest danger.

The tragic consequences that can result when violence and sport intermix are demonstrated in the case of Howard McNeill. At age fourteen he stood six-eight and dominated play on Philadelphia's ghetto courts. One of nine children in a disrupted black family, he was unusually handsome and well-mannered, and it was not surprising that he was avidly recruited by suburban high schools seeking basketball talent.

He saw the game as his best chance of escaping the harsh inner-city life and enrolled at a good prep school, but couldn't get grades which would keep him eligible. He therefore transferred to Abington, of which we read on pages 112–13, where a local postman was appointed his legal guardian. Howard not only played good basketball but also showed that he could fit into a suburban life.

His move to Abington occasioned much bitter comment in neighboring communities, and protracted legal hassles ensued, but in the end his right to play for his new team was confirmed. However, it is alleged that someone from arch-rival Norristown threatened him with serious harm if he showed up for the game against that team.

Abington, inspired by McNeill's play, had a 19–0 record, and if it could beat Norristown, it would have a good shot at the state title, so McNeill had to play. In self-protection he acquired a gun, which he kept in his duffel, and following the Norristown game he displayed it to his fellow teammate Mitchell Lee, also sixteen years old. The gun went off. The bullet struck Lee in the head and killed him. Three comments followed:

Curtis Coull, athletic director at Norristown: 'I'm very upset, bitter, about such a suggestion. No one from Norristown would make such a threat.'

Mrs. Helen Lee, mother of the dead athlete: 'It was just Mitch's time to go.'

Jim Wilkinson, much-loved coach of Abington: 'Winning doesn't seem so important any more.'

Epilogue

In the three final chapters of this book I have been preoccupied with money and violence, and I apologize. I seem to have lost sight of my preeminent criterion, that sports should be fun, but it has never been far from my mind. I should now like to conclude with several short examples of the delight one can find in the sublime nonsense of games. These are the highlights in a lifetime of following sports:

Hilarity. The most sheer fun I ever had in sports was playing volleyball, a game I commend highly. I understand that an effort is under way to establish a national league of professional volleyball teams, and if you have ever seen the great women's teams of Japan and Russia or the equally good men's teams of Cuba or East Germany, you know how exciting this playground game, which requires so little equipment, can be.

A commendable feature of the new league, and one which puts it at the head of the class in the emerging world of sports, is that each team consists of four men and two women, with the latter allowed to move freely up to the net or back.

I played for some years on a New York City YMCA team. I was a setter—the player who takes the pass from the backcourt and projects it straight upward, so that the tall spiker can put it away—and I was a fierce competitor, with one weakness. When I set the ball it often went up crooked, just outside the reach of my teammates but directly into the paws of the opposition.

We were a championship team, beating all comers, until that fatal night when we were invited to go to Harlem to play a team of black railway porters who were reputed to be rather good. When we walked onto the court they were waiting, a gang of six-foot-six stringbeans who could jump so high we wondered if they would ever come down.

We lost the first game 15–6, then pulled ourselves together, determined to save our honor. By dint of superhuman effort, and because the other side relaxed, having won the first game so easily, we squeaked out a 19–17 victory.

But we had shot our bolt. The last game was 15–3, and during the second half our side sort of stood around in amazement, staring at those superb athletes who could jump so high. At one point one of our men protested, 'Those sonsabitches are usin' sky hooks!' Everyone laughed, but my lasting memory of that third game when the porters let everything loose is of picking volleyballs out of my teeth. We were no longer champions.

I had learned volleyball in the navy, where all the captains and admirals wanted to be spikers, and I found then that a man who can subdue his own desires and master the art of serving others can make himself invaluable. In choosing sides the team captain always chose the good spikers on the first and second choice, but then the spikers would grab his arm and whisper, 'Take Michener.' I was never chosen lower than third, because I was needed. I wasn't good but I was faithful.

Revelation. Sometimes in the process of a game a man or woman will experience a moment of almost shattering revelation, about either himself or his opponent, or even about the nature of life. For me the greatest moment came in Denver in the year 1941, when I took a group of basketball players down from Greeley to see the latest sensation of the game, Hank Luisetti, recently graduated from Stanford and now playing for a California semi-pro team.

He was to play against the Denver Legion, a team which commanded the loyalties of our region because it was composed of former college stars like Jumpin' Jack McCracken and Bob Doll and was always in contention for the Amateur Athletic Union Championship. It competed against the country's top teams, like the Phillips 66ers from Bartlesville, the Fort Wayne Pistons and the Kansas City Healys, all of whom played tight defensive ball. In 1932 the Wichita Henrys had won the national championship 15–14. My crowd had seen phenoms come and go in this tough league, and we assumed haughtily that what we had been reading about Luisetti was the ordinary press agent's extravagance. We expected him to be reasonably good. We had no comprehension of how good.

When Luisetti came on the floor, there was a buzz of excitement, but he wasn't anything very special. A tallish, handsome man, not much over six feet and not very heavy. He did have graceful moves, but then so did McCracken of the Legion. In practice he showed no unusual speed, and from a distance out he missed about as many as he made.

But when the game started, with the California team moving from my right to my left, and with me in the first row of the balcony with a perfect view, something happened which left me stunned. Luisetti started from his own backcourt, flipped an ordinary pass to a teammate, then cut like lightning to about the center of the floor. There he received a pass, flipping it immediately to another teammate. He then ran in a small circle toward the left of the basket, took a pass back in stride, dribbled right through two waiting guards and leaped high into the air as the Denver center bore down on him to block the attempted shot.

It was then that the miracle happened. Somehow, Luisetti stayed up in the air, faked a shot at the basket, made the Denver center commit himself, and with a movement I had never seen before, simply extended his right arm an extra foot and banked a one-handed shot gently against the backboard and into the basket. It seemed as if he had been in the air a full minute, deceiving three different players, and ending with a delayed shot that was staggering in its beauty.

The crowd exploded! They were still cheering when he did it again, that remarkable leap, that hanging in the air, that changing direction, ending with a soft shot at the basket.

We who had come to scoff sat silent. We were seeing the end of a basketball era, the beginning of a new world. We had been taught to shoot two-handed. We had been taught to work the ball in close. We had been taught never to take a wild shot from a distance. We had been taught to manage the games so that a runaway score was 23–17. And here was the revolutionary young man from California, proving that everything we had been taught was wrong.

It was a marvelous night, one I can never forget. It demonstrated that there is always the possibility someone will come along who will be able to do old things in bold new ways. And it taught me humility. Nobody that I ever played with or against could go on the same floor with Hank Luisetti. He paved the way for Pettit and Mikan and Fulks and Chamberlain and Abdul-Jabbar. He was a revelation, and I saw him at the beginning of his professional career.

Beauty. They told me in Hawaii, 'As long as the rubber hose is attached to your midriff, and as long as the mask stays over your face, bringing oxygen, nothing really bad can happen.' They would stay in the boat and supervise the compressor, which would be pumping air to me. After affixing a heavy lead belt around my belly, so that its weight could draw me down to the bottom of the sea, I plunged overboard, ready to start my first dive. While I clung to the boat, adjusting to the temperature and learning to control the air, the experts told me, 'You should find coral at thirty feet.

If you want to risk forty-five feet, go ahead. But come up in about ten minutes.'

At thirty feet, with reassuring bubbles rising about my head, proving that the air system was functioning, I entered a fairyland of beauty: coral castles, long sweeps of bright sand, jungles of rock with eels and stingrays, and all sorts of corridors with the most graceful fish imaginable in variegated colors.

And then I fell under the spell of the ocean, the mysterious moving water that remains always the same, and the grayness of the light, and the flashing colors of the fish. I dropped to forty-five feet and discovered a more somber world, and then I was lured to sixty feet, rarely attempted on a first dive, and there I stayed for about forty-five minutes.

This was the best part of the journey, the dark-gray world where the fish moved more slowly and where new types emerged, much larger than those higher up. The coral was more pristine and the castles higher. The caves where the eels hid were like caverns in a fairy tale, and I could easily imagine that the upper world of air and sunlight existed no more.

How beautiful it was, and when I began to ascend slowly, moving always toward light and brighter colors and more lively fish, it was like being on an elevator moving upward through the evolution of the world, and when at last I left the coral behind me and the fish, and passed through the final twenty feet of clean green water, bursting at last into the free and open air, where I could breathe with my own lungs, unaided, and see the sun and the surface of the mysterious sea, I could only mutter to myself, 'How beautiful it all was.'

Solitude. It is obvious that a man's experience in sports can be divided into two types, as spectator and as participant, but it is not so obvious that the latter can also be divided into two categories, group games and solitary action. The latter is especially rewarding when it involves close contact with nature, and some of my best experiences have come in this form.

As a young man I studied in Scotland, where walking across the moors was a constant temptation. This small and congenial country produces some great hikers, and I followed in their trail. On one heroic effort, which gained me some credit in my university crowd, I hiked across Scotland in one unbroken trip.

I left Inverness, that crystal-clear city of the north, and walked westward along its loch, then cross-country to beautiful Glen Affric, then through the pass between Ben Attow and Scour Ouran and down the western slopes to Invershiel, a total of forty-eight miles. It was a journey I have never forgotten, the kind of thing a man should do when young, and one of the most rewarding things about it was that I did it alone, so that the full force of nature could impress me and give me strength as I hiked through the dark hours.

It was this long walk that committed me to constant hiking, and for the past twenty-five years, whenever I have been at home, I have left my desk almost every afternoon to walk with our dogs through the woods that surround the small plot of ground on which we live. The taxes on these splendid woods are paid by others, but they belong to me.

I walk every day, save in blizzards and cloudbursts, between two and three miles across open wheat fields and through cool, tall woods. I pursue the same path, year after year, and neither I nor the dogs ever tire of it. I watch the deer, and the fox, and the rabbits, and the squirrels, and the skunks, and especially the birds, and I have never seen the same scene twice. There are several small waterfalls whose white-plunging waters vary from real torrents to almost nothing; some trails border streams that carry fish in wet seasons, sand in dry.

Within this short walk the infinite variety of nature is compressed. I must have traveled it more than a hundred and fifty times a year for a quarter of a century. When my writing goes poorly it is always because I have not walked enough, for it is on these uneventful and repetitious walks that I do my best thinking.

But it isn't all thinking. The dogs find such constant joy in these walks that through them I discover nature afresh each day. They love to chase squirrels, and course after rabbits which they seem never to catch, and dig for groundhogs, or track down moles with their radar, or leap wildly after deer. They have been invaluable to me, these dogs, because every afternoon, at about four o'clock, they come pestering me to take them out.

They could go alone, but they need the presence of a human being to serve as a kind of checkpoint. They are like children in a swimming pool: 'Hey, Mom! Watch! Mom, watch!' We all require that fixed reference point, and they are mine as much as I am theirs, for I deplore walking in the country without them.

They come tugging at my ankles as the day ends. 'Come on, Mitch. It's time to get down to serious work.' I have walked with them and their predecessors about three hundred and fifty miles a year for twenty-five years, and to them, and the solitude into which they drag me, I owe much of my good health and the re-creation I find in nature.

Power. Sometimes it is through the presence of overwhelming power that we attain an appreciation of terror and awe. The sheer power of Babe Ruth allured the baseball fan. The unmatched power of Taiho exhilarated the Japanese sumo crowd. Football fans reveled in the power of Dick Butkus. I found power in auto racing.

On three occasions at the Pocono Raceway near my home I helped start

Indianapolis-type races, and after standing with Tony Hulman twice as he intoned, 'Gentlemen, start you-rrrrengines!' I became blasé. But the third time an accident in the pits behind us kept me trapped on the small starting platform, level with the track and only a few inches from it, I elected to stay there until the warm-up rounds were completed.

The thirty-three powerful cars, their engines sputtering, their wheels twisting purposefully to roughen the rubber, jockeyed for position behind the lead car, and moved around the oval as a compact unit. Once, twice. The man with the green flag wanted them just a little better bunched, so he sent them around a third time. Perfect. At the farthest turn the lead car accelerated to well over a hundred and left the track, roaring in behind me.

Now the thirty-three monsters were alone. For a brief spell they hesitated. Then the starter waved his green flag and the moment of supreme power arrived. The cars leaped forward, accelerating explosively. All restraint gone, they rushed toward me at a speed I could barely conceive, hurtling cars, inches apart, rushing like a tornado at my little stand, roaring past at speeds of up to a hundred and forty, and all bound together in a violent power, each life dependent upon the cool judgment of the men in the other cars.

It was the most power-filled moment I have ever known in sports, and when it passed, I was numb.

Exquisite grace. But my most treasured experience with sports has been of a gentler kind, and I could wish no man or woman better luck than to share the fun I have had playing tennis with three zany companions.

Our doubles foursome convened three or four times a week for a dozen years, and never once did we find the game dull or ordinary. I could go on playing for another dozen years with no fear of satiety. People have asked, 'Doesn't it get tiresome, playing with the same people week after week?' And I have explained, 'Those three are so ornery, so filled with tricks, that a lifetime of competing against them wouldn't be monotonous.'

Ed Swann was the Madison Avenue public relations man who coined the immortal 'Let's run it up the flagpole and see if anybody salutes.' He also launched the best good-news–bad-news joke, one with a sporting angle: 'This Roman galley was plying the Mediterranean when the hortator stopped banging his drum to inform the slaves, "I've got some good news and some bad news. The good news is that for lunch the captain has ordered an extra ration of wine." A feeble cheer rose from the benches. "The bad news is that after lunch he wants to water-ski again." ' For some years Ed served as whipping boy for one of the cruelest of the tobacco magnates, kowtowing to the monster and saving his money until that glorious day when he was able to say, 'Don't call me. I'll call you.' He was invariably my opponent, a man without mercy, a man so filled with guile and drop shots as to break the heart of any honorable competitor.

His partner was a remarkable woman, Sue Carnwath, who had not played tennis before the age of forty. After a few lessons she was proficient. She could run tirelessly and with astonishing bursts of speed. It was almost impossible to put a ball out of her reach, but her delight was to rush madly at the net, catch a low bouncing ball, and drive it with full force at a spot right between the eyes of whoever was playing net on the opposing team. She also had a very dirty chuckle when scoring on such a play. I played against her interminably, and she would test me again and again at the net. I would put away some of her best shots, but then she would catch me between the eyes, and her day was made. (On the few occasions when Sue and I played together, we beat everyone, but we were destined to be lifelong opponents.)

My partner was one of the most delightful women ever to walk on a tennis court. Mary Place, wife of the cartoon animator, did not look like an athlete. Short and round, with never an orthodox shot, she deceived newcomers into believing that here was a patsy. But she had instantaneous reflexes and she could stand in one spot and with amazing dispositions of her racket get back everything hit within her orbit. She had a flick shot that drove opponents crazy, and a sneaking return of service that dumped the ball about six inches from the net. In defending her half of the court she was remorseless.

Well, this foursome took the court weekly throughout the year. In winter we played at eighteen degrees, with snow piled high around us. We dressed in ski suits and heavy gloves until Mary Place came up with a sensational invention. She knitted what might be termed 'blizzard gloves,' woolen tubes about a foot long, small at one end, larger at the other. Around each opening she sewed tight elastic, and the rest was simple. We slipped the small end over the handle of the racket, bringing it to rest down where the handle joins the curved rim of the racket. Into the larger opening we slipped our right hand, allowing the elastic to grip our wrist snugly.

Now we could play with our hand in contact with the racket handle, yet protected from the wind. Just the other day I had a fine game with the thermometer at twenty, and we have played that way for the past dozen winters.

Our games were brutal. No one of us had real put-away shots, nor screaming drives down the sidelines. But we could all place the ball, and it was not unusual for a single point to last two or three minutes before someone was able to smack the ball out of reach.

A famous tennis expert came upon us one Sunday morning when the score was 11–12 and deuce in the critical twenty-fourth game. He saw us knocking the ball from side to side, utilizing slices and smashes and lunging recoveries. He covered his face with his hands and said, 'This is too painful to watch.' He was accustomed to games in which a man served a rocket, ran to the net, and put the ball away. To watch us straining for points through twenty and thirty exchanges, each more cliff-hanging than the preceding, was too enervating.

Sometimes, in the excitement of such a game, I would catch the true meaning of tennis: the lovely, shifting figures; the poetic flight of the ball now here, now there; the unexpected drop shot, the arching lob; and always the relation of one player to the other, the figures changing, moving, falling into postures of delicate grace. And I would experience such an overwhelming sense of kinesthesia that when the play finally ended I and the others would cry, 'What a great point!' regardless of who had won.

Then, at the far end of the court, from a grove of pine trees a herd of sixteen or seventeen deer would slowly appear, rather close to us and watching us as if we were irresponsible intruders into their world, and we would halt the game and watch them as they watched us, and very slowly they would come closer, the wild things that shared our country world with us, and they would feel secure, and when we resumed our game they would remain there, staring at us with their unblinking eyes, and after a long while one of us would shout at some outrageous act on our court, and the deer would flick their white tails and leap away, as beautiful in their motion as the tennis game had been in its.

It is such experiences—the sea, the woods, the excitement of watching an honest game, the dance of life—that have kept me interested in sports. I want our country to protect, and augment, and make available such experiences to others. For it is this enlarging of the human adventure that sports are all about.

Index

Aaron, Henry, 153, 370, 373, 426, 427
Abdul-Jabbar, Kareem, 153, 156, 157, 167–8, 169, 171, 295, 366, 367, 368, 370, 372, 390, 446
Abington High School, 112–13, 442
Ackermann, R., 90
Adult Physical Fitness (President's Council on Physical Fitness, Washington, D.C., 1965), 277
Aerobics, 75–6, 270
Aerobics (Cooper, New York, 1968), 76
Agnew, Spiro, 100, 266, 399
Alabama High School Athletic Association, 113
Alabama Sports Hall of Fame, 221
Alcindor, Lew, *see* Abdul-Jabbar, Kareem
All-Americans, 247–8
Allen, Cedric, 353
Allen, Dick, 370
Allen, George, 43, 100, 370, 414, 421, 432
Allen, Johnny, 436
Allen, Mel, 310
Allott, Gordon, 423
Aloha Stadium, 352–3
Alvarez, Carlos, 195
Amateur Athletic Act, 402–3
Amateur Athletic Union, 396–401, 403–4
American Basketball Association, 294, 295, 326–7, 364, 365, 411; *see also* Basketball, professional
American Broadcasting Company, 205–6, 298, 308, 310, 312, 323, 331–2; *see also* Television
American Council on Education, 150
American Football League, 390, 391; *see also* Football, professional
American Medical Association, 64
Amherst College, 213
Amritraj, Vijay, 292
Anderson, Dave, 317, 329
Anderson, Dick, 60, 199, 311
Andros, Dee, 256–7
Angell, Roger (*The Summer Game,* New York, 1972), 324
Arcaro, Eddie, 322
Archery: children, 108; physical demands, 72, 76, 79

Archibald, Nate, 370
Arizona State University, 259, 260
Arledge, Roone, 136, 323
Arlington Stadium, 348, 356
Arlott, John, 328
Armstrong, James, 204
Arnold, Bill, 84
Arnold, Judy, 439
Arond, Henry, 228
Arrowhead Stadium, *see* Harry S Truman Sports Complex
Arroyo, Eddie, 228–9
Ashe, Arthur, 149, 326
Association of American Colleges, 132
Athletes, 229, 265–8: character-building, 12–16, 246–7; intelligence, 241; in literature, 225–8, 229–31, 234–5, 236–7, 238–40, 246–7; political activities, 240; post-sports career, 236–8, 270–2, 283–4; psychological adjustment, 241–2; salaries, 279, 288, 366–74; social adjustment, 234–5, 241–2; *see also* Black athletes; Drugs, use by athletes; Politics and sports; names of individual sports
Athletic Institute of Chicago, 141
Atlanta Falcons, 209, 362, 415
Atlanta Stadium, 355
Atlantic City Race Track, 26, 32, 342
Atlantic Coast Conference, 200
Attles, Al, 165
Atwell, Robert H., 196
Auburn University, 207, 209, 221, 332
Austin Peay State University, 187
Auto Racing, 448–9: children, 93–6; peak athletic performance, 271; physical demands, 72, 79
Avenick, Joseph, 320–1
Avery, Earle, 73
Axthelm, Pete (*The City Game,* New York, 1970), 168

Badminton: physical demands, 72, 75, 76, 79
Bailar, Richard J., 384–5
Baker, Home Run, 19, 20, 25, 250
Bakken, Jim, 431
Ball, Donald (*Sport and the Social Order,*